Impact of Divorce, Single Parenting, and Stepparenting on CHILDREN

Impact of Divorce, Single Parenting, and Stepparenting on CHILDREN

Edited by

E. Mavis Hetherington
University of Virginia

Josephine D. Arasteh
University of California, Berkeley

LEA LAWRENCE ERLBAUM ASSOCIATES, PUBLISHERS
1988 Hillsdale, New Jersey   Hove and London

Lawrence Erlbaum Associates, Inc., Publishers
365 Broadway
Hillsdale, New Jersey 07642

Production and interior design: Robin Marks Weisberg

Cover design: John Eagleson

Library of Congress Cataloging in Publication Data
Impact of divorce, single parenting, and stepparenting on children /
editors, E. Mavis Hetherington, Josephine D. Arasteh.
p.   cm.
Papers, revised and updated, originally presented at a conference
sponsored by the National Institute of Child Health and Human
Development, May 6-7, 1985.
Includes Index.
ISBN 0-8058-0186-3.   ISBN 0-8058-0187-1 (pbk.)
1. Children of divorced parents—United States—Congresses.
2. Stepchildren—United States—Congresses. I. Hetherington, E.
Mavis (Eileen Mavis), 1926–   II. Arasteh, Josephine D., 1925–
III. National Institute of Child Health and Human Development
(U.S.)
HQ777.5.I52 1988   87-33175
306.8'74—dc19   CIP
Printed in the United States of America
10 9 8 7 6 5 4 3 2 1

Contents

PART II   DIVORCE AND THE LEGAL SYSTEM: MEDIATION AND CUSTODY

3 Mediation and the Settlement of Divorce Disputes   53

Robert E. Emery

4 A Comparison of Joint and Sole Legal Custody
Agreements   73

*Amy Koel, Susan C. Clark, W. P. C. Phear,
and Barbara B. Hauser*

5 Custody of Children Following Divorce   91

*Eleanor E. Maccoby, Charlene E. Depner,
and Robert H. Mnookin*

PART III   DIVORCE AND SINGLE PARENTING

14   Children's Development During Early Remarriage   279

James H. Bray

15   Family Relationships and Children's Psychological Adjustment in Stepmother and Stepfather Families   299

Eulalee Brand, W. Glenn Clingempeel, and Kathryn Bowen-Woodward

16   Behavior, Achievement, and Health Problems Among Children in Stepfamilies: Findings From a National Survey of Child Health   325

Nicholas Zill

Contributors

Kathryn Bowen-Woodward Department of Psychology, The Pennsylvania State University, Capitol Campus, Middletown, PA 17057

Eulalee Brand Department of Psychology, The Pennsylvania State University, Capitol Campus, Middletown, PA 17057

James H. Bray Department of Psychology and Philosophy, Texas Women's University, 1130 MD Anderson Boulevard, Houston, TX 77030

Gene H. Brody Department of Child and Family Development, University of Georgia, Dawson Hall, Athens, GA 30602

Kathleen A. Camara Eliot-Pearson Department of Child Study, Tufts University, Medford, MA 02155

Susan Clark Middlesex Probate Court—Family Serivce, Harvard Medical School—Cambridge Hospital, 40 Thorndike Street, Cambridge, MA 02141

W. Glenn Clingempeel CPC Mental Health Center, 59 Broad Street, Eatontown, NJ 07724

Shauna Corbin Center for the Family in Transition, 5725 Paradise Drive, Building B, Suite 300, Corte Madera, CA 95925

Charlene E. Depner Stanford Center for the Study of Youth Development, Stanford University, 128 Margaret Jacks Hall, Stanford, CA 94305

Robert E. Emery Department of Psychology, University of Virginia, Charlottesville, VA 22901

Rex Forehand Department of Psychology, University of Georgia, Athens, GA 30602

M. S. Forgatch   Oregon Social Learning Center, Suite 202, 207 East 5th Avenue, Eugene, OR 97401

Frank F. Furstenberg, Jr.   Department of Sociology, University of Pennsylvania, McNeil Building, 3718 Locust Walk, Philadelphia, PA 19104

Barbara B. Hauser   Middlesex Probate Court—Family Service, Harvard Medical School—Cambridge Hospital, 40 Thorndike Street, Cambridge MA 02141

Cathy L. Healow   Human Development & Family Relations, Colorado State University, Fort Collins, CO 80523

Donald J. Hernandez   Marriage & Family Statistics Branch, Population Division, FOB-3 Room 2264, U.S. Bureau of the Census, Washington, DC 20233

Amy Koel   Middlesex Probate Court—Family Service, Harvard Medical School—Cambridge Hospital, 40 Thorndike Street, Cambridge, MA 02141

Luis M. Laosa   Educational Testing Service, Research Building, Princeton, NJ 08541

Julia M. Lewis   1616 Castro Street, San Francisco, CA 94114

Nicholas Long   Department of Psychology, University of Georgia, Athens, GA 30602

Eleanor E. Maccoby   Stanford Center for the Study of Youth Development, Stanford University, 128 Margaret Jacks Hall, Stanford, CA 94305

Robert H. Mnookin   Stanford Center for the Study of Youth Development, Stanford University, 128 Margaret Jacks Hall, Stanford, CA 94305

Kay Pasley   Human Development & Family Relations, Colorado State University, Fort Collins, CO 80523

G.R. Patterson   Oregon Social Lelarning Center, Suite 202, 207 East 5th Avenue, Eugene, OR 97401

W. P. C. Phear   Middlesex Probate Court—Family Service, Harvard Medical School—Cambridge Hospital, 40 Thorndike Street, Cambridge, MA 02141

Gary Resnick   Eliot-Pearson Department of Child Study, Tufts University, Medford, MA 02155

M. L. Skinner   Oregon Social Learning Center, Suite 202, 207 East 5th Avenue, Eugene, OR 97401

Timothy F. L. Tolson   Department of Psychology, University of Virginia, Charlottesville, VA 22901

Judith S. Wallerstein   Center of the Family in Transition, 5725 Paradise Drive, Building B, Suite 300, Corte Madera, CA 95925

Melvin N. Wilson   Department of Psychology, University of Virginia, Charlottesville, VA 22901

Nicholas Zill   Child Trends, 2100 M. Street, Suite 411, Washington, DC 20036

Preface

The chapters presented in this volume grew out of a conference, "The Impact of Divorce, Single Parenting and Stepparenting on Children," sponsored by the National Institute of Child Health and Human Development (NICHD) and held in Bethesda, Maryland, May 6–7, 1985. Since its inception in 1965, the NICHD has strongly supported research on the family, particularly changes that affect the well-being of children. This conference provided an opportunity for two Institute behavioral programs, the Human Learning and Behavior Branch and the Demographic and Behavioral Sciences Branch, to bring together a broad team of experts to examine demographic trends affecting the living arrangements of parents and children, developmental and clinical evidence of how such transitions affect children, and legal issues surrounding these changes.

Chaired by E. Mavis Hetherington and Josephine D. Arasteh, the conference addressed issues concerned with divorce, divorce mediation and custody arrangements, single parenting and stepparenting as they impact on the well-being of children. Developmental psychologists, clinicians, demographers, and legal experts joined in examining current findings on how such transitions in family life are affecting both the adjustment of parents and of children as well as the legal measures being tried to make such transitions easier for families. Unanswered questions and areas that need further research were identified. At the conference, some participants presented only preliminary findings pending further data collection and analysis. The chapters in this volume offer more fully developed findings supplemented by new chapters that provide other relevant information that was cited by the conference participants.

E. Mavis Hetherington
Josephine D. Arasteh

Part I

THE DEMOGRAPHICS OF DIVORCE AND REMARRIAGE

I

Demographic Trends and the Living Arrangements of Children

Donald J. Hernandez
United States Bureau of the Census

The living arrangements of American children have shifted dramatically during recent decades due to major demographic and socioeconomic changes. This chapter begins by describing the most important demographic trends that have influenced the familial and socioeconomic circumstances of children. Next, the chapter discusses the most important changes in the parental living arrangements of children that have occurred during recent decades, and that are projected to occur during the next few decades. Finally, the chapter presents data collected by the Census Bureau in 1987 describing in considerable detail the social, economic, and demographic circumstances of children as they relate to the parental living arrangements of children. Whereas this chapter focuses on basic data for children, Hernandez (1986) thoroughly reviewed past sociodemographic research on children and their families, and Watts and Hernandez (1982) presented a conceptual framework for child and family indicators, as well as an overall assessment of the availability of statistical data for a comprehensive set of child and family indicators.

DEMOGRAPHIC TRENDS

Begining with basic demographic trends, four major variables pertain directly to the parental living arrangements of children: (a) the substantial rise in the number of births occurring to unmarried mothers as a ratio of births to all mothers, (b) the associated rise in the number of post-birth marriages among never-married women who have borne at least one child out-of-wedlock, (c) the great increase in the divorce rate, and (d) the associated increase in the proportion of divorced women with children who remarry.

Although the biological union of a mother and a father is a prerequisite to a birth, the postpartum family support and living arrangements of the child need not involve both or, indeed, either parent. In the United States many children are born to unmarried mothers, with the result that the father is not available to fulfill the social or economic functions that are typically associated with parenthood.

For Whites and non-Whites, Fig. 1.1 shows births to unmarried women as a ratio of births to all women. These data show for Whites that betweeen 1940 and 1985, the ratio rose from about 20 per 1,000 births to 145 per 1,000 births. This is an increase of 725% in 45 years. For non-Whites, the ratio rose from 168 per 1,000 to 514 per 1,000, a 306% increase. These results imply that 14.5% of all White children and 51.4% of all non-White children born in 1985 were born to unmarried mothers. For Black children the figure was 60.1%, or 3 in 5. During the last 45 years, then, marked increases have occurred in the proportion of both White and non-White children who were born into a family situation in which the father was not available to perform the social, emotional, and economic functions of parenthood.

This situation changes as time passes, however, and these unmarried mothers marry, bringing a stepfather into the household. Figure 1.2 shows the proportion of never-married women with an out-of-wedlock birth who subsequently had married by 1985 when they reached a specified age. These data indicate that marriage increases substantially with increasing age for women who were never married at the time of their first birth. A small minority of such women 15–19 years old,

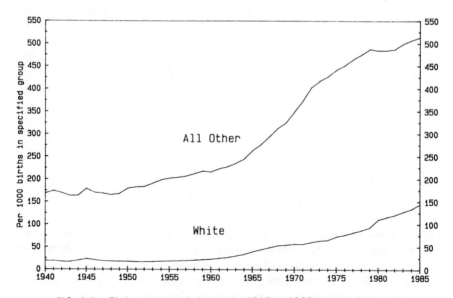

FIG. 1.1.   Births to unmarried women: 1940 to 1985 (source: National Center for Health Statistics, 1986a, 1987a, 1987b)

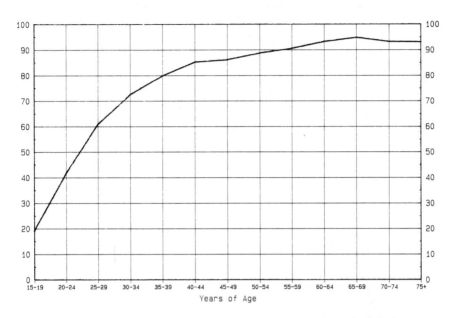

FIG. 1.2.   Proportion of never-married women with an out-of-wedlock birth who had subsequently married by 1985 by age of woman

19%, had remarried by 1985, but the proportion rises rapidly to a large minority, 42%, for women 20–24 years old, and then to a substantial majority, 61% for women 25–29 years old, and finally to very large majorities of 80% or more for women 35 years and over. As result of such marriages, many children who enter life in a one-parent family later enter a two-parent situation when the mother marries.

Divorce is the third major demographic variable that has influenced the extent to which children live with two parents or with one parent. Figure 1.3 shows that with temporary peaks following the two world wars and a temporary trough during the Great Depression, the annual divorce rate has risen from about 1 divorce per 1,000 married women age 15 and over in 1860 to 22.8 in 1979. After 1979 the trend in the divorce rate turned around, falling about 5% between 1979 and 1985. The long-term rise in divorce, and the especially rapid rise begining in 1968 tended to increase the proportion of children living with only one parent, as is shown later. The recent decrease in the divorce rate should lead eventually to a halt and perhaps a turnaround in the rising proportion of children experiencing a parental divorce. Perhaps more likely than a sharp future decline in divorce, however, is a leveling off. If the divorce rate does not decline notably during the coming years, the proportion of children who experience a parental divorce will remain relatively high, at least by long-term historical standards.

Remarriage among divorced women with children is the fourth major demo-

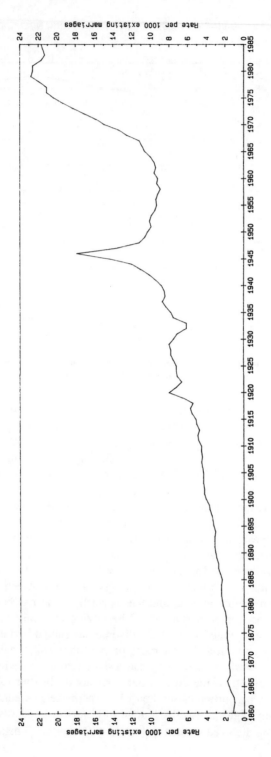

FIG. 1.3. Divorce rate: 1860 to 1985 (source: Jacobson, 1959; National Center for Health Statistics, 1986b, 1987c, 1987d)

6

graphic variable that has influenced the extent to which children live with one or with two parents, and in particular the extent to which they live with a divorced mother but no father in the home or with a remarried mother and a stepfather. Figure 1.4 shows overall that remarriage occurs for the majority of women who divorce and who have at least one child at the time of the divorce. The results as of 1985 range from a small majority of 57% remarried among women who had four or more children at the time of their divorce to a substantial majority of 68% of women who had one child at the time of the divorce. Because many of these women were relatively young at the time of the survey, the proportion who will ever remarry is larger still. Figure 1.4 also shows that the proportions remarried are much larger among the younger cohorts of women, ranging for women who are under age 30 from 72% to 82% remarried, depending on the number of children at the time of the divorce (see Norton & Moorman, 1987, for an extended discussion of marriage, divorce, and remarriage trends between 1970 and 1985). These results indicate that many children who spend time in a one-parent family due to divorce will subsequently spend time in a two-parent family with their mother and a stepfather.

Marriages of single parents and remarriages of divorced parents lead to blended families with stepparents and stepchildren, but as Cherlin (1981) suggested, such blended families can involve complications and difficulties for the parents, stepparents, and stepchildren involved. Historically, the increase in the proportion

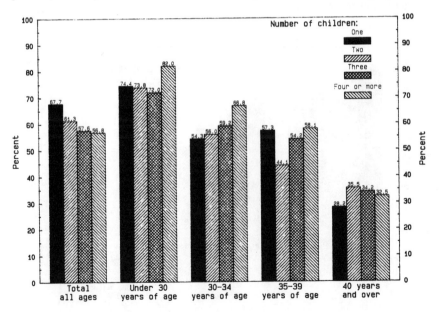

FIG. 1.4. Proportion of ever-divorced women with children at the time of divorce who had remarried by 1985 by age of woman and by number of children at the time of divorce

of children who live with a stepparent is the result of (a) the sharp rise in the proportion of all births that are accounted for by births to unmarried women, and the associated increase in the number of post-birth marriages among women who have borne one or more children out-of-wedlock; and (b) the great increase in the divorce rate, and the associated increase in the number of remarriages among women with children.

This review of four major demographic trends suggest, in a general way, how and why the living arrangements of children changed during recent decades. But a more precise understanding of the implications of demographic changes for the parental living arrangements of children requires an analysis focused directly upon these living arrangements.

PARENTAL LIVING ARRANGEMENTS OF CHILDREN

Glick and Norton (1979; Glick, 1979) used data from the Decennial Census and the Current Population Survey to develop early analyses and projections of long-term trends in the parental living arrangements of children under 18 years of age. As shown in Fig. 1.5, which summarizes their results, marked changes have occurred and may continue to occur in the family situation of children.

In 1960 about 88% of all children were living with two parents, including natural, step- and adoptive parents. But by 1978 this figure fell to 78%, and Glick's

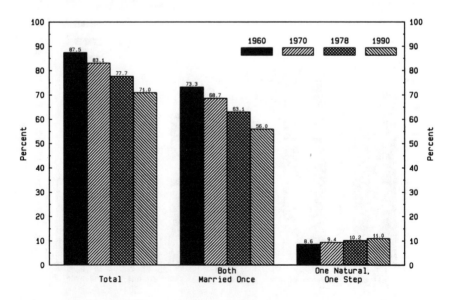

FIG. 1.5. Percent of children under 18 years living with two parents, by marital history of parents (source: Glick, 1979; Glick & Norton, 1979)

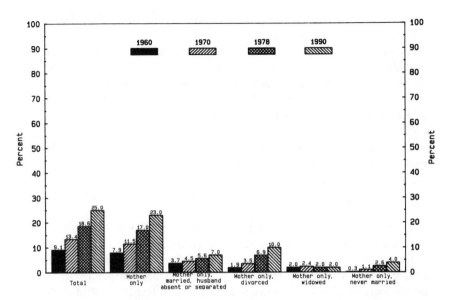

FIG. 1.6. Percent of children under 18 years living with one parent
(source: Glick, 1979; Glick & Norton, 1979)

projections suggest a further decline to 71% by 1990. Figure 1.5 shows that the
decline in the percentage of children living with two parents is accounted for mainly
by a decline in the percentage living with two natural parents, both of whom are
married only once. In 1960 approximately 73% of all children were living with
two natural parents both married once, but this figure fell almost to 63% in 1978,
and is projected to fall further to 56% by 1990. This represents a remarkable
shift for children away from the parental living arrangements that often are viewed
as the normal or traditional arrangements.

Part of this shift, as shown in Fig. 1.5, is due to increases in the proportion
of children living with two parents, one of whom is a natural parent, the other
of whom is a stepparent. These data show that 8.6% of children in 1960 were
living with a natural parent and a stepparent. By 1978 the figure rose to 10.2%,
and the projected value for 1990 is 11%. These results suggest that about 1 in
10 children are living with a stepparent as a result of the marriage of a parent
to someone other than the biological parent of the child. Such marriages may
be the first marriage for a never-married parent, or a remarriage for a divorced
parent.

Figure 1.6 shows that much of the overall decline in the two-parent living arrangement is accounted for by a sharp increase in the proportion of children living with one parent. In 1960 about 9% of all children were living with one parent.
By 1978 the figure doubled to 19%, and by 1990 the figure is projected to rise
further to 25%. Most of this increase is accounted for by children living with

their mother but not their father. The percentage rose from 7.9% in 1960 to 17% in 1978, with a projected value of 23% in 1990.

The increase in the proportion living with only their mothers is, in turn, accounted for mainly by a rise in the proportion living with a mother who is divorced, and secondarily by the increases in the proportions living with a mother who is never married or who is separated or married spouse absent. The proportion of children living with a divorced mother increased from 1.9% in 1960 to 6.9% in 1978 with a projected value of 10% in 1990. Similarly, children living with a never-married mother acounted for 0.3% of all children in 1960, but this rose rapidly to 2.6% in 1978, and a projected 4% in 1990. Finally, the proportion of children living with a mother who was separated, or who was married but not living with her husband, rose substantially from 3.7% in 1960 to 5.6% in 1978 with a projected value of 7% in 1990.

These basic statistics prepared by Glick and Norton demonstrate that major changes are occurring in the parental living arrangements of children as a result of shifts in the fertility and marital behavior of their parents. More specifically, because of the increasing proportion of births that occur to unmarried women and the increasing divorce rate, children are much less likely than in the past to be living with two natural parents in their first marriage, and considerably more likely to be living in a household where the only parents are (a) a never-married mother, (b) a mother who is separated or divorced (or still married but the husband is not present in the household), or (c) a natural parent and a step-parent.

Three recent sets of projections portray possible future changes in the family living arrangements of children. Bumpass (1984) used 1980 June Current Population Survey data to project that about 49% of all children born between 1977–1979 will spend some time in a one-parent family by age 16. Hofferth (1985) used data from the Panel Study of Income Dynamics to develop projections that suggest that substantially larger proportions of chidlren born in 1980 may live in a one-parent family. She projected that 70% of White children born in 1980 and 94% of Black children born in 1980 will have lived in a one-parent family by age 18. Most recently, Norton and Glick (1986) derived projections, based on various data sources, which lie about midway between those Bumpass and Hofferth. Because the projections of Norton and Glick appear to rest near the center of current expert opinion, they may be viewed as the current best guess about likely trends in the future.

Taken as a whole then, recent projections suggest for children born in the late 1970s and early 1980s that at least 50%, and possibly 75% will spend at least 1 year in a one-parent family, with ranges of 40%–70% for White children and 85%–95% for Black children (see Hernandez, 1986, for further discussion of these projections). In addition, although formal projections are not available, because the mothers of many children living in one-parent families will subsequently marry, bringing a stepfather into the household, it seems likely that between one–

third and one–half of all children born around 1980 will eventually spend at least 1 year in a two-parent family including a stepfather.

Using methods that yielded the high end projections, Hofferth also projected that White children born in 1950–1954 spent, on average, about 8% of their childhood in a home without two parents, but White children born in 1980 may spend 31% of their childhood in a home without two parents. The results for Black children are comparable, but more remarkable. Black children born in 1950–1954 spent about 22% of their childhood without two parents in the home, but Black children born in 1980 are projected to spend about 59% of their childhood in a home without two parents. Furthermore, although numerical estimates are not presented, Hofferth compared projections for the 1950–1954 and 1980 birth cohorts, finding that the proportion of time spent living with two parents is increasingly comprised of time spent living with one natural parent and one stepparent, instead of two natural parents.

Because these results pertaining to number of years spent in one-parent families were derived using methods that yield high-end estimates of the proportion of children ever living in a one-parent family, they too probably represent high-end estimates. If so, they suggest that White children may spend, on average, as many as 6 of their first 18 years without two parents in the home, and Black children may spend, on average, as many as 11 of their first 18 years without two parents in the home.

Even if the actual time spent by the 1980 cohort in one-parent families turns out to be less than that projected by Hofferth, the lower but still very large proportions that Bumpass and Norton and Glick projected to ever live in a one-parent family suggest that recent cohorts may spend at least twice as many years as the 1950–1954 cohort in one-parent families. At the extreme, Hofferth's projections suggested that recent cohorts may spend three times as many years as the 1950–1954 cohort in one-parent families.

SOCIAL, ECONOMIC, AND DEMOGRAPHIC CIRCUMSTANCES

The third part of this chapter presents data from the March 1987 Current Population Survey to provide an overall assessment of the current social, economic, and demographic circumstances of children (for further detail see U.S. Bureau of the Census, 1988). These data, which are presented in Fig. 1.7 through Fig. 1.13, focus specifically on children who are under 18 years old and who are living with one or two parents, where parents include natural, step-, and adoptive parents. Data for White and Black children are presented separately.

Before turning to these results, however, it should be noted that perhaps the most important limitation of these data for present purposes is that it is not possible to distinguish children who are living with two natural parents from those who are living with a natural parent and a stepparent or who are living with two adoptive parents. Similarly, it is not possible to distinguish children who live in families with only natural children from families that include only stepchildren, only adopted children, or some more complicated constellation of parent–child relationships. The reason for this limitation is that the major data collection efforts of the Census Bureau have not heretofore distinguished between natural, step-, and adopted children.

To overcome this limitation in current data, I have been leading an effort to expand current Census Bureau data collection procedures. The situation is improving quickly because a full complement of information about natural, step-, and adoptive relationships in households is in the process of being obtained in the Census Bureau's new Survey of Income and Program Participation, and because we are now planning to distinguish stepchildren from other children in the 1990 Decennial Census and in the March Current Population Survey as of 1988.

In addition, through extensive computer manipulations, some existing data also can be re-organized in a fashion that sheds light on the presence of natural, step-, and adoptive relationships, and I should let you know about two such ongoing projects that will extend and considerably enrich the results presented in this chapter. The first research effort is the census monograph on children that I am writing based on microdata from the Decennial Censuses of 1940, 1950, 1960, 1970, and 1980 under grants awarded by the Russell Sage Foundation, the Social Science Research Council, and the National Science Foundation. This study will provide a comprehensive assessment of changes in the social, economic, and demographic circumstances of children from the Great Depression to 1980.

In the second research effort, we are using data from the Marital and Fertility History Supplements of the Current Population Survey for June 1980 and June 1985 to study more recent changes. As the first step in this latter effort, we conducted a preliminary study of the social, economic, and demographic characteristics of families which differed in terms of the types of parent-child relationships present in the family home (Moorman & Hernandez, 1987). Using data from the Marital and Fertility History Supplement of the June 1980 Current Population Survey, we identified biological, step, and adopted children in the home, and then classified families as being one of nine types including (a) purely biological, where all children were biological children of both parents, (b) biological mother–stepfather, where all children had a bilogical mother and a stepfather in the home, and (c) joint biological–step families, where at least one child was the biological child of both parents, where at least one child was the stepchild of one parent and the biological child of the second parent, and where no adopted children were present in the home. Our results showed that these stepfamilies tended to differ from purely biological families along various dimensions, including the following. The stepfamilies tended to have lower family income, and the parents in these stepfamilies tended to be younger and to have completed fewer years of schooling than was true of purely biological families. The results of this research demonstrate that stepfamilies differ demographically and socioeconomically from other family living arrangements.

Turning to the most recent currently available results in Fig. 1.7–1.13, results pertaining to the social, economic, and demographic circumstances of children are presented separately for children who live in four distinct types of parental living arrangements. First are children who live with two parents. Second are children who live with their mother, but not their father, and the mother is ever married, that is, she is divorced, separated, married spouse absent, or widowed. Third are children who live with their mother, but not their father, and the mother is never married. Fourth are children who live with their father, but not their mother.

In assessing the importance of these results for children, it is necessary to bear in mind the proportion of children who find themselves in each type of parental living arrangement. In 1987 for White children, 81% lived with two parents, 14% lived with an ever-married mother but no father, 3% lived with a never-married mother but no father, and 3% lived with a father but no mother. For Whites, then, the most important categories, in terms of size, are (a) living with two parents and (b) living with an ever-married mother only. Among Black children however, only 43% lived with two parents, 26% lived with an ever-married mother only, 28% lived with a never-married mother only, and 3% lived with a father only. The largest and most important categories for Black children, then, are (a) living with two parents, (b) living with an ever-married mother only, and (c) living with a never-married mother only. Because most children live with either one or two parents, statistics presented here focus mainly on these children.

Siblings in the home of a child can act as competitors for critical resources, but they can also provide important emotional resources. Figure 1.7 shows for White and Black children that those living with a never-married mother or with a father only are more likely to have no siblings in the home than are children living with an ever-married mother. Among White children, those living with two parents are least likely to have no siblings in the home, whereas among Black children those living with two parents or with an ever-married mother are least likely to have no siblings in the home. Furthermore, within parental living arrangements, White children are more likely than Black children to have no siblings in the home.

To the extent that siblings compete for parental and economic resources, then, within specific parental living arrangements, White children are less likely than Black children to be competing with siblings for scarce parental time and economic resources. Within racial groups, children living with a never-married mother or with a father only are less likely to be competing with siblings for scarce parental time and economic resources than are other children. On the other hand, Black and White children living with a never-married mother or with a father only are less likley to have siblings available in the home to provide emotional and affective support. Figure 1.7 shows that the differences are sometimes substantial.

Another factor that influences the situation of children is the age of the par-

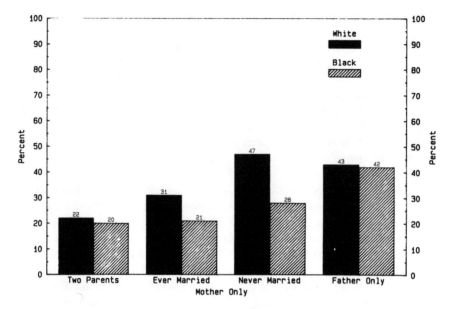

FIG. 1.7.   Percent of children under 18 years living with no siblings by
presence of parents and race: 1987 (children under 18 living with one
or two parents)

ents with whom they live, because parental age is related to parental maturity.
Figure 1.8 shows that both White and Black children living with a never-married
mother are considerably more likely than other children to be living with a relatively young parent. Forty-three percent of these White children and 34% of these
Black children are living with a mother less than 25 years old, compared to
3%–15% of children in other parent situations who are living with parents this
young.

For many children, however, parents are not the only adults in the home available to provide child care. Figure 1.9 shows, for both Whites and Blacks, that
children living with a never-married mother are more likely than other children
to have at least one additional adult relative in the home. The figure is 34% for
both Whites and Blacks. Next most likely to have another adult relative in the
home are children with ever-married mothers, 23% for Whites and 30% for
Blacks, and children living with their father but not their mother, 22% for Whites
and 20% for Blacks. Finally, children living with two parents are least likely
to have other adult relatives in the home, 15% for Whites and 19% for Blacks.

These data suggest that for many children living with only one parent, but
especially for children living with a never-married mother, an additional non-
parental adult relative is available in the home as a potential source of child care
and emotional support. On the other hand, between 66% and 80% of these children have only one adult relative, namely a parent, to provide the child care and

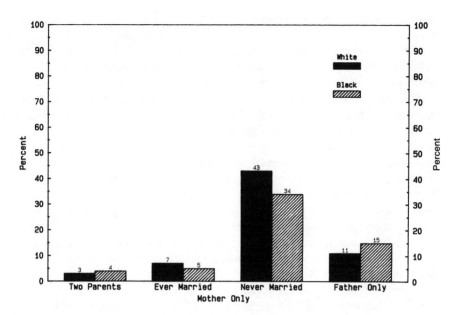

FIG. 1.8. Percent of children under 18 years living with a parent 15-24 years old, by race: 1987 (children under 18 years living with one or two parents)

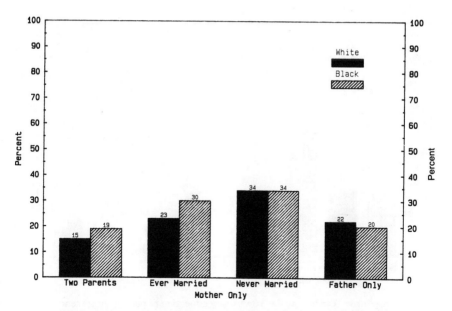

FIG. 1.9. Percent of children under 18 years living with one or more non-parental adult relatives, by presence of parents and race: 1987

emotional support that children need, whereas children in two-parent households have, by definition, two parents to provide for these needs.

Although the number of adults in the household is of obvious importance to a child, the characteristics of these adults also are important, particularly the educational attainment of the parent. One important reason is that educational attainment is a major determinant of the socialization values of parents, particularly parental preferences for autonomy versus obedience in child behavior. Educational attainment is positively related to parental preferences for children who think for themselves (Alwin, 1984).

Figure 1.10 shows that parental educational attainment varies substantially, depending on the parental living arrangements of children. Among Whites, children living with two parents are most likely to be living with parents who have completed at least 4 years of college, and they are least likely to be living with parents who have not graduated from high school. The largest differences across parental living arrangements are between children living with two parents and children living with a never-married mother. One of every two White children and two of every five Black children living with a never-married mother have a mother who has not graduated from high school. It is important to remember, however, that only 3% of White children but 28% of Black children in 1987 lived in this parental living arrangement.

Across parental living arrangements, the pattern of differences in parental educational attainment for Black children is generally the same as the pattern for

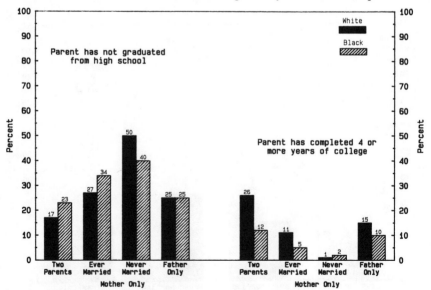

FIG. 1.10.   Children under 18 years by education of parent, by presence of parents and race: 1987 (children under 18 living with one or two parents)

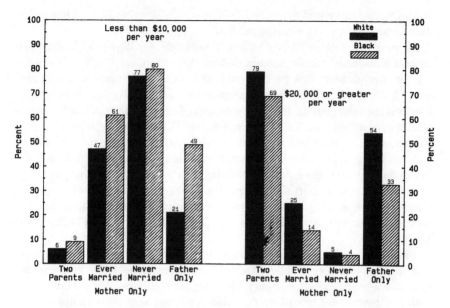

FIG. 1.11. Percent of children under 18 years by family income, by presence of parents and race: 1986 (children under 18 years living with one or two parents as of March 1987)

White children. But racial differences do exist. The most prominent differences are that Black children living with two parents are about one-half as likely as White children living with two parents to be living with parents who have completed at least 4 years of college.

Parental educational attainment is important not only because it influences parental socialization values, but also because it influences parental occupation and income, and hence the economic resources available to children from their parent's work. Figure 1.11 shows that startling differences exist in the family incomes of children depending on their parental living arrangements. For Whites in 1986, the percentage of children with family incomes of less than $10,000 per year was about 6% for children living with two parents, 47% for children living with ever-married mothers, and 77% for children living with never-married mothers. For Black children the pattern is the same, but the first two figures are substantially larger than for Whites. In 1986 the percentage of Black children with family incomes less than $10,000 was 9% for children living with two parents, 61% for children living with an ever-married mother, and 80% for children living with a never-married mother.

It should be emphasized here that, regardless of race, about four out of five children living with never-married mothers have annual family incomes below $10,000, despite the earlier finding that these children are more likely than other children to have at least one additional adult relative in the household. It also should be re-emphasized that only 3% of White children but 28% of Black children lived with a never-married mother.

Turning to the top end of the income distribution, for White children the percentage with annual family incomes of $20,000 or more is 79% for children living with two parents, 26% for children living with an ever-married mother, and only 5% for children living with a never-married mother. Again, the pattern for Blacks is the same, but the figures are smaller. The percentage of Black children with family incomes of $20,000 or more is 69% for children living with both parents, 14% for children living with an ever-married mother, and only 4% for children living with a never-married mother. The economic disadvantage of living with one parent, but especially of living with a never-married mother, is apparent from these data. It should be noted, however, that these results pertain to family income. They do not include government noncash transfer payments, such as food stamps, Aid to Families with Dependent Children (AFDC), and the like.

Finally, to round out this discussion of the social, economic, and demographic living circumstances of children in 1987, basic residential living arrangements of children are described. Figure 1.12 shows for both races that children living with two parents are less likely than children living with their mother only to be living in a central city, and for both Whites and Blacks that children living with an ever-married mother are less likely than children living with a never-married mother to be living in a central city. Moreover, within parental living

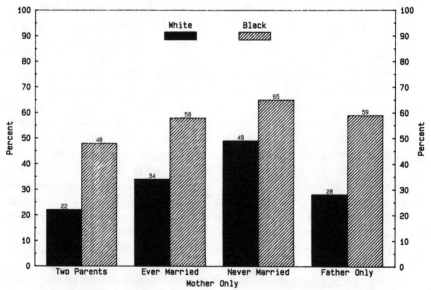

FIG. 1.12. Percent of children under 18 years living in central cities, by presence of parents and race: 1987 (children under 18 years living with one or two parents)

arrangements, White children are less likely than Black children to be living in a central city.

Furthermore, Fig. 1.13 shows for both races that children living with an ever-married mother are more likely than children living with two parents to be living in rented housing and in public housing, and children living with never-married mothers are more likely than children living with two parents or with an ever-married mother to be living in rented housing and in public housing. In addition, within parental living arrangements, Black children are generally more likely than White children to be living in rented housing and in public housing.

CONCLUSIONS

In conclusion, the dramatic rise in the divorce rate and the dramatic rise in the proportion of children born to unmarried mothers have profoundly shifted the living arrangements of children. The proportions of children living with two parents and with two parents who were both married only once have fallen considerably during recent decades, and corresponding increases have occurred in the proportions of children living with a natural parent and a stepparent and with a mother only. Furthermore, recent projections suggest for children born around 1980 that at least 4 in 10 and perhaps as many as 7 in 10 White children will spend part of their childhood living in a home without two parents, and they sug-

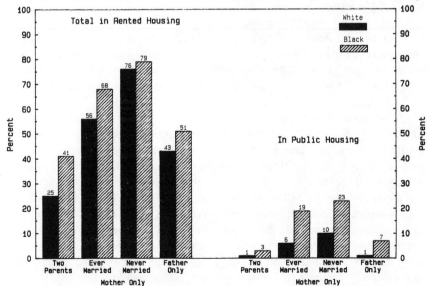

FIG. 1.13   Children under 18 years living in rented housing unit by presence of parents and race: 1987 (children under 18 living with one or two parents)

gest for Black children that about 9 in 10 will spend some time during childhood living with one parent only. It also seems likely that one-third to one-half of children born around 1980 will spend at least 1 year in a family with a stepparent.

The disruptions associated with a divorce and/or a marriage that brings a stepparent into the home are apparent. Preliminary results for 1980 also suggest that many social, eonomic, and demographic circumstances of stepfamilies tend to differ from those of families without a stepparent in the home. For example, compared to purely biological families, biological mother-stepfather families and joint biological-step families tend to have lower family income, and they tend to have parents who are younger and who have lower educational attainments.

Turning to more recent results for 1987 concerning the living arrangements of children who live with at least one parent, 81% of White children live with two parents, and 14% live with an ever-married mother but no father. In sharp contrast, among Black children who live with at least one parent, only 43% live with two parents, whereas 26% live with an ever-married mother, and 28% live with a never-married mother. Within a specific type of parental living arrangement, White children are less likely than Black children to be competing with siblings in their home for parental time and resources. Comparing across parental living arrangements, children living with a never-married mother or with a father only are less likely to be competing with siblings for parental resources. At the same time, children living with a never-married mother are somewhat more likely than other children to have one or more additional adult relatives in the household available to provide child care.

Children living with a never-married mother also are 2 to 10 times more likely than other children to be living with a relatively young mother, under age 25, and they are substantially more likely than other children to be living with a parent who has not graduated from high school. Fifty percent of White children and 40% of Black children living with a never-married mother have a mother who has not graduated from high school.

Differences in family income also are notable. For both races, approximately four of every five children living with a never-married mother have an annual family income of less than $10,000, and only 1 out of every 20 have a family income greater than $20,000 per year. At the other extreme, for both races 6%-9% of children living with two parents have incomes of less than $10,00 per year, and about 7 of every 10 Black children and 8 of every 10 White children living with two parents have family incomes greater than $20,000 per year. Children living with an ever-married mother or a father only fall between these two extreme groups with regard to income, but children living with a father only are more than twice as likely as children living with an ever-married mother only to have family incomes of $20,000 per year or more.

These basic results concerning the social, economic, and demographic circumstances of children demonstrate the critical importance of studies that delve deeply into the social, psychological, and legal consequences of divorce, single parenting, and stepparenting. In closing, I remind the reader of two ongoing projects that will extend and considerably enrich the results presented in this chapter. One research effort is the census monograph on children that I am writing based on analyses using microdata from the Decennial Censuses of 1940, 1950, 1960, 1970, and 1980 under grants awarded by the Russell Sage Foundation, the Social Science Research Council, and the National Science Foundation. The second is a research effort that we are conducting at the Census Bureau using the Marital and Fertility History Supplements of the Current Population Survey for June 1980 and June 1985.

In addition, we now have in place plans for improving the information obtained by the Census Bureau about children living in two-parent families. We currently are collecting detailed data about the full array of natural, step-, and adoptive relationships of children in the new Survey of Income and Program Participation, and we will be distinguishing stepchildren from other children in the March Current Population Survey begining in 1988, and in the 1990 Decennial Census.

ACKNOWLEDGMENTS

The author is indebted to Arlene Saluter, Edith Reeves, Jeanne E. Moorman, Steve Rawlings, Gerda Mudd, Terry Lugaila, and Debra Middleton for their assistance in the preparation of this chapter.

REFERENCES

Alwin, D. F. (1984). Trends in parental socialization values: Detroit, 1958–1983. *American Journal of Sociology, 90,* 359–382.

Bumpass, L. L. (1984). Children and marital disruption: A replication and update. *Demography, 21,* 71–82.

Cherlin, A. J. (1981). *Marriage and remarriage.* Cambridge, MA: Harvard University Press.

Glick, P. C. (1979). Children of divorced parents in demographic perspective. *Journal of Social Issues, 35,* 170–182.

Glick, P. C., & Norton, A. J. (1979). Marrying, divorcing, and living together in the U.S. today. *Population Bulletin, 32,* No. 5. Washington, DC: Population Reference Bureau.

Hernandez. D. J. (1986). Childhood in sociodemographic perspective. *Annual Review of Sociology, 12,* 159–180.

Hofferth, S. L. (1985). Updating children's life course. *Journal of Marriage and the Family, 47,* 93–115.

Jacobson, P.H. (1959). *American marriage and divorce.* New York: Rinehart.

Moorman, J. E., & Hernandez, D. J. (1987). *Estimates and characteristics of married-couple families with biological, step and adopted children.* Unpublished manuscript.

National Center for Health Statistics. (1986a). Advance report on final natality statistics, 1984. *Monthly Vital Statistics Report, 35*(4), Supp. DHHS Publ No. (PHS) 86–1120. Public Health Service Hyattsville, MD, July 18, 1986.

National Center for Health Statistics (1986b). Advance report on final divorce statistics, 1984. *Monthly*

Vital Statistics Report, *35*(6), Supp. DHHS Publ No. (PHS) 86–1120. Public Health Service Hyattsville, MD, September 25, 1986.

National Center for Health Statistics (1987a). *Vital Statistics of the United States, 1983, Vol. I, Natality*. DHHS Pub. No. (PHS) 87–1113. Public Health Service,Washington, DC. U.S. Government Printing Office.

National Center for Health Statistics (1987b). Advance report on final natality statistics, 1985. *Monthly Vital Statistics Report*, *36*(4), Supp. DHHS Publ No. (PHS) 87–1120. Public Health Service Hyattsville, MD, July 17, 1987.

National Center for Health Statistics (1987c). *Vital Statistics of the United States, 1983, Vol. III, Marriage and divorce*. DHHS Pub. No. (PHS) 87–1103. Public Health Service, Washington, DC. U.S. Government Printing Office.

National Center for Health Statistics (1987d). Advance report on final divorce statistics, 1985. *Monthly Vital Statistics Report*, *36*(8), Supp. DHHS Publ No. (PHS) 88–1120. Public Health Service Hyattsville, MD.

Norton, A.J., & Glick, P. C. (1986). One-parent families: A social and economic profile. *Journal of Family Relations*, *35*, 9–17.

Norton, A. J., & Moorman, J. E. (1987). Marriage and divorce patterns of U.S. Women. *Journal of Marriage and the Family*, *49*, 3–14.

U.S. Bureau of the Census. (1988). Current Population Reports, Series P-20, *Marital Status and Living Arrangements: March 1987*. Washington, DC: U.S. Government Printing Office.

Watts, H. W., & Hernandez, D. J. (Eds.). (1982). *Child and family indicators: A report with recommendations*. New York: Social Science Research Council.

2

Ethnicity and Single Parenting in the United States

Luis M. Laosa
Educational Testing Service

As Donald Hernandez points out in chapter 1 of this volume, the conventional family form in the United States has undergone rapid modifications in recent decades. An outcome of these normative alterations of family behavior is that a large proportion of children now live in some form of household other than the two-parent family. Consider the incidence of single-parent families. In 1970, 85% of children under the age of 18 lived with two parents, but in 1985 that figure had dropped to 74%; in the same 15-year period, the percentage of children living in a one-parent family has risen from 11.9% to 23.4% (U.S. Bureau of the Census, CPR P-20, No. 389, 1984a; U.S. Bureau of the Census, personal communication, 1986). Given its prevalence as a family form, single parenting is the personal circumstance and lifestyle of many parents and children.

Although representative and valid for the nation as a whole, the aforementioned observations and figures hide striking differences among the various ethnic and racial groups that make up our society. Single parenting is only rarely encountered among members of certain ethnic and racial groups, whereas in other groups it is encountered so frequently as to constitute virtually the normative family form. This and other ethnic or racial group differences in family behavior are more than anthropological curiosities. The history of the United States is really a history of distinct ethnic and racial groups with contrasting patterns of cultural traditions, historical circumstances, and access to societal resources (Laosa, 1984; Sowell, 1981). If we assume that the evolution of family forms is the outcome of a process of adaptation to cultural, social, and economic circumstances, it then seems reasonable to hypothesize that each U.S. ethnic and racial group will show its own characteristic pattern of contemporary family forms. This is the general hypothesis of this chapter, serving as a stimulus to exploratory inquiry rather than as a source of specific predictions. Specific predictions now seem premature; we need to know each group in much greater depth than we presently do before realistically feeling confident that our a priori hypotheses are more than just extensions of a researcher's ethnic stereotypes. In the course of the inquiry I also focus on the implications of single parenting for the economic standing of the various ethnic and racial groups, paying particular attention to the impact of this family form on the financial well-being of children and thence on the range of their likely developmental trajectories.

Data on sufficiently large and representative samples of families from certain ethnic and racial groups are always difficult and often impossible to obtain. Whereas it is now routine to report national data separately for Whites and Blacks, other ethnic and racial groups often are ignored. An encouraging sign is the emerging tendency to include Hispanics as a category in some databases. However, even such categories as Black, Hispanic, or White are so broad as to mask important dimensions of ethnic diversity within them, a point I attempt to demonstrate. For my observations and analyses here I rely primarily on data officially reported by the U.S. Bureau of the Census from its decennial census and population surveys. Although fraught with problems and limitations, the last decennial census (1980) is the best available source of family data for comparative analyses involving a relatively large number of U.S. ethnic and racial categories. In addition, because the government's databases do not contain data on religion, I turn to private surveys in an attempt to glean information on ethnoreligious groups. Because my approach here is synchronously comparative (that is, I seek to compare the characteristics exhibited by different groups at the same point in history), the fact that the data from the last decennial census and the other, supplemental information analyzed in this chapter are now several years "old" is, of course, irrelevant to the purpose at hand.

MEASURES OF SINGLE PARENTING

One's definition of what constitutes a *family* will determine the structure of the data one collects, which in turn will constrain how one measures the incidence of particular family forms. The U.S. Bureau of the Census defines a family as follows. The census taker first designates one resident of each household as the *householder*; this is usually a person in whose name the living quarters are owned or rented. A *family*, then, consists of the householder and one or more other persons living in the same household who are related to the householder by birth, marriage, or adoption. Not all households contain families, because a household may be composed by a group of unrelated persons or one person living alone. A *spouse* is a person married to and living with the householder; this category includes persons in formal marriages as well as persons in common-law marriages. *Own children* in a family are sons and daughters, including stepchildren and adopted children, of the householder who have never been married and are under 18 years of age. The number of *children living with their two parents* includes stepchildren and adopted children as well as children born to the couple regardless of the child's marital status.

The vast majority of single-parent families in the United States are headed by the mother—specifically, 87% of all single-parent families with own children under 18 years old were headed by the mother in 1980 (U.S. Bureau of the Census, PC80-1-C1, 1983a). Accordingly, I give slightly greater emphasis in the analyses to those single-parent families that are headed by mothers. However, I also conduct analyses comparing the incidence of single-father families across ethnic and racial groups.

Given the census definition of a family, I use the following measures to index single parenting. The first three measures, each calculated as a percentage of all families with own children, are respectively the number of families with own children headed by (a) a woman with no husband present, (b) a man with no wife present, and (c) either a man or a woman with no spouse present. A fourth measure is the percentage of children living with two parents. The first three measures reflect the situation from the view of women, men, and marriages, whereas the fourth one is an indicator from the perspective of children. Each index thus permits a different view of the situation. In addition, I use other indices when needed to expand or clarify the results of the analyses based on these four measures.

BROAD ETHNIC AND RACIAL CATEGORIES

The vast majority of the U.S. population is generally classified as belonging to one of four race categories—American Indian, Asian, Black, or White. In addition, an increasingly large proportion of the population is classified as Hispanic. The concept of race as used by the Census Bureau reflects self-identification by the respondents; it does not denote any clearcut scientific definition of genetically determined biological stock. The category Hispanic (or Spanish-origin) reflects the respondent's self-reported nationality group, lineage, or country in which the person or the person's parents or ancestors were born before arriving in the United States; as such, Hispanics may be of any race. Although these five broad categories mask important sources of ethnic diversity within them—a point to which I return later—they nevertheless are widely used for classifying individuals in our society and therefore significant politically and psychologically. For these reasons, let us begin the analyses by comparing the incidence of single parenting across these five ethnic and racial categories, shown in Table 2.1.

Regardless of which measure of single parenting is used, the analyses reveal striking differences across the five broad ethnic and racial categories at the time of the 1980 census. Only 14.4% of White families with own children were single-parent families, and 82.9% of all White children lived with their two parents.

TABLE 2.1
Incidence of Single Parenting for Five Broad U.S. Ethnic and Racial
Categories: 1980

Group	Percent of families with own children under 18 years old headed by a woman with no husband present	Percent of families with own children under 18 years old headed by either a man or a woman with no spouse present	Percent of children under 18 years old living with 2 parents
Black	41.8	45.8	45.4
American Indian	24.3	28.6	62.6
Hispanic[a]	20.4	23.5	70.9
Total U.S.	16.2	18.7	76.7
White	12.2	14.4	82.9
Asian[b]	9.5	11.5	84.7

[a]Hispanics may be of any race. [b]Includes Pacific Islanders.
Source: U. S. Bureau of the Census (PC80-1-C1, 1983a).

In sharp contrast, nearly half of all Black families with own children were single-parent families, and fewer than half of all Black children lived with their two parents. Single parenting was more prevalent among American Indians and Hispanics than among Whites, although not as prevalent as among Blacks. Of the five ethnic and racial categories, single parenting was most prevalent among Blacks. Whites did not have, however, the lowest incidence of single parenting. Contrary to commonly held conceptions, there is a racial minority group for which the incidence of single parenting is lower than even that of the total White population. Asians had the lowest incidence of single-parent families. Only 11.5% of Asian families with own children were single-parent families, and 84.7% of Asian children lived with their two parents. Clearly, then, the statistics describing the nation as a whole are hardly descriptive of families in each major ethnic and racial group.

RESIDENTIAL ECOLOGY

Ethnic and racial groups in the United States are unevenly distributed across residential ecologies. Families from some ethnic and racial groups tend to be concentrated in highly urbanized areas, whereas families from other groups are more likely to reside in suburban or rural areas. The best known instance of this observation is the fact that Blacks are more likely to reside in inner-city areas than are Whites. Specifically, 58.1% of Black families but only 23.5% of White families lived in central cities in 1980 (U.S. Bureau of the Census, PC80-1-C1, 1983a). Are such ethnic and racial group differences in patterns of residential ecology related to the incidence of particular family forms? And if so, are then the ethnic and racial group differences in the incidence of single parenting that we observed in the preceding section merely an analytic artifact, a confounding with residential ecology? Might the data on single parenting show a different pattern of results if each ethnic and racial category were broken down by type of residential ecology? Previous research concerned with differentiating the residential ecology of families (for a review see Bronfenbrenner, Moen, & Garbarino, 1984) suggests that certain family forms might occur more frequently in some types of environment than in others along a continuum ranging from urbanized centers to rural settings. To test this hypothesis, Table 2.2 shows the incidence of single parenting by broad ethnic and racial category separately for central cities, urban fringes, rural areas, and farms.

The incidence of single parenting clearly is related to residential ecology. There is a dramatic increase in the incidence of single parenting as one moves away from rural areas and into urbanized settings. This trend is generally true for all the ethnic and racial groups examined. The point I emphasize here, however, is that the differences across residential ecologies are so wide that ethnic or racial comparisons of the incidence of particular family forms must be qualified accordingly. Thus, Whites located in central cities in 1980 had a higher incidence of single-mother families than did (a) Hispanics residing in either urban fringes or rural areas and (b) American Indians and Blacks living on farms. For each of the five broad ethnic and racial categories, the incidence of single parenting generally becomes progressively higher toward the urban end of the rural-urban continuum. But at every point along this residential ecology continuum there are marked ethnic and racial group differences in the incidence of single parenting.

TABLE 2.2
Incidence of Single Parenting for Five Broad U.S. Ethnic
and Racial Categories, by Residential Ecology: 1980

	Percent of families with own children under 18 years old headed by a woman with no husband present				Percent of children under 18 years old living with 2 parents			
	Urban		Rural		Urban		Rural	
Group	Central cities	Urban fringe	Total	Farm	Central cities	Urban fringe	Total	Farm
Black	47.9	34.9	26.2	14.2	40.3	53.0	55.3	61.5
American Indian[a]	34.3	22.9	19.3	5.2	54.3	65.0	66.0	77.9
Hispanic[b]	26.2	16.2	9.8	3.2	65.2	75.3	79.6	86.4
Total U.S.	26.1	14.2	8.8	2.3	64.9	80.4	84.0	92.8
White	17.5	12.4	7.6	2.1	76.9	83.4	87.0	93.7
Asian[c]	10.9	7.8	9.7	3.5	82.6	87.3	84.3	89.9

[a]Includes Eskimos and Aleuts. [b]Hispanics may be of any race. [c]Includes Pacific Islanders.
Source: U.S. Bureau of the Census (PC80-1-C1, 1983a).

At each point Blacks show the highest incidence of single-parent families, followed by American Indians. However, the position of some groups relative to the others shifts across points. In other words, when one uses the incidence of single parenting as the dependent variable, there is a statistical interaction between ethnic or racial group and type of residential ecology. Specifically, although the positions of Blacks and American Indians on the single-parenting measures remain high relative to other groups at every point in the residential ecology continuum, the position of Asians relative to Whites and Hispanics shifts between points in this continuum. In urban settings, the Asians—compared to the other groups—had by far the lowest incidence of single parenting; but in rural areas, the Whites had the lowest incidence of this family form, followed in ascending order by the Asians who in turn were very closely followed by the Hispanics. These findings indicate that residential ecology should be included as a variable in theoretical models that attempt to explain ethnic or racial group differences in the incidence of particular family forms.

ANTECEDENTS OF SINGLE PARENTING

A child may be living in a single-parent family as a result of any one of a variety of causes. These include being born to an unwed parent, parental separation, divorce, or the death of a parent. Each of these causes is accompanied by its own unique set of circumstances, experiences, and changes in family life. When one considers the nation as a whole, divorce is by far the most frequent cause of single parenting. Of all U.S. children under 15 years old living with their single mothers in 1980, 40.4% were doing so because the mother was divorced, 27.8% because she was separated from her husband, 18.3% because she had never married, and 8.9% because she was widowed (U.S. Bureau of the Census, CPR P-23, No. 114, 1982a). Is this causal pattern generalizable to particular ethnic and racial categories? Are the antecedents of single parenting generally the same across ethnic and racial groups? To answer these questions, Tables 2.3 and 2.4 display statistics on children's living arrangements and parents' marital status separately for three broad ethnic and racial categories.

It is clear from these data that ethnic and racial groups differ markedly from one another not only in the incidence of single parenting, as we saw in the preceding section, but also in the causes giving rise to single parenting when this family form occurs. Of all White children under 15 years old living with their single mothers in 1980, over half were living with a divorced mother, one fourth were living with a mother who was separated from her husband, one-tenth with a widowed mother, and fewer than one-tenth with a never-married mother. These figures contrast sharply with those for Blacks and Hispanics. Of Black children living with their single mothers, over one third were living with a never-married mother, another one third with a separated mother, fewer than one fourth with

TABLE 2.3
Living arrangement, Presence of Parents, and Marital Status of Mother,
for Children Under 15 Years Old, for Three Broad U.S. Ethnic and Racial
Categories: 1980

	Total U.S.[a]	Black	Hispanic[b]	White
Total Children	100.0	100.0	100.0	100.0
In households	99.8	99.5	100.0	99.8
Living with both parents	77.2	42.6	77.2	83.5
Living with mother only				
Total[c]	17.8	43.1	18.7	13.2
Mother never married	3.2	14.8	4.1	1.2
Mother separated	4.9	14.2	7.0	3.3
Mother widowed	1.6	3.3	1.2	1.3
Mother divorced	7.2	9.8	5.4	6.8
Living with father only	1.4	1.8	1.3	1.3
Living with neither parent	3.4	12.0	2.8	1.8
Not in households[d]	0.2	0.5	0.0	0.2

Note: Figures in percentages. Noninstitutional population. [a]Includes racial categories not shown separately. [b]Hispanics may be of any race. [c]Includes those living with a mother who was "married, husband absent" (including separated), not shown separately (see text). [d]Noninstitutional living arrangements for groups not living in conventional housing units or groups living in housing units containing 5 or more persons unrelated to the person in charge.
Source: U.S. Bureau of the Census (CPR P-23, No. 114, 1982a).

TABLE 2.4
Marital Status of Single Mothers With Children Under 15 Years Old, for
Three Broad U.S. Ethnic and Racial Categories: 1980

Marital status	Total U.S.[a]	Black	Hispanic[b]	White
Total children living with mother only[c]	100.0	100.0	100.0	100.0
Mother never married	18.3	34.2	22.1	8.8
Mother separated	27.8	32.9	37.2	24.8
Mother widowed	8.9	7.6	6.2	9.5
Mother divorced	40.4	22.8	28.7	51.1

Note: Figures in percentages. Noninstitutional population.
[a]Includes racial categories not shown separately. [b]Hispanics may be of any race. [c]Includes those living with a mother who was "married, husband absent" (including separated), not shown separately (see text).
Source: U.S. Bureau of the Census (CPR P-23, No. 114, 1982a).

a divorced mother, and fewer than one-tenth with a widowed mother. Of Hispanic children living with their single mothers, over one third were living with a separated mother, fewer than three-tenths with a divorced mother, about one fifth with a never-married mother, and fewer than one-tenth with a widowed mother. Thus, although the most frequent precursor of single-parenting for Whites was divorce, it was out-of-wedlock births for Blacks, and marital separation for Hispanics (Table 2.4).

These findings strongly suggest that when parents have serious marital problems, Whites are more likely than Blacks or Hispanics to resolve them by becoming divorced and therefore to remarry if that option appeared better than remaining single. That this might indeed be so can be seen more clearly in Table 2.5, which breaks down the population of children living with their *ever*-married single mothers in 1980 into those whose mothers were separated, divorced, and widowed, separately by ethnic and racial category. The proportion of children living with ever-married single mothers who were separated (rather than divorced or widowed) is almost twice as high for Blacks and Hispanics as for Whites.

Persons reported as *separated* include only those with legal separations, those living apart with intentions of obtaining a divorce, and other persons permanently or temporarily separated because of marital discord, with or without a legal separation. There is an additional marital status category in the census data, labeled *other married, spouse absent*, which excludes those persons in the previously mentioned categories and includes married persons living apart because either the husband or wife was employed and living at a considerable distance from home, was serving away from home in the Armed Forces, had moved to another area, was an inmate of an institution, or had a different place of residence for any other reason except separation as just defined. The percentages of children under 15 years old living with a mother in this category were respectively 1.1%, 1.1%, and 0.8% for Blacks, Hispanics, and Whites in 1980 (U.S. Bureau of the Census, CPR P-23, No. 114, 1982a).

Only a small proportion of children now live with a widowed parent, as the

TABLE 2.5

Marital Status of Ever-Married Single Mothers With Children Under 15 Years Old, for Three Broad U.S. Ethnic and Racial Categories: 1980

Marital status	Black	Hispanic[a]	White
Total children living with their ever-married single mothers[b]	100.0	100.0	100.0
Mother divorced	34.7	36.9	56.0
Mother separated	50.0	47.7	27.2
Mother widowed	11.5	7.9	10.4

Note: Figures in percentages. Noninstitutional population.

[a]Hispanics may be of any race. [b]Includes those living with a mother who was "married, husband absent" (including separated), not shown separately (see text).

Source: U.S. Bureau of the Census (CPR P-23, No. 114 1982a).

mortality rate for adults of childrearing age has fallen over the years. Although the proportion of children living with a widowed mother is small in each ethnic and racial group, this proportion is higher among Blacks than among Whites or Hispanics (Table 2.3). Group differences in this regard may reflect in part differential death rates. Consider that in 1980, the number of deaths per 100,000 Black men between the ages of 25 and 34 years was 407, whereas the corresponding figure for White men of the same age was only 171 (U.S. Bureau of the Census, *Statistical abstract of the United States: 1984*, 1983b).

CHILDREN LIVING WITH NEITHER PARENT

Another family characteristic that distinguishes the Black population from other ethnic or racial groups is the relatively high proportion of children living with neither parent. Fully 12% of Black children under 15 years old were living with neither parent in 1980. In contrast, the corresponding figures for Hispanics and Whites were only 2.8% and 1.8%, respectively (Table 2.3). These figures represent children living in family households with grandparents, other relatives, or nonrelatives. Why do ethnic or racial groups differ in this respect? In discussing Black families, it is sometimes asserted that the *informal* adoption of children by nonrelatives as well as relatives is one of the various contemporary Black family forms. This practice is seen as a means of providing mutual help and support between members of extended social networks, which encompass both kin and nonkin. These social networks are viewed as important components of Black social structure. Also in this regard, one wonders to what extent parental mortality rates might explain ethnic and racial group differences in the living arrangements of children. Consider that the number of maternal deaths per 100,000 live births from deliveries and complications of pregnancy, childbirth, and the puerperium was 21.5 for Blacks but only 6.7 for Whites in 1980 (U.S. Bureau of the Census, *Statistical Abstract of the United States: 1984*, 1983b).

ETHNIC DIVERSITY WITHIN BROAD ETHNIC AND RACIAL CATEGORIES

Considerable ethnic diversity exists *within* each of the ethnic and racial categories considered thus far. In the same way that the statistics calculated on the nation as a whole fail to describe accurately families in each of these ethnic and racial categories, so do the statistics tabulated for these categories hide significant ethnic heterogeneity within them. It is therefore important to define ethnic and racial group membership with greater precision and in finer detail than these commonly used categories permit. Let us now turn to some of the major ethnic groups that are included in these categories.

Hispanic Ethnic Diversity

The Hispanic population in the United States is composed of several different ethnic groups, each with its own cultural and economic characteristics and historical circumstances. The three major groups are the Mexican (or Chicano), Puerto Rican, and Cuban. Although these groups share characteristics in common, they also differ markedly from one another along a number of dimensions (see, e.g., Laosa, 1975). Especially in analyzing the incidence of diverse family forms, it is important to consider each Hispanic ethnic group separately. Specifically, an exceedingly high incidence of single-parent families distinguishes mainland Puerto Ricans[1] from other U.S. Hispanic groups. The incidence of single parenting is over twice as high among mainland Puerto Ricans as among the other two major Hispanic groups. Of all mainland Puerto Rican families with own children under 18 years of age, the percentage headed by either a man or a woman with no spouse present was 42.6% in 1980. In contrast, the corresponding figures for Cuban Americans and Mexican Americans were, respectively, 16.5% and 18.9%. Thus, the incidence of single parenting among mainland Puerto Ricans was virtually as high as in the Black population, whereas the incidence of single parenting among Cuban Americans and Mexican Americans was only slightly higher than in the total White population (Tables 2.1 and 2.6).

We do not yet know what factors account for the very high incidence of single parenting among Puerto Ricans. It is significant, however, that the incidence of single parenting is different between mainland Puerto Ricans and those living on the island of Puerto Rico. Of the families with own children under 18 years of age living in Puerto Rico in 1980, 16.1% were headed by a woman with no husband present and 18.1% were headed by either a man or a woman with no spouse present. Thus, the incidence of single parenting among island Puerto Ricans was less than half of what it was among mainland Puerto Ricans (Tables 2.6 and 2.7). Also interesting is the further finding that the incidence of single parenting in Puerto Rico was almost identical to that of Mexican Americans and Cuban Americans. The difference in the occurrence of single parenting between mainland and island Puerto Ricans is redolent of another finding, discussed previously, revealing that the incidence of particular family forms varies greatly between types of residential ecology. Indeed, because Puerto Ricans on the mainland tend to concentrate in highly urbanized areas,[2] the question then arises: Is the incidence of single parenting in the highly urbanized areas of Puerto Rico as high

---

[1]Because of Puerto Rico's status as a U.S. Commonwealth, Puerto Ricans possess U.S. citizenship. The adjective *mainland* is used, therefore, to distinguish the Puerto Ricans living in the 50 States from those on the island of Puerto Rico.

[2]Ninety-six percent of mainland Puerto Rican families lived in metropolitan areas in 1982, compared to only 65.5% of nonHispanic U.S. families; further, 76% of mainland Puerto Rican families lived in the central cities of metropolitan areas, compared to only 24.6% of nonHispanic U.S. families (U.S. Bureau of the Census, CPR P-20, No. 396, 1985).

TABLE 2.6
Single Parenting in U.S. Hispanic Groups: 1980

Group	Percent of families with own children under 18 years old headed by a woman with no husband present	Percent of families with own children under 18 years old headed by either a man or a woman with no spouse present	Percent of children under 18 years old living with two parents
Cuban	14.4	16.5	78.1
Mexican	15.8	18.9	74.8
Puerto Rican[a]	39.3	42.6	50.9
Other Hispanic	21.1	24.2	72.0

[a]Mainland.
Source: U. S. Bureau of the Census (PC80-1-C1, 1983a).

as that of mainland Puerto Ricans? The answer to this question is negative. Within Puerto Rico, as one moves away from farms and other rural settings and into urbanized areas, the incidence of single parenting increases dramatically. Nevertheless, even in Puerto Rico's central cities the incidence of single parenting was much lower than among mainland Puerto Ricans (Tables 2.6 and 2.7). The difference in the incidence of single parenting between mainland and island Puerto Ricans might indicate family disruption resulting from the stresses involved in coping with and adapting to the mainland environment, or it might reflect a higher migration probability among single-parent than two-parent families, or perhaps a combination of these and other as yet unidentified factors.

Asian Ethnic Diversity

The designation *Asian* and the census category *Asian and Pacific Islander* include a number of distinct ethnic groups. Both culturally and linguistically as well

TABLE 2.7
Incidence of Single Parenting in Puerto Rico, by Residential Ecology: 1980

Ecology	Percent of families with own children under 18 years old headed by a woman with no husband present	Percent of families with own children under 18 years old headed by either a man or a woman with no spouse present
Urban		
Central cities	22.1	23.9
Urban fringe	15.1	17.0
Rural total	12.1	14.2
Farm	5.9	8.7
All ecologies	16.1	18.1

Source: U.S. Bureau of the Census (PC80-1-C53A, 1984b).

as in their historical circumstances these groups differ from one another in significant respects. It is possible to examine family data separately for several Asian and Pacific Islander groups living in the United States, as Table 2.8 shows. The data show wide variability in the incidence of single parenting across groups, indicating clearly that the various U.S. Asian ethnic groups are by no means a homogeneous entity with regard to family characteristics. At one end of the range indexed by the measures of single parenting are the Asian Indians, whereas Hawaiians occupy the opposite end. Only 4.7% of Asian Indian families with own children under 18 years of age were headed by a parent with no spouse present in 1980. In contrast, the corresponding figure for Hawaiians is 25.4%—a five-fold difference between these two groups.

Thus, not all the Asian and Pacific Islander groups had lower incidences of single parenting than did the Whites. The Japanese showed an incidence of single parenting very similar to that of the total White population. And although the Asian Indians, Chinese, Koreans, and Filipinos did have lower incidences than the Whites, the latter group was surpassed by the Vietnamese, Guamanians, Samoans, and Hawaiians in the incidence of this family form. Further, not all the Asian and Pacific Islander groups had less single parenting than the Hispanics. The Hawaiians and Samoans had a higher incidence of single parenting than the Cubans and Mexicans (Tables 2.1, 2.6, and 2.8).

TABLE 2.8
Single Parenting in U.S. Asian and
Pacific Islander Groups: 1980

Group	Percent of families with own children under 18 years old headed by a woman with no husband present	Percent of families with own children under 18 years old headed by either a man or a woman with no spouse present	Percent of children under 18 years old living with two parents
Hawaiian	21.5	25.4	68.7
Samoan	18.7	21.0	69.2
Guamanian	14.2	17.4	75.3
Vietnamese	13.8	18.5	74.1
Japanese	12.0	13.6	87.3
Filipino	10.0	11.9	84.5
Korean	9.7	11.2	89.4
Chinese	6.5	8.2	88.2
Asian Indian	3.7	4.7	92.7
Other Asian and Pacific Islander	9.3	11.7	82.0

Note: Population in the 50 States.
Source: U.S. Bureau of the Census (PC80-1-C1, 1983a).

TABLE 2.9
Single Parenting in Six U.S. European-Ancestry Groups: 1980

Group	Percent of families with own children under 18 years old headed by a woman with no husband present	Percent of families with own children under 18 years old headed by either a man or a woman with no spouse present	Percent of children under 18 years old living with two parents
French	12.3	14.8	77.8
Irish	12.2	14.6	78.5
English	11.5	13.9	79.8
Italian	9.8	11.9	83.2
Polish	9.7	11.7	82.3
German	8.9	11.1	83.7

Source: U.S. Bureau of the Census (PC80-1-C1, 1983a).

White Ethnic Diversity

Even within the White population there is considerable ethnic diversity, because this racial category contains numerous ancestry groups. The 1980 census was the first time that a general open-ended question on ancestry (ethnicity) was asked in a decennial census. Respondents reported their ancestry group regardless of the number of generations removed from their country of origin. Although some respondents reported two or more ancestry categories, a large number reported their ancestry by specifying a single ancestry. Although persons in these categories can be of any race, it probably can be safely assumed that almost all in certain categories are White. Accordingly, the availability of census data on European single-ancestry groups provided the opportunity to observe the incidence of single parenting in various White ethnic groups. Table 2.9 shows the incidence of single-parent families in each of six U.S. White ethnic groups. The differences across these groups are not large. Nevertheless, the differences are of sufficient magnitude to conclude that White ethnic groups are not homogeneous with regard to the incidence of this family form. Of the six U.S. White ethnic groups examined, the Irish and the French had the highest incidence of single parenting, whereas the Germans had the lowest. If the measure of single parenting used is the percentage of families with own children under 18 years old headed by a woman with no husband present, then single parenting occurred less frequently among the Germans than even in the total Asian and Pacific Islander population (Tables 2.1 and 2.9), and indeed less frequently than in any but two Asian and Pacific Islander groups (Tables 2.8 and 2.9). Using this measure to rank order the 20 U.S. ethnic and racial groups examined here (Tables 2.1, 2.6, 2.8 and 2.9), only the Asian Indians and the Chinese had a lower incidence of single parenting than the Germans.

Black Ethnic Diversity

The U.S. Black population is also ethnically heterogeneous, although precise data on this diversity are difficult to find. As Sowell (1978) pointed out, the history of Black people in the United States is really the history of three distinct groups, with contrasting patterns of socioeconomic distribution and even fertility rates. The first of these broad groups to have an independent history in the American economy were the antebellum "free persons of color." In the 1830s this group constituted only 14% of the North American Black population, but they and their descendants have played a major role in the history of U.S. Blacks. Another broad group, the largest component of the U.S. Black population, has consisted of those Blacks emancipated by the Civil War and their descendants. The third group consists of Black immigrants, principally from the West Indies. Particularly the latter group today is noticeably diverse, containing as it does a variety of national-origin groups, each with its own distinctive language and culture. Family data broken down by the various Black groups are elusive. Whether the statistics on the incidence of single parenting calculated for the total U.S. Black population, which we saw in an earlier section, can be generalized to each of the Black ethnic groups is a question that warrants empirical research.

Jewish Americans

One important group, Jewish Americans, is almost always left out of statistical analyses of ethnic group differences in the United States. The reason for this omission is that they are not included as a category in the government's databases because of alleged constitutional limitations on religious inquiries by the U.S. Bureau of the Census. Although comprehensive and accurate data on Jewish American families are elusive, the data that do exist from privately conducted surveys suggest that single parenting occurs less frequently among Jewish Americans than in the total U.S. White population.

Although limited for purposes of comparisons with the other data examined in this article, the General Standard Survey (GSS) of the University of Chicago's National Opinion Research Center is probably the best available source for extending the present inquiry to include the Jewish American population. Conducted since 1972, the GSS is a personal interview sampling of the U.S. adult noninstitutional English-speaking population that asks its respondents to identify their religious preferences. Cherlin and Celebuski (1982) compared the answers to questions about family characteristics given by White GSS respondents who identified themselves as Jewish, Protestant, or Catholic. In order to obtain a sufficiently large sample of Jewish respondents for analytic purposes, these researchers pooled eight annual GSS waves (1972–1978 and 1980), treating them as one large national survey; their approach is thus very similar to the one used earlier by S. M. Cohen (1981). Cherlin and Celebuski (1982) found the following ethnoreligious group differences, which confirmed the hypothesis of a comparatively low incidence of divorce among Jewish Americans. Among the ever-married adults in the GSS, 24% of the White Protestants and 17% of the White Catholics, but only 12% of the Jews, had divorced or separated at some time since they were married. These results are congruent with those reported by Cohen (1981) using the same database, as Table 2.10 shows. The comparatively low incidence of divorce among Jewish Americans gains in significance when one considers that members of this group are concentrated in highly urbanized areas. More than 90% of Jewish Americans are located in the largest cities or their immediate suburbs, whereas fewer than 10% are found in places with less than 50,000 population (Bogue, 1985). After attempting to control statistically for variations in education, urban residence, region of residence, and time elapsed since first marriage, Cherlin and Celebuski (1982) found that a significant portion of the Jewish versus Protestant difference in divorce and separation remained.

Just as there is diversity within the other broad ethnic and racial categories examined here, so is there ethnic heterogeneity within the Jewish American population. The aforementioned statistics on the incidence of divorce for Jewish Americans as a whole might not generalize, therefore, to each of the distinct subgroups that compose the Jewish American population. A salient dimension of diversity among Jewish Americans is religion itself. Brodbar-Nemzer (1984) analyzed data from a 1981 survey of the greater metropolitan New York City's Jewish population and, comparing the divorce rates of Orthodox, Conservative, and Reform Jews, found that the Orthodox had the lowest divorce rate, the rate among Conservatives was higher, and the Reform Jews divorced at a rate twice that of the Orthodox, whereas religiously unaffiliated Jews divorced at four times the Orthodox rate. Another important dimension of Jewish diversity reflects the immigration of Jews to America, which occurred in three historical waves involving people from three broad national locations: Sephardic Jews from Spain and Portugal; German Jews from the Germanic states; and East European Jews, largely from Poland and Russia but also from Rumania, Hungary, and Lithuania. Although they overlapped, these three waves of immigration define three distinct cultural, social, and economic patterns that have tended to differentiate Jews in America (Farber, Mindel, & Lazerwitz, 1976). Because there are historical circumstances and cultural, social, and economic characteristics that distinguish Jewish ethnic

TABLE 2.10
Divorce in Three U.S. White Religious Groups, by Age

Group	18–24	25–34	35–44	45–54	55–64	65+
Jews	–	8	10	7	5	8
Catholics	4	10	15	13	18	11
Protestants	5	15	20	20	16	17

Note: Figures are percentages of White ever-married persons who were ever divorced.
Source: General Social Survey of the National Opinion Research Center, conducted annually 1972–1978; reported in Cohen (1981).

groups from one another, it would be worthwhile to compare in future studies the incidence of various family forms across these groups.

SINGLE FATHERS

Relatively few single-parent families with children are headed by a man. This observation holds true across ethnic and racial groups. In none of the ethnic and racial groups examined here did the number of single-father families with own children under 18 years old constitute more than 5% of all families with own children of the same age. Examined from another perspective, in none of the ethnic and racial groups examined here did the number of single-father families with own children under 18 years old constitute more than 26% of all *single-parent* families with own children of the same age. Within this range there are, however, wide ethnic and racial group differences in the percentages of single-parent families that are single-father families, as Table 2.11 shows. These per-

TABLE 2.11
Single-Father Families, for Selected U.S. Ethnic and Racial Groups: 1980

	Percent of families with own children under 18 years old headed by a man with no wife present	Percent of single-parent families with own children under 18 years old headed by a man
American Indian	4.3	15.0
Asian Indian	1.1	22.5
Black	4.0	8.7
Chinese	1.8	21.3
Cuban	2.0	12.3
English	2.4	17.1
Filipino	2.0	16.4
French	2.5	17.0
German	2.2	19.5
Guamanian	3.2	18.5
Hawaiian	3.9	15.4
Irish	2.4	16.6
Italian	2.1	17.7
Japanese	1.7	12.4
Korean	1.5	13.3
Mexican	3.1	16.4
Polish	2.1	17.6
Puerto Rican[a]	3.3	7.8
Samoan	2.3	11.1
Vietnamese	4.8	25.7
Total U.S.[b]	2.5	13.4

[a]Mainland. [b]Includes groups not shown separately.
Source: U.S. Bureau of the Census (PC80-1-C1, 1983a).

centages ranged from a low of 7.8% to a high of 25.7% for the 20 groups included in the analysis. At the high end of the range are the Vietnamese, Asian Indians, Chinese, and Germans; in these groups, between 20% and 26% of the single-parent families were single-father families. At the low end of the range are the Puerto Ricans and Blacks; in these two groups, fewer than 10% of the single-parent families were single-father families. These differences in the percentages of single-parent families that are headed by men are intriguing because they might reflect ethnic group differences in family behavior generally or in men's parenting roles in particular, and they therefore warrant future research attempts to explain them.

Compared to the number of children living with their single mothers, the number of children living with their single fathers is very small. Consider the statistics for Blacks, Hispanics, and the total White population. In each of these groups, fewer that 2% of children under 18 years of age lived with their single fathers in 1980 (Table 2.3). Although the proportions of children living in single-father families is indeed small, it should be noted that the actual numbers involved are large. Over 1 million children under 18 years of age were living with their single fathers in 1980—of these, 819,000 were White; 183,000 Black; and 80,000 Hispanic.

ECONOMIC IMPLICATIONS
OF SINGLE PARENTING

The observation that single parenting, or, more specifically, the raising of children without a spouse, is a role largely relegated to women in our society, should be juxtaposed to the further observation that the average woman still earns a lower income per hour than does the average man (Fuchs, 1986), and both should be kept in mind as we examine the economic implications of single-parenting.

Although the repercussions of single parenting on children may occur along a number of dimensions (e.g., psychological), the most palpable impact is financial. The total income of single-mother families with children, including sources such as public assistance, alimony, and child support, but excluding noncash income, is considerably lower than for two-parent families. For the nation as a whole, the year preceding the last decennial census, the median annual income of single-mother families was about one third that of married-couple families with children. Among those with children under 6 years old, the income of single-mother families was about one fourth that of two-parent families. The significance of these findings increases when one considers that generally the number of children per family is remarkably similar between the two family forms (Table 2.12). It seems reasonable to infer, as others also do (e.g., Easterlin, 1983), that so far as the economic circumstances of children are concerned, the absence of a father from the household affects them adversely by lowering household income

TABLE 2.12
Average Number of Children Per Family With Children,
by Family Form: 1981

Family form	Total U.S.[a]	Black	Hispanic [b]	White
Married couple	1.91	2.04	2.21	1.89
Female householder, no husband present	1.79	2.00	2.00	1.69

Note: Own children under 18 years old.
[a]Includes racial and ethnic groups not shown separately. [b]Hispanics may be of any race.
Source: U.S. Bureau of the Census (CPR P-20, No. 371, 1982b).

more than it reduces demands on that income due both to the absence of the father and the slightly smaller number of children in single-mother families.

It can be concluded that the average child in a single-mother family lives in an economically disadvantaged environment relative to his or her counterpart in a married-couple family. This conclusion seems to hold true for each of the ethnic and racial groups examined here. The data, summarized in Table 2.13, compare the annual incomes of single-mother and married-couple families with children, separately for 20 U.S. ethnic and racial groups. Without exception, in each of the 20 groups the median income of single-mother families with children under 18 years old was less than half that of married-couple families with children of the same age; in nearly all groups the ratio was closer to one third than to one half. The economic disadvantage of single-mother families appears even greater at younger than at older ages. Among those with children under 6 years old, single-mother families in the vast majority of the groups had a median income totaling less than one third that of two-parent families; the ratio was about one fourth in half of the groups.

Given that the economic well-being of a U.S. family depends on the number of providers (primarily parents), their capacity to acquire income, and the number of dependents it must support (primarily children), the economically disadvantageous position of the single-mother family, compared to its two-parent counterpart, becomes starkly predictable. It is not only that two parents have greater earning capacity than one, but also that men's wages tend to be higher than women's, which determines the difference in income between the two family forms. Moreover, not only the level but also the flexibility of the family economy is typically curtailed when only one adult is present, because a family with a second actual or potential earner can adapt better to economic vicissitudes than a single parent, whether the vicissitudes are external to the family (e.g., recession, inflation) or internal (e.g., illness, disability).

It is important to note, however, that the size of the sex differential in earnings varies across ethnic and racial groups. Consider the case of Blacks and Whites. Although women's hourly earnings are on the average lower than men's in both

TABLE 2.13
Median Annual Income of Single-Mother and Married-Couple Families With
Children, for Selected U.S. Ethnic and Racial Groups: 1979

Group	Married-couple families		Female householder, no husband present	
	With own children under 6	With own children under 18	With own children under 6	With own children under 18
American Indian[a]	14,704	16,874	5,000	6,618
Asian Indian	26,283	27,359	7,155	10,326
Black	16,991	19,036	4,711	6,448
Chinese	23,329	24,580	6,807	10,761
Cuban	20,334	21,537	5,757	8,017
English	19,171	22,244	5,279	8,469
Filipino	24,391	26,647	7,746	10,743
French	19,377	22,259	5,290	8,170
German	20,402	23,580	6,374	9,693
Guamanian	17,042	20,253	6,554	8,864
Hawaiian	18,708	22,352	5,912	7,344
Irish	20,592	23,886	5,832	9,327
Italian	21,161	24,567	5,428	9,323
Japanese	25,926	30,208	7,154	11,199
Korean	20,697	22,461	5,586	8,165
Mexican	14,855	16,675	5,054	6,627
Polish	22,141	25,640	5,886	10,294
Puerto Rican[b]	13,428	15,177	4,044	4,593
Samoan	14,485	16,167	5,231	6,526
Vietnamese	13,209	14,836	5,378	6,851
Total U.S.[c]	19,630	22,569	5,229	8,002

Note: The data on income represent the sum of the amounts reportedly received from wages and salaries, self-employed work, public assistance and welfare, alimony, child support payments, unemployment and workers' compensation, Social Security, contributions received periodically from persons not residing in the household, and interest, dividend, royalty, and rental income. Not included as income are the value of "in kind" income from food stamps, public housing subsidies, medical care, and employer contributions for pensions, etc.
[a]Includes Eskimos and Aleuts. [b]Mainland. [c]Includes groups not shown separately.
Source: U.S. Bureau of the Census (PC80-1-C1, 1983a).

racial groups, this sex gap is considerably narrower for Blacks than for Whites (Fuchs, 1986). Blacks earn less on the average than Whites, and this is true for each sex; however, the men's earning advantage over women is appreciably smaller among Blacks than among Whites. The importance of examining the sex differential in earning capacity separately for each ethnic and racial group is that when the size of this sex differential varies across groups, so will the economic implications of single parenting vary accordingly across groups. The economic implications of single parenting will vary across ethnic or racial groups as a function of the size of the sex differential in earning capacity. For example, from the finding just given showing the Black–White difference in the sex differential in earnings, it seems reasonable to infer that the economic disincentive to becoming a single mother, as opposed to a married one, is weaker for Black than for White women. Having or not having a spouse makes less of a difference to the Black mother's situation, economically speaking, than it does to the White mother's situation. Might this difference in the apparent strength of the economic disincentive to becoming a single mother help explain the higher incidence of Black than White single-mother families? Analyses intended to model the economic impact of single parenting on families and theoretical models seeking to explain ethnic or racial group differences in the incidence of single parenting should incorporate the finding that the size of the sex differential in earning capacity is not invariant across groups.

The economic pressures and the coping reactions to them doubtlessly mean, other things equal, a more stressful environment for the single mother and her children than for their counterparts in the two-parent family. Is the manner of coping with the economic pressures of single parenting and its attendant stresses generally uniform across ethnic and racial groups? Data on Black and White mothers' labor force participation suggest that there may be group differences in how single mothers cope, as indicated by the following statistical interaction between race and family form: Of the children living in two-parent families, a larger percentage of Blacks (62%) than of Whites (51%) had mothers working outside the home in 1980; however, of the children in single-mother families, a smaller percentage of Blacks (57%) than of Whites (67%) had working mothers (Hill, 1983, p. 14). Needed is comparative research aimed at examining the coping reactions to the stresses of single parenting and studies of the actual and perceived constraints on the range of possible coping strategies in the different ethnic and racial groups.

For children, the significance of the relationship between family composition and economic position lies in the linkage between economic position and child development. Along one dimension are the material resources available to children, which can have immediate and possibly long-term effects on their physical health. On another dimension, research repeatedly has shown a correlation between children's socioeconomic status and such factors as their parents' behavior toward them, their teachers' attitudes toward them, and the children's own school performance and intellectual development (for reviews see Brophy & Good, 1974; Deutsch, 1973; Hess, 1970). On yet another crucial dimension, economic adversity may severely restrict opportunities for education and thence the range of future employment options. Insofar as family income affects access to education and therefore future occupational options, equality of opportunity is lacking between children in single-mother families and those living with two parents.

Because of the ethnic and racial differences in economic standing that exist in our society, the financial implications of single parenting for children actually differ across ethnic and racial groups. This can be discerned more readily by using as the dependent variable the percentage of children below the poverty level; Table 2.14 shows this statistic for three broad ethnic and racial categories calculated separately for two family forms. Four of every 10 White children in single-mother families lived below the poverty line in 1980. High as this figure is, it is much higher for Hispanics and Blacks. Three of every five Hispanic and Black children in single-mother families were below the poverty level. Nevertheless, in going from a two-parent to a single-mother family the White child increased his or her chances of being poor more so than the Hispanic or Black child—because poverty in the latter two groups is so prevalent even among two-parent families. Specifically, the chances of a White child's being poor were almost five times higher if living with a single mother than if living with two parents, whereas the chances of a Hispanic or Black child's being poor were only about three times higher if living with a single mother than if living with two parents. These poverty statistics of a few years ago are not very different from what they are today, and, indeed, in some respects the situation is now even worse (Table 2.14). If the decision to become a single parent were to hinge at all on economic considerations, might these findings help explain ethnic and racial differences in the incidence of diverse family forms? The next section examines three hypotheses that have been advanced to explain ethnic and racial differences in the incidence of single parenting.

EXPLANATORY HYPOTHESES

What accounts for the startling ethnic and racial group differences in the incidence of single parenting that, as we observed in the preceding sections, exist

TABLE 2.14

Percent of Children Below the Poverty Level in Single-Mother and All Other Families, for Three U.S. Ethnic and Racial Groups: 1979 to 1985

	Year		
Family type and group	1979	1980	1985
Children in families with female householder, no husband present			
Hispanic	62.2	65.0	72.4
Black	63.1	64.8	66.9
White	38.6	41.6	45.2
Children in all other families[a]			
Hispanic	19.2	22.9	27.4
Black	18.7	20.3	18.8
White	7.3	9.0	10.4

Note: Children under 18 years old and related to the householder. Hispanics may be of any race.

[a]All but a very small percentage of the children in the category labeled *all other families* are in two-parent families (see Table 2.3).

Source: U.S. Bureau of the Census (CPR P-60, No. 154, 1986).

in our society? Three major hypotheses have been advanced to explain ethnic and racial differences in the incidence of single parenting. One hypothesis implicates slavery in American history as a causative factor in the high incidence of single parenting among contemporary Black Americans. Another hypothesis posits that it is each group's economic circumstances that are responsible for its pattern of family forms. The third hypothesis points to each group's cultural traditions and their role in the maintenance of traditional family forms. How does the evidence stack for or against these hypotheses?

Slavery is indeed a dominant fact in the history of Black Americans; no other U.S. racial or ethnic group was comparably treated (Laosa, 1984). Among the most tragic consequences of slavery were the forcible breakups of slave families by the sale of individuals (Bremner, 1970; Sowell, 1983). It is sometimes suggested, therefore, that slavery is responsible for "broken matriarchal homes," or, more to the point here, for the exceedingly high incidence of single parenting among contemporary Black Americans. The slavery hypothesis appears plausible when we limit the analysis to broad racial categories, as is typically done. That is, typically the Black population is compared only to the total White population. The historical fact that one group but not the other was subjected to slavery is then taken as the cause of the contemporary difference between the two populations' incidences of single-parent families. The slavery hypothesis is contradicted, however, by the results of comparative analyses that examine ethnic groups in greater detail. Specifically, the slavery hypothesis is difficult to reconcile with the findings showing that the incidence of single parenting among contemporary Black Americans is not much higher than among nonslaved groups such as the impoverished Irish Americans of an earlier era (Sowell, 1978) or the mainland Puerto Ricans today (Tables 2.1 and 2.6).

An additional argument is sometimes brought to bear against the slavery hypothesis. The contention is that a high incidence of female-headed families among Black Americans seems to be a development that emerged well into the twentieth century—well after emancipation. This temporal hiatus between slavery and the emergence of single-parenting as a prevalent Black family form is seen as difficult to reconcile with the slavery hypothesis. However, a relatively late emergence of the Black–White difference in the incidence of single parenting does not, by itself, constitute definitive evidence against the slavery hypothesis, because it can be argued that the influence of slavery on Black family forms slowly manifested itself. A more powerful argument against the slavery hypothesis appears to be the one given in the preceding paragraph.

The economic hypothesis posits that poverty leads to "family disorganization," or more specifically, to a high incidence of single parenting. Sowell (1978) favors this hypothesis, adducing as confirmatory evidence the fact that certain groups with a high incidence of impoverished families also have a high incidence of single parenting. Compared to the total White population, Blacks and mainland Puerto Ricans indeed have both a lower average income and a higher incidence of single parenting, a pattern resulting in a perfect rank-order correlation between the incidence of this family form and the economic level of these three groups. However, when one considers more than Sowell's few exemplars, the magnitude of this rank-order correlation becomes attenuated, as Table 2.15 shows. It can be seen, for example, that the Japanese, while enjoying a higher average income than the Chinese, nevertheless also have a higher incidence of single parenting. These data suggest that more than economic factors are needed to explain the observed ethnic and racial group differences in the incidence of single-parent families. It is plausible, however, that economic variables other than income, such as the group's unemployment rate or the size of the sex differential in earning capacity, might help explain the ethnic and racial group differences in the incidence of single parenting, and such variables should be included in future, more thorough tests of the economic hypothesis.

Whereas the focus of the economic hypothesis is on the causes of ethnic and racial group differences in the incidence of particular family forms, its obverse is the question of whether the ethnic and racial group differences in the incidence of particular family forms cause the ethnic and racial group differences in economic level. Can we explain the economic inequalities that exist among the nation's ethnic and racial groups on the basis of the ethnic and racial group differences in the incidence of single parenting? Is a group's high incidence of single parenting responsible for its low standing on the society's economic ladder? Children in some ethnic and racial groups fare much worse economically, on the average, than do children in other groups, as the per capita income figures in Table 2.15

TABLE 2.15
Relationship Between Incidence of Single Parenting and
Economic Well-Being of Selected U.S. Ethnic and Racial Groups: 1980

Group	Percent of families with own children under 18 years old headed by a woman with no husband present	Percent of families with own children under 18 years old headed by either a man or a woman with no spouse present	Per capita income[a] ($)	Median income of all families[a] ($)
Chinese	6.5	8.2	7,476	22,559
Korean	9.7	11.2	5,544	20,459
Filipino	10.0	11.9	6,915	23,687
Japanese	12.0	13.6	9,068	27,354
Total White	12.2	14.4	7,808	20,835
Irish	12.2	14.6	8,534	20,719
Vietnamese	13.8	18.5	3,382	12,840
Puerto Rican[b]	39.3	42.6	3,905	10,734
Total Black	41.8	45.8	4,545	12,598

[a]Annual income in 1979. [b]Mainland.
Source: U.S. Bureau of the Census (PC80-1-C1, 1983a).

indicate. To what extent are the group differences in children's economic well-being the result of corresponding group differences in the incidence of single-parent families? A cross-group analysis of the economic circumstances of two-parent families suggests an answer to these questions. Specifically, sizable differences in income can be observed across ethnic and racial groups even when one considers only families with two parents (Table 2.13). It can be inferred, therefore, that equalizing the percentages of children in two-parent families across ethnic and racial groups would not, by itself, eliminate or even greatly reduce the ethnic and racial group differences in the economic well-being of children (or adults). Means other than equalizing the proportions of two-parent families are required to bring about ethnic and racial group equality in economic well-being. It seems reasonable to argue, however, that an increase in a group's proportion of children in two-parent families could, across generations, yield a beneficial effect on the group's economic well-being. Such an effect would result from a break in the cycle that is presumably reflected in the observed intercorrelations among family composition, income, children's education, and their future occupational opportunities. It appears unlikely, however, that even a break in this cycle can bring about complete ethnic and racial group economic equality in the absence of modifications in the society and perhaps other alterations in the groups themselves (cf. Laosa, 1982).

A third hypothesis emphasizes cultural traditions. It is generally agreed that a group's cultural traditions influence that group's individual behavior and especially family behavior. It is therefore reasonable to hypothesize that ethnic group differences in the incidence of particular family forms stem from group differences in cultural traditions. For example, Huang (1976) has suggested that Chinese cultural traditions account for the very low incidence of single parenting among Chinese Americans. She pointed out that

> traditionally the Chinese considered divorce a great shame and tragedy. . . . The Chinese, in general, disapprove of divorce no matter how open-minded or educated they are. This attitude is not related to any religious convictions; . . . rather, it is that few could afford to experience the serious social ostracism that was usually the consequence of this action. Few Chinese young men today, either American born or foreign born, would consider going with a girl who had been engaged or gone steady with another man before, let alone a divorcée. . . . It is not uncommon for unhappy couples to remain together for fear of public opinion and social disgrace. (p. 133)

It is likely, however, that more inheres in the cultural influences on the incidence of particular family forms than merely the attitudes toward divorce. Likely, it is a whole complex of attitudes toward one's role as a family member in relation to one's role identity as an individual plus a set of cultural beliefs about the meaning of the concept *family*, which result in the relative saliency and emphasis given by a group's culture to the integrity of the two-parent family. The cultural hypothesis thus appears plausible. However, although cultural traditions almost certainly account for diversity between U.S. ethnic groups along some dimensions of family behavior, the evidence thus far bearing on the specific hypothesis that cultural traditions account for the observed ethnic group differences in the incidence of single-parent families is for the most part only anecdotal. More research is needed to determine the reasons for the observed ethnic and racial group differences in the incidence of particular family forms.

CONCLUDING SUMMARY

In this chapter I have attempted to provide a panoramic, although detailed, view of the ethnic and racial diversity that exists in the United States, specifically as this diversity reflects itself in the incidence of single parenting as a family form. The analyses revealed startling ethnic and racial group differences in the incidence of single-parent families. At one end of the range are ethnic and racial groups in which single parenting is nearly the norm; at the other end are groups in which single parenting is an exceedingly rare occurrence. Clearly, then, the statistics descriptive of U.S. families, when calculated for either the nation as a whole or even such broad ethnic and racial categories as Black, White, and even Hispanic or Asian, mask wide ethnic variations composing these aggregations and hence hide the striking differences in the incidence of single parenting that exist between detailed ethnic groups. Little is known yet about the causes that give rise to the observed ethnic and racial group differences in the incidence of single-parent families. Several hypotheses have been advanced to explain the differences. Some of these hypotheses appear untenable in light of the empirical evidence examined, but more thorough tests of their tenability are warranted, and more research is needed to understand the reasons for the observed ethnic and racial group differences in the incidence of particular family forms. The rich ethnic diversity and pluralistic character of our society provide both a challenge and a unique opportunity for expanding our knowledge and increasing our understanding of the historical, social, cultural, and economic circumstances that continually impinge on families and trigger and shape the evolution of varied family forms.

The analyses also revealed that single parenting typically has dire financial consequences, particularly for the single mother and the children living with her. This appears to be true irrespective of ethnic or racial group. Single mothers and the children living with them are, on the average, economically disadvantaged compared to those in two-parent families. The significance of this disadvantage for children lies in the influence that growing up in relative economic deprivation may have on the child's development. A consistent finding in behavioral and social science research is the inverse correlation between the socioeconomic level of the home, on the one hand, and, on the other, the child's academic achievement and educational attainment and thence his or her future occupational options and societal opportunities. For this and other reasons, single parenting is a profoundly consequential issue facing this society generally and particularly those ethnic and racial groups with a high prevalence of this family form. On at least one critical dimension, it is an issue of equality of opportunity, which this society must address in the context of its social policies toward children. The family is a crucial source of inequality in modern society and should not remain unexamined in discussions of distributive justice.

ACKNOWLEDGMENT

Work on parts of this chapter was supported by a grant from the William T. Grant Foundation, which the author gratefully acknowledges.

REFERENCES

Bogue, D. J. (1985). *The population of the United States: Historical trends and future projections.* New York: The Free Press.

Bremner, R. H. (Ed.). (1970). *Children and youth in America: A documentary history* (Vol. 1). Cambridge, MA: Harvard University Press.

Brodbar-Nemzer, J. (1984). Divorce in the Jewish community: The impact of Jewish commitment. *Journal of Jewish Communal Service, 61,* 150–159.

Bronfenbrenner, U., Moen, P., & Garbarino, J. (1984). Child, family, and community. In R. D. Parke (Ed.), *Review of child development research. Vol. 7: The family* (pp. 283–328). Chicago: University of Chicago Press.

Brophy, J. E. & Good, T. L. (1974). *Teacher-student relationships: Causes and consequences.* New York: Holt, Rinehart & Winston.

Cherlin, A. J., & Celebuski, C. (1982). *Are Jewish families different?* New York: American Jewish Committee.

Cohen, S. M. (1981). The American Jewish family today. In M. Himmelfarb, D. Singer, & M. Fine (Eds.), *American Jewish yearbook: 1982* (Vol. 82, pp. 136–154). New York and Philadelphia: American Jewish Committee and Jewish Publication Society of America.

Deutsch, C. P. (1973). Social class and child development. In B. M. Caldwell & H. N. Ricciuti (Eds.), *Review of child development research* (Vol. 3, pp. 233–282). Chicago: University of Chicago Press.

Easterlin, R. A. (1983). The impact of demographic factors on the family environment of children, 1940–1995. In R. R. Nelson & F. Skidmore (Eds.), *American families and the economy: The high costs of living* (pp. 260–293). Washington, DC: National Academy Press.

Farber, B., Mindel, C. H., & Lazerwitz, B. (1976). The Jewish American family. In C. H. Mindel & R. W. Habenstein (Eds.), *Ethnic families in America: Patterns and variations* (pp. 347–378). New York: Elsevier.

Fuchs, V. R. (1986). Sex differences in economic well-being. *Science, 232,* 459–464.

Hess, R. D. (1970). Social class and ethnic influences on socialization. In P. H. Mussen (Ed.), *Carmichael's manual of child psychology* (Vol. 1, pp. 457–557). New York: Wiley.

Hill, M. S. (1983). Trends in the economic situation of U.S. families and children: 1970–1980. In R. R. Nelson & F. Skidmore (Eds.), *American families and the economy: The high costs of living* (pp. 9–53). Washington, DC: National Academy Press.

Huang, L. J. (1976). The Chinese American family. In C. H. Mindel & R. W. Habenstein (Eds.), *Ethnic families in America: Patterns and variations* (pp. 124–147). New York: Elsevier.

Laosa, L. M. (1975). Bilingualism in three United States Hispanic groups: Contextual use of language by children and adults in their families. *Journal of Educational Psychology* , *67*, 617–627.

Laosa, L. M. (1982). School, occupation, culture, and family: The impact of parental schooling on the parent-child relationship. *Journal of Educational Psychology*, *74*, 791–827.

Laosa, L. M. (1984). Social policies toward children of diverse ethnic, racial, and language groups in the United States. In H. W. Stevenson & A. E. Siegel (Eds.), *Child development research and social policy* (Vol. 1, pp. 1–109). Chicago: University of Chicago Press.

Sowell, T. (1978). Three black histories. In T. Sowell (Ed.), *American ethnic groups* (pp. 7–64). Washington, DC: Urban Institute.

Sowell, T. (1981). *Ethnic America: A history*. New York: Basic Books.

Sowell, T. (1983). *The economics and politics of race: An international perspective*. New York: Quill.

U.S. Bureau of the Census. (1982a).*Characteristics of American children and youth: 1980* (Current Population Reports, Series P–23, No. 114). Washington, DC: U.S. Government Printing Office.

U.S. Bureau of the Census. (1982b). *Household and family characteristics: March 1981* (Current Population Reports, Series P–20, No 371). Washington, DC: U.S. Government Printing Office.

U.S. Bureau of the Census. (1983a). *1980 census of the population. General social and economic characteristics: United States summary* (PC80-1-C1). Washington, DC: U.S. Government Printing Office.

U.S. Bureau of the Census. (1983b). *Statistical abstract of the United States: 1984* . Washington, DC: U.S. Government Printing Office.

U.S. Bureau of the Census. (1984a). *Marital status and living arrangements: March 1983* (Current Population Reports, Series P–20, No. 389). Washington, DC: U.S. Government Printing Office.

U.S. Bureau of the Census. (1984b). *1980 census of population. Characteristics of the population. General social and economic characteristics: Puerto Rico* (PC80-1-C53A). Washington, DC: U.S. Government Printing Office.

U.S. Bureau of the Census. (1985). *Persons of Spanish origin in the United States: March 1982* (Current Population Reports, Series P–20, No. 396). Washington, DC: U.S. Government Printing Office.

U.S. Bureau of the Census. (1986). *Money income and poverty status of families and persons in the United States: 1985—advance data from the March 1986 Current Population Survey* (Current Population Reports, Series P–60, No. 154). Washington, DC: U.S. Government Printing Office.

Part II

DIVORCE AND THE LEGAL SYSTEM:
Mediation and Custody

3

Mediation and the Settlement of Divorce Disputes

Robert E. Emery
University of Virginia

There has been an explosion of interest in divorce mediation in the last several years. Since January 1, 1981, California law has mandated that all parents who petition the court for a child custody or visitation hearing must first attempt to resolve the dispute in mediation. By 1984, Delaware and Maine also had enacted mandatory custody mediation laws, and many other states had established various mediation programs through legislation, court rule, or other means (Comeaux, 1983; Freed & Foster, 1984). The rapid growth of divorce mediation is perhaps most evident in a survey of both private and public services conducted in 1981 only a few years after the new method of negotiating divorce disputes was first advanced. In this survey, over 300 divorce mediation programs were identified (Pearson, Ring, & Milne, 1983).

The extent of interest in divorce mediation and the speed with which the concept has been embraced suggest that it promises advantages over adversarial alternatives. As is discussed in this chapter, there are a number of areas in which research findings provide support for the optimism of mediation advocates. Nevertheless, field research on mediation is quite sparse and implementation of mediation programs and policies has proceeded well in advance of empirical findings. Mediation cannot be expected to always lead to a mutually acceptable agreement, and there will continue to be a need to settle some divorce disputes through the legal system. Still, as data reviewed here suggest, as the mediation option becomes increasingly available, it should reduce need for formal judicial intervention in divorce disputes.

Because adversarial procedures are well established and mediational alternatives are quite new, proponents of mediation often have had to become vigorous advocates in order to successfully establish new programs. Unfortunately, the potential for hyperbole is a danger that accompanies such advocacy. Now that divorce mediation at least has gained a foothold as an alternative means of dispute resolution, it would seem that some of most optimistic claims about mediation need to be tempered. Otherwise, mediation advocates run the risk of promising more than they can deliver. Mediational and adversarial procedures are likely to be more or less appropriate methods of dispute settlement depending on a variety of factors related to the family situation and to the value that is placed on different elements of the dispute settlement. Athough there are a number of solid reasons for pursuing the mediation alternative, a number of cautions about its limitations must also be acknowleged.

MEDIATIONAL AND ADVERSARIAL APPROACHES

Adversarial Settlements

In order to understand the mediation alternative, it is necessary to briefly consider the process by which divorce settlements are typically reached. In a traditional adversarial settlement, two opposing attorneys are engaged, each of whom is expected to advocate only for the interests of his or her client. The lawyer's task is to attempt to reach a settlement that is most advantageous to the client. The competition between the two parties that results from this adversarial approach to dispute settlement is designed, in theory, to be a way of insuring that a fair settlement is reached. Importantly, equity in the competitive negotiations is thought to be maintained, because both sides are represented by skilled advocates who conduct the dispute resolution process as representatives of their clients.

A divorce case that goes to trial may require that opposing evidence be presented in open court, a process than can be extremely painful to members of the divorcing family. Relatives and mutual friends may be called as witnesses who are asked to testify for one spouse against the other in an attempt to substantiate the grounds for seeking a divorce, advocate for a favorable financial settlement, or support a certain childrearing arrangement. If custody is disputed, the children also may be asked to testify. Moreover, in some circumstances children are represented by a third lawyer whose duty is to advocate for their interests independently of the parents' desires concerning the custody arrangement. Although there has been remarkably little research on divorce litigation and its effects on family members, many judges (Matrimonial Law Commission, 1983), attorneys (McHenry, Herrman, & Weber, 1978), and divorcing spouses (Spanier & Anderson, 1979) feel that it can be an extremely difficult process that can have an unnecessarily negative impact on the members of the divorcing family.

In about 90% of all divorce cases settled in the adversary system, the partners' attorneys negotiate an agreement out of court (Foster & Freed, 1973). This statistic indicates that attorney negotiation is a successful way of reaching a settlement for most divorcing spouses, but attorneys have been criticized as being expensive (Cavanaugh & Rhode, 1976), unnecessarily adversarial (McHenry et al., 1978), and unskilled in dealing with the emotional aspects of divorce (Callner, 1977). Although such criticisms of attorney negotiations are common, systematic research on this important subject is only beginning (Maccoby, Depner, & Mnookin, this volume). Nevertheless, as is the case with a number of other areas in the law (Burger, 1982; Kressel & Pruitt, 1985; Sander, 1976), there is sufficient dissatisfaction with in-court and out-of-court adversarial procedures to prompt interest in exploring alternative methods of resolving divorce disputes.

Mediated Settlements

Mediation is a cooperative method of dispute resolution that operates on assumptions that differ markedly from the adversarial approach both on logistical and psychological dimensions. In mediation, both partners meet with a single professional who attempts to help them to negotiate their own settlement. The partners communicate more directly in mediation than in attorney negotiations, either in face to face meetings or by exchanging information through the mediator. Mediators operate on the assumption that certain disputes are best resolved in a cooperative rather than a competitive manner, and they view their primary role as one of facilitator rather than as an advocate or decision maker. For this reason, the mediator's goal is to encourage negotiation, but the former marital partners are expected to rely on outside experts such as lawyers, financial planners, or mental health professionals for specific advice about the details of their agreement. Thus, although mediators may control much of the process of dispute settlement, in comparison to legal professionals, they have relatively little direct influence over its outcome.

As is the case with adversarial approaches, many criticisms have been leveled against divorce mediation. Important questions have been raised about the training of mediators (Folberg & Taylor, 1984), their knowledge of the law (Silberman, 1982), and the appropriate standards of practice for family mediators (Standards of Practice, 1984). Perhaps the most important objections that have been raised about mediation relate to the agreements that are negotiated. Adversarial approaches are designed to protect individual rights, and questions have been raised as to whether these rights are adequately protected in mediation.

One common and basic fear is that the more powerful party will impose his or her preferences on the weaker one in mediation. Although this is a concern about mediation in general, issues about protecting women in mediation have been raised in particular (Schulman & Woods, 1983). Feminists have worked to empower women in the family context by encouraging legal intervention in areas such as domestic violence. Some fear that mediation may be a step backward in this regard, as it represents a delegalization of one area of family dispute. Others are concerned that women simply will be less tenacious negotiators in mediation than men are likely to be. Because of the financial plight of many divorced mothers and their children (Weitzman, 1985), particular concern is focused on the financial settlements that may be reached in mediation. As is the case with many criticisms of the adversary system, such objections are based primarily on conceptual rationales and case reports, rather than empirical evidence. Moreover, numerous questions can be raised as to whether the adversary system in practice achieves the sort of equity that it is designed to achieve in theory. Nevertheless, the objections that have been raised about mediation constitute important concerns that relate both to policy considerations and to the standards of practice of divorce mediators (for further discussion of these issues see Emery & Wyer, 1987a).

CUSTODY MEDIATION

Although many concerns about the outcome of mediation have focused on the financial settlements that are reached, the vast majority of mediators who work in the public sector limit the scope of their services to disputes that involve child-rearing concerns, namely disagreements about custody and visitation. Because public programs currently serve much larger numbers of clients than do private mediators and because of the present focus on children's adjustment to divorce, what is sometimes called *custody mediation*—mediation that is limited to custody, visitation, and other child-care issues—is the focus of the remainder of this chapter.

There are at least two broad reasons why child custody is the primary or sole focus of mediation in the majority of divorce cases (cf. Emery & Wyer, 1987a). The evolution of family law provides one rationale, as changes in the law have created particular dilemmas that provide incentives for the judiciary to encourage parental self-determination when custody is disputed. In addition, psychological research in the 1970s and 1980s has underscored the important role that continuing family relationships play in influencing children's adjustment to divorce, and the critical need for continued parental cooperation around issues concerning child-rearing has been highlighted.

Psychological rationales for mediation begin with research that has documented the stressful nature of divorce, as both adults (Bloom, Asher, & White, 1978) and children (Zill, 1978) from divorced families have been found to be over-represented in mental health patient populations. In attempting to understand the negative impact of divorce, increasingly psychologists have shifted their focus from the event of divorce per se to a more systemic view (Emery, in press). Various family processes and social and economic factors that often accompany or follow marital dissolution have been identified as the primary correlates of difficulties in children's adjustment (e.g., Block, Block, & Gjerde, 1986; Herzog & Sudia, 1973; Hess & Camara, 1979; Hetherington, 1979). With this shift in emphasis, concern has been raised that the adversarial settlement of divorce disputes may only serve to further undermine family relationships that have already been disrupted (Emery, Hetherington, & DiLalla, 1984). This concern is particularly acute in regard to children's postdivorce adjustment, as conflict in the co-parental relationship consistently has been found to be associated with an increase in child behavior problems, especially aggression, disobedience, and related conduct problems (Emery, 1982). Although there has been little systematic research on the effects of court hearings and attorney negotiations on family relationships and individual adjustment, to those who have observed or participated in this process, it seems reasonable to hypothesize that adversary procedures increase conflict and stress to the detriment of family members. From this perspective, mediation has been suggested to be a method of dispute resolution that will place less strain on postdivorce family relationships both in the short-term and in the long run.

Although this systemic view enjoys considerable research support and seems to becoming the dominant perspective in psychological research on children's divorce adjustment (Emery, in press), psychological views are not uniform. In this light, Jacobs (1986) has made an interesting observation about how the theoretical orientation of the mental health professional interfaces with mediational and adversarial approaches in family law. He notes that adversary approaches appear to be most compatible with psychoanalytic traditions. Adversary and psychoanalytic approaches both focus on the individual, emphasize internal influences over behavior, view people as acting consistently over time, and are more concerned with mothering than with fathering. Mediational approaches, on the other hand, are more consistent with family systems theory. In mediational and family systems approaches, there is a common focus on interpersonal relationships, ecological factors, change over time, and the mutual influence of mothers and fathers on the children and each other. In support of these views, Jacobs (1986) makes an intriguing and appealing observation. He notes that it is as equally rare to see an analytically oriented mediator as it is to see a family therapist doing a custody evaluation for one or the other parent. The converse situations are quite common, of course. Thus, although there are important psychological theories and a substantial body of research on children's postdivorce adjustment that both provide rationales for the movement toward custody mediation, it should be noted that there is not complete consensus in psychological opinion.

In addition to the psychological rationales, changes and problems in family law provide incentives for exploring alternative methods of dispute resolution. One incentive stems from the introduction and rapid spread of "no fault" divorce in the 1970s. No fault laws have allowed divorce to become a private rather than a public matter because neither party must prove to the state that there are acceptable grounds for dissolving the marriage. Mediation can be viewed as another step in the trend toward the "private ordering" of divorce, as divorcing couples are not only allowed but, in fact, are encouraged to negotiate their own settlements (Mnookin, 1975).

A particularly strong legal incentive for encouraging mediation exists in the area of child custody. Judicial custody determinations are guided by the best interests of the child standard, a vague doctrine that impels judges to make custody determinations based on what is likely in the future to be in the best interests of the children involved. Although the standard is laudible in intent, it can present impossible dilemmas in practice (Mnookin, 1975). Psychologists have been only mildly successful in predicting individual children's future development based on their family circumstances, but even if such predictions were perfect, the dilemma remains as to which future course is "best." Is it better for a child to live with the parent who will strongly encourage achievement but cause a child to be anxious about failure, or is it preferable to be reared by the parent who is more lax about achievement but more supportive regarding emotional development?

Not only does the standard present such impossible questions, but it also creates other problems. Because the best interests standard makes the outcome of a custody hearing unpredictable, it is likely to (a) increase the potential for bias in the exercise of judicial discretion, (b) encourage litigation, and (c) exacerbate the anger that parents feel toward each other because virtually any derogatory evidence against one or the other may be deemed relevant to a hearing (Mnookin, 1975). If such reasoned speculation is correct, custody hearings themselves may be contrary to the child's best interests.

The difficulties encountered in settling disputes concerning children and the influence of continuing postdivorce family relationships are both evident in one final aspect of divorce litigation. Although only 10% of all families proceed to court at the time of divorce, over 30% end up in court for *postdissolution* litigation involving the children (Foster & Freed, 1973). Thus, there are a variety of reasons behind the current interest in the exploration of mediation as an alternative to adversary procedures for resolving divorce disputes that involve children.

RESEARCH ON MEDIATION

Rhetoric in support of or opposition to divorce mediation far exceeds research on the topic. This is unfortunate because many of the issues that have been raised about mediation are amenable to investigation. At least, three levels of questions about mediation need to be addressed. First, can mediation be used to divert a substantial number of cases from the custody hearing? Second, do parents prefer this dispute resolution process to the adversary system? Third, does mediation, in comparison to adversary procedures, have a salutory psychological impact on the members of divorcing families? Data pertaining to each of these questions are addressed here. Although the global answers to these questions are of interest, because different dispute resolution procedures are likely to be more or less appropriate for different families, the issue of predicting successful outcome in mediation also is examined in each of the following three subsections.

Diversion from Court

Most existing mediation programs, such as those in California, are housed in a court setting, deal solely with child custody or visitation disputes, and work only with parents who request a court hearing. Thus, mediators in these programs are working with a narrow subset of the divorcing population that is likely to be considerably more acrimonious than the average. Nevertheless, statistics indicate that in most of these programs between 50% and 75% of families reach a settlement in mediation. For example, in Los Angeles county, where mediation is mandatory and thousands of couples have been seen, approximately 55% of those couples who request a custody hearing reach an agreement in mediation (McIssac, 1982).

Some attorneys object to data such as these as indicators of the extent to which mediation diverts cases from the custody hearing (Levy, 1984). They point out that many lawyers file a petition for a court hearing only to "up the ante" in their negotiations. It is argued that, because the filing of a petition often is used as a bargaining tactic, the same percentage or more cases would be settled before the court hearing even without mediation.

The issue of how many cases are settled between the filing date and the court hearing without mediation is an important consideration in interpreting mediation settlement rates, but it does not negate the conclusion that mediation is successful as a diversion procedure. The director of the Los Angeles County Court's mediation service has indicated that custody hearings have been reduced by 75% since the introduction of California's mandatory mediation law (H. McIssac, personal communication, June 5, 1985). In my own study in Virginia, where families who requested a court hearing were randomly approached about mediation or allowed to proceed through the usual court procedures following the filing of a petition for a custody hearing, 15 of the first 20 families settled out of court as a result of mediation, whereas only 5 out of 20 control group families settled out of court. This translates into a 67% reduction in court hearings as a result of mediation (Emery & Wyer, 1987b). Thus, a substantial number of settlements are reached in custody mediation, and this results in a significant number of custody disputes being diverted from court (cf. Emery & Wyer, 1987a).

Who Settles in Mediation?   The issue of who is and who is not likely to reach an agreement in mediation is important for a number of reasons. From a purely practical standpoint, if those divorcing partners who are most likely to reach an agreement can be identified beforehand, it might be possible to screen for the families who will benefit most from mediation. Although issues concerning equal protection under the law could be raised if screening criteria were used in a court-based mediation program, discretionary referrals to mediation based on prescreening are a policy alternative to mandatory or completely voluntary mediation (cf. Emery & Wyer, 1987a).

At a more theoretical level, the question of who is more or less likely to reach an agreement in mediation is highly relevant to conceptual issues about the emotional experience of divorcing partners and the nature of the conflict between them. As an example of this latter interest, one important area of postdivorce adjustment that may be relevant to outcome in mediation is the extent to which continuing emotional attachment remains between former spouses. Clinicians, in particular, have observed that one and sometimes both spouses continue to feel emotionally tied to their former partner even after the marriage has been dissolved (Hetherington, Cox, & Cox, 1982; Weiss, 1975). Lingering emotional attachment may remain between both former spouses, or one spouse may continue to long for the other even when the feelings are not reciprocated. For many divorced adults yearning for one's former mate, or for what that mate represented, is hardly a trivial issue. Researchers have found that the extent to which one member of the dyad is unable to disengage from the relationship is associated with increased problems in their postdivorce adjustment, particularly depression (Spanier & Thompson, 1984).

In conducting mediation, the issue of continuing emotional involvement between former marital partners often is an obstacle to effective negotiating. When one or both of the former spouses experiences lingering attachment to their former spouse and remorse about the dissolution of the marriage, their continuing emotional investment often interferes with the negotiations. In fact, an attempt to maintain contact or have an emotional relationship with the former marital partner sometimes appears to be the real issue which underlies a superficial dispute over custody (Emery, Shaw, & Jackson, 1987; Hetherington et al., 1982). To put it in terms sometimes used by game theorists, the emotional turmoil over whether or not to accept the end of the marriage sometimes is the latent conflict, although a dispute over the children is the manifest conflict (Deutsch, 1973). Children represent one of the few sources of continuing connection between separated or divorced parents, and they sometimes serve as an avenue that one partner uses to remain in contact with the other.

Even if the former spouses are extremely antagonistic, a dispute over the children does serve the function of forcing them to maintain contact with one another. In extreme cases, it is actually necessary for one or both spouses to maintain the dispute and avoid settlement. To agree to a settlement would mean losing the point of contact with the former spouse. In fact, a couple whose extreme animosity at first glance appears to suggest that they are emotionally disengaged, in reality may reflect their continuing emotional enmeshment. The emotional intensity of their anger may be fueled by a sense of desperate longing rather than by feelings of mutual hostility (Emery et al., 1987; Hetherington et al., 1982). It has been proposed that much of the apparently irrational conflict following divorce is a way of sustaining an intense affective relationship with the former spouse, albeit a negative relationship. For some divorced spouses, negative affect is preferable to apathy or disengagement (Hetherington et al., 1982).

We have attempted to test some of these speculations empirically in our study comparing the outcomes of the mediation and litigation of custody disputes. Consistent with the clinical observations just outlined, we hypothesized that it would be more difficult to mediate those custody disputes in which one or both spouses continued to feel intense emotional commitment to the marriage. Specifically, we predicted that for those partners for whom our measures indicated that continuing emotional attachment was higher, the likelihood of reaching an agreement in mediation would be lower.

In an attempt to examine this issue, Susan Peterman (1986) studied a number of variables related to continuing emotional attachment and outcome in mediation in a sample of 30 couples. Although the overall pattern of findings was not always consistent with the predictions, some support for the displaced conflict notion was found. For women but not for men, a significant correlation ($r = .48, p < .01$) was found between an expression of continuing emotional attachment to one's spouse as indexed by Kitson's (1982) Acceptance of Marital Termination Scale and whether or not the couple reached an agreement in mediation. Those women who reported more continuing emotional commitment to the marriage were less likely to reach an agreement in mediation. This finding is consistent with the clinical speculation just outlined, and what makes it particularly intriguing is that it is counterintuitive. It was the women who rated their former spouse more negatively who were more likely to reach an agreement in mediation.

Other researchers have successfully predicted outcome in mediation based on less complex hypotheses. For example, couples who have better communication, less intense conflict, and fewer disagreements about finances have been found to be more likely to reach an agreement in mediation (Pearson, Thoennes, & Vanderkooi, 1982; Watson & Morton, 1983). In addition, contrary to the idea that mediation will be preferred primarily by the verbal middle class, we and others (Pearson & Thoennes, 1984; Peterman, 1986) have not found socioeconomic status to predict whether or not agreements are reached. Although such findings are of interest, there is a considerable need for further research to addresss the straightforward and important question of what types of partners with what types of disputes are more or less likely to reach an agreement in mediation.

Agreements as a Measure of Outcome.   Before leaving this topic, some questions need to be raised about the adequacy of using the number of agreements reached in mediation as a measure of the success of the process. Whether or not an agreement is reached in mediation is not the only or necessarily the best measure of outcome. Although diverting a family from a custody hearing is a concrete, helpful, and very important outcome for many families, concern has been raised that parties should not be pressured into reaching a settlement in mediation. As noted earlier, this concern may be particularly relevant for women, who may feel powerless in negotiating with a dominant or even abusive husband (Cohen, 1984; Schulman & Woods, 1983). More generally, mediators must refrain from evaluating their success based on whether or not they "got an agreement."

This caution is of particular concern for mediators who work in court settings. Court mediators are likely to experience institutional pressures to divert as many cases as possible from the custody hearing. At the broadest level, the concern is that mediators not allow themselves to be a party to agreements that they deem to be grossly inappropriate or coercive, a tricky ethical judgment to make given the mediator's primary role as a facilitator of process not as an evaluator of outcome (Standards of Practice, 1984).

The opposite concern about using agreement rates as an index of success also deserves careful consideration. Cases in which mediation does not result in an agreement are not necessarily failures. Informally, I have been impressed by the large number of couples—and their attorneys and therapists—who have reported that mediation was helpful to them even though they failed to reach a specific custody agreement. Many of these "unsuccessful" mediation clients have said that mediation made them re-evaluate their thinking about their divorce, the need for cooperation with their former spouse, or their approach to negotiating a settlement.

Data from one research study offer some important support for these informal observations. In the Denver Mediation Project, partners who tried mediation but who failed to reach an agreement were found to be more likely to settle out of court through attorney negotiations than were couples who never attempted mediation at all (Pearson et al., 1982). It may be that mediation promotes parental cooperation and provides an opportunity for education about divorce even when it does not directly result in a settlement.

Consumer Satisfaction with Mediation and Adversary Procedures

The question as to whether clients prefer mediation to adversary procedures cannot be completely answered. As reviewed in more detail elsewhere (Emery & Wyer, 1987a), at least five research groups who used random assignment to the two conditions have found clients to prefer mediation over adversary procedures (Emery & Wyer, 1987b; Irving, 1980; Margolin, 1973; Pearson & Thoennes, 1984; Watson & Morton, 1983). Each study has employed somewhat different methodology, used various measures of outcome, and suffered from common and unique flaws. Still, the pattern of findings is consistent across the five research projects. In one investigation, parents randomly assigned to mediation felt that it was less biased and more suited to the family than did parents assigned to undergo the usual custody evaluation conducted by the court staff (Watson & Morton, 1983). Another researcher found that parents randomly assigned to mediation rather than a custody hearing were more likely to report that things had gotten much better 6 weeks later (Irving, 1981). A third group reported that parents assigned at random to mediate their custody settlements reported greater satisfaction, felt that the process was more fair, and indicated a more positive impact on their relationship with their former spouse when compared to parents who settled through adversary procedures (Pearson & Thoennes, 1984). Finally, lower relitigation rates were found for the families who attempted mediation in two studies employing random assignment to conditions. In one investigation the rate of relitigation following mediation was one half of the rate found for the litigation group (Pearson & Thoennes, 1984), and a second investigator found relitigation to be only one-sixth as frequent following mediation as it was following an adversary settlement (Margolin, 1973).

It should be noted that all of these investigations suffer from potentially important methodological flaws, despite their straightforward experimental designs. The external validity of the findings can be questioned for each investigation, although some studies at least employed samples that were representative of the courts that were studied (Emery & Wyer, 1987b; Irving, 1981; Watson & Morton, 1983).

The two major threats to internal validity in this set of studies both involve problems with possible self-selection biases. Some self-selection occurred when families were randomly assigned to the different conditions, as a subgroup of the parties refused to participate either in the mediation intervention or in the evaluation of the usual adversary procedures (litigation controls). The potential for self-selection bias was again introduced when the data were collected, as there may have been selective attrition from the sample. Both of these concerns are relevant since as many as half of all subjects refused mediation when assigned to that condition in one study (Pearson et al., 1982), and an even higher percentage was lost when outcome measures were obtained in another investigation (Watson & Morton, 1983). Nevertheless, each of these concerns appears to have been adequately addressed in at least two of the studies (Emery & Wyer, 1987b; Irving, 1981), and the results of these investigations generally indicated support for mediation over adversary procedures. Thus, the basic finding that parents prefer mediation to adversary procedures seems internally valid, although a number of questions about external validity can be raised.

Predicting Satisfaction with Mediation.   One important issue related to consumer satisfaction with mediation was not addressed until recently, however. Data were analyzed separately for mothers and for fathers in only one of the five studies reviewed previously (Emery & Wyer, 1987b). In our experimental evaluation of the mediation and litigation of child custody disputes, considerable differences in the experiences of men and women were found.

In agreement with the findings from the other studies, *fathers* in mediation were considerably more satisfied with their contact with the legal system than were fathers in litigation. According to their responses to a series of structured questions, fathers in mediation reported greater satisfaction with the process of resolving the custody dispute, with the effect of the process on themselves, and with the impact of the court contact on their relationship with their former spouse.

Differences between the two groups of fathers were statistically significant and substantial in magnitude. Moreover, preference for mediation was expressed by fathers in areas that reflected the legal as well as the psychological aspects of the dispute resolution process. For example, fathers in mediation were more likely than fathers in litigation to feel that their rights had been protected. In fact, on every item on the questionnaire used, fathers in mediation were more positive than fathers in litigation (cf. Emery & Wyer, 1987b).

Quite different results were obtained for *mothers*, however. For the most part, there were fewer and more inconsistent differences between women in the mediation and litigation groups. Mothers in mediation were significantly more positive about the impact of the process on their children, but mothers in *litigation* were more satisfied with the decisions that were reached. Specifically, mothers who went through a court hearing felt that they won more and lost less than did mothers in mediation. Still, for most of the questionnaire items there were relatively few between group differences for mothers, especially in comparison to the effects found for fathers (cf. Emery & Wyer, 1987b).

In order to understand these results, one other aspect of the findings must be noted. When the mediation and litigation groups were combined, it was found that mothers were consistently and significantly more satisfied with their experiences in achieving a custody settlement than were fathers. This finding extended across a wide variety of domains. When the results were examined across mediation and litigation groups, a clear pattern emerged: fathers who went through litigation formed an outlying group. They were consistently less satisfied with their contact with the legal system than were fathers in mediation or mothers in either group. Fathers in mediation, in contrast, reported mean satisfaction ratings that were somewhat lower but generally comparable to mothers in both mediation and litigation (cf. Emery & Wyer, 1987b).

In order to interpret these findings, it is necessary to return to a consideration of child custody law. Although the tender years presumption, the legal rule that preceded the best interests standard, has been eliminated from statutory law, the tradition appears to have a continuing influence on the exercise of judicial discretion under the best interest standard. According to this earlier doctrine, children of "tender years" were to be placed in the custody of their mothers following divorce. The rationale for the doctrine was a simple one: Mother–child relationships were believed to be considerably more important than father–child relationships to insuring children's healthy emotional development. Questions of sex discrimination, among other issues, have led to the elimination of the tender years doctrine as a legislative policy, but its historical influence continues in practice. In fact, despite sex-neutral legislation, the Supreme Court of Virginia has suggested that there remains a preference for mother custody in serving the child's best interests, and this preference apparently is not limited to Virginia. It has been reported that after the enactment of sex-neutral custody legislation in California, 81% of the judges surveyed still felt that mother custody was in the child's best interest (Weitzman, 1985).

The recognition of the continuing influence of the tender years presumption helps in the interpretation of the findings from our study. As was suggested in the general discussion at the beginning of the chapter, mediational and adversarial procedures differ not only in terms of the process of arriving at dispute settlements, they also differ in terms of likely outcomes. Because of the historical influence of the tender years presumption, mothers who go to court with a custody dispute are likely to win the contest. Not surprisingly, they are likely to have few complaints about the experience, at least in comparison to fathers. By going into mediation, however, mothers run the risk of giving up control in an area where the court, at the present time, tends to favor them. On the other hand, fathers who go through mediation are likely to be given a greater voice in an area where they traditionally have had little influence. But the data that we have obtained do not suggest that fathers in mediation necessarily gain at the expense of mothers. It should be noted that mothers who went through mediation were about as satisfied as the mothers who went through litigation, and, in fact, they were more satisfied in certain areas. Moreover, although 4 out of 20 agreements made in our mediation group specified that the parents would share joint legal custody, the remainder of the mediated agreements, like all but two of the judicial determinations, were "traditional" in that the greatest rights and responsibilities in regard to child care were given to mothers.

One integrative interpretation of these findings is that mediation, in comparison to litigation, led to increased psychological satisfaction for the families in this group. However, because mothers in both groups were near the ceiling on their satisfaction ratings and because mediation gives fathers a stronger voice in regard to childrearing, most of the increased satisfaction was experienced by men. Mediation appears to have brought the satisfaction of fathers up to the level experienced by mothers, whether they were in mediation or in litigation. To put this another way, although the ratings of mothers and fathers in litigation were widely disparate, mothers and fathers expressed quite similar levels of satisfaction after mediation. This suggests that the parents who went through mediation may ultimately develop a more cooperative working relationship in regard to postdivorce childrearing. If this happens, both mothers and fathers who went through mediation should, in the long run, be more satisfied than the parents who reached a settlement through adversary procedures.

Psychological Impact of Mediational and Adversarial Procedures

To this point, legal and psychological rationales, evidence on diversion from custody hearings, and evaluations of the satisfaction of mothers and fathers all are generally supportive of mediation, at least in the area of child custody. This review sets the stage for the final question: Does mediation have a relatively more positive (or less negative) impact on the psychological status of the members of divorcing families in comparison to adversary procedures?

Unfortunately, this question has been addressed empirically even less than the above issues. To my knowledge, the only investigation in which it has been studied in any detail is our own, and here the findings are not supportive of mediation. When assessed an average of four weeks following the dispute settlement, parents randomly assigned to either mediation or litigation were found to be no different in terms of self-reported conflict over co-parenting or acceptance of the termination of the marriage. This was true for both men and women, and fathers in the two groups did not differ in terms of their ratings on the Beck Depression Inventory. For women, however, mothers in litigation reported significantly less depression than did mothers in mediation (Emery & Wyer, 1987b). Unlike the findings for consumer satisfaction, in comparing across groups and sexes litigation mothers appeared to constitute the outlying group, as indicated by the following means and standard deviations which were obtained on the Beck Depression Inventory: litigation mothers, 5.32 (1.24); mediation mothers 11.37 (2.57); litigation fathers, 12.19 (2.77); and mediation fathers, 9.75 (2.31).

Certainly, the finding of lower depression among the women in the litigation group is inconsistent with the idea that mediation involves lower psychological costs for all of the members of the divorcing family. The finding is inconsistent with much of the other evidence reviewed on custody mediation, and it is especially troubling in light of some of the concerns that have been raised about mediation and women.

The finding clearly deserves very careful attention and further research, but some questions about its validity are worth raising. For one, the finding may be artifactual, resulting from a tendency for women to be more honest in their self-reports following mediation than they were following litigation. Alternatively, the depression that was reported may have been transient, as the mediation forced the women to confront the sadness they felt as they came to recognize that their marriage was ending. It also may be erroneous to conclude that the women were more depressed following mediation. Rather, it may be that the women who went to court became less depressed. Their victory in court may have led them to feel vindicated, reducing the amount of depression they normally would be expected to experience. Unfortunately, the study employed a post-only design, making it impossible to test such speculations. One-year follow-up data may reveal support for one or more of these alternatives, however, because each explanation focuses more on short-term than long-term effects.

The most straightforward conclusion about the finding that women experienced more depression following mediation than following litigation deserves the most attention, however. As was discussed earlier, it may be that women are at least somewhat disadvantaged relative to men in mediation. Women may be more depressed following mediation than litigation because they feel that they were unable to negotiate the type of settlement that they wanted. In considering this interpretation, it is important that process and outcome not be confused. It may well be that the women were more unhappy with the outcome of mediation, but their consumer satisfaction ratings suggest that they were about as satisfied with the process.

Caution is probably the best interpretation of the different experiences of men and women in mediation. The whole topic of the global psychological impact of mediational and adversarial dispute settlement procedures is one that is in need of much further investigation. The topic is of interest both in terms of how the alternatives compare to one another, and in terms of how each intervention impacts on individuals during the proceedings, immediately afterward, and at longer term follow-up intervals. These findings underscore the need for researchers to search for both positive and negative effects of mediation relative to adversary procedures and to attempt to untangle the effects of process and outcome in evaluating the impact of the two alternative interventions.

COMPARING SOME ASSUMPTIONS
OF THE DISPUTE RESOLUTION ALTERNATIVES

Although the focus of this chapter has been on the findings of field research on custody mediation and litigation, in closing the discussion, it is worthwhile to raise a few more general issues about alternative forms of dispute resolution. Some of the issues raised in discussions of the resolution of other forms of social conflict may contribute to our understanding of dispute resolution in divorce.

As alluded to at the beginning of this chapter, a basic distinction between mediational and adversarial approaches is the relative emphasis on process and outcome. Adversary methods of dispute resolution emphasize outcomes and focus concern on the individual's rights and on obtaining the best possible settlement for that individual. The impact of the process of dispute resolution on the relationship between disputants is of comparatively little concern. What is most important about the process is that it be designed to maximize the protection of the individual's rights. In contrast, the impact of the process of dispute resolution on the disputants is of utmost importance in mediation. This is true, in part, because of the mediator's philosophical position that preservation of disputants' future relationship is an essential outcome of the dispute resolution procedure. It is also true because the mediator's authority to determine outcomes is virtually nonexistent. The only way for the mediator to effect an agreement is to help the parties to negotiate a mutually acceptable settlement.

One way of conceptually equating the process approach of mediation and the outcome focus of adversarial settlements is to think of the two alternatives in economic terms. In so doing, when evaluating a given settlement, it is essential to include the ''transaction costs'' involved in reaching the settlement in evaluating the outcome. The transaction costs involved in settling a dispute include time, money, and emotional investment, all of which are factors that can influence each party's satisfaction with the agreement that is reached.

Transaction costs clearly are important elements to consider in evaluating a given outcome. From a purely rational point of view, it would be ludicrous if attorneys' fees equaled or exceeded the total value of a property settlement decided in court, for example. To the extent that transaction costs are kept to a minimum, both of the parties in dispute stand to benefit because they have a larger "pie" to divide. More to the point, an alternative method of dispute resolution that is more efficient than adversarial procedures in terms of financial costs, time, and emotional expense should be preferred, assuming, of course, that a similarly high standard of fairness in regard to outcome is maintained in both procedures.

Although the transaction costs approach suggests a way of comparing alternative methods of dispute resolution, many outcomes and transaction costs are extremely difficult to quantify. In divorce, issues such as property settlements, spousal support, and child support all involve money, and this allows for the two sides of a settlement to be more easily compared. Other outcomes such as custody, visitation, and emotional strain present much greater difficulty. The value of custody and visitation arrangements may be impossible to quantify, but at least some general assumptions can be made about the possible outcomes for settling these two types of disputes.

Assuming that compliance with the settlement does not depend on the cooperation of the adversary (an assumption that may well be inappropriate in the case of divorce), financial disputes can be thought of as distributive issues that are best modeled by zero sum games. What one side wins, the other loses by the same amount. Disputes that require integrative solutions would quite obviously seem to involve nonzero sum solutions, however. In the area of child custody, for example, parental cooperation is vital to the family's postdivorce adjustment, and one parent's time with the child can be the other parent's respite. In general, distributive conflicts may be best resolved by competitive methods of dispute resolution, whereas conflicts for which there are potential integrative solutions (such as child custody arrangements) may be better settled in a cooperative manner.

As is the case with other types of disputes (Sander, 1976), even disputes that involve distributive solutions can be thought of as nonzero sum games when the two parties' are expected to have ongoing relationship. Although its exact value cannot be determined, if the disputants relationship is assigned any value at all, all conflicts are nonzero sum games because the effects of the dispute resolution procedures on the disputants' relationship becomes a part of the outcome. From this perspective, childrearing disputes in divorce again seem to be best suited for cooperative means of dispute settlement, because the children necessitate future contact between the parents.

In summary, if mediational approaches promise equal or greater protection of rights than adversarial ones, they are to be preferred. On the other hand, if adversary approaches involve equal or lower transaction costs than mediational ones, they are to be preferred. Given the emphasis on process, mediation would seem to involve potentially lower transaction costs. Given the emphasis on outcome, adversary approaches would seem to be more likely to protect the parties from unfair settlements. Because each approach therefore would seem to hold some advantage over the other, the question is how the relative strengths average out in divorce negotiations. As the evidence from our study of custody mediation suggested, some averaging does occur, although the influences of process and outcome can be difficult, if not impossible, to untangle empirically.

The process/outcome distinction suggests some general conclusions about preferences for mediational and adversarial settlements in divorce. Different methods of dispute resolution may be preferred depending on the possible outcomes of the dispute and the transaction costs involved in arriving at a settlement. The extent to which individual rights are protected, the possibility of arriving at integrative or distributive solutions, the emotional impact of the dispute resolution procedure on the parties, and the nature of the relationship between the two disputants are some of the elements that need to be considered in weighing the alternatives. In divorce, when (a) an ongoing relationship will not be maintained between the former spouses, (b) the disputes center on distributive issues such as property division, (c) the economic transaction costs are low relative to the value of the settlement, and (d) the controversy at hand is not symbolic of underlying emotional issues, adversarial methods of dispute resolution may be preferred. However, when disputes include issues of child custody or visitation, mediation would seem to be particularly appropriate because the co-parental relationship is an ongoing one, child custody is hardly a zero-sum issue, emotional consequences become important transaction costs, and underlying issues often appear to fuel disputes which are superficially about childrearing. Thus, it may be that we are beginning to recognize some of the limitations, as well as the strengths of divorce mediation. It is no panacea, and the alternative will not survive if it is portrayed as one. This would be unfortunate, because rationales and research suggest that the mediation alternative should be there as an alternative, perhaps as a first step.

ACKNOWLEDGMENT

Preparation of this paper was supported in part by grants from the William T. Grant Foundation.

REFERENCES

Block, J. H., Block, J., & Gjerde, P. F., (1986). The personality of children prior to divorce: A prospective study. *Child Development, 57,* 827–840.

Bloom, B. L., Asher, S. J., & White, S. W., (1978). Marital disruption as a stressor: A review and analysis. *Psychological Bulletin, 85,* 867–894.

Burger, W. B., (1982). Isn't there a better way? *American Bar Association Journal, 68,* 274–277.

Callner, B. W., (1977). Boundaries of the divorce lawyer's role. *Family Law Quarterly, 10,* 389–398.

Cavanaugh, R. C., & Rhode, D. L., (1976). The unauthorized practice of law and pro se divorce. *Yale Law Journal, 86,* 104–184.

Cohen, H. N., (1984). Mediation in divorce: Boon or bane? *The Women's Advocate, 5,* 1–2.

Comeaux, E. A., (1983). A guide to implementing divorce mediation in the public sector. *Conciliation Courts Review, 21,* 1–25.

Deutsch, M., (1973). *The resolution of conlict.* New Haven, CT: Yale University Press.

Emery, R. E., (1982). Interparental conflict and the children of discord and divorce. *Psychological Bulletin, 92,* 310–330.

Emery, R. E. (in press), *Marriage, divorce, and children's adjustment.* Beverly Hills: Sage.

Emery, R. E., Hetherington, E. M., & DiLalla, L. F., (1984). Divorce, children, and social policy. In H. W. Stevenson & A. E. Siegel (Eds.), *Child development research and social policy* (pp. 189–266). Chicago: University of Chicago Press.

Emery, R. E., Shaw, D. S., & Jackson, J. A., (1987). A clinical description of a model of child custody mediation. In J. P. Vincent (Ed.), *Advances in Family Intervention, Assessment, and Theory* (Vol. 4, pp. 309–333). Greenwich, CT: JAI.

Emery, R. E., & Wyer, M. M., (1987a). Divorce mediation. *American Psychologist, 42,* 472–480.

Emery, R. E., & Wyer, M. M., (1987b). Child custody mediation and litigation: An Experimental Evaluation of the Experience of Parents. *Journal of Consulting and Clinical Psychology, 55,* 179–186.

Freed, D. J., & Foster, H. H., (1984). Divorce in the fifty states: An overview. *Family Law Quarterly, 17,* 365–447.

Folberg, J., & Taylor, A., (1984). *Mediation: A comprehensive guide to resolving conflicts without litigation.* San Francisco: Jossey-Bass.

Foster, H. H., & Freed, D. J., (1973). Divorce reform: Breaks on breakdown. *Journal of Family Law, 74,* 443–493.

Herzog, E., & Sudia, C. E., (1973). Children in fatherless families. In B. M. Cadwell & H. N. Ricciuti (Eds.), *Child development research* (Vol. 3, pp. 141–232). Chicago: University of Chicago Press.

Hess, R. D., & Camara, K. A., (1979). Post-divorce relationships as mediating factors in the consequences of divorce for children. *Journal of Social Issues, 35,* 79–96.

Hetherington, E. M., Cox, M., & Cox, R. (1982). Effects of divorce on parents and children. In M. E. Lamb (Ed.), *Nontraditional families: Parenting and child development* (pp. 233–288). Hillsdale, NJ: Lawrence Erlbaum Associates.

Irving, H. H., (1981). *Divorce mediation: A rational alternative to the adversary system.* New York: Universe Books.

Jacobs, J. W., (1986). Divorce and child custody resolution: Conflicting legal and psychological paradigms. *American Journal of Psychiatry, 143,* 192–197.

Kitson, G. C., (1982). Attachment to the spouse in divorce: A scale and its application. *Journal of Marriage and the Family, 44,* 379–391.

Kressel, K., & Pruitt, D. G., (1985). Themes in the mediation of social conflict. *Journal of Social Issues, 41,* 179–198.

Levy, R. J., (1984). Comment on the Pearson-Thoennes study on mediation. *Family Law Quarterly, 17,* 525–538.

Margolin, F. M., (1973). *An approach to the resolution of visitation disputes post-divorce: Short-term counseling.* Unpublished doctoral dissertation, United States International University.

Matrimonial Law Commission Report. (1983, May). *Florida Bar Journal,* 290–298.

McHenry, P. C., Herrman, M. S., & Weber, R. E., (1978). Attitudes of attorneys toward divorce issues. *Conciliation Courts Review, 16,* 11–17.

McIssac, H., (1982). Court-connected mediation. *Conciliation Courts Review, 21,* 49–56.

Mnookin, R. H., (1975). Child-custody adjudication: Judicial functions in the face of indeterminacy. *Law and Contemporary Problems, 39,* 226–292.

Pearson, J., Ring, M., & Milne, A., (1983). A portrait of divorce mediation services in the public and private sector, *Conciliation Courts Review, 21*, 1–24.

Pearson, J., & Thoennes, N., (1982). The mediation and adjudication of divorce disputes: Some costs and benefits. *The Family Advocate, 4*, 26–32.

Pearson, J., & Thoennes, N., (1984). *Final report of the divorce mediation research project.* Available from authors, 1720 Emerson St., Denver, CO.

Pearson, J., Thoennes, N., & Vanderkooi, L., (1982). The decision to mediate: Profiles of individuals who accept and reject the opportunity to mediate contested custody and visitation issues. *Journal of Divorce, 6*, 17–35.

Peterman, S. E., (1986). *Predicting outcome in mediation.* Unpublished masters thesis, University of Virginia, Charlottesville, VA.

Sander, F. E. A., (1976). Varieties of dispute processing. *Federal Rules Decisions, 70*, 111–134.

Schulman, J., & Woods, L., (1983). Legal advocacy v. mediation in family law. *The Women's Advocate, 4*, 3–4.

Silberman, L. J., (1982). Professional responsibility problems of divorce medition. *Family Law Quarterly, 16*, 107–145.

Spanier, G. B., & Anderson, E. A., (1979). The impact of the legal system on adjustment to marital separation. *Journal of Marriage and the Family, 41*, 605–613.

Spanier, G. B., & Thompson, L., (1984). *Parting: The aftermath of separation and divorce.* Beverly Hills, CA: Sage.

Standards of practice for family mediators, (1984). *Family Law Quarterly, 17*, 455–460.

Watson, M. M., & Morton, T. L., (1983). *Mediation as an alternative to social study in child custody disputes.* Unpublished evaluation report of the family court of the First Circuit Court, Honolulu, Hawaii.

Weiss, R. S., (1975). *Marital separation.* New York: Basic Books.

Weitzman, L. J., (1985). *The divorce revolution.* New York: Free Press.

Zill, N., (1978, February). *Divorce, marital happiness and the mental health of children: Findings from the FCD national survey of children.* Paper presented at the NIMH workshop on Divorce and Children, Bethesda, MD.

4

A Comparison of Joint and Sole Legal Custody Agreements

Amy Koel
Susan C. Clark
W.P.C. Phear
Barbara B. Hauser
Middlesex Divorce Research Group, Cambridge, MA

INTRODUCTION

For children, custody arrangements are the most critical legacy of divorce. Yet, our knowledge of custody remains substantially incomplete, compared with our understanding of other aspects of divorce and divorcing families. Marital dissolution, and its consequences for children, has been studied extensively (Emery, 1982; Guidubaldi, Perry, & Cleminshaw, 1985; Hess & Camara, 1979; Hetherington, Cox, & Cox, 1978; Rutter, 1971; Tuckman & Regan, 1966; Weiss, 1975) and the complexities of postdivorce family experience have been examined (Ferreiro, Warren, & Konanc, 1986; Hetherington, 1987; Weitzman, 1985). The legal aspects of the divorce process and the effects of laws upon the family's negotiations prior to their appearance in court are also current topics of concern (Chambers, 1984; Foster, 1983; Mnookin, 1975; Mnookin & Kornhauser, 1979). Social policy and legal procedures must be altered to support optimal postdivorce familial relationships (Emery, Hetherington, & DiLalla, 1984).

Scholars have begun to note the significance of custody arrangements and to clarify their impact on the lives of the children involved in divorce (Ahrons, 1980; Luepnitz, 1982; Santrock & Warshak, 1979; Shiller, 1986). However, this process is just beginning. There has been a dearth of research documenting the frequency of various permutations of custodial arrangements and the contents of divorce agreements (Phear, Beck, Hauser, Clark, & Whitney, 1983); the types of postdivorce fiscal arrangements encountered in the population (Weitzman & Dixon, 1979); the correlation between the legally sanctioned arrangements and actual custodial practices; the implications of these arrangements for family reorganization (Furstenberg & Nord, 1985); and postdivorce relitigation (Ilfeld, Ilfeld, & Alexander, 1982).

The inadequacy of our knowledge about custody has consequences in a number of areas. Insufficient understanding of the intricacies and varieties of possible custodial arrangements hinders the development of relevant theory, as well as the planning of research that adequately captures the realities of postdivorce life for parents and children. Other consequences are more direct and practical. Lawyers, judges, and other professionals must rely on limited empirical data, anecdotal evidence, and their sense of the judicial experience as they help divorcing parents reach the formal agreements that will define their children's future.

Recent social trends have further complicated our understanding of legal and familial aspects of custody arrangements. Since Kansas and Oregon adopted the first joint custody statutes in 1979 (Folberg, 1983), many other states have adopted similar laws with the hope that joint legal custody would decrease interparental conflict and would improve the children's postdivorce adjustment and development. These statutory changes have been enacted with little or no knowledge of how they would affect societal expectations of the divorce process, statutory and case law, and divorcing parents and their children. Public, legislative, and judicial concern about how our courts should deal with postdivorce custodial and financial arrangements is increasing. Such developments point to a need for empirical research in these areas.

This chapter addresses the need for information on: (a) the frequency of joint and sole custodial arrangements in the population; (b) the court process and procedures leading up to the divorce; (c) the content of divorce agreements; (d) the comparison of joint and sole legal custody families; and (e) the rate at which families with various custody arrangements return to court to either enforce or change their agreements.

In discussing custodial arrangements, we distinguish between legal and physical custody. *Legal custody* refers to parental rights and responsibilities of decision making with regard to a minor child. In joint legal custody, both parents retain the right and responsibility to make major decisions about their child. Although there is no clear definition of what constitutes "major" decisions, they are usually thought to include the areas of education, medical care, and childrearing. Sole legal custody sanctions, but does not mandate, unilateral decision making.

Physical custody stipulates living arrangements for a minor child and, by implication, which parent is responsible for day-to-day decisions regarding the child. Joint physical custody indicates that the child lives with both parents, although the time division is often unequal. Parents are assumed to share daily decision making and provision for the child's needs, although frequent consultation between parents does not always occur. Sole physical custody indicates that the child lives with one parent and visits with the other. This chapter focuses primarily on legal custody, comparing families with joint legal custody to families with sole legal custody. Therefore, our use of the term *custody* refers to legal custody, unless otherwise noted.

Divorce agreements are developed in various ways. There are agreements that parents work out with the help of attorneys, agreements that parents and attorneys work out under the guidance of a judge during a court hearing, and "agreements" that are actually judicial orders in the absence of an agreement by the parties. Although the manner in which an agreement is reached may have significant consequences for the family, this distinction is beyond the scope of this chapter.

METHOD

Data Collection and Coding

Public documents of 700 divorces were abstracted and tabulated from the public records of the Middlesex Probate and Family Court, located in Cambridge, Massachusetts.[1] The data were collected in three different samples, each consisting of the first 100 divorces (each including at least one minor child) filed in the target months. Study A (300 families) divorces were filed in January 1978, 1979, and 1980; Study B (200 families) divorces were filed in May 1980 and January 1981; and Study C (200 families) divorces were filed in January 1983 and 1984. Where equivalent, data were collected for all three studies, $N = 700$. Data-collection refinements were made in studies B and C, resulting in the incomparability of some information with study A. Therefore, for some data, $N = 400$. No attempt was made to obtain missing data from sources other than the public records. In Massachusetts, in most cases, the only financial information included in the divorce agreement is the support award (child support and/or alimony). Because financial statements are confidential and are filed separately, socioeconomic, employment, and other financial data were not available.

On the basis of the judicial order, a family's custodial arrangements were coded as SOLE if the agreement specified sole legal custody or JOINT if the agreement specified joint legal custody. SOLE was further divided into mother-custody and father-custody families. Physical custody was coded in a similar manner.

Data Analysis

Some families in the original sample of 700 had a custody designation other than joint or sole (split custody, no custody mentioned, custody to other parties). These families were not included in the analysis. Group comparisons were based on 199 joint legal custody cases (JOINT) and 479 sole legal custody cases (SOLE).[2]

---

[1]A detailed summary of the first 500 cases in this study is available in Phear et al. (1983).

[2]Where data are only available on the last 400 cases, the sample consists of 155 joint families and 231 sole families.

Differences between the JOINT and SOLE groups were analyzed using *t* tests and chi-squares. All tests were two tailed. Two standard statistical packages, SAS and Systat, were used. Some of the comparisons reported here were statistically significant. Significance levels are given in the tables. Comparisons that failed to attain statistical reliability but that seem to have psychological significance are also discussed.

RESULTS AND DISCUSSION

The most compelling of the findings concern the distinctions between JOINT and SOLE families in custody provisions and court process, the comprehensiveness of the agreements, and the content and extent of relitigation. In reporting and discussing these findings, we consider the intricacies of the custodial agreements and suggest possible interrelationships among these agreements, court process, social changes, and the characteristics of the families. We also suggest likely areas for future research.

Middlesex County and Description of the Sample

All the divorces summarized in this study were granted in Middlesex County, the most populous county in Massachusetts. The county's one and a third million residents (U.S. Census, 1980) live in 11 cities and 43 towns, ranging from densely populated inner cities to affluent commuter suburbs to sparsely populated rural communities. The sample was distributed throughout Middlesex County, with all but 1 of the 54 cities and towns represented. The population is geographically, educationally, and ethnically diverse. No official records are available, but, from an informal, random sample of 4 months prior to 1981, we estimate that minor children are involved in 60% to 65% of all divorces filed in the county.

At the time of the target marriage, the mean age of the 700 husbands in this sample was 23.5 years, and that of their wives was 21 years (see Table 4.1). The average age at the birth of their first child was 22.9 for mothers and 25.5 for fathers. At the time of their separation, the parents had a total of 1,311 minor[3] children, 651 girls and 660 boys. The range was from one to seven children, with a mean of 1.87. At separation, the children ranged in age from 0 (born after separation) to 20 years.

Demographics, Court Process

There were no differences between JOINT and SOLE families for the parents'

---

[3]This number includes minor children and a few children who were older but still covered in the provisions of the divorce agreement.

TABLE 4.1
Ages of Parents at Marriage and First Child

Age (in Years) At	Legal Custody Designation		
	All (N = 700)	Sole (n = 479)	Joint (n = 199)
Marriage			
Mother			
Mean	21.0	20.5	21.1
SD	5.3	4.4	4.2
Father			
Mean	23.5	23.5	23.5
SD	5.3	6.6	7.0
First Child			
Mother			
Mean	22.9	22.5	23.7
SD	5.3	6.6	5.6
Father			
Mean	25.5	25.1	26.1
SD	7.9	6.6	9.9

ages at marriage or at the birth of their first child (see Table 4.1). Before separating, parents with joint custody had been married over 2 years longer than had parents with sole custody (see Table 4.2). JOINT families filed for divorce more rapidly upon separation than did SOLE families (1.0 vs. 1.7 years). The JOINT group was also more likely to have filed under a no-fault provision (56.8% vs. 32.8%; see Table 4.3).

The meaning of these differences is unclear. We do not know whether the

TABLE 4.2
Marriage and Divorce Chronology

	Legal Custody Designation		
	All (N = 700)	Sole (n = 479)	Joint (n = 199)
Years married before separation			
Mean	9.8	9.0	11.3
SD	13.2	10.9	8.4
Separation to filing interval*			
Mean	1.5	1.7	1.0
SD	5.3	2.2	1.4
Filing to final divorce hearing			
Mean	0.38	0.36	0.42
SD	.8	.9	.8

Note. Time is given in years.
*$p < .001$

TABLE 4.3
Filing Behavior: Spouse Initiating Divorce and Grounds

	Legal Custody Designation				
	All (N = 700) N (%)	Mother (n = 441) n (%)	Father (n = 38) n (%)	Joint (n = 199) n (%)	Other (n = 22) n (%)
FILED BY					
Mother	534 (76.3)	376 (85.3)	14 (36.8)	124 (62.3)	19 (86.4)
Father	166 (23.7)	65 (14.7)	24 (63.2)	75 (37.7)	3 (13.6)
GROUNDS*					
Fault	419 (59.9)	292 (66.2)	30 (78.9)	86 (43.2)	11 (50.0)
No fault	281 (40.1)	149 (33.8)	8 (21.1)	113 (56.8)	11 (50.0)

*$p < .005$

apparent deliberateness of the longer marriages and shorter filing time of the JOINT group results from interpersonal characteristics or some other factor. We have observed that, in the past, couples who requested joint custody were characterized by an interpersonal style more compatible with recognizing mutuality, not only in wishes for childrearing, but also in their assessment of responsibility for marital breakdown. The choice of the ''no-fault'' option might indicate a decision to avoid assigning public blame for the marital breakup, thereby maintaining or creating a civil postdivorce environment in which continued shared parenting is possible.

Custody

The frequencies of legal custody requests and the custody arrangements finally granted are summarized in Table 4.4. Sole legal custody was requested much more frequently (81.9%) than was joint custody (5.1%).

TABLE 4.4
Legal Custody Arrangements Requested and Granted

	Legal Custody Granted				
Legal custody requested	All (N = 700) N (%)	Mother (n = 441) n (%)	Father (n = 38) n (%)	Joint (n = 199) n (%)	Other (n = 22) n (%)
Mother	515 (73.6)	380	8	109	18
Father	58 (8.3)	7	26	23	2
Joint	36 (5.1)	4	1	31	0
No request	91 (13.0)	50	3	36	2

TABLE 4.5
Joint Custody Designations by Year of Divorce Hearing

Years of Divorce Hearing	Sample N	Custody Designation	
		Joint legal n (%)	Joint physical n (%)
1978–1980	346	55 (15.9)	7 (2.0)
1981–1982	154	54 (35.1)	4 (2.6)
1983–1985	200	90 (45.0)	9 (4.5)
TOTAL	700	199 (28.4)	20 (2.9)

Note. Percentages given are based only on the sample N for the years of divorce.

The incidence of joint legal and physical custody arrangements varied by year (see Table 4.5). Our data indicate that both joint legal and joint physical custody are becoming more common. However, throughout all of the 6 years of the study, joint legal custody was much more common than joint physical custody. The rate with which joint legal custody was awarded increased substantially (29.1%) between 1978 and 1985. Percentages for joint physical custody increased at a rate of only 2.5% during that same period. The inital difference between the percentages of joint legal and joint physical custody was 13.9% in 1978 but had increased to 40.5% by 1985.

In all cases, if a parent was granted sole legal custody, that parent also received sole physical custody (see Table 4.6). There was no similar association between joint legal and joint physical custody. Of the 199 joint legal custody cases, only 10% received joint physical custody. In the families granted joint legal custody, most mothers received physical custody (71.4%), whereas few fathers did (13.6%).

This distinction between legal and physical custody is becoming increasingly important to make. Historically, there was no need to discriminate between the two aspects of custody. States assumed they were synonymous, giving one par-

TABLE 4.6
Legal Custody by Physical Custody

Physical custody	Legal Custody Designation				
	All (N = 700) N (%)	Mother (n = 441) n (%)	Father (n = 38) n (%)	Joint (n = 199) n (%)	Other (n = 22) n (%)
Mother	584 (83.4)	441 (100)	0 (0)	142 (71.4)	1 (4.5)
Father	65 (9.3)	0 (0)	38 (100)	27 (13.6)	0 (0)
Joint	20 (2.9)	0 (0)	0 (0)	20 (10.1)	0 (0)
Other	31 (4.4)	0 (0)	0 (0)	10 (5.0)	21 (95.5)

ent complete responsibility for both principal decision making and day-to-day care for a minor child. However, when parents began to share postdivorce decision making, the question of where the child should live became a relevant issue. Physical custody needed to be addressed as a separate and distinct entity. Currently, divorce decrees cover living arrangements for children (physical custody), as well as parental rights and responsibilities with regard to decision making (legal custody). However, divorce statutes and the legal process often blur this distinction. In spite of the fact that the courts make awards of physical custody, Massachusetts law does not mention, much less define, physical custody. In addition, much of the research literature and most of the popular press fail to differentiate between legal and physical custody.

Agreement Content: Specific Arrangements and Completeness

We examined the divorce agreements to see how frequently 17 specific child-related issues were included. These issues were: legal custody, physical custody, visitation, vacations, holidays, child support, alimony, insurance on primary support provider, insured health-care costs, uninsured health-care costs, orthodontic costs, current and future educational costs, summer camp costs, property division, parental relocation, and resolution of parental disputes.

There was considerable variation in how thoroughly the agreements made formal provision for the children's current and future needs (see Table 4.7). No agreement addressed more than 15 of the 17 issues, and the majority dealt with 8 or fewer items. Comparing JOINT and SOLE families for the presence or absence of the 17 specific child-related issues, we found substantial within-group variation (JOINT, 2–15 issues covered; SOLE, 2–12 issues covered). There was also a between-group distinction; JOINT families had more complete agreements (a mean of 9 issues covered) than did SOLE families (a mean of 6.3 issues covered).

The agreements were examined to determine how extensively they specified the amount of time that the children would spend with their noncustodial parent. Few agreements included both parents as regular participants in their children's daily lives; children were seldom scheduled to spend a mid-week night with their noncustodial parent. The SOLE agreements listed nonspecific provisions for visitation more often (65.8%) than did the JOINT agreements (59.3%; see Table 4.8). Specific visitation arrangements were contained in more of the JOINT agreements (28.1%) than in the SOLE agreements (18%). Visitation was prohibited in 13 of the SOLE cases but in none of the JOINT cases. The JOINT agreements were also significantly more likely to contain definite plans for how children spend holidays and vacation time than were the sole agreements (see Table 4.7). The JOINT agreements more reliably addressed alteration in provisions for children in the event of parental geographic relocations (see Table 4.7). How the parents

TABLE 4.7
Issues Mentioned in Divorce Agreements

Issue	Totals (%)	Legal Custody Designation		
		Joint (%)	Sole (%)	Other (%)
Legal custody♦♦	685 (97.9)	199 (100)	479 (100)	8 (36.4)
Physical custody♦♦	683 (97.6)	196 (98.5)	479 (100)	9 (40.9)
Child support♦♦	572 (81.7)	167 (83.9)	391 (81.6)	14 (63.6)
Visitation♦♦	608 (85.4)	181 (91.0)	417 (87.1)	10 (45.5)
Health insurance♦♦	469 (67.0)	172 (86.4)	289 (60.3)	8 (36.4)
Uninsured health costs♦	210 (52.5)	118 (76.1)	91 (39.4)	1 (7.1)
Orthodonture♦	61 (15.3)	43 (27.7)	18 (7.8)	0 (0)
Vacations♦♦*	159 (22.7)	86 (43.2)	72 (15.0)	1 (4.5)
Holidays♦♦*	134 (19.1)	70 (35.2)	63 (13.2)	1 (4.5)
Future education♦♦	150 (21.4)	73 (36.7)	75 (15.7)	2 (9.1)
Life insurance♦♦	223 (31.9)	83 (41.7)	135 (28.2)	5 (22.7)
Geographic relocation♦				
regarding child*	44 (11.0)	32 (20.6)	12 (5.2)	0 (0)
regarding house only	7 (1.8)	3 (1.9)	4 (1.7)	0 (0)
Future dispute				
resolution♦♦*	58 (8.3)	33 (16.6)	25 (5.2)	0 (0)

Note. Frequencies given are number of families in which the issue was mentioned in the divorce agreement. Issues not listed here were mentioned very infrequently in the divorce agreements.
♦Total Sample of 400 (155 JOINTS, 231 SOLES, 14 OTHERS)
♦♦Total Sample of 700 (199 JOINTS, 479 SOLES, 22 OTHERS)
*$p < .005$

would attempt to resolve serious disputes was specified in 16.6% of the JOINT cases and 5.2% of the SOLE cases.

The considerable diversity in the extent to which these agreements included issues relevant to the future of children is notable. Some important needs of divorcing families, such as custody and child support, were nearly always covered. However, guidelines for restructuring children's lives in the event that one of their parents moved and settling future familial disputes were specified much less frequently. The agreements also varied considerably in the completeness of their coverage of holidays and vacation time, all known to be emotional and frequently problematic issues. Families spend a large percentage of court time negotiating where, and with whom, the children will spend Thanksgiving, Christmas, and other holidays. Most agreements were noteworthy for their vagueness and inconclusive language, leaving a considerable amount of uncertainty regarding future contacts between children and their noncustodial parent (Furstenberg & Nord, 1985).

Economic resources may be a factor in the greater agreement specificity seen in the JOINT group in two ways. Making provisions for future education, health and dental costs, and life insurance is necessary for families who can afford these options. These provisions are irrelevant for poorer families who could not afford

TABLE 4.8
Varieties of Visitation Granted: Joint and Sole Custody

	Legal Custody Designation			
	All *(N = 678)* N *(%)*	*Mother* *(n = 441)* n *(%)*	*Father* *(n = 38)* n *(%)*	*Joint* *(n = 199)* n *(%)*
Nonspecific visitation provisions				
Reasonable visitation, reasonable times, with reasonable notice	317 (46.8)	229 (51.9)	18 (47.4)	70 (35.2)
Prior category plus other, unspecified times	116 (17.1)	65 (14.7)	3 (7.9)	48 (24.1)
Specific visitation provisions*				
Specific weekends and holidays	90 (13.3)	56 (12.7)	5 (13.2)	29 (14.6)
Prior category plus one or more weekday evenings	35 (5.2)	21 (4.8)	0 (0)	14 (7.0)
One or more week nights with each parent	17 (2.5)	4 (.9)	0 (0)	13 (6.5)
Other visitation arrangements				
Arrangements not included in above categories	10 (1.5)	3 (.7)	0 (0)	7 (3.5)
No visitation allowed	13 (1.9)	12 (2.7)	1 (2.6)	0 (0)
Visitation not mentioned in custody agreement	80 (11.8)	51 (11.6)	11 (28.9)	18 (9.1)

Note. Families with other than joint or sole legal custody are not included in this table. Therefore, N = 678, not 700.
   *p < .005

them even before divorce. Also, court procedures and comprehensive legal representation often are costly. Most parents require extensive, and usually expensive, advice to arrive at agreements that carefully detail postdivorce responsibilities.

Although complete socioeconomic data on our specific sample are unavailable, we have two indications that our JOINT families had more money. In comparison with the SOLE families, they more often mentioned a house in their divorce agreements. Their support awards were also higher (see Table 4.9).[4] Because a few families had very large awards, the average is not an informative measure here. The median amount for joint families was around $6,000, and for sole families was somewhat lower than $4,000.

---

[4]The support awards reported here for the combined custody groups are higher than the national average (Espenshade, 1979).

TABLE 4.9
Support Awards: Child Support and Alimony Combined

	Custody Designation		
	All (N = 400)	Sole (n = 231)	Joint (n = 155)
Minimum annual amount	600	720	600
Maximum annual amount	78,000	30,000	78,000
Mean annual amount*	6,467	5,049	8,450
SD	16,755	10,749	11,952

Note. Data for families with other than joint or sole custody (n = 14) are not available.
*$p < .001$

A critical question raised by these data is the extent to which, and for whom, custody arrangements should remain ambiguous and flexible. Are divorce agreements that carefully define future duties and responsibilities, and that leave little room for negotiation, effective in creating stable, conflict-free, environments for children? Or, do rigid agreements fail to provide for the changing needs of developing children and their parents? These questions cannot be answered without a greater understanding of the extent to which agreement content reflects parental intent and influences familial behavior. It is possible that, despite legal ambiguities, parents with incomplete agreements can negotiate successfully with each other and readily communicate a sense of security and continuity to their children. It is also possible that incomplete agreements (particularly in the areas of living arrangements and visitation) promote interparental conflict and relitigation, and leave children anxious and confused about their continuing relationship with the noncustodial parent and/or the future structure of their daily lives. In spite of our limited knowledge about the impact of various types of agreements, we do know that postdivorce custody arrangements are of considerable concern to children (Wallerstein & Kelly, 1980).

Relitigation

At the time the records were examined, less than 20%[5] of the 700 cases had returned to court for one or more complaints[6] (see Table 4.10). Most families who returned to court had done so only once; no family returned more than seven

---

[5]Examination of the records after a longer interval will yield considerably higher relitigation rates. We have not found a point beyond which families stop relitigating. More recent, unpublished data indicate that families divorced since 1978 are still returning to court. The relitigation rate is over 40% for a subsample consisting of the 400 families who filed for divorce in January 1978 through May of 1980.

[6]Legal complaints include both contempts and modifications. Filing to declare someone in contempt is the first step toward enforcing an existing court order. Filing a modification is done when one of the parties believes the original order needs to be changed. It is the first step toward changing an existing court order.

TABLE 4.10
Frequency of Postdivorce Litigation:
Numbers of Families Filing Complaints

Number of petitions	Legal Custody Designation				
	All (N = 700) N (%)	Mother (n = 441) n (%)	Father (n = 38) n (%)	Joint (n = 199) n (%)	Other (n = 22) n (%)
0	578 (82.6)	358 (81.2)	36 (94.7)	165 (82.9)	19 (86.4)
1	89 (12.7)	64 (14.5)	1 (2.6)	23 (11.6)	1 (4.5)
2	22 (3.1)	13 (2.9)	1 (2.6)	8 (4.0)	0 (0)
3	8 (1.1)	5 (1.1)	0 (0)	2 (1.0)	1 (4.5)
4–7	3 (.4)	1 (.2)	0 (0)	1 (.5)	1 (4.5)
Total Number of relitigating families	122 (17.4)	83 (18.8%)	2 (5.3%)	34 (17.1%)	3 (13.6%)

times. Relitigation rates were lowest for father-custody families (5.3%), and highest for mother-custody families (18.8%). The reported grounds for relitigation occurring in the 400 divorces filed between May of 1980 and January of 1984 are summarized in Table 4.11. Fifty contempts and 26 modifications were filed. Occasionally, contempts and modifications were filed simultaneously, and, as previously noted, some families were responsible for several filings. Most of the relitigation (65.8%) centered on complaints about financial problems (child support and alimony). More families went back to court to attempt to enforce

TABLE 4.11
Content of Postdivorce Litigation: Numbers of Petitions

	Legal Custody Designation				
	All (N = 400)	Mother (n = 210)	Father (n = 21)	Joint (n = 155)	Other (n = 14)
CONTEMPTS:					
Custody	1	0	0	1	0
Visitation	8	0	0	8	0
Child support	35	22	1	10	2
Alimony	6	4	1	1	0
(Sub total)	(50)	(26)	(2)	(20)	(2)
MODIFICATIONS:					
Custody	12	5	0	6	1
Visitation	5	1	0	3	1
Child support	8	2	0	6	0
Alimony	1	0	0	1	0
(Sub total)	(26)	(8)	(0)	(16)	(2)
Total Petitions	76	34	2	36	4

existing financial orders (82%) than to change them (34.6%). Of the modifications filed, the single most frequent request was in the area of custody (46.2%).

There was no difference in the overall frequency with which the two groups returned to court during the postdivorce period encompassed by the study (JOINT 17.1% vs. SOLE 17.7%; see Table 4.10). However, in the final 200 cases, despite the relatively short interval (16 months or less) between the final divorce and data collection, 15 JOINTS had returned to court at least once (16.7%), as opposed to 9 SOLES (8.7%).

Of 50 contempts, SOLE families filed 28 (56%) and JOINT families filed 20 (40%). SOLE families were responsible for 8 of 26 modifications (30.8%), JOINT families for 16 (61.5%). All of the contempts filed by SOLE families were for enforcement of financial matters (child support and alimony). Of 20 contempts filed by JOINTS, 11 (55%) were about financial issues. Seventy-five percent of the modifications filed by the SOLE group dealt with child-related matters (custody and visitation), whereas the percentage was 56.3 for the JOINTS.

Relitigation of child support reaffirms the knowledge that we have a national problem in this area. Sole mother-custody families, in particular, are suffering (Weitzman, 1985). We do not yet understand why families come to court to modify custody arrangements so often. This may be a response to the changing needs of developing children or other alterations in family circumstances, such as geographic relocation. Initial agreements, forged in the stress of marital separation, may no longer reflect the needs of the family whose relationships have been altered by the divorce itself and by time. Alternatively, such relitigation may be a measure of parental conflict and retaliation.

The extent to which relitigation is an accurate index of postdivorce distress is also unknown. Different types of data yield different answers. Clinical experience tells us that many families will tolerate a great deal of noncompliance, ambiguity, and tension rather than seek judicial resolution. Relitigation, therefore, is but one measure of postdivorce stress and dissatisfaction experienced by many families. On the other hand, examination of the legal divorce process in Massachusetts reminds us that relitigation may be the only way to effect changes in divorce agreements. Other than relitigation, there are few widely available services that can achieve these changes. Using the court thus remains the only process for instituting a legal and enforceable modification.

Regardless of the etiology and underlying significance of returning to court, that action in itself is cause for concern because "contacts with the legal system tend to intensify family problems as the divorcing couple attempts to settle issues of custody, visitation, and divorce" (Hetherington & Camara, 1984, p. 409). A minority of the families were responsible for a substantial number of complaints, indicating that we must be more concerned about some families than about others.

We found no differences in relitigation rates between JOINT and SOLE families. These data are not consistent with the lower joint custody relitigation rates reported by Ilfeld et al. (1982) in California. We have no explanation for these distinctions, other than possible differences between the populations and/or in the local court procedures. Our results also seem incompatible with our clinical impressions of families with joint custody as being more cooperative and less litigious. Again, it is important to take into account the economic and legal advocacy differences that may allow the joint custody families to return to court more easily.

In the last 2 years of our study, relitigation rates for JOINT families increased substantially. These data, considered together with recent statutorial changes, raise a number of issues. This increase may be an aberration, peculiar to this particular population at this particular time. However, it may also be an indication that the population of joint custody families is changing. Historically, the first joint custody families appeared to be a small minority with significant resources, dedicated to shared parenting, and willing to endure considerable sacrifice toward this end. Our data indicate that joint legal custody is steadily increasing. Since 1984 when the Massachusetts legislature made joint custody a rebuttable presumption prior to a formal hearing, joint custody has become even more prevalent than we have shown in this paper (Middlesex Divorce Research Group, 1986). Therefore, the population receiving this designation is likely to become less unique and singleminded, and possibly more willing to relitigate.

This situation is exacerbated by the particular requirements of the joint custody designation. Joint custody necessitates more interparental contact than does sole custody. Greater contact requires greater cooperation and affords more opportunities for conflict. If, with the current level of social support for divorcing families, these requirements cannot be met by most couples who choose or are assigned joint custody, we would expect relitigation rates to increase. This situation requires careful monitoring to assess changing needs of parents and children. It is also a natural, transforming experiment (Bronfenbrenner, 1979). As such, it offers a rare opportunity to study the interplay of social policy and divorcing families, and to make the former more responsive to the latter.

As the rate of joint custody increases, reports in the media have promoted the popular impression that it is both the optimal and desirable postdivorce parenting behavior. Although we believe that children benefit from the involvement of both their parents, it is likely that only certain families can make joint legal custody a positive and relatively stress-free experience (Steinman, 1981). The danger inherent in the broad assumption of joint custody is that families will be pushed to accept this norm, even when it is unsuitable, and will then have to struggle, both within and outside of the court system, to arrive at an arrangement that is suited to their circumstances. This reordering process is often both protracted and stressful. We believe that it effectively delays the needed psychological adjustment to the divorce and creates new levels of interparental conflict and distrust. Within the context of refining social policies, it is crucial to encourage and to assist families to undertake serious and productive exploration of how best to restructure their unique postdivorce relationships.

Future Considerations

We have presented and discussed data on court process, custody designations, content of custody agreements, and relitigation. We have raised questions suggested by these data. However, a more fundamental issue remains to be considered. To really understand the impact of custody on families, researchers must first come to a consensus about what is meant by various custodial terms.

Custody can have several components (dimensions): (a) a designation or label (usually joint or sole); (b) a prescription for parental behavior written into a divorce agreement; and (c) the actual behavior of divorced parents caring for their children. These components have very different implications for families and for research on custody. Future work should distinguish among them.

Our work suggests that terms like *joint legal custody* and *sole physical custody* are sometimes ambiguous. We do not know the extent to which the formal custodial designations are simply labels, or whether they actually indicate parental approaches toward childrearing. Choosing a custody designation is not always the careful decision on the part of the parents that we may imagine. In our experience with divorcing families, we have noted that the specifics of filing (such as type of custody requested, time of filing, and type of grounds) more often reflect legal requirements for filing, attorney preferences, negotiation strategies, and prevailing societal norms than they do parental wishes. We do not know to what extent the content of the final agreement reflects these factors.

Grouping families by their custody designation can be misleading. The populations of joint and sole families are changing as divorce laws and social norms evolve. Joint legal custody is becoming the social ideal and the legal presumption in an increasing number of states. The joint legal custody population seems to encompass a broader spectrum of personal characteristics and parenting styles than it did a decade ago. The sole legal custody population seems to be increasingly more homogeneous. As the composition of these groups of families continues to change, interpreting these, and similar, data will become increasingly difficult.

The specifics of families' written agreements often do not reflect their custody designations. Our data revealed considerable variability of agreement content within one custody type. In addition, further examination of the agreements indicates that different custody designations occasionally mask considerable similarity in parental rights and responsibilities. In some cases, the specifics of SOLE agreements give both parents the right to be actively involved in making all meaningful and necessary parenting decisions. Thus, although they are theoretically different, some of the SOLE agreements are actually indistinguishable from the JOINT agreements.

We have also observed that the official designations and the schedules, rights, and responsibilities specified in custody agreements are not always reflected in families' actual behavior. In our other work (Clark, Whitney, & Beck, in press; Hauser, 1985), 25% to 33% of the families contacted at various intervals after their divorce reported that they were not following the physical custody arrangements detailed in the court records. The number of families not following the legal custody arrangements listed in their agreements may be even greater. Some joint custody families indicated that they did not share decision making, whereas some sole custody families reported that they did. Some of those interviewed said that what they had agreed to (and were doing) was never reflected in the court-sanctioned agreement. There is little research in this area (Brown, 1984).

Further refinement of the interrelationship between the legal and the psychological aspects of the divorce process is another critical task. Future research must, therefore, address the extent to which divorce behaviors and the content of custody agreements are consequences of family attributes and goals or are consequences of the legal environment. If laws and court requirements have a causative role, and we believe that they do, we must also examine the ways in which the legal environment influences custody agreements, relitigation, family behaviors, and the well-being of parents and children. In order to do this, examination of the actual divorce process and the experiences of families as they negotiate the legal system is necessary. It is also important for data on divorce to be collected in different jurisdictions. Such data will answer questions about generalizability and will further our understanding of relationships between families and the legal system.

Because so little is known about custody in divorcing families, it is difficult to make specific public policy recommendations. Legislative change should be responsive to future research findings. In addition, divorcing families need educational programs about custodial and legal options; more clinical and legal court-based services as they enter the legal process; institutionalized ways to develop individualized custody plans; and mediation and other supports for alternative means of dispute resolution.

REFERENCES

Ahrons, C. (1980). Joint custody arrangements in the postdivorce family. *Journal of Divorce, 3,* 189–204.

Bronfenbrenner, U. (1979). *The ecology of human development: Experiments by nature and design.* Cambridge, MA: Harvard University Press.

Brown, S. (1984). Changes in laws governing divorce: An evaluation of joint custody presumptions. *Journal of Family Issues, 5,* 200–223.

Chambers, D. L. (1984). Rethinking the substantive rules for custody disputes in divorce. *Michigan Law Review, 83*(3), 477–569.

Clark, S., Whitney, R., & Beck, J. (in press). Discrepancies between custody arrangements and practices. *Journal of Divorce, 11*(4).

Emery, R. E. (1982). Interparental conflict and the children of discord and divorce. *Psychological Bulletin, 92*(2), 310–330.

Emery, R. E., Hetherington, E. M., & DiLalla, L. F. (1984). Divorce, children, and social policy. In H. W. Stevenson & A. E. Siegel (Eds.), *Child development research and social policy* (Vol. 1, pp. 189–266). Chicago: University of Chicago Press.

Espenshade, T. J. (1979). The economic consequences of divorce. *Journal of Marriage and the Family, 41*(3), 615–625.

Ferreiro, B. W., Warren, N. J., & Konanc, J. T. (1986). ADAP: A divorce assessment proposal. *Family Relations, 35*(3), 439–449.

Folberg, J. (1983). *Joint custody statutes and judicial interpretations (as of 1983).* Unpublished manuscript.

Foster, H. H. (1983). Child custody and divorce: A lawyer's view. *Behavioral Science and the Law, 22,* 392–398.

Furstenberg, F. F., & Nord, C. W. (1985). Parenting apart: Patterns of childrearing after marital disruption. *Journal of Marriage and the Family, 47*(4), 893–904.

Guidubaldi, J., Perry, J. D., & Cleminshaw, H. K. (1985). The legacy of parental divorce: A nationwide study of family status and selected mediating variables on children's academic and social competencies. In B. B. Lahey & A. E. Kazdin (Eds.), *Advances in clinical child psychology* (Vol. 7, pp. 109–151). New York and London: Plenum Press.

Hauser, B. B. (1985). Custody in dispute: Legal and psychological profiles of contesting families. *Journal of the American Academy of Child Psychiatry, 24*(5), 575–582.

Hess, R. D., & Camara, K. A. (1979). Post-divorce family relationships as mediating factors in the consequences of divorce on children. *Journal of Social Issues, 35*(4), 79–95.

Hetherington, E. M. (1987). Family relations six years after divorce. In K. Pasley & M. Ihinger-Tollman (Eds.), *Remarriage and stepparenting today: Research and theory.* (pp. 185–205). New York: Guilford.

Hetherington, E. M., & Camara, K. A. (1984). Families in transition: The process of dissolution and reconstruction. In R. Parke (Ed.), *Review of child development research* (Vol. 7, pp. 398–439). Chicago: University of Chicago Press.

Hetherington, E. M., Cox, M., & Cox, R. (1978). The aftermath of divorce. In J. H. Stevens, Jr., & M. Mathews (Eds.), *Mother-child, father-child relations.* Washington, DC: National Association for the Education of Young Children.

Ilfeld, F. C., Jr., Ilfeld, H. Z., & Alexander, J. R. (1982). Does joint custody work? A first look at outcome data of relitigation. *American Journal of Psychiatry, 139*(1), 62–66.

Luepnitz, D. A. (1982). *Child custody: A study of families after divorce.* Lexington, MA: Lexington Books.

Middlesex Divorce Research Group, (1986). [Content of divorce agreements]. Unpublished raw data.

Mnookin, R. (1975). Child custody adjudication: Judicial functions in the face of indeterminancy. *Law and Contemporary Problems, 39,* 226–293.

Mnookin, R., & Kornhauser, L. (1979). Bargaining in the shadow of the law: The case of divorce. *Yale Law Journal, 88,* 950–996.

Phear, W. P. C., Beck, J. C., Hauser, B. B., Clark, S. C., & Whitney, R. A. (1983). An empirical study of custody agreements: Joint versus sole legal custody. *Journal of Psychiatry and Law, 11,* 419–441.

Rutter, M. (1971). Parent-child separation: Psychological effects on the children. *Journal of Child Psychology and Psychiatry, 12,* 233–260.

Santrock, J. W., & Warshak, R. A. (1979). Father custody and social development in boys and girls. *Journal of Social Issues, 35*(4), 112–125.

Shiller, V. M. (1986). Joint versus maternal custody for families with latency age boys: Parent characteristics and child adjustment. *American Journal of Orthopsychiatry, 56*(3), 486–489.

Steinman, S. (1981). The experience of children in a joint-custody arrangement: A report of a study. *American Journal of Orthopsychiatry, 51,* 403–414.

Tuckman, J., & Regan, R. (1966). Intactness of home and behavioral problems in children. *Journal of Child Psychology and Psychiatry, 7,* 225–233.

U.S. Department of Commerce, 1980 Bureau of the Census. (1981). *Census of Population (Vol. 1) Characteristics of the population* (Chap. B, general population characteristics. Part 23, Massachusetts. p. 23–275. Table 44). Washington, DC: U.S. Government Printing Office.

Wallerstein, J. S., & Kelly, J. B. (1980). *Surviving the breakup: How children and parents cope with divorce*. New York: Basic Books.

Weiss, R. S. (1975). *Marital separation*. New York: Basic Books.

Weitzman, L. J. (1985). *The divorce revolution: The unexpected social and economic consequences for women and children in America*. New York: The Free Press.

Weitzman, L. J., & Dixon, R. B. (1979). Child custody awards: Legal standards and empirical patterns for child custody, support and visitation after divorce. *University of California at Davis Law Review, 12*(3), 472–521.

5

Custody of Children Following Divorce

Eleanor E. Maccoby
Charlene E. Depner
Robert H. Mnookin
Stanford University

Legal reform and social experimentation are introducing dramatic changes in the possibilities for child custody after divorce. Thirty-one states have adopted some form of joint custody legislation (Freed & Walker, 1985). Divorcing couples are now faced with an array of options for custodial arrangements ranging from sole custody to elaborate time sharing between parents. What are parents in fact doing? In this chapter, we describe the several forms of legal custody, but most of the chapter concerns the *de facto* residential custody of the children—where they were living at the time of our initial interview, shortly after filing for divorce. We are particularly interested in how much the children were moving back and forth for overnight stays in each of the parental households, and how family size and characteristics of the child covary with the kind of custody arrangements adopted by the family.

Data are taken from the Stanford Child Custody Study, a longitudinal study of 1,129 families with 1,884 children. Most of the information has been obtained by telephone interviews with the parents, although a subsample of parents responded to a shorter mail questionnaire. In 43% of the families, both parents provided information; in the remainder, one parent was the informant. We begin with a brief overview of the background of the study, including the status of divorce law in California, where the study is taking place.

CHANGES IN DIVORCE LAW

In recent years, laws concerning the custodial arrangements for children following divorce have been undergoing rapid change in two important respects. First, there is an increased acknowledgment that parents, not judges, should be encouraged to decide what custodial arrangements best serve the needs of a particular family. For many years, divorce laws reflected a restrictive and regulatory attitude toward divorce. The courts not only had to decide who was "at fault," but they were assumed to have both the right and the obligation to decide which parent should have custody of the children. Laws even assumed that courts would have ongoing supervisory responsibility for the children after the divorce decree was formalized. With the onset of no-fault divorce, courts have become less and less regulatory, leaving as many decisions as possible to the private agreements of the parties concerned. It would appear that courts are no longer in the business of trying to govern the conduct of parents who are able to agree on a particular form of custody after divorce. Rather than have a state court judge determine on an individual basis what is best for a particular child, the state now follows the wishes of the parents. A primary function of the law now is to endorse whatever arrangement is negotiated by the divorcing parents—a move away from regulation to acknowledgment of "private ordering" (Mnookin, 1985; Mnookin & Kornhauser, 1979). No doubt, the retreat of the courts from a more regulatory stance has stemmed in part from a recognition of the fact that making a choice between two fit parents, in the absence of clear presumptions and rules, strained the competence of even the most conscientious judges and their staffs.

A second fundamental change involves the move away from sex-role stereotypes, and an increasing insistence that a mother and father stand on an equal footing before the law. Until recently, the law reflected traditional sex-role ideology that characterized the father as head of the household and breadwinner, and the mother as homemaker, primarily responsible for children's care and nurturance. Thus, mothers were expected to care for children after divorce, and absent extraordinary circumstances (such as a demonstration that the mother was "unfit"), the father's role was seen as limited to visitation and the fulfillment of his support obligation. But in recent years a strong preference in favor of maternal custody following divorce has given way to new laws that require that there be no preference based on a parent's sex. Disputes are resolved on a case-by-case determination of the child's bests interests. Since 1981, the laws of many states have gone the further step to authorize and encourage joint custody (i.e., an arrangement where the parents share resonsibility for the children following divorce). The statutes take widely varied form ranging from: (a) an adoption available to the court; (b) a presumption that must be overcome; (c) an alternative available only upon petition or agreement of the parties; or (d) an even split into joint legal custody and joint physical custody (Freed & Walker, 1985).

The notion that divorced parents should share the reponsibilities for raising a child after divorce is a radical departure from the traditional doctrine that the law's function was to select a sole custodian through the application of some substantive custody standard. Indeed, it flies in the face of some strong psychological and legal advice to the contrary (Goldstein, Freud, & Solnit, 1973, 1979).

Today the law permits a number of alternative forms of custody, in which parental rights and responsibilities can be allocated in different ways.

CALIFORNIA LAW TODAY

California, the location of our study, is an ideal place to explore the causes and consequences of these legal changes. Its laws very much reflect these trends and assumptions. Indeed, California has often been among the first states to adopt a legal change later accepted across the country. For example, it was in the vanguard of the no-fault revolution (Wheeler, 1974), and under current California law, one spouse can end the marriage, in spite of the objections of the other.

California's legal standards for child custody have evolved from a maternal preference through a neutral best interest standard to a preference for joint custody. In 1969, the Family Law Act, which introduced no-fault divorce, provided that custody was to be awarded "to either parent according to the best interests of the child, with a preference for maternal custody if the child is of tender years." This preference for maternal custody was softened in 1970 (California Statute 1970, Chapter 1545, Paragraph 3139, Section 2) and eliminated in 1972 (California Statute, 1972, Chapter 1007, Paragraph 1855, Section 1) in favor of a neutral "best interest of the child" standard. In 1979, California became the first state to adopt a statute that not only specifically authorized a joint custody award upon divorce, but established a presumption in favor of joint custody when both parents request it. The 1979 statute also explicitly stated the policy goal of assuring children "frequent and continuing contact with both parents," and re-affirmed the state's policy that gender of a parent could not be a basis for a preference. The state not only created a presumption in favor of joint custody when both parents requested it, but authorized the court to order joint custody in a disputed case where one parent sought it (California Civil Code Sections 4600, 4600.5). In September 1983, the legislature refined these joint custody provisions by explicitly differentiating joint physical custody (i.e., arrangements where both parents have "significant periods" of reponsibility for the day-to-day care of the child) and joint legal custody (where both spouses have "the right and responsibility to make decisions relating to the health, education and welfare of the child"). The presumption applies to each of these aspects of custody.

Legal Labels: The Trend Toward "Joint" Custody

The changes in the California law appear to have been accompanied by changes in the legal custodial arrangements requested by petitioners for divorce, and in the kinds of custody awards specified in divorce decrees. At the present time, the most common combinations of legal and residential custody are:

1. *Mother physical and legal custody*: This is the traditional arrangement. The

mother has sole responsibility for the care and custody of the child, along with the various legal rights of a custodial parent. The father usually has the right to visit his children on a "reasonable" basis.

2. *Mother physical custody with joint legal custody*: Under this arrangement, the mother has ongoing day-to-day responsibility for the care of the child, but the father has the legal right to participate in various important decisions that may affect the child's life.

3. *Joint physical custody*: Both parents retain full legal rights and responsibilities, including the physical custody of the child. In this form of custody the child resides, for some amount of time, in the home of each parent. There is a considerable range of actual arrangements under this label. The period of alternation can vary on a weekly, monthly, or even yearly schedule. In many arrangements labeled *joint physical custody* the child does not spend equivalent amounts of time with the two parents.

4. *Father physical custody*: The father is the primary custodian, and the child resides in his household. The mother usually has visitation rights, and sometimes has joint legal custody.

Table 5.1 illustrates recent trends in the forms of custody requested by parents in one California county. The first two columns of the table show data from pilot work for the present study. The court records of divorce decrees granted in Santa Clara County during October 1979 (before joint custody legislation went into effect) and October 1981 (shortly after the law was enacted) were tabulated. There was evidence at that time that a decline in the traditional "mother custody" was already under way; an increase in awards of joint custody could be discerned. Column three shows data collected for the present study. Court records of Santa Clara County divorce filings over a 7-month period (September 1984 through March 1985) were scanned. We collected data from 1,551 petitions in that county. At this time, only about one third of the petitioners were asking for traditional "mother custody," and the proportion specifying both joint legal and physical custody was nearly one-fifth.

The final column of Table 5.1 shows the legal labels of arrangements adopted by Santa Clara County families in our study who had reached agreement about custody by the time of the first interview. About 58% of the interviewed families reported agreement by that time. Among those who have agreed, proportions of joint custody exceed those in the petitioners' request. (This may mean that families predisposed to joint custody settle more quickly. However, our analysis of this subgroup who have reached agreement, documents substantial shifts from sole custody requests to joint custody agreements.)

Table 5.1 indicates a continuing trend toward some form of joint custody and a continuing decline in exclusive custody to one parent. Particularly striking is the fact that the majority of families divorcing in 1984–1985 expect to have joint legal custody (with either joint residential or mother residential custody). Although

TABLE 5.1
Legal Labels for Custodial Arrangements
Santa Clara County, California
(Percent of Families in Each Category)

Form of Custody	Final decrees Oct., 1979	Final decrees Oct., 1981	Petitioners' requests Sept., 1984– March, 1985	Agreement at Time 1
N =	321	138	1551	476
Mother physical and legal custody	56.7	44.2	30.8	20.8
Mother physical with joint legal custody	21.2	23.9	39.3	49.0
Joint physical custody	4.4	13.0	19.4	21.6
Father custody	14.0	14.5	9.5	6.9
Other[a]	3.7	4.3	1.1	1.7
Total	100%	100%	100%	100%

[a]"Other" includes special arrangements, such as split custody.

residential custody is still assigned to the mother in the majority of the cases, more families seem to be moving toward arrangements that permit fathers to participate in day-to-day childrearing.

Do these changes reflect the impact of the concurrent changes in the divorce law? Perhaps so. We know that even when custodial decisions are not contested in the courts, the kind of private bargaining that goes on between couples who are not initially in agreement depends on their understanding of the legal endowments of each party (Mnookin & Kornhauser, 1979). Thus, merely knowing that the law now sanctions joint custody might encourage families to consider it who might otherwise not have done so. It is possible, however, that both changes in the law and changes in the choices of individual families reflect changes in a third factor: namely, the ideology surrounding custody. In particular, there appears to be a growing belief that both parents should remain involved with the children and that some form of joint custody is feasible.

Psychological research has contributed to the weight of opinion favoring joint custody. Two major studies of families with traditional maternal custody (Hetherington, Cox, & Cox, 1982; Wallerstein & Kelly, 1980) have reported that the children in these families fare worse if their fathers do not continue to be involved in their lives following the divorce. A study by Steinman (1981) with a small group of families who chose joint custody before the legal preference was established was also influential. This study indicated that joint physical custody was a viable arrangement, at least for the first year or two following divorce.

However, the couples included in the Steinman study were, for the most part, exceptionally well-educated people with fairly "friendly" divorces, and both parents were intensely committed to maintaining a supportive role in the lives of their children even if this entailed some personal sacrifice. It is not clear to what extent these results would apply to a broader population of divorcing families. And in the two major studies of the impact of divorce on children in maternal custody, it may have been the case that the fathers who remained involved with their children were from the families in which there had been less intense conflict between the spouses prior to and immediately following the divorce. If this were so, it may not have been the father's continued involvement per se that benefited the children, but the lower level of interparental discord to which the children had been exposed.

ISSUES AND QUESTIONS

Although it is possible to document some rapid changes in the nature of the legal labels for the custodial arrangements, little is known concerning the realities that underlie these legal labels. It is possible that some of the changes are more apparent than real. For example, a decree of joint legal custody with maternal physical custody may not mean that families live their lives differently than they did under the traditional pattern of maternal custody with father visitation. On the other hand, having a legitimized role—even a *pro forma* one—in decisions concerning the child may sustain a father's interests and prevent the "father dropout" that so commonly occurs (Furstenberg, Nord, Peterson, & Zill, 1983).

Further questions concern interspousal conflict. In some number of cases, joint custody—physical or legal—is being settled upon by the couple despite the fact that one of the parents might have preferred an alternative arrangement. It is reasonable to suppose that there may be more conflict, at least initially, in these cases than for the couples who fully agreed on the form of custody they preferred. Some writers assume that joint custody implies more than increased father–child interaction. They present a picture of shared parenting. Furstenberg and Nord (1985) challenged the assumption of co-parenting, reporting that they found evidence for "parallel parenting" at best. In her sample of parents with joint physical custody, Steinman (1981) also reported that parents operate in an independent fashion with little consultation on routine childrearing activities. Ahrons (1981) found that parents often avoid consultation about the child in order to suppress conflict. What kind and degree of shared parenting is possible between parents who separate under conditions of high conflict (over custody or other issues)? We need to know more about the conditions under which co-parenting can actually occur, and what role is played in this by the degree of initial agreement or conflict between the divorcing couple. Do hostility and conflict drop away over time? Do they drop faster, or more slowly, if the parents remain in contact because of their mutual involvement with the child? Our study is designed to obtain information relevant to these questions.

Our study includes the full range of custodial arrangements currently being chosen by families. The families are being followed over a 3-year period, and information will be forthcoming concerning the aforementioned questions, as well as others. At the time of this writing, only the first preliminary data are available. The purpose of the present chapter is to provide a description of the existing *de facto* arrangements for physical custody, and to examine how these arrangements vary according to the age and sex of the children and the number of children in the family. The existing studies of divorce give some intriguing indications that the impact of family disruption may be different for children of different ages (see Wallerstein & Kelly, 1980), and the work of Warshak and Santrock (1983) has highlighted the possibility that the children's welfare may in part depend on whether they are in the custody of the same-sex versus opposite-sex parent. We lack baseline information, however, concerning the custodial decisions that are being made in the lives of children of different ages and sexes and the factors that underly such decisions. The present study has a large enough sample to permit separate study of the custodial decision made for boys and girls, and for the full age range of minor children.

We begin with a brief description of our sample selection and our data collection procedures.

THE SAMPLE

We reviewed nearly 7,000 court records of filings for divorce that were entered into the records of two California counties between September 1, 1984 and March 31, 1985. Of these, an estimated 1,990 met the eligibility requirements of the study: that there was at least one child under 16 years of age from this marriage and that the couple had been separated for no more than 14 months before filing. Because the primary mode of data collection is via telephone interview, a search was made for telephone numbers, and a valid telephone number was found for at least one of the parents in 1,327 families. A telephone interview was obtained for a least one parent in 858 of these families. (The primary reason for nonresponse was inability to reach a parent by phone after repeated calls. Only 11.3% of individuals reached declined to be interviewed.) Mail questionnaires were sent to eligible parents whom we were unable to reach, and an additional 271 families were added to the sample via these mail questionnaires. Thus, the sample size for the first round of interviewing is 1,129 families. In 491 of these, information was obtained from both parents, for the remainder, from only one. The total number of individual parents reporting, then, is 1,620. The families included in the sample have 1,884 children.

About 72% of the sample live in Santa Clara County, a large and diverse urban and suburban county including the city of San Jose and the smaller cities of Cupertino, Santa Clara, Sunnyvale, Mountain View, and Palo Alto. The remainder of the sample live in San Mateo County, including East Palo Alto, Menlo Park, Redwood City, San Mateo, Belmont, Burlingame, San Carlos, and Milbrae. The modal period of separation prior to filing was 2 months, and the modal Time 1 telephone interview took place 2 to 3 months after filing. Thus, in the most common case, our Time 1 interview occurred 4 to 5 months after the couple separated.

Parents with a wide range of ages, education levels, occupations, and incomes are included in the study. For example, 28% of the parents interviewed have high school education or less; 41% have some college; and 30% have completed college or gone on to graduate work. The mean earnings reported in the Time 1 interview were $16,049 for mothers and $34,932 for fathers. The range is very wide—from those currently unemployed to one respondent with an annual income of $250,000. When the characteristics of our sample are compared with those of the adult populations of the two counties, our respondents on the average are younger (the modal age is in the early 30s), somewhat better educated, and somewhat more affluent. However, the counties include substantial numbers of people beyond childrearing age. We do not have information that would permit comparing our sample's socioeconomic status with that of nondivorcing parents.

The children in the sample range in age from under 2 (one child was yet unborn at the time of the first interview) to 18. Although a family was included in the sample only if there were children under age 16, older, minor children (aged 16 to 18) in sample families were included in the analysis. Family size varied from one minor child to over six, with 28% of the children in the study being in one-child families, 49% in two-child families, and 23% in families with three or more children.

Determining Time 1 De Facto Residential Custody

As previously noted, families seek a variety of legal custodial arrangements, but these do not always define the actual living arrangements of the children. We asked parents to fill out a diary for the last 2 weeks for each child in the family, indicating what portions of each 24-hour period were spent with each of the parents. We then asked whether the situation prevailing in the past 2 weeks was typical of the usual visitation and alternation arrangements. Approximately half the respondents said that the last 2 weeks were *not* typical. For these respondents, we asked whether there was a regular pattern (one that differed from the last 2 weeks) and if they said yes, we obtained a detailed report of the regular pattern. For the minority who said there was no regular pattern (e.g., that the nonresidential parent was free to see the children whenever convenient) we asked how much time this parent usually spent with the children in terms of daytime and overnight visits.

We also asked parents a simple question: "Do your children now live with you, your spouse, both of you or someone else?" There is a strong correspondence between the diary information and this measure of the child's *de facto* residence. If the child spent three or fewer nights with the father, over 90% of parents said that the child resided with the mother; if three or fewer overnights were spent with the mother, over 90% of parents said the child resided with the father. The relationship between residence and overnights is not equivalent for children who spend 4 to 11 overnights with the father. The majority of them are characterized as living with both parents; but many others are described as residing primarily with the mother.

When both parents were interviewed, there was slightly more discrepancy in reports concerning the last 2 weeks than in reports about the regular or usual pattern—an understandable finding, in view of the fact that the two parents were almost never reporting about the same 2-week period. For the analyses reported here, we have chosen the number of overnights spent with each parent in a usual or regular 2-week period as the best index of the child's *de facto* residence. Note that in the majority of the cases, this "usual" pattern places the child in the same residential category as the measure of overnights reported for the last 2 weeks.

There were a number of cases in which the question concerning which parent the child was living with was not relevant. Most of these were cases in which the parents were still living in the same residence although they had filed for divorce. A few such parents may reconcile. More often, however, it appears that these are genuine divorces-in-progress in which neither of the parents had been willing or able to move out by the time of the first interview. In some cases, attorneys advised parents that to move out would jeopardize their chances of getting custody or being awarded the house. More often, the problem was either that the couple could not agree on who was to move out, or they had agreed but the parent planning to leave had not yet been able to find affordable separate housing. The tensions involved in such cases are illustrated by a family with two children in which the mother occupied the house from 8 a.m. to 7 p.m. each day, at which point the mother departed and the father arrived to spend the night. The two parents did not speak to one another. Each had obtained a restraining order from the court, forbidding the other to approach the house during the in-house parent's official residence time. Each parent wanted to keep the house, and each wanted custody of the children. The father said: "I just want her to get out and leave me and the children here where we belong. I never want to see her again." The mother, in her interview, was equally outraged over her husband's behavior and charged him with trying to throw her bodily out of the house. Both expressed worry concerning the effect that the situation must be having on the children, but the couple was unable to resolve the impasse. We have put the cases of continued co-residence, along with the much smaller group of families whose children were living with relatives or friends, into an "other" category.

In a few cases—approximately 1% of the families in our sample—the children's residences had been split, so that both parents were providing a primary residence for at least once child and siblings were living apart. In the analyses that follow, tables are based on children, not families, and individual children are shown according to their residential location regardless of the location of their siblings.

Table 5.2 shows that the distribution of the number of overnights is very similar whether one uses the last 2 weeks or interpolates the usual pattern for those cases in which the last 2 weeks were said not to be typical.

Nevertheless, there were more children who did not spend any overnights with the secondary parent during the last 2 weeks than the number who "usually" spent no overnights, according to their parents' reports. We interpret this slight discrepancy to reflect the fact that occasionally unusual circumstances arise that prevent the expected visitation pattern from occurring. Thus, if the secondary parent is ill or away on a trip, or the primary parent has a 2-week vacation and wishes to take the children along, the usual overnights with the secondary parent would not occur in a given 2-week period even though they do occur most of the time. Of course, the converse can be true as well—that special circumstances produce an additional overnight or two, beyond what the normal agreed-upon pattern of visitation calls for. For purposes of estimating the total amount of involvement by the two parents, unusual circumstances should of course be averaged in. For purposes of placing families into our major categories of overnight visitation, however, we have elected to designate families according to their most usual practice, whenever this differed from the last 2 weeks.

In the large majority of cases, however, the two kinds of reports yielded the same categorical placement for a family, and the correlation between the number of overnights reported for the last 2 weeks and that reported for the "usual" 2-week period is .96.

TABLE 5.2
Number of Overnights Spent With Father
Comparison of Last 2-Weeks and
Respondent's Report of Usual 2-Week Period
(Percent of Children)

# Overnights with father	Last 2 weeks	Usual 2 weeks
None	38.3	37.0
1–3	28.8	31.3
4–10	14.1	13.2
11–13	4.9	5.5
14	7.6	7.2
Other	6.3	5.8
	100%	100%
N =	1,884	1,884

Where the Children Were Living at Time 1

Table 5.2 shows the distribution of children according to the number of overnights they spent with their fathers. The converse of these numbers is, of course, the number of overnights spent with mothers. That is, the category "14 nights with father" is equivalent to the "none" category, in that it indicates that the child is sleeping exclusively at one parental residence, and spends no overnights with the other parent. The numbers can be grouped into categories that we believe represent fairly distinct residential arrangements. Children designated as living with their mothers include those who spend either no overnights or 1 to 3 overnights with their fathers. Children designated as living with their fathers include those who spend more than 10 overnights with their father during a 2-week period. *Divided residence* refers to arrangements in which children usually spend 4 to 10 overnights with their fathers. Clearly, any grouping based on the number of overnights with each parent is arbitrary. We have chosen these cut-off points because, on the question "Where are the children living?" parents who reported three or fewer overnights with father almost always answered "with mother." When the child spent between greater than 3, but less than 11 nights with father, however, the answers were usually "with both of us." Our cut-off points were chosen, in other words, in order to represent as closely as possible the descriptive labels the parents themselves applied. In a family where the children were spending 4 or 5 overnights with father, for example, there would usually be one or more school-aged children; the children would sleep at their mother's house during the school week, and spend every weekend night with their fathers. We (and most of the parents) regard this as a considerable sharing of residential custody between the two parents.

We find that over a third of the children in our sample were spending no overnights with father at the time of our Time 1 interview, and 6% were spending no overnights with mother. We hasten to point out, however, that the absence of overnights does not imply a total lack of contact with the secondary parent.

Nearly three quarters of the group shown as having no overnights with the secondary parent saw this parent for at least one daytime visit during the 2-week period; and other children received phone calls. Our estimate of the proportion of children who had no contact of any kind with the secondary parent is lower than 15%. In terms of residence, however, 70% of the children in our sample were with their mothers and only 13% were with their fathers. Another 12% spent enough overnights in both residences so that they may be considered to be in shared or joint residential custody.

Why do most parents continue to choose maternal residence? The reasons are various. Some of them are illustrated by the following excerpts from interviews:

Father of two children, aged 3 and 5:

My wife is more suited to bring up the kids than myself under the circumstances.

It's the woman's role to bring up the kids. She is the guiding force behind the children. A large portion of her time is with the kids. My wife doesn't work. She has more desire to be a mother—more prepared to take on the kids than me. I couldn't give the kids the kind of time they need to bring them up.

Father of three children, aged 3, 5, and 8:

I have three children and do not have sufficient space at this time. My job requires frequent out of state travel and child care would be difficult. The chances are slim to none that a court would award me custody.

Father of two:

The younger one needs a mother. The older one is about old enough to make his own choice.

Mother of a 4-year-old daughter:

I want her to live with me because of selfishness. I don't want any other woman to raise her.

Father of daughter aged 6, son aged 3:

The hours I work leave only weekends. I want a weekend for myself and one for the kids. I can't afford babysitters, so I didn't take the kids to live with me. I feel I'm a better person to raise the children. She does a good job, but I disagree with some of what she does.

Father of three children, aged 10, 13, and 15:

I'm not a very good parent. Parenting is a difficult role that I am not willing to handle at this point.

Mother of son aged 3:

I have been a consistent parent. I have a better understanding of my son's needs.

A number of mothers told us that their former husbands suffered from drug or alcohol problems, and that they did not consider it safe for the children to spend time at their father's residence. In addition, of course, there were cases in which the father's new woman friend represented an impediment to visitation by the children, either because of the mother's jealousy, or because of disinterest on the part of the father or his woman friend in integrating the children into their household.

We do not yet have counts that would enable us to know the frequency with which these various factors underly the choice of maternal custody. However, the excerpts serve to illustrate the range and complexity of these factors. There is a mix of practical and interpersonal considerations. Parents make assumptions concerning which of them would be the better parent, and these may be implicitly agreed upon even if never discussed. Beyond the individual skills of the parents involved, many parents of both sexes assume that mothers have a natural talent for childrearing, especially for children of "tender years," and that fathers do not understand young children as well. Also, there are many parents who seem to assume that it is natural for fathers to give higher priority to their work than mothers will do. These views are by no means universal, however, and a number of fathers (especially those who either had or wanted custody) told us that their former wives were too immature to manage the care of children on their own, or mentioned drug or alcohol problems that rendered the mother's capacity for childrearing doubtful. Fathers also were sometimes concerned about the influence of a mother's male friend upon the children.

The practicalities of the father's situation often led to maternal custody, at least in the short run. More often than not, it was the father who had moved out, leaving the mother and children in the family dwelling. The father might initially have moved in with relatives or stayed in some other temporary residence where there was no room for the children. Even if he was more permanently housed, he might be in a place poorly set up for children (e.g., with an unfenced pool).

With children of school age, both parents usually saw advantages to keeping them in their familiar school, and the father's residence was seldom close enough to make this convenient. Parents frequently spoke of the importance of maintaining as much stability as possible for the children. As long as the mother stays in the family home, this implies maternal custody.

The attitudes parents expressed about joint physical custody were mixed, as indicated here:

Father of 2-year-old son:

I'm coming from the point of view that I feel it's important for the child to have the benefit of both parents. That a father has just as much equal stake in raising the child and influencing the child's growth. I also feel it's important for both parents to have time for themselves to do whatever they need to do. It's not good for a child to be with one parent continuously where that parent feels tied down and unable to do what they want to do with their lives. So, I'm trying to strike a balance where our son gets the benefit of both of us and at the same time we are able to pursue our own interests.

Mother of 3-year-old son:

I find joint custody totally unfair to the child. A child needs certain grounding, stability and roots. Bouncing from one home to the other does not allow that stability.

Mother of three:

I think this 50–50 stuff is crazy. It's not practical. My two oldest are in school. They have to leave the house an hour earlier (at father's house) to get to school. That's no way to live.

Mother of 2-year-old son who is currently in shared custody but for whom mother wants maternal custody:

> His father wants as much time as I have. I miss my son. I'm so used to having him here. The actual leaving—seeing him go—is so hard. It wasn't my idea to split. (Interviewer asks why she wants mother custody) Selfishness? I try to think what's best for my son. I've always been around. If being with his father would be proven to be better, I'd do it, but it would be hard. His room is here, this is his house. At his father's, he doesn't even have a room. But . . . a father should be responsible too. The father and mother originally should guide and provide a family for the child. Both should have input to what happens in his life.

In the cases of father residential custody, once again the situations are highly varied. In some cases, both parents say the arrangement is temporary. In others, the father considers that the mother (or her male friend) provides an unfit environment. This includes several cases in which the father says the mother uses drugs or alcohol to excess. In a few cases, the mother simply left, rejecting what she saw as the burdens of child and household care. As one mother put it: "I resigned as maid." The housing of the two parents also makes a difference. In one family, for example, the father initially left, and the children remained in the family apartment with the mother. Then the mother was evicted from the apartment, and took the children to her parent's house. When the father was settled in a stable residence, the children went to stay with him. In several cases, the housing issue was of a different kind: the children wanted to remain in the house, and the mother could not afford to keep up the house payments, whereas the father could. She, therefore, was the one who left. The father's ability to offer a stable physical environment was also noted as a reason for father custody by Keshet and Rosenthal (1978).

Another theme emerges in cases in which the father is resentful over his wife having left him, and keeps the children as an act of retaliation against her, knowing she wants them. And out of guilt, she may agree.

Sometimes, there are indications of power plays by the father during the bargaining over custody. As an example: A mother of three children, aged 7, 8, and 10, says that father residence was the only arrangement the father would agree to. When she said she would take the children, the father said he would not pay child support. The mother did not want to fight with him any more, and "gave in." The father in this family says that his wife moved out because of involvement with another man, and the children are angry with their mother, "reacting violently" to her dating. In this and many other cases, involving either father or mother residential custody, there are overtones of the children being used as pawns in the emotional struggle between the parents.

Custody of Boys and Girls

Table 5.3 shows the residential patterns separately for boys and girls. Out of our

TABLE 5.3
Number of Overnights Spent With Father
Usual 2-Week Period, Time 1
By Sex of Child
(Percent of Children of Each Sex)

# Overnights with father	Girls	Boys
None	39.9	34.2
1–3	32.2	30.4
4–10	10.9	15.7
11–13	4.5	6.5
14	5.7	8.6
Other	6.8	4.6
N =	940	942

1,884 children, half (942) were male, and half (940) were female (the gender of two children could not be established at Time 1). Although the patterns are on the whole very similar, there is a tilt in the direction of children residing with the same-sex parent.

Table 5.4 is the same table within age categories. The trend toward living with the same-sex parent is characteristic of all ages, although it is strongest for children age 11 or older. At this age, there are over twice as many boys as girls

TABLE 5.4
De Facto Residential Custody
Usual 2-Week Period, Time 1
(Percent of Children in Each Age-Sex Group)

	Under 2	2–4	5–7	8–10	11–13	14–16
Primarily with mother (0–3 overnights)						
Boys	78.7	69.0	67.2	65.4	62.4	58.9
Girls	79.3	75.3	69.0	73.1	77.5	76.8
Divided residence (4–10 overnights)						
Boys	8.5	18.2	16.7	14.1	7.7	8.9
Girls	6.9	13.4	12.8	10.3	6.3	5.4
Primarily with father (11 or more overnights)						
Boys	12.8	9.9	13.1	13.5	24.8	25.0
Girls	1.7	6.7	12.3	12.4	10.8	8.9
Other						
Boys	0	2.9	3.0	7.0	5.1	7.2
Girls	12.1	4.6	5.9	4.2	5.4	8.9

residing primarily with their fathers. Between the ages of 2 and 11, the numbers of boys and girls residing with father are very similar. However, at these ages, there are considerably more boys than girls who spend a substantial number of overnights in both parental residences.

Differences between boys and girls residing primarily with one parent or the other are pictured in Fig. 5.1.

Research conducted when mother custody was the norm showed an overwhelming trend toward father disengagement from the family. This was true uniformly for fathers of sons and daughters (Furstenberg et al., 1983). New child-custody options offer fathers the opportunity for greater involvement without assuming sole custody. Our data show that fathers, particularly those with boys, seem to be taking advantage of this option. Hetherington et al.'s (1982) long-term follow-up data show that fathers are more likely to sustain visitation with boys. These trends are interesting in view of the work of Santrock, Warshak, and their colleagues on same-sex custody assignment (Santrock & Warshak, 1979; Santrock, Warshak, & Elliott, 1982; Warshak & Santrock, 1983). Their research points out advantages of father custody for the social development of boys, at least until the father remarries. In our research, we hear respondents expressing related themes of identification with the same-sex parent and the father's superior ability to exercise control over older boys. Such issues are raised as explanations for divided residence as well as residence exclusively with the father. Numerous in-

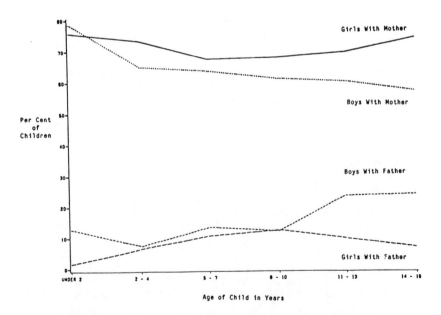

FIG. 5.1.   De facto residential custody by age and sex of child

vestigators have noted that mothers are more likely than fathers to encounter behavior problems with sons (Ambert, 1982; Hetherington, Cox, & Cox, 1978, 1979; Wallerstein & Kelly, 1980). Mothers and fathers in our study report that fathers are sometimes better able to keep older boys in line. One father of a 14-year-old son with a history of discipline problems said that if his wife had had sole responsibility for the child she would have had a "nervous breakdown."

The trend toward more divided residence of young boys and more residence with fathers among older ones may also be a reflection of the father–son bond. One mother who relinquished custody said, "I really couldn't take my son away from him. I couldn't split them up." Orthner, Brown, and Ferguson (1976) also noted the strong attachment between sole custody fathers and their children.

The higher incidence of residence with fathers among teenaged boys sometimes reflects the children's choices as well as those of their parents. In a family in which three teenaged boys lived with their father, the parents said this represented mainly the boys' choice. They and their father were all intensely involved in sports, and the mother could see the children only on the one night when the boys did not have athletic practice or games scheduled. It should be noted, however, that even in the teenage years, a substantial majority of both boys and girls reside with their mothers.

Both mothers and fathers in a number of families assume that girls need to be with their mothers, whereas boys benefit especially from contact with their fathers. One father of three daughters aged 16, 11, and 9 said: "They are better off with their mother because they are girls." However, as previously noted, considerations of gender by no means override deep-seated assumptions many parents make about mothers being better parents for children of both sexes.

The lower incidence of divided residence for girls aged 2 to 10 undoubtedly has multiple roots. In previous studies (e.g., Newson & Newson, 1968) it has been found that girls are subject to closer chaperonage than are boys, at least from the beginning of the school-age years, and perhaps both parents assume that mothers are in a better position than fathers are to maintain the needed degree of surveillance.

Residence of Children of Different Ages

Not surprisingly, Table 5.5 shows that children under the age of 2 are more likely than any other age group to be living with their mothers—79% of this youngest group have maternal residence, as compared with about 67% of the other age groups. Divided residence, where the child regularly spends a substantial number of overnights with each parent, is highest for the children aged 2 through 7, and drops off after that age to a very low level among teenagers. Residence with father is most common among teenagers, although as noted previously this applies to boys only.

In Fig. 5.2, we have combined the children who reside with mothers and have

TABLE 5.5
Number of Overnights Spent With Father
Usual 2-Week Period, Time 1
By Age of Child
(Percent of Children in Each Age Group)

	Age					
Overnights with Father	Under 2	2–4	5–7	8–10	11–13	14–16
None	50.5	36.8	27.2	34.2	37.7	46.2
1–3	28.6	32.1	38.4	33.6	29.4	22.0
4–10	6.7	18.0	16.2	13.6	9.7	6.4
11–13	1.9	3.2	6.2	5.7	9.7	6.4
14	4.7	4.9	7.5	6.6	7.5	11.0
Other	7.6	5.0	4.5	6.3	6.0	8.0
	100%	100%	100%	100%	100%	100%

no father overnights with those who live with fathers and have no overnights with mothers. (This group is labeled, *No Overnights*.) In a similar way, we have combined the children who reside primarily with either mother or father and visit the other overnight from one to three times during the usual 2-week period. (This group is labeled, *One to Three Overnights*.) A clear and curvilinear relation with age appears: The youngest and oldest children are the ones who most commonly sleep exclusively in a single dwelling. Making one to three overnight visits to the secondary parent is most common at age 5 through 7, and drops off there-

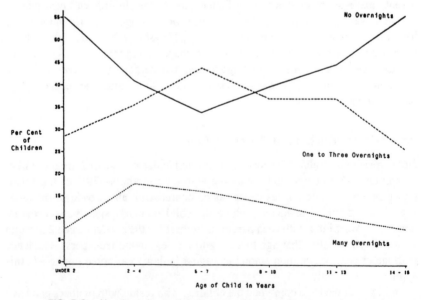

FIG. 5.2.   Number of overnights spent with secondary parent by age of child

after. The frequent alternation of overnights between parental households is most common at age 2 through 7.

We may speculate as to what lies behind these age trends. The low incidence of overnight visits and divided residence for children under 2 reflects a number of logistical problems, such as the need for special equipment for a very young child—crib, stroller, potty chair—all of which would need to be transferred or replicated in a second household. One mother of two children aged 18 months and 3 years said: "He originally asked for two weekends a month. I want no overnights because of (youngest child's) age. His father has no place for him to sleep and he doesn't sleep well as it is." Perhaps a more pervasive issue is the nature of the child's attachment to the mother in the first 2 years. One father of a 1-year old says: "I don't know how to be with a baby very well. She's very attached to her mother. I don't really like to be with her. She screams a lot and I'm not used to that. She doesn't like being away from her mother. She doesn't like being here. It's more sensible (for her to be with her mother). She doesn't know who I am."

Why are overnight stays and divided residence most frequent at age 2 through 7, and why do they decline thereafter? The logistics of having children spend time in two households appear to become more complex as children develop their own activity agendas and grow old enough to go back and forth to friends' houses without being accompanied by a parent. We suspect that with increasing age, children have more and more voice in where they will reside, and that when they do have a choice, many prefer to have a single residence for sleeping and to use as a base of operations. One father described his children's attachment to their home as follows: "The kids don't care who's in the house, but they want to be there."

Residential Custody and Family Size

Whether or not children live with their mothers following divorce does not appear to depend on the number of children in the family. The kind and amount of residence with father, however, does vary according to family size.

Approximately 66% of the children reside primarily with their mothers, and this is true for "only" children as well as for children with one or more siblings. Approximately 25% of the children in each family-size group spend substantial residential time with their fathers (i.e., divided residence or residence with father), but, as illustrated in Fig. 5.3, how this time is allocated does depend on family size.

It appears that maintaining divided residential arrangements for children, where they spend a substantial number of nights in each household, is more difficult for larger families than it is with only one child. Nearly 20% of the "only" children have a shared residential pattern, whereas this pattern is found in only 4% of the children who have two or more siblings. When the children in such families do not live primarily with their mothers, they live primarily with their fathers. The group of children in families with three or more children who live with their fathers (20% of the large-family children) come from only 21 families. The rea-

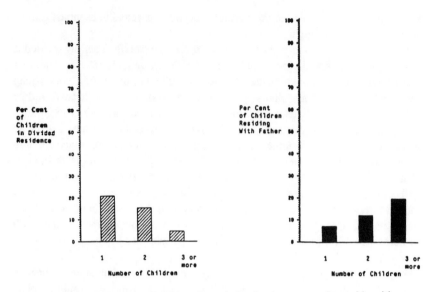

FIG. 5.3.   Percent of children in each family size group who reside with father or have divided residence

sons for father residence in these relatively rare cases are various, but the most common case appears to be that the mother has moved out of the house without attempting to take the children with her, leaving the father to assume full-time responsibility for the children whether he wanted it or not.

We need to consider how age and family size intersect. We previously noted that children's residence following divorce was related to the children's age, in that the youngest and oldest children were the ones least likely to engage in substantial overnight visits or to have divided residence. As might be expected, family size and age of children are related. That is, children in larger families are older on the average than "only" children or those in two-child families.

It is possible that the age trends noted here are more a function of family size than of the children's age per se. The older children in our sample are much more likely than the younger ones to be in larger families. And as Table 5.6 shows, children in larger families have lower rates of visitation and alternation. Indeed, only 4% of children in families with three children or more are in divided residences, as compared to 15% of children in two-child families and 19% of "only" children.

When we examine the age trends separately for children who are in families with different numbers of children, as shown in Table 5.7, we find that the curvilinear relation between age and visitation-alternation holds up within family size groups.

About 25% of the children in the study have a great deal of contact with their fathers. Family size is a key determinant of the way in which that contact is af-

TABLE 5.6
Number of Overnights Spent With Father
Usual 2-Week Period,
By Family Size
(Percent of Children in Each Family Size Group)

	One-child families	Two-child families	Three or more children
None	35.6	36.2	38.1
1–3	32.8	32.2	30.3
4–10	19.0	15.0	3.7
11–13	2.6	6.3	7.2
14	4.3	5.9	12.2
Other	5.7	4.4	8.5
	100%	100%	100%

TABLE 5.7
Number of Overnights Spent With Secondary Parent
Usual 2-Week Period, Time 1
Family Size and Age of Child
(Percent of Children in Each Age and Family Size Group)

Overnights with secondary parent	Age					
	Under 2	2–4	5–7	8–10	11–13	14–16
None						
One-child families	57.9	38.0	32.2	33.3	31.7	43.3
Two-child families	60.6	46.7	32.9	33.2	37.3	43.1
Three-child families	—	47.0	39.1	43.7	56.5	52.8
1–3 (Visits)						
One-child families	29.8	34.8	36.7	36.7	34.2	33.3
Two-child families	26.3	32.4	45.7	45.8	41.4	39.8
Three-child families	—	34.8	45.7	43.7	32.5	38.6
Divided Residence						
One-child families	5.3	22.1	24.4	25.6	26.8	16.7
Two-child families	10.5	18.7	18.3	18.2	14.2	11.4
Three-child families	—	3.0	3.3	3.5	7.2	4.3
Other						
One-child families	7.0	5.1	6.7	4.4	7.3	6.7
Two-child families	2.6	2.2	3.2	2.8	7.1	5.7
Three-child families	—	15.2	12.0	9.2	3.6	4.3

fected. In smaller families, divided residence is more common. In larger ones, it is more likely that at least some children in the family will reside with their father.

To a considerable extent, age and family size function independently as factors affecting the custodial arrangements for children. It is true that the relatively high rate of divided residence characteristic of 2 to 7 year olds is continued to a later age when there is only one child in the family than in larger families; and this rate is very low at all ages for the families with three or more children. But the "no visit" pattern shows its lowest level at age 5 through 7 for every family-size group. This is evident in the relationship between family size, age, and the absence of overnight visitation, graphed in Fig. 5.4.

SUMMARY AND CONCLUSIONS

With new changes in the laws governing child custody and attendant re-thinking of old notions governing parental responsibilities we find increasing numbers of parents electing postdivorce child custody arrangements that maintain the involvement of both parents. These range from forms of legal custody that retain the rights of both parents to take part in decisions affecting the child to arrangements involving alternation of the child between parental residences. Our data also show that this trend toward joint arrangements varies with the characteristics of the child. Divided residence between parental households is most likely for children aged 2 through 7. Boys are more likely than girls to have overnight visits with their fathers, and if they are 11 or older are more likely to have their primary residence with their fathers. This pattern holds regardless of family size, although the level of visitation and alternation is lower for large families.

Our findings reflect interesting compromises between opposing viewpoints in the joint custody debate. Parents appear to be embracing the norm that fathers should remain involved with their children after divorce. Still, they are not rejecting the idea that children, particularly very young ones, should have their major residence with their mothers. The level of father physical custody is not increasing; but joint physical custody is. Most parents elect an arrangement that assigns physical custody to the mother and legal custody to both parents.

Another key debate about joint custody centers on whether the stability of a single-home environment should be compromised in order to permit frequent contact with each parent. The families in our study seem to weigh stability versus contact differently depending on the age and gender of the child. Very young children are less often alternated between parental households. Divided residence is also less frequent among older children, who have established ties to school and friends. Considerations of parental contact versus a stable environment also seem to be weighed somewhat differently for boys and girls. Boys are more likely than girls to divide their time between two parental households. As boys grow older, however, the need for the stability of a single home environment seems

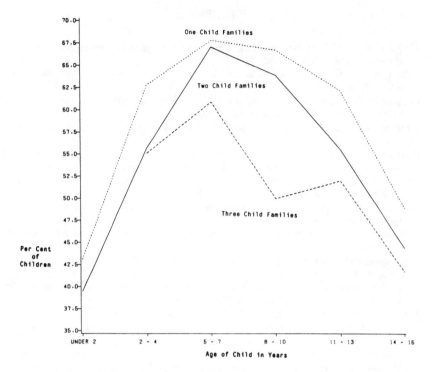

FIG. 5.4. Children spending overnights with secondary parent, by age and family size

to be added to the need for father contact. Consequently, more adolescent boys live with their fathers.

It is important to remember that these findings are drawn from interviews taken shortly after filing for divorce. We do not know whether arrangements that involve the participation of both parents can be sustained over time. These early data already highlight two important factors that may affect the viability of arrangements; the wishes of the child and the parents' involvement in new relationships. Can these be integrated with the goal of dual parental involvement? We will follow such issues in subsequent interviews with the families.

ACKNOWLEDGMENTS

© E. Maccoby, C. Depner, and R. Mnookin, 1987. This research is supported by Grant #1R01 HD 19386 from the National Institute of Child Health and Human Development and by Stanford University's Center for the Study of Families, Children and Youth. The authors wish to thank Sue Dimiceli for her assistance in data analysis.

REFERENCES

Ahrons, C. R. (1981). Continuing coparental relationship between divorced spouses. *American Journal of Orthopsychiatry, 5*(3), 415–428.

Ambert, A. M. (1982). Differences in children's behavior toward custodial mothers and custodial fathers. *Journal of Marriage and The Family, 44*(2), 73–86.

Clingempeel, W. G., & Reppucci, N. D. (1982). Joint custody after divorce: Major issues and goals for research. *Psychological Bulletin, 91*(1), 102–127.

Freed, D., & Walker, T. (1985). Family law in the fifty-states: An overview. *Family Law Quarterly, 18*(4), 361–471.

Furstenberg, F. F., & Nord, C. W. (1985). Parenting apart: Patterns of childrearing after marital disruption. *Journal of Marriage and The Family, 47*(4), 893–905.

Furstenberg, F. F., & Nord, C. W., Peterson, J. L., & Zill, N. (1983). The lifecourse of children of divorce. *American Sociological Review, 48*(5), 656–668.

Goldstein, J., Freud, A., & Solnit, A. (1973). *Beyond the best interests of the child.* New York: The Free Press.

Goldstein, J., Freud, A., & Solnit, A. (1979). *Before the best interests of the child.* New York: The Free Press.

Hetherington, E. M., Cox, M., & Cox, R. (1976). Divorced fathers. *Family Coordinator, 25,* 417–428.

Hetherington, E. M., Cox, M., & Cox, R. (1978). The aftermath of divorce. In J. H. Stevens, Jr. & M. Mathews (Eds.), *Mother-child, father-child relations* (pp. 149–176). Washington, DC: National Association for the Education of Young People.

Hetherington, E. M., Cox, M., & Cox, R. (1979). The development of children in mother-headed families. In D. Reiss & H. Hoffman (Eds.), *The American family* (pp. 117–145). New York: Plenum Press.

Hetherington, E. M., Cox, M., & Cox, R. (1982). Effects of divorce on parents and children. In M. Lamb (Ed.), *Nontraditional families* (pp. 233–288). Hillsdale, NJ: Lawrence Erlbaum Associates.

Keshet, H. F., & Rosenthal, K. M. (1978). Fathering after marital separation. *Social Work, 23*(1), 11–18.

Luepnitz, D. A. (1982). *Child custody: A study of families after divorce.* Lexington, MA: D. C. Heath.

Mnookin, R. H. (1985). Divorce bargaining: The limits of private ordering. *University of Michigan Journal of Law Reform, 18*(4), 1015–1037.

Mnookin, R. H., & Kornhauser, L. (1979). Bargaining in the shadow of the law: The case of divorce. *Yale Law Journal, 88*(5), 950–977.

Newson, J. & Newson, E. (1968). *Four years old in an urban community.* Chicago: Aldine.

Orthner, D. K., Brown, T., & Ferguson, D. (1976). Single-parent fatherhood: An emerging family lifestyle. *The Family Coordinator, 25,* 429–37.

Santrock, J. W., & Warshak, R. (1979). Father custody and social development in boys and girls. *Journal of Social Issues, 35*(4), 112–125.

Santrock, J. W., Warshak, R. A., & Elliott, G. L. (1982). Social development and parent-child interaction in father-custody and stepmother families. In M. E. Lamb (Ed.), *Nontraditional families* (pp. 289–314). Hillsdale, NJ: Lawrence Erlbaum Associates.

Steinman, S. (1981). The experience of children in a joint-custody arrangement: A report of a study. *American Journal of Orthopsychiatry, 51*(3), 403–414.

Wallerstein, J., & Kelly, J. (1980). *Surviving the breakup.* New York: Basic Books.

Warshak, R. A., & Santrock, J. W. (1983). Children of divorce: Impact of custody disposition on social development. In E. J. Callahan & K. A. McCluskey (Eds.), *Life-span developmental psychology: Non-normative life events* (pp. 241–263). New York: Academic Press.

Wheeler, M. (1974). *No-fault divorce.* Boston: Beacon Press.

PART III

DIVORCE AND SINGLE PARENTING

6

Multiple Determinants of Parenting:
Research Findings
and Implications
for the Divorce Process

Gene H. Brody
Rex Forehand
University of Georgia

Students of divorce have traditionally directed their attention toward describing its effects on the social and cognitive development of children and adolescents. Although great effort has been expended in studying the consequences of divorce as a global concept, less attention has been given to understanding the specific aspects of divorce that directly compromise parent–child relations and indirectly impact social and cognitive developmental outcomes. The classic work of Hetherington and her colleagues provides much of the large quantity of empirical information that addresses the latter issue (see Hetherington, Cox, & Cox, 1979a, 1979b, 1980, 1981).

It is the basic premise of this essay that research on families with conduct-disordered children has much to contribute toward an understanding of the influence of divorce on parenting and, accordingly, on developmental outcomes. Because conduct disorders often are displayed by young children, particularly males, following divorce, the study of their etiology in nondivorced families should help to identify family processes that lead to changes in parenting behavior, and consequently child behavior, following divorce.

To facilitate this analysis, this chapter is organized around the presentation of recent studies performed by our research group with conduct-disordered children and their mothers. Subsequently, we apply these data to develop and substantiate a model of the determinants of parent–child relations in families with a conduct-disordered child. We conclude by examining the utility of this model in understanding the ways in which the dynamics of divorce compromise the parent–child relationship.

"SETTING THE STAGE"—PRELIMINARY STUDIES

Study 1

This study (Forehand & Brody, 1985) examined the relationship between two areas of parent functioning, personal adjustment (as measured by depression level) and marital adjustment, and the development of conduct disorders in the child. Although these two areas of parental functioning have been found to contribute to individual differences in the mother–child relationship in clinic populations, their relative and additive effects are not known; this study examined these effects on three aspects of the relationship between the parent and her noncompliant child: parent behavior, child behavior, and parent perceptions of child adjustment.

Subjects included 25 mother–child (7 females and 18 males) pairs, in which the children had been referred to the University of Georgia Psychology Clinic for treatment of noncompliant behavior. The modified form of the Locke Marital Adjustment Test (MAT; Kimmel & Van der Veen, 1974) was used to assess marital satisfaction. Adequate reliability and validity data have been reported for this scale (see Gottman, 1979). The Beck Depression Inventory (BDI; Beck, Rush, Shaw, & Emery, 1979) was used to assess maternal depression. This instrument consists of 21 self-report items designed to assess the presence and severity of various depressive symptoms. The authors have reported adequate reliability and validity data. Based on scores on the MAT and BDI, four groups were formed using median splits: Group 1—high MAT, low BDI; Group 2—high MAT, high BDI; Group 3—low MAT, low BDI; Group 4—low MAT, high BDI. The groups did not differ on age, gender composition, or socioeconomic status (SES).

Behavioral observations, used to assess child and parent behavior, and a parent-completed questionnaire, used to determine maternal perceptions of child adjustment, served as dependent measures. Mother–child interactions were coded in the home by naive observers during four 40-minute observations, only one of which occurred per day for any mother–child pair. All observers received at least 20 hours of training in the coding system prior to beginning observations. Coders were required to attain at least 80% agreement with a prescored key for a 5-minute videotape of an actual mother–child interaction. Weekly 1-hour training sessions were held throughout the study. The observers were naive concerning the purpose of the study. The mother was instructed to follow her daily routine within the following limitations: to remain in two adjoining rooms with her child during observations, to ignore the observer, and to avoid having visitors, making telephone calls, or watching TV. Behavioral measures for the parent include rewards (praise or positive description of child behavior) and beta commands (commands to which the child does not have an opportunity to comply), and the child behavioral measure was compliance to alpha commands (commands to which the child has an opportunity to comply). Three scales of the Parent Attitude Test (PAT;

Cowen, Huser, Beach, & Rappoport, 1970), Home Attitude, Behavior Rating, and Adjective Checklist, were completed by the mothers to assess parent perceptions of child adjustment. The Home Attitude Scale (HAS) consists of 7 items that reflect the parents' perception of the child's adjustment in the home; the Behavior Rating Scale (BRS) consists of 25 items, each of which refers to a behavior problem; and the Adjective Checklist Scale (ACS) consists of 34 adjectives, each describing a child behavior-personality characteristic. Cowen et al. (1970) have presented adequate reliability and validity data for the PAT. Because the three scales' intercorrelations are high (Cowen et al., 1970), they were combined to yield one score for each mother assessing her perception of her child's adjustment.

Each dependent measure was analyzed via a 2(MAT: High and Low) × 2(BDI: High and Low) analysis of variance. The analyses of maternal behavior revealed that mothers reporting less marital satisfaction used fewer rewards than mothers reporting higher levels of marital satisfaction. The children of mothers reporting higher levels of marital satisfaction were more compliant to alpha commands than those of mothers in the low satisfaction group. In regard to the parent perception measure (PAT), mothers in the high BDI group perceived their children as more maladjusted than did those in the low BDI group. These results indicated that depression and marital satisfaction were related to different aspects of the parent–child relationship. Depression was associated only with the measure of parent perception of child adjustment, whereas marital satisfaction was related to child and parent behavior. Furthermore, the two parent adjustment variables did not interact on any of the dependent measures, suggesting that the effects of depression and marital satisfaction are not additive.

These results indicated that depression and marital distress, both of which accompany divorce (Hetherington et al., 1981), may affect different components of the parent–child relationship during the divorce process. The conclusions that can be reached in this study are of course limited by the relatively small sample size and by the fact that the dynamics involved for divorced mothers and their children may be quite different from those occurring in nondivorced families; however, the results indicate the role that parental perceptions of their children might play in the development and maintenance of conduct disorders. In addition to reinforcing the hypothesis that marital difficulties make effective parenting more difficult, these data indicate that depression may indirectly influence child behavior by influencing the parental labelling process.

Study 2

Research that addresses the relationship between parental perceptions of deviance and child behavior falls into one of two categories. The first category includes studies designed to determine whether parent perceptions reliably discriminate clinic from nonclinic children, whereas the second category examines the unique contributions of parent adjustment variables to parental perceptions of deviance. The results of the studies in the first category demonstrate that parental perceptions of child deviance discriminate clinic from nonclinic children, and that clinic-referred children actually display more independently observed noncompliant and deviant behavior than do nonclinic children (Doleys, Cortelli, & Doster, 1976; Forehand, King, Peed, & Yoder, 1975; Griest, Forehand, Wells, & McMahon, 1980; Lobitz & Johnson, 1975; Patterson, 1982), suggesting that parents are reasonably accurate in their perceptions. The results of some of these studies, however, as well as data from other investigations (e.g., Delfini, Bernal, & Rosen, 1976; Rickard, Forehand, Wells, Griest, & McMahon, 1981), indicate a considerable overlap in the behavior of clinic and nonclinic children. Although parents of clinic-referred children perceived their children as more deviant, the children could not invariably be differentiated behaviorally from those of nonclinic status.

Studies in the second category have examined the covariation of measures of parental psychological adjustment with parental perceptions of child behavior. The approach taken by these researchers has been to relate levels of parental distress (depression) with parental perceptions of deviant child behavior (Christensen, Phillips, Glasgow, & Johnson, 1983; Forehand, Wells, McMahon, Griest, & Rogers, 1982; Griest et al., 1980; Griest, Wells, & Forehand, 1979; Rickard et al., 1981). The results of these studies have indicated that parents, almost exclusively mothers, who report higher levels of depression perceive their children as more deviant. In several studies, measures of personal distress accounted for more variance in parental perceptions of child adjustment than did objective evaluations of child behavior (Christensen et al., 1983; Forehand et al., 1982; Griest et al., 1979). Such results prompted speculation that the objective nature of child behavior, compared to assessments of parental pathology, is relatively unimportant in the labeling process (Christensen et al., 1983).

Our approach (Brody & Forehand, 1986) to examining the contributions of parental distress and child behavior to the labeling process differs from that of previous researchers. Our analysis suggests that particular characteristics of parents, such as depression, combine with behavioral characteristics of the child to produce perceptions of maladjustment. This approach was influenced by Hetherington et al.'s (1981) divorce data, which indicated that the quality of parent-child relations following divorce was determined by the combined influence of child temperamental characteristics and maternal emotional functioning. We therefore hypothesized that parental perceptions of a child's maladjustment will be greater when the mother is depressed *and* the child is highly noncompliant than when only depression or only noncompliance occurs. Accordingly, we propose that a highly noncompliant child will foster different perceptions in a depressed mother than would a compliant child.

To assess these hypotheses, 60 clinic-referred children (37 males and 23 females) were observed with their mothers during four 40-minute in-home observations. Their interactions were quantified via a behavioral coding system identical to the one described in the aforementioned study. In addition, an assessment of depression (BDI) was obtained for each mother. Based on the behavioral observation data, collected in the home, subjects were assigned to groups which differed with respect to the child's rate of noncompliant behavior, within which maternal depression was categorized into two levels. The mothers' perceptions of child deviance measured by their PAT scores were analyzed using a 2(Child Compliance: High vs. Low) × 2(Depression: High vs. Low) analysis of variance.

A significant main effect for the maternal depression parameter was found, indicating that high maternal depression was associated with greater perceptions of child maladjustment than low maternal depression; however, this main effect was qualified by a significant child compliance by maternal depression interaction. The post hoc analyses revealed that children in the *low compliance/high maternal depression group* were perceived to be more maladjusted than children in the *high compliance/high maternal depression group*, the *low compliance/low maternal depression group*, and the *high compliance/low maternal depression group*.

The findings refined the results of previous studies designed to investigate the contributions of parent psychological functioning and child characteristics to maternal perceptions of child maladjustment. The main effect for high versus low maternal depression in this study supports earlier findings. Of primary importance, however, was the significant interaction that confirmed the combined influence of the child's behavior and maternal depression: Children were perceived as more maladjusted when they displayed high rates of noncompliant behavior *and* their mothers reported high levels of depression. As both maternal depression and child conduct problems are common following divorce, single parents will be likely to label their children as maladjusted. Such a process may have serious implications for these children. It is plausible that the finding of Hetherington and her colleagues (1981) that temperamentally difficult children recover from divorce more slowly may have been mediated by the development of parental labels of maladjustment that in turn governed the single mother's behavior. These data suggest that such a dynamic would be especially likely to occur for mothers who experience higher levels of depression or anxiety.

In summary, the findings from this study, as well as from Study 1, provide evidence that parental distress, particularly depression, may exert a powerful influence on a parent's perception of her child's functioning. It appears plausible that depression might indirectly influence parental behavior via its effect on the parental labeling processes. If indeed such a path of influence can be demonstrated, it will have important implications for basic research and clinical interventions.

TESTING A MODEL
OF PARENT–CHILD RELATIONS IN FAMILIES
WITH A CONDUCT-DISORDERED CHILD

This section presents the results of a study by our research group designed to test a model of the respective contributions of maternal personal/marital adjustment, maternal labeling processes, parenting behavior, and child noncompliant behavior to parent–child relations in families with a conduct-disordered child. We present supporting evidence for our model, describe the methodology of this study in detail, and present the results of the test of the proposed model as well as tests of alternative models.

The Model and Rationale

This section presents a model of parent–child relations in families with a conduct-disordered child, as well as the rationale that led us to test this particular formulation over others that are plausible. Basic to this model is the assumption that the presence of preschool children in the home is associated with a high frequency of negative interactions directed toward the primary caretaker, in most instances the mother. Patterson (1982) clearly documented that mothers with young noncompliant children are subjected to a high frequency of negative behaviors from both their children and their husbands; these accumulate over time, resulting in reports of maternal mood dysfunctions and depression. Because depressed persons are more negative and pessimistic than those who are not depressed (e.g., Beck et al., 1979; Layne, 1983), we conjecture that such a state will directly affect the mother's perception of her marital adjustment and the adjustment of her child. Prior research (Rickard, Forehand, Atkeson, & Lopez, 1982) indicated a relationship between maternal depression and marital dissatisfaction. Although directionality of this relationship has not been examined, we would hypothesize that depression leads to marital difficulties rather than vice versa.

Our model further predicts that marital dissatisfaction and perceptions of child functioning each directly affect the mother's behavior with her child. Support for the link between marital distress and parenting behavior can be found in our aforementioned study as well as several other recent investigations. The results of these research efforts have been consistent in demonstrating that supportive husband–wife relationships facilitate the adaptation of mothers and fathers to their parental roles during the transition to parenthood (Grossman, Eichler, & Winickoff, 1980; Russell, 1974; Shereshefsky & Yarrow, 1973). Using observational methodologies, other studies found maternal feeding competence with 1-month-old infants to be positively associated with the husband's esteem for his wife as a mother (Pedersen, 1975) and marital support of his wife (Price, 1977), and negatively associated with the amount of tension and conflict between husband and wife (Pedersen, 1975). Similarly, Pedersen, Andersen, and Cain (1977) found that increased rates of negative behavior directed by husbands toward their wives predicted increased rates of negative behavior directed by wives toward their 5-month-old infants. Goldberg and Easterbrooks (1984) found high marital quality to be associated with sensitive parenting, which in turn forecasts mother-infant and father-infant attachments. Brody, Pellegrini, and Sigel (1986) found marital distress to be associated with fathers' use of less positive feedback and more intrusive teaching styles; mothers in turn appeared to compensate for a less than satisfactory marriage by becoming more actively involved with their school-aged children during teaching interactions.

Maternal parenting behavior has been more clearly linked to marital quality than to perceptions of child maladjustment. Recently, however, several pieces of evidence have been found that converge to support the latter association. Gottman (1979) found that, within the marital relationship, distressed couples are significantly more likely than nondistressed couples to misattribute a negative valence to an intended positive message. From this evidence it appears that such negative misattribution is a fundamental component of the relationships of people engaged in daily conflict, often serving as the antecedent to the exchange of negative affect and behavior between spouses. Research that has focused on the parent-child relationship has produced similar results. Lorber, Reid, and Felton (1982) compared the performance of mothers of conduct-disordered children to that of mothers of nonproblem children on a laboratory task that required them to identify aversive child behaviors on a videotape. In addition, all families were observed in their homes, and parent daily report data were collected from the mothers over a 2-week period. The mothers of conduct-disordered boys perceived more deviant behaviors than did the mothers of nonproblem boys on the same videotape. In addition, the degree to which mothers labeled as aversive those behaviors recorded as neutral or positive by trained observers was positively associated with the number of problems she reported having with her child on a daily basis. The observational data indicated that mothers who described neutral and positive behaviors as aversive in the laboratory task were more likely to react immediately and punitively to the misbehavior of their children in the home. Taken together, the results of these two studies provide sufficient justification for proposing a link between maternal perceptions of child adjustment and parental behavior.

Thus far we have proposed that maternal depression directly influences perceptions of marital satisfaction and child adjustment, which in turn are conjectured to directly influence parenting behavior. The final association that we propose states that parenting behavior directly affects child noncompliant behavior. The particular parenting behavior on which we focus is the parental command. Both in laboratory research (Roberts, McMahon, Forehand, & Humphreys, 1978; Williams & Forehand, 1984) and in treatment outcome studies (Peed, Roberts, & Forehand, 1977), observational research on parent-child interactions has demonstrated the clinical importance of parental command behavior in influencing child compliance, in that a variety of parental commands are likely to lead directly to noncompliance. Four general types of such commands, termed *beta commands*, have been found to lower the rate of child compliance (Forehand & McMahon, 1981). Chain commands are a series of instructions strung together, which may require the completion of several unrelated activities (e.g., "Pick up the blocks and put them in the box, then make your bed and put the dirty clothes in the hamper"). Vague commands do not specify observable behaviors to be performed by the child, thus creating an ambiguous situation. Classic vague commands include, "Be careful," "Watch out," and "Be a good boy." Question commands occur when the parent expects compliance with a command, but phrases it as if the child had a choice. For example, parents are often surprised when they say to their 6-year-old, "Would you like to take your bath now?" and he or she says, "No." "Let's . . ." commands are stated in a fashion that includes the parent as a participant in the proposed activity ("Let's pick up the toys"). Parents often use this command style to coax the child into beginning an activity, although the parent has no intention of becoming involved. The child feels tricked, and the typical result is an uncompleted task and another round in the coercive cycle.

Methodology

Fifty-one mother–child pairs served as subjects. In all cases, the mother was married and the child had been referred to the University of Georgia Psychology Clinic for treatment of noncompliant behavior problems, the most common reason for referral of children. The sample did not include any autistic, severely retarded or brain-damaged children. The ages of the children ranged from 27 to 108 months ($X = 48.48$ months). Using occupation and educational level of the head of the household, each family was assigned a Social Class Index (Myers & Bean, 1968) ranging from 11 to 77, corresponding to a class status of I (e.g., professionals) to V (e.g., welfare recipients). The mean Social Class Index was III, with a range from I to V.

Three measures—Home Attitude Scale (HAS), Behavior Rating Scale (BRS), and Adjective Checklist Scale (ACS)—from the Parent's Attitude Test (PAT; Cowen et al., 1970) were used to assess parental perceptions of child behavior. As in the prior studies, the three scales were combined to yield one score for each mother. Higher scores indicate poorer adjustment. A modified form of the Locke–Wallace Marital Adjustment Test (MAT; Kimmel & Van der Veen, 1974) was administered to the mothers to obtain a rating of marital satisfaction.

Mother–child interactions were coded in the home by naive observers during four 40-minute observations, only one of which occurred per day for any mother–child pair. The mother was instructed to follow her daily routine within the following limitations: to remain in two adjoining rooms with her child during observations; to ignore the observer; and to avoid having visitors, making telephone calls, or watching television. From all the behaviors recorded in home observation sessions, the following mother behavior and child behavior were selected for inclusion in the proposed model: (a) maternal beta commands—vague or interrupted commands to which the child cannot comply; and (b) child compliance—an appropriate motoric response initiated within 5 seconds following a parental command [both beta commands and alpha commands (those to which the child could comply)].

Again, maternal beta commands were *preselected* as the parenting behavior to be included in the proposed model, because our research has indicated that this behavior discriminates mothers of noncompliant children from those of compliant children (Rickard et al., 1981) and serves as an excellent predictor of child noncompliance (Williams & Forehand, 1984). Compliance was preselected as the child measure because a low rate of this behavior constitutes the most frequent reason for referral of children for treatment (Forehand & McMahon, 1981). Beta commands and the command-compliance sequence were both scored on a frequency basis. For purposes of analysis, beta commands were computed on a rate per minute basis, and a percentage score was computed for child behavior (percentage of child compliance to total maternal commands = number of child compliances/number of maternal commands × 100).

Reliability checks were made by a calibrating observer on 22% of the home observations. Agreement between the observer and the calibrating observer was calculated on total session scores for each of the two behaviors using the formula, number of agreements/number of agreements + disagreements. The percentage of agreement was 89% for beta commands and 93% for child compliance to parent commands.

Procedure

Following referral, each mother was interviewed to determine whether noncompliance was the primary child problem, and a parent–child interaction was observed in a laboratory setting. The mother then completed the BDI, MAT, and PAT, and the four home observations were scheduled to occur during the next 2 weeks.

Results

Table 6.1 presents the correlation matrix among all variables included in the path analysis. A higher level of maternal depression was associated with lower marital adjustment and greater perceptions of maladjustment in the child. Greater maternal perceptions of child maladjustment were also associated with more frequent issuance of beta commands, whereas higher levels of marital adjustment were associated with lower rates of beta command issuance. Higher rates of beta commands were associated with lower rates of compliance.

A Lisrel (Jöreskog & Sörbom, 1981) path analysis was used to test the pro-

TABLE 6.1
Correlation Matrix Among Variables (*N* = 51)

	1	2	3	4	5
1. PAT		.37*	−.10	.26*	−.14
2. BDI			−.62*	−.12	.10
3. MAT				.21*	.14
4. Beta commands					−.51*
5. Compliance					

*$p < .05$, one-tailed

posed model; Fig. 6.1 shows the significant paths. The paths from depression to marital adjustment, depression to perception of maladjustment, perception of maladjustment to parenting, marital adjustment to parenting, and parenting to compliance are all significant at the .05 level (one-tailed). Visual inspection of the Q-plot indicated that the model fits the data well ($x^2 = 1.69$, $df = 4$, $p < .79$). Comparison of this model to one that included an additional path from depression to parenting showed no significant reduction in fit as a result of the elimination of this additional path. Likewise, reversing the path of influence between

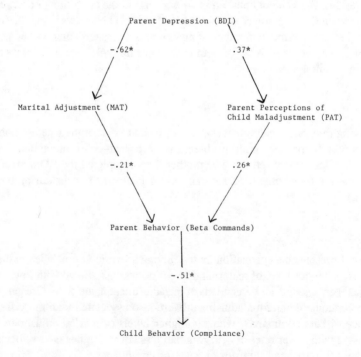

p < .05, one-tailed

FIG. 6.1   Path Analysis

depression and marital adjustment showed no significant reduction in fit. Finally, to ascertain whether a model driven by child effects, in this case child behavior, is plausible, several models were run in which child compliance leads to the other parameters. None of these models fit the data well.

Discussion

The results of this study confirm that the proposed model accounts for the dynamics of parent–child relations with a conduct-disordered child. According to this model, maternal depressive mood has a direct effect on the mother's perceptions of her marital adjustment and her perceptions of her child's adjustment, and an indirect effect on child behavior through these variables and parenting behavior. Although other models can be generated to account for the relation between maternal depression and parenting/child behavior (e.g., child behavior influences maternal depression), the analysis supports the "goodness of fit" of the present model to the data. Furthermore, a model that examined the direct effects of child behavior on the other parameters did not fit the data.

Some prior research (e.g., Rogers & Forehand, 1983) has failed to find a relationship between maternal depression and behavior toward her child. The data in this study, together with those from other studies, suggest that reported levels of maternal depression that are not considered high enough to require clinical intervention have their greatest impact on perception and the labeling processes. Had the mothers in the present study reported higher levels of depression, we may have found a direct link between maternal depression and behavior toward her child.

The importance of the link between maternal depression and perceptions of marital adjustment and child adjustment should not, however, be minimized. To the extent that maternal depression, although minimal, maintains negative perceptions of her spouse and child, we would expect a dynamic akin to a self-fulfilling prophecy to operate, in which the mother interacts with her spouse and children in a manner that confirms her perceptions. Social psychologists have termed this series of events *behavioral confirmation processes* (Synder & Swann, 1978). From this perspective, the mother may, as a result of her depression, have developed the belief that her spouse and children tend to be hostile or nonsupportive. These perceptions influence her to initiate hostile or rejecting exchanges with other family members, because such exchanges are consistent with her perceptions. Other family members would in turn reciprocate her behavior, thus confirming the mother's initial perceptions. Such dynamics pose particular difficulties for the clinician, for they suggest that it is not possible to achieve long-term reductions in conduct-disordered child behavior without changing the mother's parenting behavior and her perceptions of her child.

Few efforts have been made to examine multiple determinants of parenting behavior and child functioning. The present study used a clinical sample; we therefore do not know the extent to which the paths of influence presented in this chapter generalize to a nonclinic sample. This caution notwithstanding, the data demonstrate the importance of obtaining data that will allow delineation of the interdependencies between maternal personal functioning, her perceptions of her marriage and of her child's adjustment, her parenting behavior, and her child's behavior. Such information will have tremendous heuristic value for researchers and clinicians alike.

IMPLICATIONS AND LIMITATIONS OF THIS RESEARCH FOR UNDERSTANDING PARENT–CHILD RELATIONS AND DIVORCE

This chapter began with the assertion that insight into parent–child relations following divorce can be obtained by studying nondivorced families with a conduct-disordered child. Divorced mothers share many experiences with those who seek assistance from a clinic in managing a conduct-disordered child. Both have children who exhibit behavioral difficulties, both typically report elevated levels of depression, and both often are involved in conflicted or unsatisfactory relations with the child's father. In view of these similarities, we believe that our research endeavors with nondivorced, but somewhat atypical families is instructive regarding the mechanisms of change in parent-child relations following divorce. Based on these research efforts, we propose a refined theoretical analysis of parent–child relations during and following the divorce process, focusing in turn on the effects of elevated levels of depression and continued conflict with the former spouse.

During the separation and divorce process and continuing for at least a year after divorce, single mothers are often preoccupied with their own depression, anger, or emotional needs and are unable to respond sensitively to their children. We hypothesize that such dysfunctions in maternal adjustment result in a lowered tolerance of the child's behavior, which directly impacts maternal perceptions of her child's adjustment. Ross (1972) argued that parental perceptions are a product of both the child's behavior and the parent's tolerance level. It appears plausible that depression influences individual differences between parents in their tolerance for a range of child behaviors. Clinical symptoms that covary with depression, such as distractibility and insomnia, may increase the probability that single mothers will selectively attend to relatively low frequency inappropriate behavior, creating *impressions* of her children's adjustment that are not warranted by objective counts of behavior. Alternately, parental depression and distress may increase attention to relatively high frequency noncompliant behaviors that were not interpreted as bothersome prior to the onset of personal distress. On a behavioral level, changes in perceptions may result in the disproportionate use of ineffective child-management strategies and authoritarian control (e.g., beta commands) at a time when parents seek to limit interactions with their children. The net result of such dynamics may be the development of what Patterson (1982) has termed *coercive styles* of family interactions.

Caution must be exercised, however, in generalizing the paths of influence proposed in this chapter to divorced single-parent families; one reason for this caveat involves differences in maternal affect. Unlike divorced mothers, the mothers of clinic-referred children who participated in the present study reported depression levels that, for the most part, fell within the nondepressed to slightly depressed range. Among mothers, such as those who have recently been divorced, who report higher depression levels, the path of influence between maternal mood and child behavior may be direct rather than indirect. The work of Forgatch, Patterson, and Skinner, reported in this volume, relates to this issue. They found, as did we, that heightened levels of maternal negative affectivity indirectly influenced child behavior as a result of inept discipline; in addition, they established a direct path from the mother's affective state to the child's antisocial behavior. These mothers were separated, and reported an average of nine recent life events requiring major adjustments, whereas the mothers in our study were married and reported significantly fewer life adjustments during the preceding year. Further, the condition of the mothers in the Forgatch et al. sample appears similar to that of clinically depressed women, who have been found to be less involved with and affectionate toward their children, to feel more guilt and resentment, and to experience more general difficulty in managing and communicating with their children, compared to nondepressed mothers (Anthony & Ittelson, 1980; Cohler, Grunebaum, Weiss, Hartman, & Gallant, 1976; Hops et al., 1985; Shulterbrandt & Raskin, 1977; Weissman, Paykel, & Klerman, 1972). In addition, depressed mothers perceive themselves as ineffective and perceive their children as poorly adjusted (Brody & Forehand, 1986; Griest et al., 1979).

The severity of maternal depression following divorce, then, may help to determine whether its influence on child antisocial behavior is predominantly direct or indirect. In those instances in which maternal personal adjustment is severely compromised by an accumulation of negative life experiences, financial problems, family health problems, and conflict with the former spouse, we can expect to find direct paths between impaired personal functioning and child behavior. For other mothers, whose negotiation of divorce is less difficult, other models in which maternal depression is less salient may be appropriate. It should be noted that different direct and indirect paths of influence between maternal psychological resources, parenting, and child adjustment will be found depending on when in the divorce process the data are collected. Paths of influence described at one point in the process are not likely to be generalizable to those operating at either earlier or more distant points in time. Clearly, the interaction between time since separation and the paths of influence surrounding parenting and child adjustment merits more research.

The paths of influence in the research reported in this chapter are undoubtedly tied to the age of the children studied, because a child's age may be a particularly important moderator of his or her response to divorce and interparental conflict. Surprisingly, however, age-related differences among individual children's behavior associated with disruptions in family functioning have not been well researched. Younger children have more difficulty than older ones in exerting self-control, thus they require more structured, consistent external control (Hetherington et al., 1981). Older children, on the other hand, are able to seek support elsewhere if the home situation is chaotic and authoritarian because they spend more time in social settings outside the family. Consequently, older children have more opportunities to find outside support systems that can help to buffer the deleterious effects of a discordant home. Either cross-sectional or longitudinal studies are clearly needed to identify those factors that affect parenting and child behavior following separations and divorces for children of different ages within the same families. Such processes are an example of what Rowe and Plomin (1981) have termed *nonshared environmental influences*, and should serve as a reminder that events within families such as marital discord and divorce often are experienced very differently by members of the same family.

The sample of clinic children that we studied was comprised of young boys. Substantial research from the divorce literature suggests that boys more often than girls react with externalizing problems to family stress (Emery, 1982). This literature also suggests that girls display a propensity to respond with anxiety and withdrawal. To our knowledge, no attempts have been made to investigate the paths of influence between parental adjustment, parenting, and the adjustment of girls. At present, in the literature that addresses parental depression and child functioning, child gender has been considered in only a few studies; sufficient data are not yet available to reach any conclusions about the mechanisms that influence the development of anxiety and withdrawal in girls following divorce.

In summary, the study of nondivorced families with conduct-disordered children has provided data for testing a model of the ways in which personal adjustment, marital conflict, and parent perceptions in the divorce process are related to parent and child behavior. Our long-range goal is to test the model with families who have recently experienced a divorce in order to determine if modifications are needed.

ACKNOWLEDGMENTS

The first author's efforts were supported by Grant BNS 84-15505 awarded by the National Science Foundation and the second author's efforts were supported by a grant from the William T. Grant Foundation.

REFERENCES

Anthony, E. J., & Ittelson, B. F. (1980, September). *The effects of maternal depression on the infant.* Paper presented at the Symposium on Infant Psychiatry III, San Francisco, CA.

Beck, A. T., Rush, A. J., Shaw, B. F., & Emery, G. (1979). *Cognitive therapy of depression.* New York: Guilford.

Brody, G., & Forehand, R. (1986). Maternal perceptions of child maladjustment as a function of the combination of child behavior and maternal depression. *Journal of Consulting and Clinical Psychology, 54*, 237–240.

Brody, G. H., Pellegrini, A. D., & Sigel, I. (1986). Marital quality and mother–child and father–child interactions with school-aged children. *Developmental Psychology, 22*, 291–296.

Christensen, A., Phillips, S., Glasgow, R. E., & Johnson, S. M. (1983). Parental characteristics and interactional dysfunction in families with child behavior problems: A preliminary investigation. *Journal of Abnormal Child Psychology, 11*, 153–166.

Cohler, B. H., Grunebaum, H. U., Weiss, J. L., Hartman, C. R., & Gallant, D. H. (1976). Child care attributes and adaptation to the maternal role among mentally ill and well mothers. *American Journal of Orthopsychiatry, 46*, 123–133.

Cowen, E. L., Huser, J., Beach, D. R., & Rappoport, J. (1970). Parental perceptions of young children and their relation to indexes of adjustment. *Journal of Consulting and Clinical Psychology, 34*, 97–103.

Delfini, L. F., Bernal, M. E., & Rosen, P. M. (1976). Comparison of deviant and normal boys in home settings. In E. J. Mash, L. A. Hammerlynck, & L. C. Handy (Eds.), *Behavior modification and families* (pp. 75–94). New York: Academic Press.

Doleys, D. M., Cortelli, L. M., & Doster, J. (1976). Comparisons of patterns of mother–child interaction. *Journal of Learning Disabilities, 9*, 42–66.

Emery, R. E. (1982). Interparental conflict and the children of discord and divorce. *Psychological Bulletin, 92*, 310–330.

Forehand, R., & Brody, G. (1985). The association between parental personal/marital adjustment and parent-child interactions in a clinic sample. *Behaviour Research and Therapy, 23*, 211–212.

Forehand, R., King, H. E., Peed, S., & Yoder, P. (1975). Mother-child interactions: Comparisons of a non-compliant clinic group and a non-clinic group. *Behaviour Research and Therapy, 13*, 79–84.

Forehand, R., & McMahon, R. J. (1981). *Helping the non-compliant child: A clinician's guide to parent training.* New York: Guilford.

Forehand, R., Wells, K. C., McMahon, R. J., Griest, D., & Rogers, T. (1982). Maternal perceptions of maladjustment in clinic-referred children: An extension of earlier research. *Journal of Behavioral Assessment, 4*, 145–151.

Goldberg, W. A., & Easterbrooks, M. A. (1984). Role of marital quality in toddler development. *Developmental Psychology, 20*, 504–514.

Gottman, J. M. (1979). *Marital interaction: Experimental investigations.* New York: Academic Press.

Griest, D. L., Forehand, R., Wells, K. C., & McMahon, R. J. (1980). An examination of differences between nonclinic and behavior-problem clinic-referred children and their mothers. *Journal of Abnormal Psychology, 89*, 497–500.

Griest, D. L., Wells, K. C., & Forehand, R. (1979). An examination of predictors of maladjustment in clinic-referred children. *Journal of Abnormal Psychology, 88*, 227–281.

Grossman, F. K., Eichler, L. S., & Winickoff, S. A. (1980). *Pregnancy, birth, and parenthood.* San Francisco, CA: Jossey-Bass.

Hetherington, E. M., Cox, M., & Cox, R. (1979a). Play and social interaction in children following divorce. *Journal of Social Issues, 35*, 27–49.

Hetherington, E. M., Cox, M., & Cox, R. (1979b). Family interaction and the social, emotional, and cognitive development of children following divorce. In V. Vaughn & T. Brazelton (Eds.), *The family: Setting priorities* (pp. 94–124). New York: Science & Medicine.

Hetherington, E. M., Cox, M., & Cox, R. (1980). *Stress and coping in divorce: A focus on women.* Unpublished manuscript, University of Virginia, Charlottesville.

Hetherington, E. M., Cox, M., & Cox, R. (1981). Effects of divorce on parents and children. In M. Lamb (Ed.), *Nontraditional families.* Hillsdale, NJ: Lawrence Erlbaum Associates.

Hops, H., Breglan, A., Sherman, L., Arthur, J., Friedman, L., & Osteen, V. (1985). *Home observations of family interactions of depressed women.* Unpublished manuscript, Oregon Research Institute.

Jöreskog, K. G., & Sörbom, D. (1981). *LISREL VI: Analysis of linear structural relationships by maximum likelihood, instrumental variables, and least squares methods.* Mooresville, IN: Scientific Software.

Kimmel, D. C., & Van der Veen, R. (1974). Factors of marital adjustment test. *Journal of Marriage and the Family, 36,* 57–63.

Layne, C. (1983). Painful truths about depressives' cognitions. *Journal of Clinical Psychology, 39,* 848–853.

Lobitz, G. K., & Johnson, S. M. (1975). Normal versus deviant children: A multimethod comparison. *Journal of Abnormal Child Psychology, 3,* 353–374.

Lorber, R., Reid, J., & Felton, D. (1982, September). *Maternal tracking or childhood behaviors as mediated by family stress.* Paper presented at the meeting of the American Psychological Association, Washington, DC.

Myers, J. K., & Bean, L. L. (1968). *A decade later: A follow-up of social class and mental illness.* New York: Wiley.

Patterson, G. R. (1982). *Coercive family process: A social learning approach* (Vol. 3). Eugene, OR: Castalia.

Pedersen, F. (1975, September). *Mother, father, and infant as an interactive system.* Paper presented at the annual convention of the American Psychological Association, Washington, DC.

Pedersen, F., Andersen, B., & Cain, R. (1977, April). *An approach to understanding linkages between the parent-infant and spouse relationships.* Paper presented at the Society for Research in Child Development, New Orleans, LA.

Peed, S., Roberts, M., & Forehand, R. (1977). Evaluation of the effectiveness of a standardized parent training program in altering the interaction of mothers and their non-compliant children. *Behavior Modification, 1,* 323–350.

Price, G. (1977, April). *Factors influencing reciprocity in early mother-infant interaction.* Paper presented at the biennial meeting of the Society for Research in Child Development, New Orleans, LA.

Rickard, K. M., Forehand, R., Atkeson, B. M., & Lopez, C. (1982). An examination of the relationship of marital satisfaction and divorce with parent-child interactions. *Journal of Clinical Child Psychology, 11,* 61–65.

Richard, K. M., Forehand, R., Wells, K. C., Griest, D. L., & McMahon, R. J. (1981). A comparison of mothers of clinic-referred deviant, clinic-referred nondeviant, and nonclinic children. *Behaviour Research and Therapy, 19,* 201–205.

Roberts, M. W., McMahon, R. J., Forehand, R., & Humphreys, L. (1978). The effect of parental instruction giving on child compliance. *Behavior Therapy, 9,* 793–798.

Rogers, T. R., & Forehand, R. (1983). The role of depression in interactions between mothers and their clinic-referred children. *Cognitive Therapy and Research, 7,* 315–324.

Ross, A. O. (1972). Behavioral therapy. In B. B. Wolman (Ed.), *Manual of child psychopathology* (pp. 158–201). New York: McGraw-Hill.

Rowe, D. C., & Plomin, R. (1981). The importance of nonshared environmental influences in behavior development. *Developmental Psychology, 17,* 517–531.

Russell, C. (1974). Transition to parenthood: Problems and gratification. *Journal of Marriage and the Family, 36,* 294–301.

Shulterbrandt, J. G., & Raskin, A. (1977). *Depression in children—Diagnosis, treatment and conceptual models.* New York: Raven Press.

Shereshefsky, P. M., & Yarrow, L. J. (1973). *Psychological aspects of a first pregnancy and early postnatal adaptation.* New York: Raven Press.

Synder, M., & Swann, W. B. (1978). Behavior confirmation in social interaction: From social perception to social reality. *Journal of Experimental Social Psychology, 14,* 148–162.

Weissman, M. M., Paykel, E. S., & Klerman, G. L. (1972). The depressed woman as a mother. *Social Psychiatry, 7,* 98–108.

Williams, C. A., & Forehand, R. (1984). An examination of predictor variables for child compliance and noncompliance. *Journal of Abnormal Child Psychology, 12,* 491–504.

7

A Mediational Model for the Effect of Divorce on Antisocial Behavior in Boys

M. S. Forgatch
G. R. Patterson
M. L. Skinner
Oregon Social Learning Center

The numerous problems that are associated with separation and divorce have been well documented (Bloom, Asher, & White, 1978; Hetherington, 1979, 1980; Wallerstein & Kelly, 1980), making this transition a social problem worthy of careful research. This chapter presents a structural equation analysis for a model associating separation-related stressors to disrupted parenting skills and the development of antisocial behavior in boys.

There is a general consensus that separation and divorce rank high among the major stressors that impinge on family life (Bloom et al., 1978; Coddington, 1972; Hetherington, 1980; Olson et al., 1983). There seems to be a general relation between parent stress and children's adjustment problems (Stolberg & Anker, 1983; Wolfe, Jaffe, Wilson, & Zak, 1985). However, there is no general agreement on what the mechanism might be that enables parent stressors to be associated with problem behaviors in children.

Hetherington (1979) and Wallerstein and Kelly (1980) found a relationship between the early stages of divorce and the development of aggressive behavior in boys. In both studies, it was speculated that the effect was brought about in part by the emotional impact of the divorce on the mother (e.g., depression and anxiety), disruptions in parent practices, or both. It was not clear, however, what the relation might be between the mothers' affective states, disrupted parenting, and child problem behaviors.

Most single parents do not produce extremely aggressive children. Why do some have these problems, whereas others do not, even though they are involved in the same process of adjusting to separation and divorce? This chapter addresses these questions by introducing a mediational model that links stress for recently separated mothers and antisocial behavior in their sons. The model is sum-

135

marized in Fig. 7.1. The mediating Inept Discipline construct describes the effect of maternal stress on her discipline practices with the boy. The degree to which stressors on the mother result in antisocial child behavior depends on the degree to which she uses inept discipline practices. Of course, it is possible that the inept discipline practices may have been in place prior to the separation. In the work summarized here, a number of models were examined, ranging from a simple mediational model to variants of more complex models.

After a brief description of the sample and instruments, we review material relevant to the concept of stress as it relates to measurement models for newly separated mothers. The next section examines the rationale linking parent discipline and antisocial behavior. The final section presents findings relevant to the mediational model of stress and to two variants of more complex models.

Sample

Subjects were 64 mothers separated within the prior year and their sons. Mothers were in their early 30s (mean age = 31.3 years, SD = 4.7, range = 24 to 46). The boys were between the ages of 6 and 8 (mean age = 6.8 years, SD = .84). Most of the families were caucasoid: 92% of the mothers, 90% of the boys.

These families were living in poverty even though the mothers' education levels were moderate to high (72% had training beyond high school). Prior to the separation the average annual family income was about $14,000; after the separation it was less than half that. Of the mothers, 36% were receiving unemployment benefits; 57% of the mothers reported receiving public assistance in the prior year. The downward economic mobility that characterized this sample is in keeping with findings reported by Weitzman (1985), who has studied the effect of the no-fault divorce laws. In her recently collected sample of California families, she reported a 73% decline in the standard of living for the women and their children in the first year after the divorce. Although many of the women in her sample had received good educational training, they nevertheless did not prepare themselves for career tracks in the world of employment. In our sample, the departure of the father, who represented the loss of only one person in a family with three or more individuals, resulted in a decrease of more than 50% in the family's income.

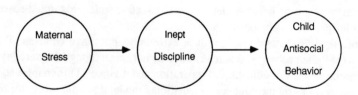

FIG. 7.1.   Simple stress model

Many of the estranged spouses maintained contact with the boys. Over 37% of the boys were reported to have had contact with their fathers at least once a week; 28% had contact once or twice a month. Slightly less than 10% of the boys were reported to have had no contact with their fathers since the separation.

Assessment Battery

The assessment, which required approximately 25 hours to complete, employed several methods and agents: separate interviews with the mother and the child in the laboratory, problem-solving interactions between the mother and her youngster and also between the mother and her confidant, observations in the home, telephone interviews and questionnaires with the mother and the child, and teacher ratings.

Constructs

Brief descriptions of the Inept Discipline and Child Antisocial Behavior constructs follow. Descriptions of the Maternal Stress and Maternal Negative Affectivity constructs are found in a later section of this report.

Inept Discipline. The home observations formed a database for deriving each of the three indicators defining this construct: nattering, explosive discipline, and observer impressions of the mother's discipline consistency. Nattering and explosive discipline are probability scores calculated directly from observation data. Nattering is the probability that the mother will direct low intensity, negative verbal or nonverbal behaviors toward the target child (e.g., scowling, scolding, disapproval). Explosive discipline is the probability that the mother will use more intense negative behaviors with the target child (e.g., hitting, humiliating remarks, threats, or yelling). The observers' impressions indicator is a composite of 13 items about parental consistency and moderation in discipline. Details about this construct have been reported by Dishion, Patterson, Yamamoto, and Skinner (1984).

Child Antisocial Behavior. This construct was defined by five indicators, reflecting the reports of three agents: mother, teacher, and the child himself. The mother's report was obtained from a series of six telephone interviews, the Child Behavior Checklist (CBC; Achenbach, 1978), and a questionnaire developed at the Oregon Social Learning Center (OSLC) concerning overt and clandestine antisocial behaviors (OCA). The teacher's report was from the CBC (Achenbach, 1978). The child's report was from a set of six telephone interviews. Details of analyses for the Child Antisocial Behavior construct have been summarized by Skinner and Gardner (1985).

A MEASUREMENT MODEL FOR STRESS

As Rutter (1983) so lucidly pointed out, the first problem to be solved in research on stress is to decide what it means. At one end of the continuum is Selye's (1978) position that to be alive is to be stressed. From this vantage point, stressors include joyful experiences as well as painful ones. In this study it was decided to assess the unpleasant stressful events that accompany the separation/divorce process. We included four major areas: negative life events, recent hassles, financial problems, and family health problems.

The classic injunction by Feigl (1956), MacCorquodale and Meehl (1948) and Cronbach and Meehl (1955) stated that most concepts in the social sciences do not lend themselves to any single score or measure. The meaning of a complex concept, such as stress, would best be established by a nomologic network, employing a variety of assessment techniques (e.g., laboratory measures, field observations, self-reports, and so on). In the general model for antisocial behavior developed at OSLC, this injunction has been interpreted to mean that each construct should be defined at the very least by multiple methods from a single agent and preferably by reports from multiple agents (Patterson & Bank, 1987).

In the case of stress, the individual's appraisal of stress can be reported best by one agent, the individual herself (Lazarus, DeLongis, Folkman, & Gruen, 1985). This makes the single agent with multiple methods approach the most appropriate. An effort was made in this chapter to develop a self-report measure that assessed variable units of time. Some of the measures sampled large units of time, whereas others sampled intermediate time frames, and still others recent events. For example, many of the items from the family health problems indicator represented long-standing conditions. The Sarason version of the Life Experiences Survey (Sarason, Johnson, & Siegel, 1978) sampled events that occurred in the past year. The recent hassles indicator defined our effort to assess more immediate, and perhaps more trivial, stressors that occurred within the past few days. The financial problems indicator also focused on recent problems.

THE MATERNAL STRESS CONSTRUCT

There were four steps in building constructs for the general model, including the Maternal Stress construct. First, it was necessary to list each of the dimensions thought to define the construct. Second, using data from the 64 recently separated mothers and their sons, each group of items, or scale, was analyzed to determine whether it was internally consistent. In this stage, items that correlated less than .20 with the corrected total score were dropped from the scale. Those scales with an alpha value above .60 were retained for the next stage. The third step involved a principal components factor analysis to determine whether the scale loaded significantly on the latent construct, or factor. Those scales with factor loadings less than .30 were dropped. Finally, each scale that survived the rigors of a confirmatory factor analysis became an indicator for that construct.

Four indicators composed the Maternal Stress construct: negative life experiences, recent hassles, financial problems, and family health problems. Three of the indicators were subjected to itemetric analysis to test for internal consistency. The negative life events indicator was excluded from this analysis because the items were not expected to form a coherent cluster. All items endorsed with a negative valence were summed, reflecting the additive nature of such stressors. The reduction process for the recent hassles indicator is described in detail.

The recent hassles indicator is a potpourri of common problems of daily living. Its items were drawn from the OSLC Family Events List. This self-report instrument included 46 trivial but unpleasant events typical for most families (e.g., child care problems, car problems, various work-related problems). Items describing family conflict, problems with youngsters and so forth were removed to eliminate a confound with information contained in the Child Antisocial Behavior construct. From the 18 items remaining in the apriori list, 12 items correlated with the total scale at the .20 level or greater; the other 6 items were dropped. Cronbach's alpha for the scale of 12 items was .75, so the recent hassles scale was elevated to indicator status.

This same process was carried out with the financial problems and family health problems indicators. Seven items were assigned a priori to the financial problems scale, and all survived the itemetric analysis, resulting in an alpha of .75. The six items assigned to the family health problems scale also survived the analysis, with an alpha of .65. These four indicators were subjected to a principle components factor analysis, and each obtained a factor loading of .3 or greater on a single factor.

Are Separated Mothers More Stressed?

A key assumption underlying our current work is that recently separated mothers represent a highly stressed group. Specifically, they should demonstrate higher scores on each of the stress indicators than mothers of intact families. Three samples of families were compared on three different indicators defining the Maternal Stress construct. The financial problems indicator was not compared because those data were not collected for all samples.

Data equivalent to that collected for the divorce sample (64 subjects) had been collected from two cohorts (approximately 100 in each) of families with boys in Grade 4 in a longitudinal study of antisocial behavior in boys (Patterson, Reid, & Dishion, in press). The families with 4th graders were recruited from schools in high crime areas in the Eugene, Oregon, metropolitan area. Because these families were not screened for high levels of stress or for family dysfunction, we assumed normal distributions of various family processes.

Table 7.1 displays comparisons of the stress scores between the recently sepa-

Table 7.1
Comparison of Stressors: Mothers of Single Versus Two-Parent Families

| | Single-parent | | Two-parent mothers | | | | | |
| | | | Cohort I | | | Cohort II | | |
	Mean	SD	Mean	SD	t	Mean	SD	t
Recent hassles	16.46	5.44	11.96	5.61	5.74*	11.86	5.15	6.01*
Life events	9.08	4.16	4.92	3.77	7.61*	5.13	3.05	8.01*
Family health problems	1.14	.56	1.11	.52	.35	1.25	.69	.25

*p < .001

rated mothers and the mothers with a spouse present from two cohorts. It can be seen that recently separated mothers were significantly more stressed on two of the three indicators. Single mothers reported having 16.5 recent hassles (minor difficulties that occurred within the prior 3-day period) versus approximately 12 reported by mothers in two-parent families. Over the prior year, the single mothers experienced approximately nine life events (changes requiring major adjustment), whereas the mothers in two-parent families had about five. It is interesting to note that mothers in all groups reported approximately the same number of family health problems, slightly more than one per family.

Comparing Factor Analyses

In order to determine the generalizability of the factor loadings for the recently separated sample, a comparable analysis was carried out for Cohort I of the longitudinal sample (Viken, in preparation).

The single-factor solution for the recently separated sample explained 44.5% of the variance in the matrix; it had an eigenvalue of 1.78. The results for the longitudinal sample were surprisingly consistent. The principal components factor analysis accounted for 50.5% of the variance and had an eigenvalue of 1.51. The factor loadings for these two analyses are summarized in Table 7.2.

Taken together, the findings suggested that we had a reasonably robust defini-

TABLE 7.2
Stress Factor Loadings for Two Samples

	Mothers in single-parent households	Mothers in two-parent households
Life events	.767	.751
Recent hassles	.722	.740
Financial problems	.691	---
Family health problems	.440	.634

tion for the Maternal Stress construct. The next step was to use it in a modeling analysis to determine whether it functioned as specified by the a priori theory.

INEPT DISCIPLINE
AND CHILD ANTISOCIAL BEHAVIOR

The social interactional stance taken here begins with the assumption that the process of socializing the child begins in the home (Cairns, 1979; Lamb, Suomi, & Stephenson, 1979; Patterson & Reid, 1984). Parents provide basic training for both prosocial and, inadvertently, deviant behavior. Both processes unfold over the course of the child's development.

Patterson and his colleagues have studied family processes over the past 2 decades, with a special focus on families with antisocial youngsters. They have conducted treatment studies in which change in the child's behavior is accomplished by teaching the parents a set of four family management skills: monitoring, positive parenting, discipline, and problem solving (Patterson, 1982; Patterson & Forgatch, 1987; Patterson, Reid, Jones, & Conger, 1975).

Several studies have shown that teaching parents these skills is effective in changing the antisocial behavior of their children (Chamberlain & Patterson, 1984; Patterson, 1985, 1986; Patterson, Chamberlain, & Reid, 1982). Discipline is considered one of the key mechanisms determining children's antisocial behavior. Parents of problem children typically nag, scold, threaten and hit but seldom follow through. Training the parents involves the use of consistent and contingent punishment that deemphasizes the use of ineffective techniques and that is nonviolent (e.g., time out, privilege removal).

Patterson and his colleagues have extended their findings from treatment studies to field studies in normal families. In a longitudinal study with boys at risk for antisocial behavior, structural models have been tested demonstrating relationships among family management skills and antisocial child behavior. Of particular importance for the current study is a model describing the relationship between poor discipline practices and antisocial behavior (Patterson, 1986), displayed in Fig. 7.2. The model was tested and replicated with two cohorts of 100 Grade 4 boys.

The figure shows that parents' use of inept discipline practices is associated with antisocial behavior in their 10-year-old boys. This process is exacerbated by the child's observed coercive behavior. It is consistent with our hypothesis that poor discipline practices lead directly to antisocial behavior. We think that parents who use ineffective discipline practices teach their children to use high rates of coercive behavior at home. This makes it even more difficult to discipline them, which makes the youngsters still more antisocial. Presumably, children's coercive behavior learned in the home generalizes to the school and other settings. This is implicit in the model because the criterion construct, Child Antiso-

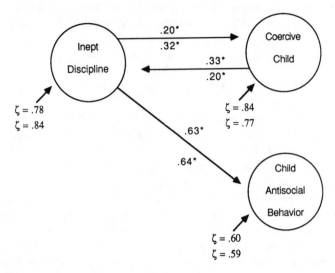

FIG. 7.2.   Direct effects model (upper numbers refers to Cohort I, lower to cohort II; * $p < .05$)

cial Behavior, is based on reports from the children's teachers and peers, in addition to parents' and self-reports.

The numbers on the arrows represent the path coefficients between the constructs. In that the path coefficients are standardized partial beta coefficients, it is possible to compare the magnitude of one path coefficient to another. In keeping with the model, developed from our clinical experience, the strongest path coefficient is from the Inept Discipline construct to the Child Antisocial Behavior construct. It is reassuring to note that the path coefficients are relatively stable across the two cohorts.

One of the prime concerns in developing a performance model is the demonstration that the model actually accounts for the majority of the variance in the criterion measure. Given the limited reliability for most psychological measures, it was decided that 30% of the variance would be a reasonable goal (Patterson et al., 1986). The zeta values for the Child Antisocial Behavior construct indicate that the model accounted for about 40% of the variance for Cohort I and 41% for Cohort II. These findings replicate an earlier model developed in a pilot study using a different sample (Patterson, Dishion, & Bank, 1984).

The general model presented by Patterson (1982) and Patterson et al. (In Press) emphasizes the dual nature of the problem. It is not only that the children are antisocial, but also that many or most of these problem youngsters are deficient in one or more crucial prosocial survival skills. Most of them are rejected by the normal peer group, many fail to develop appropriate academic skills, and many also have very low self-esteem. The child most at risk for an antisocial career is both antisocial and socially unskilled. It is interesting to note in this regard that the Hetherington, Cox, and Cox (1979) findings showed that boys in divorced families not only tended to be antisocial but were failing in academic subjects as well. For most of those families, both effects were thought to be short lived, however, so that the child did not become chronically antisocial.

MEDIATIONAL MODEL
FOR SINGLE-PARENT STRESS

It was hypothesized that several kinds of stressors experienced by recently separated mothers would lead to the mothers' use of Inept Discipline practices, and that, in turn, would result in antisocial behavior in their young sons. The results of the LISREL VI (Jöreskog & Sörbom, 1984) test of that model are shown in Fig. 7.3.

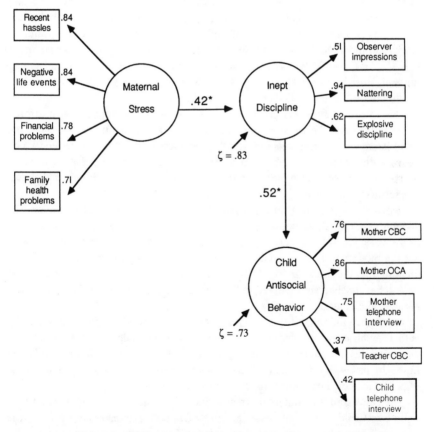

FIG. 7.3. Simple mediational model (Boys age 6 to 8, n = 64; all estimates on this FIGure are significant at the .05 level. X^2 = 68.79 p = .059)

The fit of the data to the model was acceptable. The X^2 of 68.79, with the probability level of .059 indicated that there was no significant difference between the hypothesized covariance matrix and that which was produced by the actual data. The path coefficients between constructs were both significant. This simple mediational model for stress accounted for 27% of the variance in Child Antisocial Behavior.

In this stress model the indirect effects of coercive child behavior were not described as in the Patterson model shown in Fig. 2. Nevertheless, the relationship between Inept Discipline and Child Antisocial Behavior was significant and of a similar magnitude as that found in the study by Patterson. This supports the notion that inept discipline practices are an important determinant of child antisocial behavior for families in the separation process.

The path between Maternal Stress and Inept Discipline was also significant, and 17% of the variance in the Inept Discipline construct was explained. This implies that Maternal Stress, as it is measured in this analysis, is somewhat useful in understanding inept discipline practices. The factor loadings for the two constructs provide more specific information about what is meant by Maternal Stress and Inept Discipline in this model. All of the indicators for Maternal Stress loaded strongly and within a narrow range, whereas there was a wide spread among the indicators for Inept Discipline. Apparently, nattering was the most relevant in the context of the indicators we selected.

One of the positive aspects of structural equation modeling is that it affords the ability to test the fit of competing structural relationships among the same set of latent variables. In keeping with this, an alternative model was tested, which added a direct path from Maternal Stress to Child Antisocial Behavior in addition to the relationships hypothesized in the first model tested. Figure 7.4 shows the results of that test.

When a direct path from Maternal Stress to Child Antisocial Behavior was added to the model, all path coefficients were significant and an additional 10% of the variance in the criterion was explained. The difference in the chi-squares for the models in Figs. 7.3 and 7.4 was statistically significant ($p < .03$), indicating that the model in Fig. 7.4 was preferable. This suggests that there must be another mechanism involved in the translation from Maternal Stress to Child Antisocial Behavior.

One test of the reliability of the relationships expressed in structural modeling is their endurance in the face of increasingly complex models. In this sense, there was reliability for the paths between constructs, the amount of variance explained in the Inept Discipline construct, and for the relative positions and factor loadings of the indicators in all three constructs.

The paths from the Maternal Stress to Inept Discipline and from the Inept Discipline to Child Antisocial Behavior constructs both retained significance. It is of some interest here, however, that their relative weights became more equally distributed, and that they not only became equivalent to each other but also equivalent to the path between Maternal Stress and Child Antisocial Behavior.

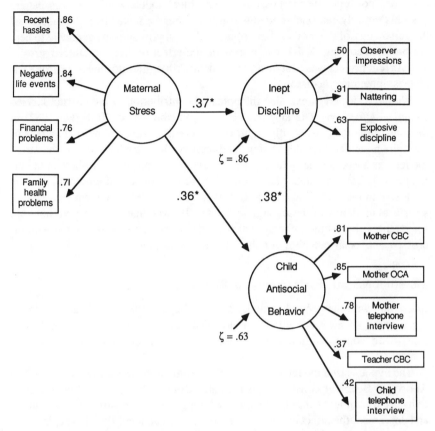

FIG. 7.4. Mediational model with direct effects (All estimates on this figure are significant at the .05 level; X^2_{51} = 64.39; p = .009)

Another sign of stability was found in the relationship between Maternal Stress and Inept Discipline. In Fig. 7.3, Maternal Stress accounted for about 17% of the variance in Inept Discipline, whereas it accounted for 14% in Fig. 7.4. More work is needed in the future to account for additional variance. Such analyses could involve structural modeling, where Inept Discipline might serve as the criterion construct and constructs other than Maternal Stress might enter into the explanation (e.g., socioeconomic status, education, substance abuse, personality traits, parenting skill prior to separation).

More Complex Models and Some Complex Problems

Bentler (1980), Pedhazur (1982), and others who have written about applications of structural equation modeling emphasized the fact that a fit between theory and data does not preclude the possibility that other models would fit even better. It seems entirely reasonable to suppose that other variables (e.g., measures of the personality of the mother, her coping skills, support systems available to her, her problem solving skills), might mediate the effect of divorce-induced stress.[1] The current project was designed to include multiple-indicator measures for each of these potential mediators.

We have elected to examine the potential contribution of a construct labeled *Negative Affectivity*. The label reflects the contributions of Tellegen (1982) in demonstrating the consistently significant intercorrelation among such personality traits as irritability, depression, and anxiety. Its introduction into the stress model was based on the findings of Elder and his colleagues that showed the ill-tempered father who, under the stress of the great economic depression, became explosive in his discipline (Elder, Liker, & Crosse, 1984). Incidentally, Elder's structural modeling of these longitudinal data showed that the effect did not hold for mothers. It was the fathers' explosive discipline that was associated with increased antisocial behavior for the boys in the family.

Maternal Negative Affectivity as Mediator

In keeping with the general formulation by Tellegen (1982), we began by defining, a priori, a wide spectrum of indicators that would define this construct: depression, drug abuse, withdrawal, irritability, self-esteem, and internal/external control.[2]

The hypothesized model was that the path from the Maternal Stress to the Child Antisocial Behavior construct was mediated through Maternal Negative Affectivity. It was thought that for mothers with a general disposition to be irritable and depressed, the effect of stressors might serve as an amplifier. In keeping with the Elder model, it was hypothesized that when irritable or depressed mothers become stressed, they become even more irritable, and thus exacerbate existing problems in discipline confrontations.

---

[1]Another hypothesis is that the stressors reported by the child himself would be directly related to his antisocial behavior. A measure of child stress correlated .43 ($p < .001$) with the Child Antisocial Behavior construct.

[2]*Depression*: The mothers' self-reported depression scale was based on seven items from diaries completed six times over the 2- to 4-week assessment period. Cronbach's alpha for this scale was .81. *Irritability*: The nine items of the irritability scale came from five different measurement modes: mother's diaries, the Spielberger, et. al (1983), the Caprara (Caprara, Renzi, Alcini, D'Imperio, & Travaglia, 1983), six telephone interviews with the mother, and a questionnaire completed at the time of the second mother interview. Cronbach's alpha for this scale was .81. *Self Esteem*: Self-esteem was assessed with a questionnaire developed from Pearlin and Schooler (1978) and interviewers' subjective ratings. These 10 questionnaire items and the global rating formed a scale with Cronbach's alpha of .88. *Internal-External*: The items for this scale were also developed from Pearlin and Schooler (1978). The items concerned helplessness, lack of control, and ability to change important life conditions. These seven items formed a scale with Cronbach's alpha of .77.

TABLE 7.3
Convergent and Discriminant Validities for Maternal Stress
and Maternal Negative Affectivity Indicators (N = 64)

Indicators	Maternal stress			Maternal negative affectivity			
	Recent hassles	Financial problems	Negative life events	Self-esteem	Internal/external	Depression	Irritability
Stress							
Family health problems	.33**	.29*	.34**	.21*	.05	.28*	.20*
Recent hassles		.50***	.54***	.20*	.19*	.42***	.42***
Financial problems	.53***	.31**	.36***	.55***	.45***		
Negative life events				.37***	.39***	.63***	.55***
Negative Affectivity							
Self-esteem					.72***	.59***	.50***
Internal/External control						.60***	.56***
Depression							.80***

*p < .05   ***p < .001
**p < .01

The first step was to look at the correlations among the indicators that defined the Maternal Stress and the Maternal Negative Affectivity constructs. There was concern with the fact that both constructs were entirely based on mothers self-reports. The convergent and discriminant validities are summarized in Table 7.3. There are two general issues here. First, is there evidence for a solid convergence in defining the two constructs? Second, are there significant across-construct correlations (discriminant validity)? The investigators hoped that both sets of correlations would be significant, but with the convergent correlations being higher than the discriminant correlations. The reason for the qualifying statement will be clea; n a moment.

The first three columns of Table 3 summarize the convergent validity data for the Maternal Stress construct. It can be seen that the mothers' self-report data of stress intercorrelated nicely; the range was from .29 to .54, with the median about .42. This is, in fact, a better convergence than that obtained for many of the other constructs in the general model of Patterson and Dishion (1985). The convergence for the Maternal Negative Affectivity construct was even better. As shown in the lower section of columns 4 through 7, the range was from .50 to .80, with a median of about .60.

It is the discriminant correlations that pose the problem. The median correlation here was about .39. Not only were there significant relations within the constructs, but the interrelation was of about the same magnitude. Within the context of negative affectivity and environmental stressors, the question becomes: Are there two factors here or simply several measures that reflect only mother's reporting style?

In order to test the hypothesis that a mother's report of negative affectivity and her report of stress were two different latent constructs, a confirmatory factor analysis was undertaken. Using the LISREL framework, two models were tested and compared for goodness of fit. The first model contained two latent constructs, or factors, with mothers report of depression, irritability, self-esteem, and internal/external locus of control loading on the first and her report of hassles, finances, life events, and family medical condition loading on the second. The second model contained only one latent construct, with all of the eight indicators loading on it. The results of this analysis led us to reject our hypothesis. The one-factor solution fit the covariance structure of the data significantly better than the two-factor model.

A total reliance on parent self-report data created a situation in which it was extremely difficult to separate methods from (construct) structure. We seriously entertain the hypothesis that parents' self-reports on their feelings, cognitions, life experiences, and their children's behavior form a matrix in which everything is inextricably bound together. Although it is possible to obtain good convergence in measuring structures, the magnitude of the interconstruct correlations (path coefficients) suggests a bipolar dimension of negative to positive (e.g., "I'm living an awful life and everything in it is awful"). In this mode, when the mother describes the external environment in essentially negative terms, we investigators note this as evidence for stress: she describes her own mood in negative terms, we note this as evidence for depression/irritability. Given that she is stressed and depressed/irritable, she also tends to describe the people living close to her in negative terms. For example, there is now a burgeoning literature that shows that depressed mothers tend to perceive their children as being more deviant, even though observations of the children's behavior are not in accord with her perceptions (Brody & Forehand, 1986). For this reason, we do not believe it is possible to build a theory of stress or of child pathology based solely on parent-report data at this time (Reid, Baldwin, Patterson, & Dishion, 1985).

This places us in the awkward position of investigating phenomenologic states such as stress, depression, and irritability that may, indeed, be interconnected. We have to ask the mother what phenomenologic state she is in, but if we are to understand what produces this state, and what its effect might be, then clearly we must step outside the mothers' self-report as the sole source of data for model building. In that most investigators building models rely solely on the individuals' self-report, it must be said that the resulting models should be approached with some skepticism.

In the present context, it should be possible to step outside the sole reliance on mothers' self-report by asking other persons to provide data, either for the Maternal Stress or for the Maternal Negative Affectivity constructs. In the present study, both the interviewers and the home observers had been asked to provide global ratings on mother mood and irritability (five and eight items, respectively). The child had also reported on these states in a series of six brief telephone interviews.

The first step in building a new Maternal Negative Affectivity construct was to determine whether these variables were internally consistent. The alphas were .79, .86, and .65 respectively. The intercorrelations are summarized in Table 7.4.

It can be seen that the child's report on mother negative affectivity correlated significantly with the mother's report but none of the other adult reports. Child report would therefore be dropped from the construct. Before assuming that the two adult reports were adequate, however, it would seem reasonable to demonstrate that the two new indicators were valid indicators of the mothers' state. The correlations of each of the three new indicators with the mothers' self-report score are listed in column 3. All correlations were significant; those for the adult raters approached the convergent validities previously demonstrated for the Maternal Negative Affectivity construct based only on mothers' self-report data.

We now have a measure of mothers' negative affectivity based on the perceptions of others that interacted with her in two interview situations and in three observations in the home. The model requires a significant path from the Maternal Stress construct (entirely mothers' appraisal) to the Maternal Negative Affectivity construct (entirely others' appraisal). The two sets of indicators have been set so that there is now no agent overlap and only partial method overlap

TABLE 7.4
The Effect of Using Alternative Measures of Maternal
Negative Affectivity

Indicators	Interviewer impressions	Observer impressions	Mother self-report	Stress indicators (mother self-report)			
				Family health problems	Recent hassles	Financial problems	Negative life events
Interviewer impressions			.54***	.17	.17	.18	.21*
Observer impressions	.22*		.33**	.25*	.13	.10	.11
Child telephone interview	.13	.17	.23*				

*p < .05
**p < .01
***p < .001

(assuming one wished to view ratings based on home observation as different from interview and questionnaire methods). In our recent work at OSLC, we have come to label this kind of drastic surgery as *model stretching*. It is assumed that selecting valid indicators that have no overlap in method and/or agent source would provide the most conservative possible estimate of what the model could be. In effect, the search is for some plausible confidence interval that could be attached to each path coefficient, in addition to its usual test of significance.

The last four columns of data in Table 7.3 define the most conservative estimate of what the path might be from Maternal Stress to Maternal Negative Affectivity. The correlation between each of the four Maternal Stress indicators with the two adult reports for Maternal Negative Affectivity ranged from .10 to .25, with a median of about .17. Given the sample size, one might say that the relation between the two constructs was not very strong. But notice that the average discriminant correlation based on mother self-report accounted for five times as much variance as this new path. Based on this more conservative estimate, one would conclude that the Maternal Stress construct accounts for only a modest 2% to 3% of the variance in Maternal Negative Affectivity.

IMPLICATIONS

It was proposed that the simple mediational model might serve as an explanation for the results of the Hetherington et al. (1979) finding that during the first 2 years following separation, single-parent families are at significant risk for producing antisocial boys. The model cast the first stages of the divorce experience as a set of stressors. In keeping with this idea, the findings showed that, indeed, recently separated mothers reported higher levels of stress than did mothers from intact families. Second, the model stipulated that the impact of Maternal Stress on Child Antisocial Behavior would be mediated by its effect on parent Inept Discipline practices. The findings supported this assumption in that the structural equation model showed that the data set was consistent with the a priori model and that the two key path coefficients were significant.

One of the virtues of the model lay in the fact that for immediately adjoining constructs there was virtually no agent or method overlap in the indicators. The objective was to use multiple agent/multiple method approaches to model building.

In the methodological study reported, the point was made that, whereas one can identify construct *structures* based solely on self-report data, there is some question as to whether the same data can also be used to specify the relation between constructs. A careful look using analyses such as confirmatory factor analysis might suggest that many of the stress models reported in the literature would collapse into bipolar self-reports about positive and negative world views.

The individual's self-report data are viewed with some suspicion, at least in the context of specifying relations among constructs. Some effort was made to explore model stretching as a means for identifying when such confounds exist. Model stretching involved the use of indicators from different measurement methods in defining adjoining constructs in the models. Presumably the path coefficients could be specified in several different ways: the most conservative (no common measurement methodology), moderate (common measurement in two out of four), and liberal (single method for all indicators).

ACKNOWLEDGMENTS

The authors gratefully acknowledge the support provided by Grant No. MH38318, from The National Institute of Mental Health, U. S. Public Health Service. The ideas developed here have grown out of ongoing dialogues with our colleagues L. Bank, T. Dishion, and J. Reid, and reflect their careful thinking and multidimensional contributions. We are also grateful to Karen Gardner, whose supervisory work made it possible to collect data of consistently high quality, Judy Evitt, for her assistance in obtaining the sample, and Judy Ray for her toils at the computer terminals.

REFERENCES

Achenbach, T. M. (1978). The child behavior profile, I: Boys aged 6 through 11. *Journal of Consulting and Clinical Psychology, 46*,(3), 478–488.

Bentler, P. M. (1980). Multivariate analysis with latent variables: Causal modeling. *Annual Review of Psychology, 31,* 419–455.

Bloom, B. L., Asher, S. J., & White, S. W. (1978). Marital disruption as a stressor: A review and analysis. *Psychological Bulletin, 85*(4), 867–894.

Brody, G. R., & Forehand, R. (1986). Maternal perceptions of child maladjustment as a function of the combined influence of child behavior and maternal depression. *Journal Clinical and Consulting Psychology, 54*(2), 237–240.

Cairns, R. B. (Ed.). (1979). *The analysis of social interaction: Methods, issues, and illustrations.* Hillsdale, NJ: Lawrence Erlbaum Associates.

Caprara, G. V., Renzi, P., Alcini, P., D'Imperio, G., & Travaglia, G. (1983). Instigation to aggress and escalation of aggression examined from a personological perspective: The role of irritability and of emotional susceptibility. *Aggressive Behavior, 9*(4), 345–352.

Chamberlain, P., & Patterson, G. R. (1984). Aggressive behavior in middle childhood. In D. Shaffer, A. A. Ehrhardt, & L. L. Greenhill (Eds.), *The clinical guide to child psychiatry* (pp. 229–250). New York: The Free Press.

Coddington, R. D. (1972). The significance of life events as etiological factors in the diseases of children: A survey of professional workers. *Journal of Psychosomatic Research, 16,* 7–18.

Cronbach, L. J., & Meehl, P. E. (1955). Construct validity in psychological tests. In H. Feigl & M. Scriven (Eds.), *Minnesota studies in the philosophy of science. Vol. 1. The foundations of science and concepts of psychology and psychoanalysis* (pp. 174–204). Minneapolis, MN: University of Minnesota Press.

Dishion, T. J., Patterson, G. R., Yamamoto, M., & Skinner, M. L. (1984). Discipline construct. *Oregon Social Learning Center Technical Report.* (Available from the Oregon Social Learning Center, 207 E. 5th, Suite 202, Eugene, OR 97401.)

Elder, G. H., Liker, J. K., & Crosse, C. E. (1984) Parent child behavior in the great depression: Life course and intergenerational influences. In P. B. Baltes & O. G. Brin (Eds.), *Life span development and behavior* (Vol. 6, pp. 109–158). New York: Academic Press.

Feigl, H. (1956). Some major issues and developments in the philosophy of science of logical empiricism. In H. Feigl & M. Scriven (Eds.), *Minnesota studies in the philosophy of science. Vol. 1. The foundations of science and concepts of psychology and psychoanalysis* (pp. 3–37). Minneapolis, MN: University of Minnesota Press.

Hetherington, E. M. (1979). Divorce: A child's perspective. *American Psychologist, 34*, 851–858.

Hetherington, E. M. (1980). Children and divorce. In R. Henderson (Ed.), *Parent-child interaction: Theory, research and prospect* (pp. 35–58). New York: Academic Press.

Hetherington, E. M., Cox, M., & Cox, R. (1979). Family interaction and the social, emotional, and cognitive development of children following divorce. In V. Vaughn & T. Brazelton (Eds.), *The family: Setting priorities* (pp. 89–128). New York: Science and Medicine.

Jöreskog, K. G., & Sörbom, D. (1984). *LISREL VI: Analysis of linear structural relationships by maximum likelihood, instrumental variables, and least squares methods*. Mooresville, IN: Scientific Software.

Lamb, M. E., Suomi, S. J., & Stephenson, G. R. (Eds.). (1979). *Social interaction analysis: Methodological issues*. Madison, WI: The University of Wisconsin Press.

Lazarus, R. S., DeLongis, A., Folkman, S., & Gruen, R. (1985). Stress and Adaptational Outcomes: The problem of confounded measures. *American Psychologist, 40*,(7), 770–779.

MacCorquodale, K., & Meehl, P. E. (1948). On a distinction between hypothetical construct and intervening variables. *Psychological Bulletin, 55*, 95–107.

Olson, D. H., McCubbin, H. I., Barnes, H., Larsen, A., Muxen, M., & Wilson, M. (1983). *Families: What makes them work*. Beverly Hills, CA: Sage.

Patterson, G. R. (1982). *Coercive family process*. Eugene, OR: Castalia Publishing.

Patterson, G. R. (1985). Beyond technology: The next stage in developing an empirical base for parent training. In L. L'Abate (Ed.), *The handbook of family psychology and therapy* (pp. 1344–1379). Homewood, IL: Dorsey Press.

Patterson, G. R. (1986). Performance models for antisocial boys. *American Psychologist, 41*(4), 432–444.

Patterson, G. R., & Bank, L. (1987). When is a nomological network a construct? In D. R. Peterson & D. B. Fishman (Eds.), *Assessment for decision* (pp. 249–279). New Brunswick, NJ: Rutgers University Press.

Patterson, G. R., Chamberlain, P., & Reid, J. B. (1982). A comparative evaluation of a parent-training program. *Behavior Therapy, 13*, 638–650.

Patterson, G. R., & Dishion, T. J. (1985). Contributions of families and peers to delinquency. *Criminology, 23*(1), 63–79.

Patterson, G. R., Dishion, T. J., & Bank, L. (1984). Family interaction: A process model of deviancy training. In L. Eron (Ed.), *Aggressive Behavior, 10*, 253–267 (special ed.).

Patterson, G. R., & Forgatch, M. S. (1987). *Parents and adolescents: Living together. Part 1, The basics*. Eugene, OR: Castalia Publishing.

Patterson, G. R., & Reid, J. B. (1984). Social interactional processes within the family: The study of moment-by-moment family transactions in which human social development is imbedded. *Journal of Applied Developmental Psychology, 5*, 237–262.

Patterson, G. R., Reid, J. B., & Dishion, T. J. (in press). *Antisocial boys*. Eugene, OR: Castalia Publishing.

Patterson, G. R., Reid, J. B., Jones, R. R., & Conger, R. E. (1975). *A social learning approach to family intervention. I. Families with aggressive children*. Eugene, OR: Castalia Publishing.

Pearlin, L. I., & Schooler, C. (1978). The structure of coping. *Journal of Health and Social Behavior, 19*, 2–21.

Pedhazur, E. J. (1982). *Multiple regression in behavioral research: Explanation and prediction* (2nd ed.). New York: Holt, Rinehart & Winston.

Reid, J. B., Baldwin, D. V., Patterson, G. R., & Dishion, T. J. (1985). *Some problems relating to the assessment of childhood disorders: A role for observational data.* Manuscript prepared for ADAMHA (A. Hussain Tuma, Project Officer), NIMH, U.S. PHS.

Rutter, M. (1983). Stress, coping, and development: Some issues and some questions. In N. Garmezy & M. Rutter (Eds.), *Stress, coping, and development in children* (pp. 1–43). New York: McGraw-Hill.

Sarason, I. G., Johnson, J. H., & Siegel, J. M. (1978). Assessing the impact of life changes: Development of the life experiences survey. *Journal of Consulting and Clinical Psychology, 46*(5), 932–946.

Selye, H. (1978). *The stress of life* (rev. ed.). New York: McGraw-Hill.

Skinner, M. L., & Gardner, K. (1985). Antisocial construct. *OSLC Technical Report for Completed Analysis.* (Available from the Oregon Social Learning Center, 207 E. 5th, Suite 202, Eugene, OR 97401.)

Spielberger, C. D., Crane, R. S., Westberry, L. G., & Russell, F. (1983). Assessment of anger: The state-trait anger inventory. In J. N. Butcher & C. D. Spielberger (Eds.), *Advances in personality assessment* (Vol. 2). Hillsdale, NJ: Lawrence Erlbaum Associates.

Stolberg, A. L., & Anker, J. M. (1983). Cognitive and behavioral changes in children resulting from parental divorce and consequent environmental changes. *Journal of Divorce, 7*(2), 23–41.

Tellegen, A. (1982). *Brief manual for the Differential Personality Questionnaire.* Unpublished manuscript. (Available from the Dept. of Psychology, University of Minnesota, Minneapolis, MN.)

Viken, R. (in preparation). *Stress, family process, and child antisocial behavior.* Manuscript in preparation. (Available from the Oregon Social Learning Center, 207 E. 5th, Suite 202, Eugene, OR 97401.)

Wallerstein, J., & Kelly, J. B. (1980). *Surviving the breakup: How children and parents cope with divorce.* New York: Basic books.

Weitzman, L. J., (1985). *The divorce revolution: The unexpected social and economic consequences for women and children in America.* New York: The Free Press.

Wolfe, D. A., Jaffe, P., Wilson, S. K., & Zak, L. (1985). Children of battered women: The relation of child behavior to family violence and maternal stress. *Journal of Consulting and Clinical Psychology, 53*(5), 657–665.

8

Divorce and Marital Conflict:
Relationship to Adolescent Competence and Adjustment in Early Adolescence

Rex Forehand
Nicholas Long
Gene Brody
University of Georgia

The effect of parental divorce on children has, over the last 2 decades, become a major area of concern to both professionals and the general public, paralleling the alarming rise in the divorce rate during that time. A substantial amount of research has addressed the effect of divorce on children, resulting in the conclusion that children often are affected negatively; however, most investigators are now moving beyond the notion that parental divorce has the same effect on all children. Numerous factors associated with divorce are being proposed as important mediators of child adjustment (Atkeson, Forehand, & Richard, 1982; Emery, 1982; Hess & Camara, 1979; Santrock & Madison, 1985) and will likely prove critical in understanding the effects of parental divorce. Studies that do not control for such variables (e.g., interparental conflict, age) may be masking many significant relationships. Wallerstein and Kelly (1974), for example, reported that the effects of divorce on child adjustment vary according to the child's age, thus identifying one distinct contributor to adjustment.

Many investigators believe that the most important mediating variable associated with divorce and child adjustment may be interparental conflict (Atkeson et al., 1982; Block, Block, & Gjerde, 1986; Emery, 1982; Lupenitz, 1979). Several authors have discussed the importance of determining the relative significance of parental conflict and divorce per se (ie., the change in the family structure) on various areas of child adjustment (Emery, 1982; Hall & Hare-Mustin, 1983). Emery (1982) stated:

> A critical question is whether separation from a parent per se or the interparental conflict that is concomitant with divorce is more strongly related to child behavior problems. This distinction is particularly relevant because it bears on such issues as whether parents should stay together for the children's sake. (p. 313)

Several reviewers have concluded that the emotional climate of the home may be a more important factor than divorce per se in regard to child behavior problems, particularly aggression (Bane, 1976; Herzog & Sudia, 1973; Rutter & Madge, 1976). Some studies suggest that frequent expression of parental conflict, in particular, appears to be more strongly associated with childhood aggression than is father absence (Block et al., 1986; Herzog & Sudia, 1973; Marotz-Baden, Adams, Bueche, Munro, & Munro, 1979).

Contrary to popular belief, parental conflict does not always dissipate following divorce and may in fact increase (Ahrons, 1981; Emery, 1982). Hetherington, Cox, and Cox (1976) reported that 66% of the exchanges between ex-spouses 2 months after divorce were conflictual. The major areas of conflict were reported to be finances, visitation, childrearing, and intimate relations with others. There is also evidence that frequent conflictual contact between ex-spouses can continue for several years after divorce (Kressel, 1980; Weiss, 1975). There are, however, many divorced couples who interact in a nonconflictual and positive manner following their divorce (Ahrons, 1981). Several studies have found that children from such homes have fewer problems than children from high-conflict divorced families (Hetherington et al., 1976; Jacobson, 1978; Kelly & Wallerstein, 1976; Power, Ash, Schoenberg, & Sorey, 1974). Wallerstein and Kelly (1980) also concluded that parents' ability to resolve conflictual issues after their divorce was related to beneficial postdivorce adjustment of children.

At the present time, available evidence suggests that parental conflict may prove to be one critical mediating variable affecting the postdivorce adjustment of children. Evidence further suggests that it is not necessarily the occurrence of parental conflict, but rather the occurrence of parental conflict in the presence of the child, that is associated with the most detrimental effects on children (Hetherington, Cox, & Cox, 1979a; Jacobson, 1978; Porter & O'Leary, 1980).

Our research efforts, which are delineated in this chapter, address the role of marital conflict in the divorce process as well as in family functioning in nondivorced families. It is important to recognize that this work is still in its infancy as data collection has begun only since mid-1985. Nevertheless, with the support of the William T. Grant Foundation, several studies have been completed that are summarized here. (Each of these studies has been published; therefore, for a more complete report, the reader can request reprints, as well as preprints of more recent work, from the first author.)

The first study addresses the association of marital conflict and divorce with early adolescents' social and cognitive competence. The second study expands on the first by examining not only the effects of marital conflict and divorce, and particularly their interactive effects, but also the degree to which nondivorced couples have considered divorce. Finally, the third study examines the interaction of adolescent gender with marital conflict and its association with adjustment. Although adolescents from divorced homes were not included in the third study, the results have implications (which are discussed later) for divorced populations, as some data suggest that boys and girls differ in the same way in their reactions to marital conflict and to divorce (for reviews see Atkeson et al., 1982; Emery, 1982).

Our research is restricted to early adolescent subjects, both as a control for the effects of child age (Wallerstein & Kelly, 1974) and as a means of extending our knowledge of the effects of parental divorce beyond latency age children, who most often are the targets of such studies. Adolescence might prove to be a particularly important period for such investigations as it is generally considered to be a time of developmental stress (Montemayor, 1983). Regarding the child's functioning within the family, Robin (1985) has indicated that major shifts occur in the parent–child relationship during adolescene. The adolescent typically assumes more independence, decision-making authority, and freedom to move in and out of the family system. If parental divorce occurs, these transitions may well be disrupted, leading to adjustment difficulties. Thus, the "normal" changes associated with adolescence, as well as the stress typically associated with these changes, may exacerbate the negative effects of parental divorce. Recent evidence indicating that older children (fifth grade) may experience more problems associated with parental divorce than younger children (Guidubaldi, Perry, & Cleminshaw, 1984) supports this notion.

Our research is also restricted to an examination of child adjustment during the first year following divorce, because length of time since divorce has been identified as an important factor in postdivorce child adjustment. Wallerstein and Kelly (1980) found that parental divorce appears to have both acute and chronic effects on children. Their data suggest that, for the first 2 years following parental divorce, children tend to display increased behavior problems, whereas other difficulties, such as feelings of anger, persisted past this period. Hetherington, Cox, and Cox (1978, 1979a, 1979b) also stated that the greatest child adjustment problems occur during the first year following parental divorce. Therefore, the first 1–2 years following parental divorce appears to be the period of greatest stress for children.

GENERAL METHODOLOGY

As the general methodology is similar for all three studies, this section delineates the common methods employed. Each sample was drawn from a pool of 89 families, 69 of which were intact and 20 of which were divorced for 1 year or less. All families included an adolescent between 11 and 15 years of age, and were recruited through newspaper ads and announcements that were distributed at schools and posted in public places. In addition, some divorced families' participation was directly solicited after they were identified through the examination of divorce records at area courthouses. In all families, the mother and adolescent participated in a 2-hour data-gathering session at a local university during which they were administered a series of questionnaires presented in a randomized order. After they had completed these instruments, the adolescent and mother were instructed to discuss and resolve the issue of cleaning the adolescent's bedroom, one that is frequently disputed in many families. This 3-minute interaction was videotaped through a one-way window. Subsequently, naive observers viewed the videotapes and independently rated the adolescent and the parent–adolescent interaction on several dimensions using a 7-point Likert scale (Robin & Canter, 1984). Following the data-collection session at the university, a packet of questionnaires was sent to both the adolescent's father and social studies teacher, each of whom was requested to complete the forms and return them in an enclosed envelope.

Study 1

The purpose of the first study, conducted by Long, Forehand, Fauber, and Brody (1987), was to examine the association of marital conflict and divorce with self-perceived and independently observed social and cognitive competence of young adolescents. Marital conflict and divorce were hypothesized to be differentially associated with adjustment of young adolescents. Divorce per se (i.e., the actual change in family structure) was predicted to have a short-term distress-type effect on children, which would be manifested in a lowering of the adolescent's perception of his or her own competence. Assuming that competence in various skill areas was achieved prior to the divorce and that the skills are an established part of the adolescent's repertoire, such distress would probably not significantly affect an adolescent's actual competence as assessed by others. In contrast, because of inadequate parental modeling or problem-solving strategies and communication skills, as well as inconsistant discipline resulting from interparental conflict, marital conflict would probably be associated with adolescent behavior problems as long as the conflict continues. These problems may lead to, or occur concomitantly with, impaired social and cognitive competence, which may further lead to accurate reductions in self-perceived competence. It was, therefore, expected that both divorce and marital conflict would be associated with lowered self-perceived competence, whereas only marital conflict would be related to lowered independently observed competence.

Forty (20 females and 20 males) young Caucasian adolescents, their mothers, and their social studies teachers participated in this study. The adolescents ranged in age from 11 years, 1 month to 15 years, 1 month, with a mean age of 13 years, 1 month. Half of the subjects were from recently divorced families (biological parents divorced within the last 12 months), whereas the other half were from intact families (biological parents still married). The average time since parental divorce was 5.6 months.

Parental conflict was assessed using the O'Leary–Porter Scale, which measures overt parental conflict that occurs in the presence of the adolescent (Porter

& O'Leary, 1980). Within the divorced group, a median split was performed on the mothers' O'Leary-Porter scores to form high and low conflict subgroups. A group of 20 intact families, matched with the divorced families on O'Leary-Porter scores, adolescent's age and gender, and family socioeconomic status (SES) was selected from the available pool of 69 intact families and divided into high and low conflict subgroups. In order to assure that the groups differed as planned on the conflict dimension, a two-way analysis of variance (high vs. low conflict; intact vs. divorced family) was conducted on mothers' O'Leary-Porter scores. As expected, a significant effect existed only for the conflict dimension.

Each of the four subgroups in the study included 5 male and 5 female adolescent subjects. A two-way analysis of variance indicated that no significant differences existed among subgroups for adolescent age; however, there was a significant marital status effect for SES, based on the standing of the parent with the highest occupational and educational level in each household, indicating lower SES among divorced than intact families.

The dependent measures included the cognitive and social subscales of the Perceived Competence Scale for Children (PCSC; Harter, 1982), the Teacher's Rating Scale of Child's Actual Competence (TRS; Harter, 1982), the teacher completed Conduct Disorder factor of the Revised Behavior Problem Checklist (RBPC; Quay & Peterson, 1983), the adolescent's grade-point average and ratings of problem-solving ability and level of positive communication obtained from the videotaped observation of the mother–adolescent interaction. The data were analyzed using two-way multivariate and univariate analyses of covariance (ANCOVA). The independent variables for these anlyses were parental marital status and level of parental conflict, and the covariate was SES. Initial analyses indicated no main or interactive effects for adolescent gender on any of the dependent variables; therefore, this variable was not included in the primary analyses.

Self-perceived cognitive and social competence among adolescents from divorced homes was lower than that of adolescents from nondivorced homes; however, no association was found for level of marital conflict. With the exception of the behavioral rating for positive communication, all of the independent ratings of cognitive competence (teacher ratings and grade-point average) and social competence (teacher ratings and behavioral observational data) indicated a significant effect for parental conflict but not for marital status, as adolescents from high parental conflict homes were functioning less well than those from low conflict homes. Significant interactions between marital status and parental conflict did not emerge for any of the dependent measures.

These findings confirm the hypothesis that parental marital status and conflict are differentially associated with adolescent adjustment. Marital status was associated with adolescents' perceptions of their cognitive and social competence, whereas parental conflict was associated with independently assessed competence. Contrary to expectations, conflict was not associated with self-perceived competence. Although their grades, their teacher's perceptions, and their interactions with their mothers suggest that adolescents from high conflict homes are less competent, the adolescents do not view themselves as such.

Recent divorce independent of parental conflict appears to be primarily associated with adolescent self-perceived competence. As hypothesized earlier, if an adolescent has developed adequate social and cognitive skills prior to the divorce, the immediate influence of the divorce per se will be limited to the adolescent's self-perception. Any long-term effects on actual competence that may take place cannot be determined from the present results; it is, however, important to note that detrimental effects may result if the adolescent continues to perceive himself or herself as incompetent.

Several possible explanations for the association between independently observed adolescent competence and parental conflict are based on social learning theory (Emery, 1982). First, when parents display conflict in an adolescent's presence, the adolescent is likely to imitate their behavior, which will interfere with social and academic functioning. Second, parental conflict may interfere with the use of consistent childrearing strategies and/or adequate supervision of the adolescent.

The results indicate the importance of examining, or at least controlling for, parental conflict level when studying the effects of divorce on children and adolescents. Because of the matching process across groups, mothers from intact and divorced families did not differ in level of parental conflict; consequently, in contrast to much of the earlier literature that did not control for this factor, no differences in independently observed levels of competence were found. These data support the importance some investigators (Atkeson et al., 1982; Emery, 1982) have placed on parental conflict in intact and divorced families.

Study 2

Whereas the results of Study 1 indicate the importance of examining parental conflict when studying the effects of divorce on children, this investigation (Forehand, Brody, Long, Slotkin, & Fauber, 1986) was undertaken to examine the singular and interactive role of parental divorce potential in adolescent adjustment. As has been noted by several investigators (e.g., Atkeson et al., 1982), divorce is not a discrete occurrence but rather is a process, one aspect of which is the degree to which couples have considered divorce a solution to their marital problems. Spouses from intact families are not homogeneous in regard to their potential for divorce. Weiss and Cerreto (1980) have recently devised a scale, The Marital Status Inventory, to measure a couple's marriage dissolution potential; this measure was used to examine the possible contribution of this variable to adolescent adjustment.

The present study was also designed to further examine the role of marital conflict, divorce, and the interaction of these two variables on young adolescent's functioning. Study 1 identified the differential effects of conflict and divorce; however, although the functioning of the divorced high conflict group was poorer for all measures, the interaction of the two independent variables did not reach significance for any of the dependent variables. By utilizing a somewhat larger sample in this study, the interactive effect of divorce and marital conflict was further examined.

Twenty adolescents from divorced families and 36 from intact families served as participants. As noted earlier, all divorces had occurred within the past 12 months. Parental conflict was assessed using the O'Leary–Porter scale, after which subjects were divided into high and low conflict groups. Within each group subjects were further divided into one of three subgroups: Intact-low divorce potential, intact-high divorce potential, and divorced. As previously noted, divorce potential was measured using the Marital Status Inventory (Weiss & Cerreto, 1980), which was completed by the adolescent's mother.

O'Leary–Porter scale scores did not differ among the three low conflict subgroup or among the three high conflict subgroups. Neither the two low divorce potential subgroups nor the two high divorce potential subgroups differed from one another. Adolescent's age did not vary significantly across groups; however, family SES did vary, indicating that adolescents from divorced homes were from lower SES families.

The dependent measures in this study included the Perceived Competence Scale for Children (PCSC), the Teacher's Rating Scale of Child's Acual Competence (TRS), and the adolescent's grade-point average (GPA). Both the social and the cognitive subscales were examined on the PCSC and the TRS.

The results of a 2 (conflict: high or low) × 3 (intact-low divorce potential, intact-high divorce potential, divorced) analysis of covariance (using SES as the covariate) on each of the dependent measures indicated a significant marital status by divorce/divorce potential interaction for the cognitive subscale of the TRS and for GPA. Simple effect analyses indicated that, relative to the other groups, adolescents in the divorced, high conflict group demonstrated more conflict with their mothers on both measures. The remaining five groups did not differ from one another. For the social subscale of the TRS, the interaction was not significant; however, exploratory analyses revealed that the divorced, high conflict group was functioning less well than the remaining groups. No differences were evident for either the cognitive or social subscales of the adolescent-completed PCSC.

The results of Study 2 suggest that parental conflict and divorce are interactive in their effects on young adolescents, as the combination of high parental conflict and divorce was associated with more parent–adolescent conflict and poorer school performance than was either factor alone. As noted previously, this finding is consistent with those derived from earlier studies (e.g., Hetherington et al., 1976; Power et al., 1974).

The available data to this point in time have indicated that continued conflict after divorce is associated with more problems for children than are low conflict divorces (Hetherington et al., 1976; Jacobson, 1978) and that children from conflicted intact homes are equally or more likely to have problems than are children from broken homes (McCord, McCord, & Thurber, 1962; Nye, 1957; Power et al., 1974). However, the present study is the first to demonstrate that the combination of high conflict and divorce is more detrimental than each of the other combinations of these two variables.

The present results do not provide support for a main or interactive (with interparental conflict) influence of divorce potential on adolescent functioning. It appears that interparental conflict, particularly in interaction with divorce, is more detrimental than divorce potential. Several possible explanations for the relative effects of these two variables can be advanced. First, interparental conflict as assessed in this study occurred in the presence of the adolescent; therefore, adolescents may have been more aware of parental conflict than of parental divorce potential. Indeed, a measure of the adolescent's perceptions of parental divorce potential may yield different findings. Second, Emery (1982) has delineated several ways in which conflict may interfere with child/adolescent functioning, including a modeling effect and disruption of monitoring and disciplinary practices. It may well be that divorce potential does not exert these effects. At this time one can only speculate on the different effects of conflict and divorce potential. Intuitively, it seems that divorce potential per se does not exert a modeling effect but may disrupt monitoring and discipline; further research is needed to explore these questions.

Study 3

Studies 1 and 2 both indicate the important role of marital conflict when examining divorce effects on adolescents. Unfortunately, the samples in both of these studies were too small to allow for an adequate test of the differential responses of boys and girls to such conflict. The available research suggests that males are more adversely affected by stress in general and marital conflict in particular than are females (Emery, 1982; Rutter, 1983); however, the outcome measures employed in most of these studies have been limited to the assessment of acting out problems, such as aggression and destructiveness. As Emery (1982) noted, female children may react just as much to parental conflict as males, but in ways other than those which involve the display of conduct disorders. For example, Emery (1982), as well as Block et al. (1986) and Cummings, Iannoti, and Zahn-Waxler (1985), suggested that girls may respond to conflict by becoming withdrawn and anxious. Parental conflict may exacerbate disorders to which a particular individual is especially prone, an hypothesis that has received some support from Cummings et al. (1985). As conduct disorders are more prevalent in boys (Graham, 1979) and anxiety disorders and complaints about physical symptoms are more prevalent in girls (Graham, 1979; Greene, Walker, Hickson, & Thompson, 1985), these types of disorders may be displayed by male and female children, respectively, in response to parental conflict.

The purpose of the present study (Forehand et al., 1987) was to examine the role of parental marital conflict with male and female young adolescents. As indicated, it has been proposed that both male and female children may be influenced by parental conflict, but in different ways by displaying different types of adjustment problems. Three areas of adjustment were, therefore, examined: Physical symptoms, externalizing behavior problems, and internalizing behavior problems. The data analyzed in this study were collected from intact families. Although this imposes limitations on their application to divorced samples, these data can, nevertheless, help to clarify the general influence of marital conflict on boys and girls, respectively.

Thirty-nine mothers and their early adolescent children participated in the study. Subjects were selected from the sample of 69 intact families on the basis of the mother's score on the O'Leary–Porter Scale. The low conflict subgroups included were 9 males and 10 females, whereas the high conflict subgroups included 10 males and 10 females. The groups were matched for SES and age of adolescent.

The dependent measures included the Conduct Disorders and Anxiety-Withdrawal factors of the Revised Behavior Problem Checklist (RBPC; Quay & Peterson, 1983), the Issues Checklist (Robin & Weiss, 1980), the Wahler Physical Symptoms Inventory (Wahler, 1969), and the Revised Children's Manifest Anxiety Scale (Reynolds & Richmond, 1978). The Revised Behavior Problem Checklist was completed by the adolescent's mother and social studies teacher, the Issues Checklist and Wahler Physical Symptoms Inventory was completed by the adolescent and his or her mother, and the Revised Children's Manifest Anxiety Scale was completed by the adolescent only.

A significant interaction between level of parental conflict and adolescent gender was found for each of the four measures of externalizing problems: Parent-completed RBPC Conduct Disorder factor, teacher-completed RBPC Conduct Disorder factor, parent-completed Issues Checklist, and adolescent-completed Issues Checklist. In all cases an increase in behavior problems occurred from low to high parental conflict groups for boys, whereas there was minimum increase, no increase, or a decrease for girls from low to high conflict groups. For the three measures of internalizing problems and the two measures of physical health, the interactions were not significant; however, as with the measures of externalizing problems, there was a trend for males more than for females to display more problems and symptoms in high conflict homes.

These results indicate that adolescent males are more reactive to parental conflict than are females. Furthermore, the reaction is primarily expressed through externalizing problems. The results were impressive as the same finding for externalizing problems was consistently reported by mothers, teachers, and adolescents.

Although there was not a significant interaction between level of parental conflict and adolescent gender for internalizing and physical problems, males, relative to females, tended to demonstrate more of an increase in difficulties as the level of conflict at home increased. Based on the lack of significant interactions, perhaps the most conservative and appropriate conclusion that can be reached is that early adolescent boys and girls do not differ in their responses to parental conflict on these measures. These results do not support Emery's (1982) contention that females may display problems other than conduct disorders, such as anxiety, in response to conflict. It is important to note that Emery suggested that females may respond to parental conflict by becoming less problematic, possibly in an attempt to reduce the friction in the home. On two of the three adolescent-completed measures (Wahler Physical Symptoms Inventory and Issues Checklist), fewer problems were reported by girls in high conflict homes compared to those in low conflict homes. Therefore, it is plausible that girls, more than boys, attempt to reduce friction in high conflict homes by reporting fewer problems.

CONCLUSIONS

Early adolescence is a time of transition, during which children begin to form their own values, as well as becoming more peer oriented and less family oriented. The need for the family to provide a safe environment—a haven from the pressures of the outside world—is critical at this time (Csikszentimihalyi & Larson, 1984). Unfortunately, for many adolescents, the family does not fulfill this need. Conflict between parents may be a part of daily home life, or the parents may choose to divorce as a way of ending their dislike for each other and their home life. Both conflict and divorce can disrupt the stable, secure home environment adolescents frequently need in order to cope with the demands of their changing world.

Although data have been gathered on preadolescent children, little is known about the relationship of parental conflict and divorce with the adjustment and functioning of adolescent-age children. The present series of studies was, therefore, undertaken to provide information about these relationships. What conclusions can be drawn from the three studies reported in this chapter? First, parental conflict is related to independently assessed competence of adolescents, whereas, at least in Study One, recent divorce appears to be related to adolescent self-perceived competence. Second, adolescents whose recently divorced parents engage in high levels of conflict function more poorly than adolescents whose parents are not divorced or have less conflict. Third, the present data suggest that divorce potential is not significantly related to adolescent functioning. Finally, boys appear to react more strongly to parental conflict than girls, particularly by displaying acting out problems. Overall, the combined results from the three studies suggest that divorce must be considered in light of parental conflict and that adolescent variables (e.g., gender) should be considered when examining the relationship between adolescent functioning and divorce or marital conflict. These conclusions are in agreement with the recent data reported by Block et al. (1986).

The influence of divorce in the present series of studies is limited to its effect during the first year after the marriage is terminated. Clearly, longitudinal data are needed. The poorer perceptions that adolescents have of their own competence, which is associated with divorce, may set in motion a series of events that can lead to a reduction in actual competence, particularly in combination with continued parental conflict.

REFERENCES

Ahrons, C. R. (1981). The continuing coparental relationship between divorced spouses. *American Journal of Orthopsychiatry, 51*, 415–428.

Atkeson, B. M., Forehand, R., & Rickarad, K. M. (1982). The effects of divorce on children. In B. B. Lahey & A. E. Kazdin (Eds.), *Advances in clinical child psychology* (Vol. 5, pp. 255–281). New York: Plenum.

Bane, M. J. (1976). Marital disruption and the lives of children. *Journal of Social Issues, 32*, 103–117.

Block, J. H., Block, J., & Gjerde, P. F. (1986). The personality of children prior to divorce: A prospective study. *Child Development, 57*, 827–840.

Csikzentimihalyi, M., & Larson, R. (1984). *Being adolescent.* New York: Basic Books.

Cummings, E. M., Iannoti, R. J., & Zahn-Waxler, C. (1985). Influence of conflict between adults on the emotions and aggression of young children. *Development Psychology, 21*, 495–507.

Emery, R. E. (1982). Interparental conflict and the children of discord and divorce. *Psychological Bulletin, 92*, 310–330.

Forehand, R., Brody, G. H., Long, N., Slotkin, J., & Fauber, R. (1986). Divorce, divorce potential, and interparental conflict: The relationship to early adolescent social and cognitive functioning. *Journal of Adolescent Research, 1*, 389–397.

Forehand, R., Long, N., Faust, J., Brody, G. H., Burke, M., & Fauber, R. (1987). Psychological and physical health of young adolescents as a function of gender and marital conflict. *Journal of Pediatric Psychology, 12*, 191–210.

Graham, P. (1979). Epidemiological studies. In H. C. Quay & J. S. Werry (Eds.), *Psychopathological disorders of childhood* (2nd ed., pp. 185–209). New York: Wiley.

Greene, J. W., Walker, L. S., Hickson, G., & Thompson, J. (1985). Stressful life events and somatic complaints in adolescents. *Pediatrics, 75*, 19–22.

Guidubaldi, J., Perry, J. D., & Cleminshaw, H. K. (1984). The legacy of parental divorce: A nationwide study of family status and selected mediating variables on children's academic and social competenacies. In B. B. Lahey & A. E. Kazdin (Eds.), *Advances in clinical child psychology* (Vol. 7, pp. 109–151). New York: Plenum.

Hall, J. E., & Hare-Mustin, R. T. (1983). Sanctions and the diversity of ethical complaints against psychologists. *American Psychologist, 38*, 714–729.

Harter, S. (1982). The perceived competence scale for children. *Child Development, 53*, 87–97.

Herzog, E., & Sudia, C. (1973). Children in fatherless families. In B. M. Caldwell & H. N. Ricciuti (Eds.), *Review of child development research* (Vol. 2, pp. 141–232). Chicago: University of Chicago Press.

Hess, R. D., & Camara, K. A. (1979). Post-divorce family relationships as mediating factors in the consequences of divorce for children. *Journal of Social Issues, 35*, 79–96.

Hetherington, E. M., Cox, M., & Cox, R. (1976). Divorced fathers. *The Family Coordinator, 25*, 417–428.

Hetherrington, E. M., Cox, M., & Cox, R. (1978). The aftermath of divorce. In J. H. Stevens & M. Mathews (Eds.), *Mother/child, father/child relationships* (pp. 110–155). Washington, DC: National Association for the Education of Young Children.

Hetherington, E. M., Cox, M., & Cox, R. (1979a). Family interaction and the social-emotional and cognitive development of children following divorce. In. V. Vaughn & T. Brazelton (Eds.), *The family setting priorities* (pp. 89–128). New York: Science & Medicine Publishing.

Hetherington, E. M., Cox, M., & Cox, R. (1979b). Play and social interaction in children following divorce. *Journal of Social Issues, 35,* 26–49.

Jacobson, D. S. (1978). The impact of marital separation/divorce on children: II. Interpersonal hostility and child adjustment. *Journal of Divorce, 2,* 3–20.

Kelly, J. B., & Wallerstein, J. S. (1976). The effects of parental divorce: Experiences of the child in early latency. *American Journal of Orthopsychiatry, 46,* 20–23.

Kressel, K. (1980). Patterns of coping in divorce and some implications for clinical practice. *Family Relations, 29,* 234–240.

Long, N., Forehand, R., Fauber, R., & Brody, G. H. (1987). Self-perceived and independently-observed competence of young adolescents as a function of parental marital conflict and recent divorce. *Journal of Abnormal Child Psychology, 15,* 15–27.

Lupenitz, D. A. (1979). Which aspects of divorce affect children. *Family Coordinator, 28,* 79–85.

McCord, J., McCord, W., & Thurber, E. (1962). Some effects of paternal absence on male children. *Journal of Abnormal and Social Psychology, 64,* 361–369.

Martoz-Baden, R., Adams, G. R., Bueche, N., Munro, B., & Munro, B. (1979). Family form or family process? Reconsidering the deficit family model approach. *Family Relations, 28,* 5–14.

Montemayor, R. (1983). Parents and adolescents in conflict: All families some of the time and some families most of the time. *Journal of Early Adolescence, 3,* 83–103.

Nye, F. I. (1957). Child adjustment in broken and in unhappy unbroken homes. *Marriage and Family Living, 19,* 356–361.

Porter, B., & O'Leary, K. D. (1980). Marital discord and childhood behavior problems. *Journal of Abnormal Child Psychology, 8,* 287–295.

Power, M. J., Ash, P. M., Schoenberg, E., & Sorey, E. C. (1974). Delinquency and the family. *British Journal of Social Work, 4,* 17–38.

Quay, H. D., & Peterson, D. R. (1983). *Revised behavioral problem checklist* (1st ed.). Unpublished manuscript.

Reynolds, C. R., & Richmond, B. O. (1978). What I think and feel: A revised measure of children's manifest anxiety. *Journal of Abnormal Child Psychology, 6,* 271–280.

Robin, A. L. (1985). Parent-adolescent conflict: A developmental problem of families. In R. J. McMahon & R. D. Peters (Eds.), *Childhood disorders: Behavioral-developmental approaches* (pp. 244–265). New York: Brunner/Mazel.

Robin, A. L., & Canter, W. (1984). A comparison of the marital interaction coding system and community ratings for assessing mother-adolescent problem-solving. *Behavioral Assessment, 6,* 303–313.

Robin, A., & Weiss, J. (1980). Criterion-related validity of behavioral and self-report measures of problem solving communication skills in distressed and nondistressed parent-adolescent dyads. *Behavioral Assessment, 4,* 339–352.

Rutter, M. (1983). Stress, coping, and development: Some issues and some questions. In N. Garmezy & M. Rutter (Eds.), *Stress, coping, and development in children* (pp. 1–36). New York: McGraw-Hill.

Rutter, M., & Madge, N. (1976). *Cycles of disadvantages.* London: Heineman.

Santrock, J. W., & Madison, T. D. (1985). Three research traditions in the study of adolescents in divorced families: Quasi-experimental, developmental; clinical; and family sociological. *Journal of Early Adolescence, 5,* 115–128.

Wahler, H. J. (1969). The physical symptoms inventory: Measuring levels of somatic complaining behavior. *Journal of Clinical Psychology, 24,* 207–211.

Wallerstein, J. S., & Kelly, J. B. (1974). The effects of parental divorce: The adolescent experience. In E. Anthony & C. Koupernik (Eds.), *The child and his family* (Vol. 3, pp. 479–505). New York: Wiley.

Wallerstein, J. S., & Kelly, J. B. (1980). *Surviving the breakup: How children and parents cope with divorce.* New York: Basic Books.

Weiss, R. S. (1975). *Marital separation.* New York: Basic Books.

Weiss, R. L., & Cerreto, M. C. (1980). The marital status inventory: Development of a measure of dissolution potential. *American Journal of Family Therapy, 8,* 80–85.

9

Interparental Conflict and Cooperation:
Factors Moderating Children's Post-Divorce Adjustment

Kathleen A. Camara
Gary Resnick
Tufts University

INTRODUCTION

Conflict is an inevitable part of family life. Whenever there are differences in interests, beliefs, values, or desires among family members, or whenever there is a scarcity of such resources as money, time, or space, conflict can occur. The assumption in much of the literature on the effects of marital conflict on children's behavior is that conflict is a destructive process that may lead to divorce, and, eventually, cause problems in children. Studies of divorce and conflicted marriages have demonstrated that high levels of discord are related to high levels of child disturbance. Aggression, social withdrawal, depression, lowered self-esteem, somatic symptoms, and noncompliance to adult authority are problems characteristic of children who are in families marked by interparental discord (Hess & Camara, 1979; Hetherington, Cox, & Cox, 1982; Wallerstein & Kelly, 1980). Research has suggested that it is the interparental conflict, and not the separation or divorce of parents, that may be the major cause of behavior problems generally associated with children of divorce (Emery, 1982; Rutter, 1971).

Although there is evidence linking disturbances in children's behavior to interparental discord in both divorced and nondivorced families, little is known about the processes by which children are affected by conflict. Several theoretical frameworks have been suggested. One explanation, based on the concept of modeling, suggests that children learn social interaction skills by observing the interactions of their parents. Studies have found that openly hostile conflict between parents is related to aggression, noncompliance, and acting-out behaviors, rather than to problems of depression or social withdrawal in children (Oltmans, Broderick, & O'Leary, 1977; Porter & O'Leary, 1980; Rutter et al., 1974).

A second explanation, derived from socialization theories, proposes an indirect influence of interparental conflict on children. Parents, in the midst of disagreement and marital turmoil, may be unable to function effectively in their parental roles due to their preoccupation with the tensions and problems in their marital relationship. Interparental disagreements about discipline, which take place in front of the children, may be related to greater inconsistency in discipline practice, and subsequently, to increased behavioral problems in children. Parents in the midst of conflict also may be less available emotionally to their children, and may be unable to offer reassurance or comfort to children who are witnessing continual tension between their parents. Poorly timed or inappropriate interactions between parents and children may impede healthy development (Emde & Easterbrooks, 1985).

A third explanation is based on a family systems perspective in which the family is viewed as an organized whole consisting of interdependent elements (Minuchin, 1985). The patterns of interaction between any two members of the system will affect other members. Marital conflict or separation and divorce may challenge prevailing interactional patterns among family members and may require a structural reorganization so that developmental progress may be achieved (Minuchin, & Fishman, 1981). It has been suggested that children may respond to conflict in the family by developing a problem themselves as a means of functionally adapting to the distressed family system (Minuchin, 1974; Minuchin et al., 1975).

It is unlikely that one explanation can describe adequately the process by which interparental conflict affects children's behavior. Dysfunctional behavior in children probably derives from a congeries of conditions and factors, such as the observation of hostile interactions between parents, reduced emotional and physical availability of parents, inconsistent discipline and challenges to the family system and to individuals within the system that are beyond the adaptive resources of family members. Whichever model best describes the paths of influence, there is substantial evidence that links interparental discord to childhood behavior problems.

Most of the research on the effects of interparental conflict has not attended to factors surrounding the conflict, such as the nature, substance, intensity, duration, or style of resolving conflicts. The assumption made in most studies is that conflict between parents is characterized by angry, hostile, and destructive behaviors. However, there is nothing inherent in conflict that precludes the achievement of healthy resolution through the use of cooperative strategies (Deutsch, 1969). Conflict can be either productive or destructive, depending on the context in which it occurs and the styles used by parents to resolve disagreements.

Conflict that is destructive is characterized by interactional processes that expand and escalate the conflict. Cooperative resolutions enable both parties to arrive at a mutually acceptable outcome by recognizing the legitimacy of the other's interests within the context of open and honest communication (Deutsch, 1969).

The application of conflict theory to family interactions would suggest that the methods for resolving conflict in families, rather than the presence or absence of conflict may be predictive of child health and adjustment. Parents who respond to disagreements and conflicts in constructive ways will tend to emphasize mutual interests, sharing of goals and ideas, and division of labor. Parents who respond to conflicts in destructive ways will tend to be suspicious and hostile with a readiness to exploit the other's needs and weaknesses. Differences between constructive and destructive strategies for resolving conflict may explain the negative effects of divorce on the child's psychosocial functioning.

In divorced families, where children may comprise the only link between parents, cooperation around child-related concerns may be possible, despite continuing conflicts in other areas of the postmarital relationship. There is evidence to suggest that some divorced couples are able to cooperate and develop a healthy "coparental" relationship, based on their continued roles as parents (Ahrons, 1981; Bohannan, 1971). The continuing relationship between former spouses who are parents implies that the family subsystem consisting of the former spouses is still operative. This "interparental" subsystem for divorced families may be an important component in the family reorganization that is ultimately related to the child's adjustment.

This chapter presents the results of a study that focuses on this notion that healthy adaptation of children in divorced families may be dependent on processes of family interaction in the postseparation period. The study, part of a larger longitudinal research study begun in 1982 (Camara, 1981), investigated the degree and nature of disharmony between the two parents in two domains of their relationship: their connection to each other as parents of the child (Interparental Cooperation) and their relationship to each other as married partners or as former spouses (Interparental Conflict). Specifically, the research addressed the following questions:

1. What are the long-term effects of parental separation on children's psychosocial behavior?
2. What is the relationship between interparental conflict and child behavior?
3. What moderating effects does interparental cooperation have on the relationship between conflict in both divorced and nondivorced families and children's social competence?

A multimethod, multiple measure approach was used to obtain data from 82 families living in communities surrounding the Boston area. Three types of family configurations were compared in this study: divorced mother-custody, divorced father-custody, and nondivorced two-parent households.

DESIGN AND METHODS

Sample Selection

Parents who participated in the study were Caucasian of middle socioeconomic background, possessed a minimum of 2 years of education beyond high school, and were working at least part time. The sample was further restricted to families with one to three children, where the target child was the biological child of both parents, was between the ages of 7 and 9 years, and did not have any serious illness or disability. The parents were not previously married and, in the case of the divorced families, the decree of divorce was final. Custodial parents had not remarried at the time of data collection.

The court records of divorces filed in the Middlesex and Norfolk Counties in Massachusetts provided the initial sample of divorced families. Potentially eligible families were identified as those where the parents were physically separated for a period of 2 to 3 years and where the custodial parent resided in Massachusetts. The parent with custody was defined as the one with whom the child resided at least two thirds of the time. Two-parent households were identified through schools and afterschool care programs, and through referrals of participating divorced and nondivorced families. Families who met the initial criteria were recruited through an initial letter and a follow-up telephone call. Of the 51 divorced families who met the criteria for sample selection, 4 declined to participate (1 father-custody and 3 mother-custody) citing as their reasons busy schedules or continued custody litigation. Of the 39 nondivorced families who met sample criteria, 4 declined, citing busy schedules as their reason. Both parents in each family were involved in the study, except in 5 of the divorced families where the noncustodial parent had not been in contact with the child since the divorce or separation.

Family Characteristics

Thirty-seven mother-custody, 10 father-custody and 35 two-parent households participated in the study. The group of 7- to 9-year-old children was composed of 41 boys and 41 girls, with approximately equal numbers of boys and girls in each family type. No significant differences were found among the three types of families on any of the background statistics of parental age, income, education, length or marriage, or length of time passed since the physical separation.

The average age of the target children was 8.25 years. Across families, the average ages of mothers and fathers were 35.5 and 38.1 years respectively, with parents having been married for an average of 10.1 years. At the time of the initial interviews, the divorced parents had been separated for an average of 2.7 years.

Procedures and Measures

The study procedures consisted of individual interviews with both parents, the target child and sibling(s), as well as parent-completed questionnaires, observations of the family at home and in a laboratory setting, observations of the child at play in school and in a laboratory playgroup setting, teachers' ratings of the child's social and academic competence, and standardized assessments of the child's cognitive and social ability and developmental level. The description of these measures is restricted to those that are the focus of the analyses contained in this chapter.

Parent and Child Interviews.   Each of the parents, target child, and siblings participated in separate, 2 to 3-hour interviews conducted by trained graduate students at Tufts University. The interviews for parents consisted of questions about family activities, schedules, childrearing expectations, and discipline methods, interparent and parent–child relationships, marital and separation history, friendship and play patterns, and social and academic competence of children, availability of familial and extrafamilial supports, and expectations for the child and family's future.

The target child was interviewed about daily schedules, family activities, parent–child and interparental relationships, participation in school and play activities, concepts of family, expectations of parents, and their wishes for their family in the future. In addition, a number of standardized measures were administered to each of the children including the Harter's Perceived Competence Scale for Children (Harter, 1982).

Five teams, each comprised of two additional graduate students, independently rated the family using the Family Rating System, 130 ordinal scales developed by Camara (1984) and Hess and Camara (1979). These scales were used to construct the family process composites. Interrater reliability estimates using Spearman's rho coefficient for all of the 82 families ranged from .80 to .93, with an average interrater agreement across scales of .86. Interteam reliability estimates between separate teams that independently rated a subset of the same families, ranged from .56 to 1.0, with an average .87 across all the scales.

Questionnaire and Inventory Manual.   Parents completed the interparental Conflict Inventory and Conflict Resolution Scales as well as standardized measures of the child's functioning, including the Achenbach Child Behavior Checklist (Achenbach & Edelbrock, 1983), Harter's Perceived Competence Scales (Harter, 1982), and Gesten's Health Resources Inventory (Gesten, 1976). Finally, information was obtained on family backgrounds, schedules and routines, and the availability of support services.

The Conflict Resolution Scales instrument (Rands, Levinger, & Mellinger, 1981) was adapted to measure the perceptions of each spouse or former spouse on how conflict or disagreement was handled by the self and by the other and to identify the typical outcomes of such conflicts. Each spouse completed a set of statements that described methods for resolving conflict in terms of how they would do so, and, in terms of what methods their spouse would use. In addition, another set of items asked each spouse to describe the outcome of the conflict. Four major conflict resolution styles (Verbal Attack, Avoid, Compromise, and Physical Anger) and two conflict resolution outcomes (Escalation of Conflict and Increased Intimacy) were produced from a factor analysis of the items. The analyses in this chapter utilized the spouse's report of the other's conflict resolution styles. Table 9.1 depicts the items and the factor loadings for the styles of conflict resolution.

Observations of Children at Play at School. Each child was observed at play during school recess by at least one member of the research team who was unaware of the child's family background. The child's play behaviors were coded at 8-second intervals for 20-minute observation periods using Parten's (1932) Levels of Social Participation scales (revised to reflect play behaviors of 7- to 9-year-old children). In addition, the number and gender of playmates with whom the child was interacting, and instances of hostile physical interaction and positive physical interaction were recorded.

The percentage of total time the child spent in each category of play behavior comprised the main dependent variables. Interobserver reliability was measured by having two observers independently code the play behavior of 77 of the 82 study children. The average percent of agreement between the observers, across all categories of play, was 87%, with none of the percentages falling below an 80% level.

Afterschool Play Groups. Each target child participated in afterschool play sessions with five unacquainted same-sexed peers who met for a 1-hour period for 3 consecutive days. An attempt was made to have each of the family groups represented in each of the playgroups. Two video cameras recorded the children's play and were augmented by separate audio-transmitters that were attached to vests worn by each of the children during the 3-day observation periods. At 5-second intervals, two independent coders, focusing on the play of each child independently, recorded the number of playmates, the type of play material used, cognitive level of play as described by Smilansky (1968) and Parten's level of social participation.

Event sampling was used to record instances of aggressive and prosocial behaviors. Both aggressive verbal (e.g., teasing, name calling, or swearing) and aggressive physical behavior (e.g., pushing, kicking, hitting, and throwing objects) were recorded. Prosocial behavior included helping, sharing, positive verbal statements, and physical expressions of affection.

TABLE 9.1.
Factor Loadings for the Conflict Resolution Scale (*N* = 82 families).

Items	Factor I Attack	Factor II Avoid	Factor III Compromise	Factor IV Phys. Anger
He/she does something to hurt my feelings	.61			
He/she gets really mad and starts yelling	.62			
He/she gets sarcastic	.50			
The more we talk, the madder he/she gets	.71			
He/she gets mad and walks out	.55			
He/she takes a long time to get over feeling mad	.67			
He/she clams up and holds in his/her feelings		.60		
He/she tries to avoid talking about it		.74		
He/she gets cool and distant and gives me the cold shoulder		.48		
He/she comes straight out and tells me how he/she is feeling		− .61		
He/she tries to work out a compromise			.50	
He/she tries to smooth things over			.61	
He/she tries to reason with me			.66	
He/she listens to what I have to say and tries to undertand how I really feel			.72	
He/she does something to let me know he/she really loves me even if we disagree			.51	
He/she really gets mad and strikes me				.95
He/she gets mad and throws things at me				.60

Notes: The fourth factor—physical anger—consists of items that did not significantly load in the Rands, Levinger, & Mellinger (1981) study.
    Factor loadings are based on a Varimax Rotation.

The dependent measures consisted of the percentage of time spent by the child within each behavior category averaged across the 3 days to yield a total composite score for each play behavior. Interrater agreement over the 3 days, for a sample of 40 children, ranged from 80% to 98% with an average of 86%.

Postplaygroup Child Interviews.   After completing the 3 days of playgroups, each of the children viewed selected videotaped episodes of their own play, as well as play episodes from a standard tape of "unfamiliar" children at play. In individual interviews that followed, the children were questioned about their concepts of play behaviors, aggression, and onlooker activity. They were also asked to identify solutions to social play dilemmas presented in the videotapes, and to evaluate the effectiveness of prosocial and aggressive strategies used by children. Interrater reliability estimates, based on the percentages of agreement between the two coders for 30 of the study children, averaged 87% for the generation of aggressive strategies and 88% for the affirmation of aggressive strategies.

Teacher Assessments. The teachers completed a shortened form of the Harter's Perceived Competence Scale, the Achenbach Child Behavior Checklist, and selected scales from the Gesten's Health Resources Inventory in order to further assess the child's academic and social functioning.

Preparation and Reduction of Data

Approximately 70 hours of data were gathered for each of the 82 participating families. In order to reduce the number of variables required for multivariate analysis, and, to increase the explanatory power of each variable, composites were developed using internal consistency analysis. The composite measures represented data gathered from multiple methods, sources, and settings.

Family Process and Child Behavior Composites

The family process composites were developed from items on the Family Rating Scales. Composites measuring two major family processes of interparental conflict and cooperation were used in the analyses presented in this chapter. As described earlier, Interparental Conflict between parents was a measure of the disharmony existing between spouses and former spouses in areas of their relationship separate from their coparental roles. Interparental Cooperation was a measure of the degree of support and cooperation between spouses or former spouses in their coparental roles. The family process composites reflect the reciprocal nature of the interparental relationship assessing separately each parent's perceptions and affective responses to the other. In addition, separate scales were used to assess positive and negative affect expressed by each parent in recognition that parents may simultaneously hold both strong negative and positive feelings toward each other. The description of the scales used in each composite and estimates of internal reliability (Cronbach's alpha) are contained in Table 9.2.

Three scales (from the Family Rating Scales) measuring the frequency and duration of visitation and the frequency of other forms of contact between noncustodial parents and their children were scored from the family interviews with the divorced sample of 47 families.

Child behaviors were treated as dependent variables in the analyses. Five composite variables were constructed to measure Aggression, Prosocial Behavior,

TABLE 9.2
Description of Family Process and Child Behavior Composites

Family Process Composites

INTERPARENTAL COOPERATION (Cronbach's Alpha = .97)
1. Father's support of mother
2. Mother's support of father
3. Father's respect & esteem of mother as a parent
4. Mother's respect & esteem of father as a parent
5. Father's evaluation of mother as a parent
6. Mother's evaluation of father as a parent
7. Exchange of information between parents regarding child
8. Parents working together to solve problems and conflicts concerning childrearing
9. Extent of shared decision making
INTERPARENTAL CONFLICT (Cronbach's Alpha = .94)
1. Positive affect expressed by father toward mother
2. Positive affect expressed by mother toward father
3. Negative affect expressed by father toward mother
4. Negative affect expressed by mother toward father
5. Degree of hostility and anger in underlying atmosphere
6. Stressful or tense conversations between parents
7. Degree of overt conflict and silent tensions currently
CONFLICT RESOLUTION STYLES
1. Father's styles, as reported by the mother on the Conflict Resolution Questionnaire:
    verbal attack
    avoidance
    physical anger
    compromise
2. Mother's styles, as reported by the father on the Conflict Resolution Questionnaire:
    verbal attack
    avoidance
    physical anger
    compromise

Child Behavior Composites

AGGRESSION (Cronbach's Alpha = .61)
1. Externalizing behavior problem subscale of Child Behavior Checklist, mother's report
2. Externalizing behavior problem subscale of Child Behavior Checklist, father's report
3. Total hostile verbal and physical acts of aggression in lab playgroup (over 3 Days)
4. Total acts of instrumental aggression in lab playgroup (over 3 days)
5. Total negative behavior acts in peer play at school
PROSOCIAL BEHAVIOR (Cronbach's Alpha = .67)
1. Proportion of prosocial acts during lab playgroups (3 days)
2. Proportion of positive play behavior during school play
3. Prosocial subscale of Harter's Perceived Competence Scale, mother's report
4. Prosocial subscale of Harter's Perceived Competence Scale, father's report
5. Prosocial subscale of Harter's Perceived Competence Scale, teacher's report
f. Prosocial subscale of Harter's Perceived Competence Scale, child self-report
g. Peer sociability subscale of the Gesten Health Resources Inventory, mother's report
h. Peer sociability subscale of the Gesten Health Resources Inventory, father's report

---

(Continued)

TABLE 9.2

(Continued)

Child Behavior Composites

GENERATION AND AFFIRMATION OF AGGRESSIVE STRATEGIES
(Pearson Product-Moment Correlation = .52, $p < .001$)
a. Ratio of aggressive acts generated by child during postplaygroup interview
b. Ratio of aggressive acts affirmed by child during postplaygroup interview
CHILD'S GENERAL SELF-ESTEEM (Cronbach's Alpha = .67)
1. General competence subscale of Harter's Perceived Competence Scale, mother's report
2. General competence subscale of Harter's Perceived Competence Scale, father's report
3. General competence subscale of Harter's Perceived Competence Scale, teacher's report
4. General competence subscale of Harter's Perceived Competence Scale, child self-report
BEHAVIOR PROBLEMS
Total behavior problem raw score on the Achenbach Child Behavior Checklist as reported by custodial parent or by mother of children in two-parent families

---

Behavioral Problems, General Self-Esteem, and the child's generation and affirmation of Aggressive Strategies to solve social conflicts with peers. The composite-building process consisted of testing interitem consistency using Cronbach's alpha and then summing the Z-score equivalents of the items. A listing of the measures comprising each of the child behavior composites and the estimates of internal reliability (Cronbach's alpha) are included in Table 9.2.

STUDY RESULTS

Comparison of Children in the Three Family Configurations

The first analysis compared outcomes for children from each of the family structures[1] using two-way analyses of variance. Even at 2 to 3 years after the separation of parents, there were significant differences in social behavior among the groups of children. Children from divorced families showed the highest levels of aggression and behavioral problems and the lowest levels of prosocial behavior, general self-esteem. They also had the lowest scores in the generation

---

[1]Because of the small size of the father-custody sample ($n = 10$) relative to the mother-custody and nondivorced samples, three sets of analyses of variance were conducted to detect differences between the father-custody and mother-custody samples. The first analysis used all three family groups while the second analyses combined the two divorced samples to compare the differences between the divorced and the nondivorced group. Finally, only mother-custody and two-parent household groups were included. However, because the results from all analyses were similar, only the comparison of the three groups is reported.

and affirmation of aggressive strategies (Table 9.3).

Most of these analyses also revealed an interaction between family type and the gender of the child. Mother-custody boys and father-custody girls revealed the highest levels of aggression and behavioral problems, and the lowest levels of general self-esteem. They also engaged in fewest instances of prosocial behavior with peers, although this effect only approached significance ($p = .10$). In addition, boys were more likely than girls to generate or affirm aggressive strategies, mother-custody girls were least likely to identify or affirm aggressive strategies whereas boys from two-parent households were most likely to do so.

In the analysis of play behaviors in the school and laboratory settings, there were only two categories that showed significant differences due to family type. Children from divorced families spent more time in associative play in the laboratory setting, compared to children from nondivorced families. In the school setting, children from father-custody homes spent more time in parallel play compared to children from mother-custody or nondivorced families.

Some gender differences also emerged from this analysis. In the laboratory playgroups, boys spent more time in cooperative play and onlooker play than did girls, whereas girls engaged in more parallel play behaviors than did their male peers. In play at school, boys, compared to girls, engaged in more cooperative play. There were no significant interactions between family type and the child's gender in the type of play behaviors in which the children engaged.

An interesting difference emerged in the analysis of children's play with opposite-sexed peers in the school setting. Mother-custody boys and father-custody girls played significantly more often with opposite-sexed peers and in mixed-gender groups of children than did their same-sexed peers from the other family groups. Mother-custody girls spent the least amount of time playing with males or in mixed-gender groups of children and spent the greatest amount of time playing with same-sexed peers, compared with girls from other family types. However, as expected for children in this developmental period, the majority of time for all children was spent playing with same-sexed peers.

Despite differences in the average scores of children from the divorced and nondivorced groups on the behavioral measures, there was a high degree of variability. Some children from divorced families showed higher levels of social competence and fewer behavioral problems than did some of the children in the nondivorced group. The next stage of analysis examined some of the family process factors that might account for the variability in child behaviors.

Analysis of Family Process Factors

The analyses just given revealed a relationship between family type and the child gender in children's play and social behavior. The high variability in scores across families suggests that factors other than family structure may be responsible for the behavior disturbances. Previous literature pointed to marital and family con-

TABLE 9.3
Means of Child Behaviors by Family Type and Child's Gender

	Mother-Custody		Father-Custody		Two-Parent		SIGNIFICANT EFFECTS
	BOYS	GIRLS	BOYS	GIRLS	BOYS	GIRLS	
AGGRESSION	2.55	-.89	-.81	1.17	-1.03	-.72	F, S, FxS
PROSOCIAL	-3.62	.73	-.49	-1.97	.62	3.09	F, S
GENERAL ESTEEM	-2.09	1.00	.79	-2.98	-.06	1.80	F, S, FxS
BEHAVIOR PROBLEMS	45.94	19.94	18.25	27.75	22.61	19.06	F, S, FxS
AGGRESSIVE STRATEGIES	-.11	-1.26	.30	.31	1.02	.26	F, S
SCHOOL PLAY							
Cooperative	39.6	21.0	30.0	25.3	37.0	16.9	S
Associative	21.9	29.4	20.0	36.0	38.4	31.6	
Parallel	1.5	2.3	9.3	13.9	1.6	5.8	F
Solitary	1.4	1.4	5.3	0.0	2.2	2.2	
Onlocker	4.9	4.3	9.4	1.6	4.9	6.7	
Unoccupied	10.7	7.6	7.5	6.5	2.8	7.0	

LAB PLAYGROUPS

Cooperative	67.2	28.5	89.2	23.0	80.5	20.1	S
Associative	31.9	38.4	36.2	25.7	28.4	14.4	F
Parallel	41.3	93.6	41.4	90.7	38.1	108.9	S
Solitary	72.3	47.2	58.8	62.5	64.9	70.2	
Onlooker	15.2	6.9	9.2	12.5	15.4	12.4	S
Unoccupied	36.2	37.0	24.9	43.6	38.0	27.4	
GENDER OF PLAYMATES							
Play with males	65.50	1.43	58.09	7.04	84.63	4.56	FxS
Play with females	1.90	90.28	.68	44.57	.29	59.83	FxS
Mixed-gender play	32.72	8.28	41.23	48.39	15.08	35.62	FxS

Notes: FxS - Significant Family Type by Child's Sex Interaction

    F - Significant Main Effect of Family Type

    S - Significant Main Effect of Child's Sex

All Significance Levels were set at $p < .05$

flict as possible influences (Anthony, 1974; Hess & Camara, 1979; Rutter, 1975). However, most studies have not examined how conflict in the family is managed and whether parents can cooperate in their parental roles, despite the hostility and anger they may feel toward each other as adults.

In our study, parents were asked to identify typical responses to disagreements that occurred between spouses or former spouses. We found that divorced parents were more likely to report that their former spouse used avoidance or verbal attacks during disagreements, whereas nondivorced parents were more likely to report compromise. There were no significant differences between the divorced and nondivorced family groups in parental reports of spousal physical abuse, an item contained in the Expressions of Physical Anger factor. Approximately 11% of the nondivorced and 14% of the divorced families identified incidents of physical attacks made by either spouse on the other.

Although the correlations between conflict styles and the interparental conflict and cooperation composites within divorced families were consistently stronger, the results for both family types were similar (Table 9.4). Parents who

TABLE 9.4

Correlations of Conflict Styles and Outcomes with Interparental Cooperation and Conflict Composites, by Family Type and Parent Report

			DIVORCED FAMILIES		NONDIVORCED FAMILIES	
			Cooperation	Conflict	Cooperation	Conflict
Conflict Resolution Styles						
Verbal Attack	-	Father	-.35‡‡	.48‡‡‡	-.28‡	.31‡
		Mother	-.51‡‡‡	.74‡‡‡	-.01	.16
Avoid	-	Father	-.02	-.05	.05	.28‡
		Mother	-.18	.33‡‡	-.03	.21
Compromise	-	Father	.48‡‡‡	-.48‡‡‡	.28‡	-.45‡‡
		Mother	.54‡‡‡	-.68‡‡‡	-.12	.06
Physical Anger	-	Father	-.22	.28‡	-.25	.27
		Mother	-.28‡	.34‡‡	-.01	-.12
Conflict Resolution Outcomes						
Intimacy	-	Father	.62‡‡‡	-.65‡‡‡	.01	-.11
		Mother	.68‡‡‡	-.68‡‡‡	.06	-.22
Escalation	-	Father	-.60‡‡‡	.54‡‡‡	-.24	.12
		Mother	-.50‡‡‡	.74‡‡‡	.09	-.11

Notes: All correlations report the Pearson Product-Moment Correlation Coefficient (r). Levels of significance are summarized as follows:
    ‡   indicates correlation is significant at $p < .05$
    ‡‡   indicates correlation is significant at $p < .01$
    ‡‡‡ indicates correlation is significant at $p < .001$
The conflict resolution style variables were comprised of each spouse's frequency of using the conflict resolution style, as reported by the other spouse. The conflict resolution outcome measures were based on each spouse's perceptions of the outcome from conflict.

reported their spouses using verbal attack, avoidance, or physical anger in resolving disagreements tended to have lower levels of interparental cooperation and higher levels of interparental conflict, and the outcome of disagreements, as reported by these parents, is more likely to be an escalation of conflict. Compromise strategies for resolving disagreements were associated with a lower degree of interparental conflict and a higher degree of interparental cooperation, and outcomes leading to greater closeness between the two adults.

The correlations support the importance of separating the assessment of parental issues from marital issues when studying the relationship between divorced spouses. Parents who are able to use compromise in resolving conflicts are more likely to cooperate on parental issues, despite disagreements in other spheres of their lives. Divorced spouses who display negative styles for resolving conflict, such as verbal attack, avoidance, and physical anger, are more likely to show increased escalation of the conflict, thereby reducing their chances of reaching agreement on parental issues.

The Relationship of Family Structure and Family Process to Children's Social Behavior

A series of stepwise regression analyses were conducted to determine the relative contribution of family structure, child's gender, interparental conflict, cooperation, and parental conflict resolution styles as predictors of child social behavior (see Table 9.5). It should be noted that the regression analyses alone cannot provide complete information about the nature and direction of the effects, especially when there are two or more significant predictors for a single dependent variable. We do not know whether the predictors act interactively or additively to explain the variance in the dependent measure. In these cases, simple correlations among the significant predictors were computed to clarify the regression results.

In general, the strong interaction between family type and child gender reported earlier emerged in these regression analyses and, in combination with cooperation and parental conflict resolution styles, explained a significant amount of variance in the children's behavior. As well, it would appear that the father's styles of conflict resolution are more predictive of the child's social behavior than are the mother's (based on spousal reports). Approximately 15% to 47% of the total variance in children's behavior was predicted by these factors.

The regression results indicated that interparental conflict was not significantly related to any of the dependent measures. Interparental cooperation was related to children's aggressiveness, but did not emerge as a significant predictor of the other dependent measures. Children in families with higher levels of interparental cooperation showed less aggressive behavior. In addition, family configuration alone (divorce vs. nondivorced) did not explain a great deal of the variance in children's behavior. The regression analyses revealed that child gender

TABLE 9.5
Stepwise Regression of Family Structure, Child's Gender, Family Process Variables on Child Behavior Scores

| DEPENDENTS | FAMILY STRUCT | CHILD'S GENDER | FATHER'S CONFLICT STYLE | | | | | | MOTHER'S CONFLICT STYLE | | | | TOTAL VARIANCE EXPLAINED |
| | | | CONFLT | COOP | VERBAL ATTACKS | AVOIDS | PHYS. ANGER | COMPROM | VERBAL ATTACKS | AVOIDS | PHYS. ANGER | COMPROM | |
	Beta	Beta	Beta	Beta	Beta	Beta	Beta	Beta	Beta	Beta	Beta	Beta	Pct.
Aggression	−.03	.16	−.09	−.31‡‡	.06	.04	−.05	.07	.11	−.04	−.04	−.16	10%
Prosocial	.21	−.34‡‡‡	−.15	.14	−.39‡‡‡	.06	−.04	.12	.04	.02	−.06	.07	27%
General Esteem	.11	−.32‡‡	.05	.01	−.33‡‡‡	.03	.04	.08	.03	.08	−.16	.15	20%
Behavioral Problems	−.09	.29‡‡	.07	−.11	.31‡‡	.01	−.06	.22	.06	.09	.01	−.10	18%
Aggressive Strategies	.45‡‡‡	.25‡	−.06	−.25	.05	.11	−.13	−.25‡	.05	.13	−.01	−.02	21%
SCHOOL PLAY													
Cooperative Associative	−.04	.23‡	.08	−.09	−.01	−.06	.02	−.04	.02	−.001	.11	−.18	5%

—NO VARIABLES WERE ENTERED—

LABORATORY PLAYGROUPS

Cooperative	−.16	.49‡‡‡	.08	.06	−.20‡	−.03	−.01	−.01	−.04	.04	.03	−.09	29%
Associative	−.27‡	.09	.06	−.05	.04	.10	−.20	−.12	−.05	.02	−.14	−.03	7%
Parallel	.21‡	−.63‡‡‡	−.10	−.23	.11	−.10	.12	.01	.29‡‡	.10	−.13	−.03	47%
Solitary	.02	.06	−.03	−.01	.10	.17	.26‡	−.05	−.02	−.27‡‡	.10	.16	14%
Onlooker	−.02	.22‡	.02	.13	−.34‡‡	.38‡‡‡	−.10	.11	−.09	.02	−.12	.05	21%
Unoccupied	—NO VARIABLES WERE ENTERED—												

Notes:

For the regression analysis, divorced families were coded 0 and the nondivorced families were coded 1.

Child's gender was entered as two separate binary (0 or 1) variables. Only the variable in which boys were coded 1 are reported in this table, as the variable in which girls were coded as 1 was not a significant predictor in any of the regressions.

The percentage of variance explained was determined by calculating the R Square for the *final set* of predictors that entered the stepwise regression.

Where 'no variables were entered,' none of the predictor variables explained a significant amount of variance (using a criterion level of $p < .05$).

Significance levels: ‡ indicates $p < .05$; ‡‡ indicates $p < .01$; and ‡‡‡ indicates $p < .001$.

and parental conflict resolution styles were the important predictors of the child's social functioning.

The results indicated no interaction between child's gender and father's conflict resolution styles, but rather, an additive effect of the two factors in explaining variation in children's levels of prosocial behavior, self-esteem, and behavioral problems. Children whose fathers used verbal attack in attempting to resolve conflicts in the family displayed lower levels of prosocial behavior, lower self-esteem, and showed more behavioral problems. Although both boys and girls were similarly affected in their prosocial behavior, self-esteem, and behavioral problems, girls overall exhibited higher levels of prosocial behavior and self-esteem, and fewer behavioral problems.

Children's generation and affirmation of aggressive strategies was predicted by family type, child's gender, and father's use of compromise to resolve conflicts. Subsequent intercorrelations revealed that boys in two-parent households where father used compromise to resolve conflicts were least likely to generate or affirm aggressive strategies.

The father's style of conflict resolution also appeared to differentially affect some social behaviors of boys and girls in the laboratory playgroup setting. In families in which fathers employed verbal attack to resolve conflict, boys were most likely to display reduced cooperative play, whereas girls were more likely to show lower levels of onlooker behavior during peer play. Conversely, boys' levels of onlooker behavior and girls' levels of cooperative play were not affected by the father's attack style. Finally, fathers who used compromise to resolve conflict were more likely to have children who exhibited lower levels of unoccupied behavior during school play, regardless of the child's gender or the family configuration.

The mother's conflict styles also predicted variance in the children's aggressive behavior, albeit to a lesser extent. In contrast to the father's conflict resolution styles, there was no relationship between mother's use of verbal attack and the children's social behavior. The only exception was in the child's parallel play with peers in the laboratory setting, where children whose mothers used verbal attack to resolve conflict displayed higher levels of parallel play. In this relationship, the contribution of child's gender primarily indicated that girls tended to have higher levels of parallel play than did boys. However, the relationship between parallel play and mother's use of verbal attack was significant for both genders.

As well, mother's use of avoidance and father's use of physical anger to resolve conflicts were related to children's levels of solitary play in the laboratory setting. Regardless of the child's gender or family configuration, families where fathers used physical anger during conflict resolution were more likely to have children who showed higher levels of solitary play. As well, families where mothers used avoidance to resolve conflict were more likely to have children who showed lower levels of solitary play. Thus, the father's use of physically expressed anger toward the mother or toward objects was positively correlated with the solitary play of children, whereas the mother's use of avoidance was negatively associated with this play behavior.

In general, the regression results supported the importance of the child's gender as a moderating factor in explaining the relationship between the family process variables and the child's social functioning. Subsequent t tests confirmed that these differences could not be explained by one gender being exposed to more parental attack, avoidance, compromise, or abuse than the other gender. The regression results also revealed that the overall amount of interparental conflict was not predictive of the child's social functioning. Thus, the social functioning of children from both divorced and nondivorced families appears to be related to how spouses, or former spouses, manage or regulate conflict and whether they can work together in a cooperative relationship as parents. It should be noted that the comparison of the two types of divorced families (mother-custody vs. father-custody) could not be analyzed in the regression results because of the few cases in the father-custody sample. However, there were few instances in which family type was a significant predictor of the child's social functioning, especially when interparental cooperation or the parent's conflict resolution styles were included in the analysis.

Variations in Interparental Relationships in Postdivorce Families

In our analyses of interparental conflict and cooperation, it was found that cooperation between parents was a significant predictor in both family groups for some of the child social competence measures. Cooperative strategies that enable parents to move beyond anger and to reconstruct their relationship to each other as parents may provide important clues to healthy postdivorce functioning.

To describe the typical patterns of cooperation and conflict in families, four family typologies were constructed using a double median split procedure. The median values for divorced families on the Interparental Cooperation and Conflict composites were used to classify the families into high or low groups. Four sets of families were produced by this procedure: high conflict and low cooperation; low conflict and high cooperation; high conflict and high cooperation; and low conflict and low cooperation (see Fig. 9.1).

Although it was expected that the majority of postdivorce families would belong to either the high conflict/low cooperation or low conflict/high cooperation categories, a significant number of families (32%) were classified into the other groups. Interestingly, among the four groups there were no significant differences in parental reports of the level of conflict present before and during the time of separation. Thus, parents reporting high levels of conflict at the time of separation were as likely to appear 2 years later in the low conflict groups as in high conflict groups. A closer examination of these families characterized by

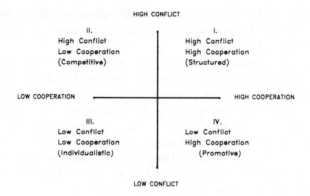

FIG. 9.1.   Interparental conflict and cooperation

varying levels of conflict and cooperation was conducted through a qualitative analysis of interview data obtained from these families.

Low Conflict/High Cooperation Families
(Promotive Families)

The postdivorce relationship of these parents could best be described as "friendly" with an absence of accusation, recrimination, and ongoing battles. Children maintained a good relationship with the noncustodial parent with full cooperation of the custodial parent. Spouses expressed respect and esteem toward each other as parents, and shared jointly in decision making concerning their child. Although these parents seemed to genuinely like each other as persons, they felt that they could not have remained married.

Visitation arrangements between the child and the noncustodial parent were generally agreed upon by parents, and not court ordered, and parents were flexible in scheduling. The children usually had free access to both parents, and the noncustodial parent could spontaneously arrange contacts.

Parents discussed mutual concerns about the child, ranging from more serious concerns relating to child health or school problems to those that were related to such daily, general issues related to the rearing of children as bedtime schedule changes, helping with homework, and considering requests for field trips. They typically discussed in advance the types of presents they were planning to buy their children and sometimes even pooled their resources to purchase gifts together. Respect was expressed for the roles each parent played in their children's lives, and, in the interviews they noted how much the child loved the other parent. Although some disagreements still occurred, these parents seemed to make a deliberate effort to support each other's decisions.

Compared to other groups of parents, these parents were also more likely to discuss their own personal concerns, such as job pressures, difficulties with co-workers, career goals, education, and even relationships with new partners. They expressed concern about each other as parents and as individuals, recognized each other's limits and strengths, and talked openly about the dissatisfaction they had felt as a married couple. Most of these parents felt that their relationship with each other had improved since the divorce.

High Conflict/High Cooperation Families
(Structured Families)

Parents in this group remained bitter toward each other as persons, and were frequently unable to forgive each other for past hurts stemming from such experiences as extramarital affairs and physical expressions of anger. They expressed dislike for each other in their adult relationships. However, active attempts were made to communicate around child-centered issues. Discussions between parents were limited to child-oriented concerns. Parents said that they tried to avoid topics of conflict, and when there was a potential disagreement, the issue was discussed during agreed-upon times when the child was not present. Most of these parents said that they refused to talk to each other about issues not related to the children.

Agreements between parents in this group were highly structured and ritualized. For example, visitation schedules were clearly spelled out and strictly adhered to. When asked whether the other parent would accomodate to changes, these parents said that it was such a hassle to change plans that they generally tried not to make changes. The noncustodial parent usually arrived on time as planned and gave advance notice if a change was needed. In one family, at least 2 week's notice was required to alter plans for visitation.

These families were characterized by each parent's commitment to their shared childrearing roles. Although business-like in their conferences about the children, they reported that they tried not to denigrate each other as parents. These parents actively attempted to separate adult and parental relationships. Although they expressed concerns about their own relationship to each other, they admitted the competence of the other as a parent. Frequently, divergent stories emerged about their experiences with each other as spouses or as divorced spouses, but the descriptions they offered of child-related incidents tended to converge, providing evidence of their communication with each other as parents.

High Conflict/Low Cooperation Families
(Competitive Families)

These parents remained enmeshed in their anger and engaged in a pattern of destructive conflict, marked by endless and inconclusive arguments. Former spouses sometimes seemed to derive psychological gratification from the continued fighting. These parents were openly critical of each other as parents and as persons. Families in which violent physical arguments took place prior to separation reported continued violent episodes, with attempts made to physically hurt the other. In some cases, more subtle attempts were made to "get back" at the ex-spouse. The anger continued to be a significant part of the relationship, and led to increased bitterness and estrangement. Many of the arguments centered on the children, the remaining link between these divorced parents. A small percentage of the parents expressed fear for their children's safety when they were in the other parent's company.

These parents did not share information with each other about their child, even when this information involved changes in visitation or contact. They were quick to criticize each other as parents, each other's discipline methods, even gifts bought for the children, and they freely shared their criticisms of each other with the children. Each spouse's descriptions of episodes in which disagreements and conflict occurred were typically contradictory. Many of these parents seemed to be engaged in what Freud has called, the "narcissism of small differences." There was bickering and squabbling over even the smallest issues related to the child (for example, differences of less than 30 minutes in the scheduling of bedtimes at each household).

Disagreements and intense arguing frequently occurred when noncustodial parents came to pick up or return the children. Contact between the noncustodial parent and child was nearly always court ordered in this group, and attempts to increase the amount of contact were ignored or denied by the custodial parent. The noncustodial parents were overwhelmingly dissatisifed with the visitation and custodial arrangements and shared their hopes for the future when their children were older and would decide to live with them.

Low Conflict/Low Cooperation (Individualistic Families)

Parents in this group were characterized by an "autistic" pattern of postdivorce interparental relations. Parents avoided each other physically and emotionally, so that overt conflict or even mild disagreements would not occur. These parents generally discussed little, if anything, about their children, and discussed nothing about their own personal lives. Contact between the two adults was limited and the custodial parent in each of these families made all decisions with regard to the child. When there was a disagreement between the custodial and noncustodial parent, the custodial parent asserted his or her authority and the other parent usually acquiesced.

Many of the parents in this group expressed the wish that there would be no contact, but because contact was court ordered, it was "out of their hands." In a few cases, the fathers or mothers had terminated contact with the children, as well as with their former spouse. Unfortunately, parents' avoidance of each other in these families resulted in a poor exchange of information regarding the child and frequently left the noncustodial parent unaware of important events and crises in his or her children's lives.

Relationship of Conflict and Cooperation
to Contact Between Noncustodial Parent and the Child

Interparental conflict was not significantly related to the frequency of visits or to the frequency of other forms of contact between noncustodial parents in mother-custody and father-custody families. However, it was significantly associated with the duration of visits between noncustodial mothers and their children ($r = -.58$, $p < .05$) and noncustodial fathers and their children, although this finding only approached significance ($r = -.22, p < .10$). In both family types, visits were shorter compared to those in families with low levels of conflict.

There were no differences in the frequency of visits or other forms of contact according to child gender. However, noncustodial parents of girls did contact their daughters slightly more often than did the noncustodial parents of sons (contact averaging once a week or every other week compared to once a month or once every 3 weeks). Noncustodial fathers had significantly more contact with their children than did noncustodial mothers (Spearman's rho $= -.30, p < .05$).

The amount of interparental cooperation was significantly related to all of the noncustodial parent measures. Noncustodial parents who had a cooperative relationship with their former spouses were likely to visit their children more frequently ($r = .47$, $p < .001$), have more frequent telephone calls and correspondence ($r = .52, p < .001$), and the visits lasted for longer periods of time ($r = .55, p < .001$). They were also more likely to have their children stay with them for weekends or extended lengths of time.

DISCUSSION

This study examined the consequences of divorce on children's social development 2 years following the event. The study also identified aspects of family processes that may act to moderate the negative effects of divorce on children. The study was designed to alleviate some major methodological problems cited in the literature (Emery, 1982; Emery, Hetherington, & DiLalla, 1984). The divorced and nondivorced families were carefully matched and the potential bias from using clinic or self-selected samples was eliminated. The measures and composite-building reflect data collected from a variety of sources and settings using multiple strategies for data collection.

Children from divorced families displayed reduced levels of social functioning, as evidenced by lower prosocial and positive interactions with peers, and lower levels of general self-esteem. These children were more aggressive, had more behavioral problems, and were more likely to engage in non-affiliative behavior during peer play. However, family type, child's gender, or the overall amount of interparental conflict was not able to account for the negative behaviors of children in the divorced families.

The degree of interparental cooperation in the postdivorce period, as well as the conflict resolution styles used by each spouse to regulate disagreements, appear to be important factors that determine the children's psychosocial adjust-ment 2 years following the divorce. Children in families in which the former spouses were able to cooperate around parental issues, despite continued animosity in other areas of their relationship, were likely to show less aggression and fewer behavior problems. Fathers who used verbal attacks to resolve conflict were more likely to have children who showed less prosocial behavior, lower levels of general self-esteem, and more behavioral problems. Mothers who used compromise to settle disputes were more likely to have children who displayed higher levels of general self-esteem.

Gender differences in the findings replicate those found in earlier studies (Fur-stenberg & Zill, 1984; Hetherington, Cox, & Cox, 1982; Santrock & Warshak, 1979). Boys from mother-custody homes and girls from father-custody homes showed the lowest levels of prosocial behavior and general self-esteem, and dis-played the highest levels of aggression and behavioral problems. The data con-cerning conflict resolution styles support a modeling explanation because fathers employed the verbal attack style more often than did mothers, and, the father's use of verbal attack predicted children's behavioral problems and aggressiveness. Perhaps, children in highly conflicted divorced families model their father's ag-gressive behaviors as a method for resolving peer conflicts.

A further explanation of the gender differences among children in the two cus-todial arrangements may be that children who lack acceptance by peers may ex-perience greater frustration or anger, and as a result, display higher levels of aggression and lower self-esteem. The study found reduced involvement by mother-custody boys and father-custody girls in affiliative behaviors with same-sexed peers in laboratory playgroups and in school settings. These children also were more likely to play with opposite-sexed peers than their peers in the other family groups, which supports earlier studies (Hetherington et al., 1982). Boys in mother-custody homes may adopt more typically feminine interactional styles that when used in play with same-sexed peers, leads to the child's ostracism or ridicule. Similarly, girls from father-custody families may engage in more mas-culine styles of interaction, such as greater use of aggression to resolve conflicts, which will lead to their alienation from same-sexed peer groups. Children dur-ing the latency age may be especially vulnerable to problems in peer relations and self-esteem because, according to Erikson (1968) the child is engaged in the struggle between industry and inferiority.

One of the difficulties in making conclusions about father-custody girls is the small sample size and the high degree of variability within this subsample. Even though the proportion of father-custody families used in this study overrepresents the population of male-headed, single-parent families in the United States, the absolute number of cases limits the statistical power. It is also important to note that the reasons for the awarding of custody to fathers are different from those used in awarding custody to mother. Fathers receiving custody either choose to assume the traditional role of primary caregiver, whereas their ex-spouses are willing to play a less significant role in their children's lives, or, the mothers have been declared unfit as parents. Nevertheless, it is interesting that a number of studies (Furstenberg & Zill, 1984; Santrock & Warshak, 1979), all having relatively small samples of father-custody families, found identical effects among children in the custody of the opposite-sexed parent.

The analyses reported in this chapter document the contribution of one family subsystem to the child's adjustment following divorce. The interparental or spousal subsystem was measured via the interparental cooperation and conflict composites. The analysis of an additional subsystem in the family, namely the parent–child subsystem, (see Camara and Resnick, 1987) broadens our understanding of family process by specifying the contribution of the quality of mother–child and father–child relationships to child behavior. Furthermore, the interaction between these two subsystems offers a more integrated systems perspective in analyzing the postdivorce family.

The study results suggest that interventions with families should not be focused on the eradication of conflict because some conflict is an inevitable element of family life. As Deutsch (1973) pointed out, there can be positive conflict, which will lead to respect for the other's perspective and the ability to cooperate despite differences. Positive conflict resolution may produce a higher level of cooperation around joint parental issues and a reduction in dysfunctional family interactions. In the long run, interventions directed toward assisting parents to resolve conflict in more productive ways will be in the best interests of parents and children.

ACKNOWLEDGMENTS

The research reported here was supported by a grant from the National Institute of Mental Health (5R01MH3571-03) and by a small supplementary grant from the Biomedical Research Awards Program, Tufts University.

We acknowledge with thanks the participation of Wendy Boynton, Janet Milley, Kevin Brennan, Cheryl Burgoyne-Perreault, and Ada Pollock in the various phases of data collection and processing.

REFERENCES

Achenbach, T. M., & Edelbrock, C. S. (1983). *Manual for the Child Behavior Checklist and the Revised Child Behavior Profile*. Burlington: University of Vermont.

Ahrons, C. R. (1981). The continuing coparental relationship between divorced spouses. *American Journal of Orthopsychiatry*, *51*(3), 416–428.

Anthony, E. J. (1974). Children at risk from divorce: A review. In E. J. Anthony & C. Koupernick (Eds.), *The child in his family* (Vol. 3, pp. 461–478). New York: Wiley.

Bohannan, P. (Ed.). (1971). *Divorce and after*. New York: Anchor Books.

Camara, K. A. (1981). Children of divorce: *Cognitive and social functioning* (Grant No. 5R01MH35751-03), Bethesda, MD: Department of Health and Human Services, National Institute of Mental Health.

Camara, K. A. (1984, March). *Children of conflict*. Paper presented at the Flowerree Mardi Gras Symposium, Tulane University, New Orleans.

Camara, K. A. (1985, May). *Patterns of conflict and cooperation in divorced and non-divorced families*. Paper presented at a meeting of the National Institutes of Health, Washington, DC.

Camara, K. A., & Resnick, G. (1987). Marital and parental subsystems in mother-custody, father-custody, and two-parent households: Effects on children's social development. In J. Vincent (Ed.), *Advances in family intervention, assessment and theory* (Vol. 4, pp. 165-196). Greenwich, CT: JAI Press.

Deutsch, M. (1969). Conflicts: productive or destructive. *Journal of Social Issues, 25*(1), 7-41.

Deutsch, M. (1973). *The resolution of conflict: Constructive and destructive processes*. New Haven, CT: Yale University Press.

Emde, R. N., & Easterbrooks, M. A. (1985). Assessing emotional availability in early development. In W. K. Frankenburg, R. N. Emde, & J. Sullivan (Eds.), *Early identification of children at risk: An international perspective* (pp. 79-101). New York: Plenum.

Emery, R. E. (1982). Interparental conflict and the children of discord and divorce. *Psychological Bulletin, 92*(2). 310-330.

Emery, R. E., Hetherington, E. M., & DiLalla, L. F. (1984). Divorce, children and social policy. In H. W. Stevenson & A. E. Siegel (Eds.) *Child development research and social policy* (Vol. 1, pp. 189-266). Chicago: University of Chicago Press.

Erickson, E. (1968). *Identity: Youth and crisis*. New York: Norton.

Furstenberg, F. F., & Zill, N. (1984). *A national longitudinal study of marital disruption . Synopsis*. Washington, DC: Child Trends Inc.

Gesten, E. L. (1976). A health resources inventory: The development of a measure of the personal and social competence of primary-grade children. *Journal of Consulting and Clinical Psychology, 44*(5), 775-786.

Harter, S. (1982). The perceived competence scale for children. *Child Development, 53*, 87-97.

Hess, R. D., & Camara, K. A. (1979). Post-divorce relationships as mediating factors in the consequences of divorce for children. *Journal of Social Issues, 35*(4), 79-96.

Hetherington, E. M., Cox, M., & Cox, R. (1982). Effects of divorce on parents and children. In M. Lamb (Ed.), *Nontraditional families* (pp. 233-288). Hillsdale, NJ: Lawrence Erlbaum Associates.

Minuchin, S. (1974). *Families and family therapy*. Cambridge, MA: Harvard University Press.

Minuchin, S., & Fishman, C. (1981). *Family therapy techniques*. Cambridge, MA: Harvard University Press.

Minuchin, S., Baker, L., Rosman, B. L., Liebman, R., Milmar, L., & Todd, T. G. (1975). A conceptual model of psychosomatic illness in children: Family organization and family therapy. *Archives of General Psychiatry, 39*, 226-293.

Minuchin, P. (1985). Families and individual development: Provocations from the field of family therapy. *Child Development, 56*, 289-302.

Oltmans, T. F., Broderick, J. E., & O'Leary, K. D. (1977). Marital adjustment and the efficacy of behavior therapy with children. *Journal of Consulting and Clinical Psychology, 45*, 724-729.

Parten, M. (1932). Social play among preschool children. *Journal of Abnormal and Social Psychology, 27*, 243-269.

Porter, B., & O'Leary, K. D. (1980). Marital discord and child behavior problems. *Journal of Abnormal Child Psychology, 8*(3), 287-295.

Rands, M., Levinger, G., & Mellinger, G. D. (1981). Patterns of conflict resolution and marital satisfaction. *Journal of Family Issues, 2*(3), 297-321.

Rutter, M. (1971). Parent-child separation: Psychological effects on the children. *Journal of Child Psychology and Psychiatry, 12*, 233-260.

Rutter, M. (1975). *Helping troubled children*. New York: Plenum.

Rutter, M., Yule, B., Quinton, D., Rowlands, O., Yule, W., & Berger, M. (1974). Attainment and adjustment in two geographic areas: III. Some factors accounting for area differences. *British Journal of Psychiatry, 125*, 520–533.

Santrock, J. W., & Warshak, R. A. (1979). Father custody and social development in boys and girls. *Journal of Social Issues, 35*(4), 112–125.

Smilansky, S. (1968). *The effects of socio-dramatic play on disadvantaged preschool children*. New York: Wiley.

Wallerstein, J. S., & Kelly, J. B. (1980). *Surviving the breakup: How children actually cope with divorce*. New York: Basic.

10

Children of Divorce:
A 10-Year Study

Judith S. Wallerstein
Shauna B. Corbin
Julia M. Lewis
Center for the Family in Transition
Corte Madera, CA

Long-term outcome of psychological trauma in childhood is inevitably difficult to trace or to identify. Many complexly interacting factors shape the lives of children, and the conceptual and methodological problems in studying any single factor or set of factors are formidable. Moreover, we have in recent years become increasingly aware of the enduring effects of psychic trauma, and that these effects may not be visible immediately or in subsequent specific behaviors or symptoms, but may forever shatter the individual's guiding conception of the world as relatively safe and reliable (Horowitz, 1976; Terr, 1983).

Theoretical issues include the lack of clarity regarding expectable continuity and discontinuity in development; perplexing individual differences and wide variation in immediate and subsequent response to what appear to be similar experiences; methodological issues of cohort problems and the confounding fact that psychological configurations discerned at any cross-sectional vantage point inevitably highlight that which is most salient at that developmental stage and may obscure patterns of behavior that become prominent at a subsequent stage. Thus, observations about children of divorce at the point of their entry into young adulthood differ significantly from observations of the same group during mid-adolescence.

Beyond the broad considerations that attach to all longitudinal investigations, the study of divorce and its long-range consequences for children within the post-divorce or remarried family poses special problems. For divorce, as we have finally recognized, is not a single circumscribed event, but a multistage process of radically changing family relationships. This process begins in the failing marriage, sometimes many years prior to the marital breakdown, may include one or more separations within the marriage, and extends over years following the decisive separation and the legal divorce.

197

Many families experience not only extended instability in family functioning, but discontinuity in their physical and social environment as well. A goodly number face major decline in their social and economic circumstances, and diminished educational opportunities for their children (Wallerstein & Corbin, 1986; Weitzman, 1985). The remarriage of one or both parents introduces a whole new set of critical factors that once again radically alters relationships and circumstances within the family.

Each of these changes in and outside of the family takes on meaning for the child within the overall context of the divorce. Altogether, these changes impose psychological tasks upon the child that represent notable additions to the usual tasks of growing up in our society. For the child, the necessary readjustments are likely, from our observations, to stretch out over the years of childhood and adolescence (Wallerstein, 1983a, 1983b). For the adult, the divorce also presents a formidable set of new tasks that must be addressed, and that cannot be deferred without unfortunate, even tragic, consequences for themselves and for the children in their care (Wallerstein, 1985d, 1986b).

A second special issue, one that is not usually remarked but that is critical in identifying the distinctive attributes of a divorce population, is that divorce and its sequelae are much more than the condition of a particular divorced family. Assessment of the differential impact of divorce on any population has been rendered infinitely more difficult by the profound impact of the divorce phenomenon on patterns of courtship, marriage, and the family in society as a whole. The high incidence of divorce has significantly raised levels of anxiety in relationships between men and women and, in many observed instances, between children and their parents, whether or not they themselves come from divorced families. There are few, if any, intact families in our society that have not been touched and changed by the high incidence of divorce.

It is within the framework of such considerations concerning the complexly interlocking factors that must be taken into account when delineating the divorce experience over time, that the perceived experiences of the children of divorce and their parents were selected as the *initial* point of entry for the study at the 10-year follow-up. Observations regarding these experiences comprise the data of three preliminary papers that are reported in this chapter.

INITIAL GOALS

The California Children of Divorce Project began in 1971, as one of the earliest psychological studies in the field.[1] The main goals of the study were (a) to exa-

---

[1]Judith Wallerstein was principal investigator and Joan Berlin Kelly was co-principal investigator from 1971–1980, during the initial assessment and the first and second follow-up phases. Dr. Kelly left the study after the publication of the 5-year follow-up.

mine the experiences and responses of children and adolescents at the decisive separation and during the immediate and long-term aftermath; (b) to trace the vicissitudes of the parent–child relationships over the same time period; (c) to examine the experiences and responses of the parents; and, finally, (d) to elucidate factors related to course, to continuity and change, and to good and poor outcome.

The investigation was longitudinal in design, and initial family contacts occurred within the first year following marital separation, with follow-up contacts conducted at 18 months, 5 years, and 10 years postseparation.

Full reports from the initial assessment, the first-year follow-up and the 5-year follow-up have already been published in numerous articles within the professional literature, beginning in 1974 (Kelly, 1981, 1982a, 1982b; Kelly & Wallerstein, 1976, 1977a, 1977b, 1979; Wallerstein, 1974, 1977a, 1977b, 1980a, 1980b, 1980c, 1981, 1983c, 1984a; Wallerstein & Huntington, 1983; Wallerstein & Kelly, 1974, 1975, 1976, 1977, 1979a, 1979b, 1980a, 1980b, 1982). A book, *Surviving the Breakup: How Children and Parents Cope With Divorce* (Wallerstein & Kelly, 1980c), summarized the major findings. The present investigation deals with the same population at the 10-year mark. Several preliminary papers have been issued (Wallerstein, 1983b, 1984b, 1985b, 1985c, 1985d, 1986a, 1986b; Wallerstein & Corbin, 1986) but the full analysis of the data is still in progress.

RESEARCH SAMPLE

To review briefly the population of the project at its inception: In 1971, each of 131 children and adolescents from 60 families, together with their parents, were studied intensively during a 6-week period near the time of the marital separation (Wallerstein & Kelly, 1980c). Each family member was reexamined at 18 months postseparation, and once again at 5 years postseparation. The 131 children were divided almost equally between male and female (48% boys, 52% girls). Slightly more than half were 8 years old or less, 47% were between 9 and 18 years old. Fifty-nine mothers and 47 fathers were interviewed initially.

At the 18-month mark, contact was reestablished with 58 of the original 60 families. Because two couples had been reconciled in the intervening year, and two other families declined to participate or could not be located, the first follow-up population included 56 families, with data derived from interviews with 41 fathers, 53 mothers, and 108 children. Forty-five percent of the returning youngsters were boys, 55% were girls.

At the 5-year mark, contact was again established with 58 of the original families. The sample for whom there were extended interviews supplying sufficient data to permit a full psychological and social assessment, consisted of 96 children from 56 families. Fifty-four mothers and 41 fathers were interviewed at the 5-year mark.

At the 10-year mark, 54 (90%) of the original 60 families were located, and members in 52 families (87%) were interviewed. Of the children, 110 were interviewed directly, and extensive data regarding another 6 were obtained from family members, surpassing the numbers reached at the 5-year mark. Of all the children reached, 113 met the criteria for inclusion in the analysis. These included 50 male and 63 female subjects, seen over the 2-year period, 1981-1983. Of the adults, 47 women and 36 men met the criteria for full inclusion in the analysis.[2] The mean length of time since the separation was 10.9 years with a range of 9.6–13.1 years.

It is important to note that the children were screened initially for chronic psychological problems. Prior to the family rupture, all of the children in the study had reached appropriate developmental milestones in the view of their parents and teachers. They were performing at age-appropriate levels within the school. Children who had ever been referred for psychological or psychiatric treatment were excluded from the study. The sample probably represented young people skewed in the direction of psychological health, because they had been able, by all accounts, to maintain their developmental pace within the failing marriage.

Demographics of the Original Sample

The average age of the men at separation was 36.9; the mean age of the women was 34.1. Couples had been married an average of 11.1 years prior to the decisive separation and averaged 2.2 children per family.

They were a well-educated group. One quarter of the men held advanced degrees in medicine, law, or business administration. One third of the women had earned a college degree, with some few holding graduate degrees. Only 18% of men and 24% of women had terminated their education with a high school diploma.

In their initial socioeconomic distribution, the families reflected the population of the suburban Northern California county in which they resided. The families were largely, but not entirely, within the middle-class range. Of the original 60 families, 88% were White, 3% were Black, and 9% were interracial, with one Asian spouse. The distribution of the families along social class dimensions was determined using the Hollingshead Two Factor Index of Social Position (Hollingshead, 1957). Forty-three percent of families fell into the two highest categories, 28% ranked in the middle category, and another 28% ranked at the two lowest levels.

---

[2]Analysis of the families who were lost to follow-up at the 18-month and 5-year mark indicates that these families did not differ from the population that remained in the study in their race or socioeconomic status, or along psychological dimensions that we were able to ascertain. However, the families lost to follow-up at the 10-year mark did differ somewhat from those in the sample, in the lower socioeconomic status and greater psychological instability of the adults. Two families, with a total of 5 children, reconciled and therefore were excluded from the analysis at each of the follow-up points.

The Population at 10 Years

The socioeconomic differences between men and women at the 10-year mark were less pronounced than those observed at the 18-month and 5-year marks, when we reported a precipitous economic decline for 60% of the women and a drop in the standard of living for the majority of the women and children. By the 10-year mark, 40% of the women and 50% of the men belonged in the two highest categories of the 5-level Hollingshead scale. Women still outnumbered men significantly in the two lowest categories, where 30% of the women were ranked, as compared with 17% of the men.

At 10 years, 42 women and 46 men were employed. With respect to type of employment, equal proportions (42%) were classified as professionals, although it is significant that, whereas the professional men were physicians, attorneys, and business executives, only one woman was a physician. The majority of female professionals were in fields such as teaching, nursing, or the arts, reflecting a substantial difference in both social status and income. One quarter of the women and somewhat less than one fifth of the men were experiencing grave financial difficulties.

Geographic Stability

Our ability to locate the children after a lapse of so many years was unexpectedly aided by the finding that 41% continued to reside in the county in which the initial study was done. An additional 36% moved out of the immediate geographical area to neighboring San Francisco Bay Area counties or elsewhere within the state, so that 77% of the young people in the study had remained in California. Of the remainder, half now live in neighboring states. None are living outside of the country. Overall, this represents an unanticipated stability in residence.

The geographical stability of the adults was also surprising. Over half of the women (53%) and almost half of the men (49%) continued to live, a decade later, in the county where the study was initiated. When mothers did move, they were as likely to move out of the state (22%) as elsewhere in California (25%). Fathers tended to remain within the state (43%). Even taking into account some degree of mobility, the majority of men and women (67% and 63%, respectively) showed considerable stability of residence. Only 14% of women and 17% of men had a history of multiple moves and instability in this regard.

METHODOLOGY

The choice of research design including measurement strategies and creation of variables from coding schemata stems from decisions about which dimensions of the phenomena under study are of greatest interest and therefore should be highlighted. This investigation was originally conceived of as a hypothesis generating study in which the goal was to uncover and track the perceptions and experiences of the individual family members, particularly the children, following divorce. The qualitative focus of the study is ideally suited to this purpose, as the emphasis is on attempting to understand the complexity and variation endemic to the long-term divorce process from the point of view of the participants. The various methods of data collection and analysis, including the use of extensive clinical interviews and development of coding categories truly reflective of the richness of the clinical data, were selected for their suitability to retain and highlight the qualitative nature of the phenomenon under investigation.

Initial Contact

Structure of the Service.   Families in the study understood from the outset that the brief planning intervention was being offered in exchange for their willingness to participate in the research project. The roles of counselor and researcher were combined. Sources of referral were primarily attorneys and the schools. Very few litigating families were included.

Each family member was seen individually. The research objective in seeing parents and children separately, and in gathering independent information from the schools, was to obtain a complex and rich set of data about each family member, as well as about the relationships within that family. The potential pitfalls of interviewing just one family member about that family's overall divorce experience were convincingly demonstrated throughout the history of the project. These multiple sets of data enabled the researchers to triangulate often apparently irreconcilable data into a meaningful psychological portrait of the family and its members in the midst of divorce.

Each parent was interviewed weekly over a 6-week period; each child was seen for three or four sessions. Parent interviews ranged from 60 to 90 minutes; most child sessions were 50 minutes. Families were not excluded if one family member refused to be involved. Generally, the same clinician saw all family members, but occasionally two staff members shared parents and children, if time considerations or particular expertise dictated such an arrangement. The average number of interviews per family was 15.

The Follow-Up Studies

Families were recontacted at 18 months, 5 years, and 10 years from the decisive marital separation. Family members were seen individually for a single follow-up interview that lasted several hours; young children were seen for extended play sessions. At 18 months and at 5 years, the same clinician who assessed the family originally was available to interview each family member. At the 10-year mark, three of the five original clinicians remained available, thus ensuring considerable continuity of contact for these young people and their parents. At the 18-month and 5-year follow-ups, independent school interviews were conducted; at the 10-year follow-up, parent and child questionnaires supplemented the interview material.

Initial Assessment

The children and their parents were seen individually by trained clinicians in semi-structured clinical interviews. The format and content of these interviews are reported elsewhere (Wallerstein & Kelly, 1980c) . Results of the interviews were transcribed, and the transcriptions were coded. (See Wallerstein & Kelly, 1980c, for details.) Reliability was established between trained clinicians by the consensus method. Those codes requiring clinical judgment were discussed and discrepancies were resolved. After consensus was reached, the same clinical raters completed coding the transcripts.

18-Month and 5-Year Assessments

The method of assessment at 18 months and at 5 years was essentially the same as has been described for the initial time period. The same interview outline was used in the semi-structured interviews, with additional portions added at each time period that addressed issues relevant to demographic and psychological status appropriate to the time elapsed. Interview portions having to do with premarital and marital history were not repeated.

Assessment at 10 Years

As at previous time periods, the interview outline was adjusted to include new areas relevant to assessment of status at 10 years. The 10-year interview outline included all items on the initial interview (minus predivorce history) and those new items added at 18 months and 5 years that were still appropriate at 10 years. Thus, the semi-structured interviews at 10 years were the most extensive of the follow-ups in the study. As at the earlier time periods, the interviews were transcribed, and the transcriptions were coded. The coding forms at 10 years contained categories used at the earlier time periods, and new categories reflecting questions added at 10 years. (See Table 10.1 for a summary of the domains of functioning reflected by these categories.)

Coding items requiring clinical judgments were reviewed extensively by trained clinical raters. Operational criteria anchoring scale points were developed and discussed thoroughly. Transcripts from 10% of the sample were selected and individually coded. Interrater reliabilities were computed using Kendall's tau b statistic for ordinal level variables and the Kappa statistic for nominal type variables. Those variables having acceptable levels of agreement ($p < .05$) constituted 62%

TABLE 10.1
Summary of Domains of Functioning Coded at the 10-Year Follow-Up*

Children	Parents**
Marital status/history	Marital status/history
Living situation (and custody)	Employment
Pattern of contact with father	Schooling/training
Pattern of contact with mother	Economic circumstances
Attitudes toward parent contact	Living situation
Schooling	Social relationships
Employment	Supports/needs
Economic situation	Parenting
Adolescent achievements	Current psychological functioning
Early/middle adolescent history	Treatment history
Later adolescent history	Attitude to the divorce
Supports	Co-parental relationship
Peer relationships	Interparental relationship
Sexual/love relationships	
Current psychological functioning	
Psychotherapy and health history	
Relationship with father	
Relationship with mother	
Attitude toward mother's remarriage	
Attitude toward father's remarriage	
Attitude toward the divorce	
Expectations/attitudes to the future	

*These domains of functioning are coded primarily in the form of clinical ratings based firstly on interview data and secondarily on questionnaire data from parents and children.
**Mother and father were rated separately.

of the ordinal codes and 54% of the nominal codes. The remaining codes were reviewed and operational criteria further defined. Where consensus on these criteria could not be reached, the codes were eliminated from formal analyses.

ANALYSIS OF THE DATA

Data Reduction

Frequencies were obtained on all of the coding categories. Those categories that did not discriminate statistically were examined and eliminated if the frequencies were not meaningful clinically. Appropriate measures of association were run between remaining categories. Categories that were associated above the .80 level were either combined or collapsed. The surviving categories provided the database.

To date, the primary method of analysis has been assessing the sample at 10 years using the chi-square statistic, as the data is of a categorical nature. The children have been assessed by sex, age group, and sibling status. Dependent measures were organized into several dimensions reflecting psychological, social, academic, and economic functioning, attitudes toward the divorce, expectations for the future, and perceived long-term residual impact of being a child of divorce.

A global measure of child outcome entitled Ego Cope has been developed by combining two codes that represent different but overlapping dimensions of functioning. One dimension, "Ego Intactness," is an assessment of the individual's internal degree of psychological integration, affective stability, and strength of defensive structure. The second dimension, "Overall Competence," represents the way in which an individual functions in various areas of the external environment including school, occupation, and social and family relationships.

The adults have been assessed by sex, age group, current marital status, and visiting patterns. Individual parent–child relationships have been analyzed along several dimensions, including overall quality, type of identification, feelings of reJection, love, trust, worry, and anger.

Profiles were developed that reflect combinations of parent characteristics within each divorced couple, such as patterns of conflict and anger, cooperation over visiting, attitude toward the ex-spouse as parent, and degree of felt responsibility for the child. The rationale behind the development of the parent profiles stems from our realization that many of the critical long-term effects of divorce are best conceptualized at a family level. Although each person's response is in part due to individual variation and exposure to certain life experiences, it is in the history of changes in the family that significant individual transformations may be best understood. The parent profiles represent an attempt to combine information from individual parents into family level variables that more accurately represent the reality of the postdivorce environment in which the child has lived. These parent profiles were then compared with measures of child functioning, in an attempt to perceive triadic or family system level relationships. (See Lewis & Wallerstein, 1987, for a complete discussion of this method of data analysis.) An analysis of longitudinal effects, including patterns of stability and change over time and prediction of long-term functioning, is currently under way.

EARLIER FINDINGS

The children's initial responses to the marital rupture, as manifest in their play, fantasy, verbal communication, and behavior, have been described in detail in the early publications of the project (Kelly & Wallerstein, 1976, 1977a, 1977b, 1979; Wallerstein, 1974, 1977a, 1977b; Wallerstein & Kelly, 1974, 1975, 1976). By and large, the symptoms of great distress—such as separation phobias, anxiety reactions, ego regressions, sleep disturbances, acute mourning reactions, intense anger, and loyalty conflicts—appeared to be governed at the outset by the age of the child or adolescent at the marital rupture, rather than by the idiosyncratic events within that particular family. Sex differences were not apparent at the separation but emerged strikingly at the first follow-up, at approximately 18 months following the marital separation, with the girls showing fairly rapid recovery and the boys showing continued difficulty or new difficulty. Children who were separated from a disturbed parent, or who had been caught in a destructive parent–child relationship, were improved at the 18-month follow-up.

It was not uncommon for the symptomatic responses of most of the children to subside before the adults had reached a state of restored equilibrium. There was no significant relation between the intensity and pervasiveness of the child's initial symptomatic response and his or her overall adjustment at the 5-year mark. But, the feelings aroused by the separation—the anger at one or both parents, the profound and sometimes pervasive sorrows, the sense of vulnerability, the concern for the custodial parent, the yearning for the departed parent, the loyalty conflict, the general sense of neediness and of being overburdened, the nostalgia for the intact family—these were all likely to remain in place and endure long after the symptomatic responses and the regressions had disappeared.

Observations at the 5-year mark showed a strong connection between the psychological adjustment in children and the overall quality of life within the postdivorce or remarried family. The age of the child at the time of the rupture and the sex of the child were no longer as critical as they had been at the outset. Instead, the relationships within the postdivorce family—and the extent to which the divorced or remarried family had been able to make use of the opportunities afforded by the divorce to create a richer, more emotionally gratifying life that included the children—had become salient. We were troubled to find moderate to severe depression in over one third of the entire original sample at the 5-year mark.

The earliest papers issued from this longitudinal study divided the children into four distinguishable groups in terms of their responses to the divorce-induced stress. Although many of the responses are, of course, overlapping or idiosyncratic, the patterns are noteworthy and have considerable usefulness as predictors. These groups comprised the preschool children, aged 3 to 5½; the early latency youngsters, aged 6 through 8; the later latency children, aged 9 to 11; and the adolescents. The responses of these youngsters have been described in detail (Kelly, 1982b; Wallerstein, 1977a, 1977b; Wallerstein & Kelly, 1974, 1975, 1976, 1980c). In accord with the same approach, the children at the 10-year mark were first examined by age groupings which corresponded, by and large, to the groupings at the earlier time-points.

The Preschool Children

Earlier Findings.   The original findings regarding the preschool children's initial responses to the separation called attention to their profound upset, to their neediness, to the high incidence of regression, and to acute separation anxieties that appeared rooted in the widespread fantasy that marital rupture augured abandonment by both parents. Although the extent and duration of regressive behavior and other symptoms varied from child to child, with very few exceptions these children were severely distressed. They appeared in many ways to be the age group most upset by the family crisis. We and others have also described the counterpart to these children's anxieties in the deterioration in parenting that so often accompanies the marital breakup (Hetherington, 1979; Hetherington, Cox, & Cox, 1978, 1982; Wallerstein, 1985a; Wallerstein & Kelly, 1980b, 1980c, 1982).

The second stage of the study, 18 months following the marital rupture, revealed new and consolidating decline among children who at first seemed to have survived the failing marriage and the conflicts surrounding the breakup without significant psychological impairment. A most dismaying finding at the 18-month mark was that almost half of the preschool children looked more troubled than they had initially. Differences between the sexes also emerged strikingly at this time. In accord with other researchers (Hetherington, 1979; Hetherington et al., 1978, 1982), it was found that little boys, whose psychological adjustment at the time of the marital rupture was only slightly below that of the little girls, were significantly *more* troubled at school, playground, and home at the 18-month mark, whereas many of the girls appeared recovered.

Observations at the 5-year mark once again reflected change, showing a strong connection between adequate psychological adjustment in children and the overall quality of life within the postdivorce or remarried family. The preschool children were fully represented within the one third of the sample who were diagnosed with moderate to severe depression at the 5-year mark, but they did not emerge, as they had at the outset, as the most vulnerable youngsters. Overall, sex differences were not significant. However, in the younger age groups who were preschool and early elementary age at baseline, sex differences continued to be a noticeable factor in adjustment.

Preliminary Findings Regarding the Preschool Child at the 10-Year Mark.   Thirty-one youngsters, between the ages of 2½ and 6 at the time of the divorce, and now ranging from almost 12 to almost 18, were located. Thirty of these young people, 14 boys and 16 girls, and 40 of their parents, were seen for 10-year follow-up interviews.

Preliminary findings show that few conscious memories of the intact family or of the marital rupture were retained by these youngsters, who were by now in mid-adolescence. Although these young people had spent two thirds of their lives within the divorced or remarried family and most were performing adequately in school, a significant number spoke sorrowfully of their emotional and economic deprivation and wistfully of the more nurturant, more protected life that they envisioned within the intact family. Reconciliation fantasies were still discernible in half of the sample. Relationships with the custodial mother often reflected closeness, appreciation, and concern for her struggles and her vulnerability, and worry over the impact of their forthcoming departure from the home, as well as some residual anger at the mother's emotional and physical unavailability over the years. Relationships with the noncustodial father had retained their emotional centrality for these youngsters, whether they were visited frequently or infrequently. Some youngsters displayed intense yearning and compassionate caring for troubled, needy fathers who showed up erratically over the years. Intense anger was expressed at fathers who had failed to provide economic support when they had the capacity to do so. A heightened need to establish relationships with absent fathers appeared to occur as these youngsters, especially the girls, reached adolescence. Finally, most of these young people looked forward optimistically to marriage and a family. They allowed, albeit reluctantly, for the possibility of marital failure and divorce. A few were openly concerned about repeating their parents' mistakes, but the majority asserted their expectations of avoiding the unhappiness that they associated with divorce in their parents' lives.

What emerges in this preliminary analysis is the very interesting possibility that children who are very young at the marital breakup are considerably less burdened in the years to come than those who were older at the time of the divorce. Certainly they carry with them fewer memories of unhappiness and conflict between the parents, and almost no memories of the intact family. Although they are no less attached in fantasy to the intact family, they appear unburdened by intensely cathected memories of parental conflict or of their own fright and suffering at the time. As a consequence, they may be less apprehensive and more optimistic about the future. This finding is especially interesting because the preschool children who were the most distressed at the time of the marital rupture, by virtue of their own immaturity at the time and the repressive processes at work, have emerged less consciously troubled than their older siblings, who had difficulty mastering or erasing the memory of the family travail. Some of these attitudes may, of course, reflect the adolescent stage at which the 10-year study found these youngsters.

Late Latency and Adolescent Children

Earlier Findings.   Youngsters who had been between the ages of 9 and 18 at the initial assessment included two groups: those who were in late latency and those who had already reached adolescence. There were distinguishable differences between these two groups. The later latency or preadolescent youngsters felt especially powerless, as well as frightened, at the marital rupture. Most striking, however, was their intense anger at one or both parents for precipitating the divorce. They were more inclined at this age to align with one parent, to take sides in the parental conflict, and to join with one parent in a bitter, even mischievous harassment of the other. About half of the boys and girls in this group suffered a severe drop in their school work that lasted throughout the year following the marital rupture (Wallerstein & Kelly, 1976). Initial responses in the adolescent group were of concern because so many youngsters showed acute depression, acting out, and regression that included emotional and social withdrawal from involvement with friends and investment in school. The anxiety of almost all of the adolescents with regard to their own futures ran very high. A significant subgroup of the adolescent young people also showed an impressive developmental spurt. Many were mature, compassionate, and genuinely helpful to one or both parents during the height the marital crisis (Wallerstein & Kelly, 1974).

The second stage of the study, 18 months following the marital separation, revealed psychological decline among children and adolescents who at first seemed to have survived the failing marriage and the conflicts surrounding the marital breakup without significant psychological dysfunction. Differences between the sexes emerged strikingly at this time. Young boys below the age of adolescence were significantly more troubled in their performance and behavior at school, playground, and home, than were the girls. In fact, many of the girls seemed to be well on their way to recovery from their initial distressed reactions. It should be noted that almost all of these youngsters were in the custody of their mothers. Few differences between the sexes in the incidence of new or continuing distress were noted in the adolescent group at that time.

As with the preschool children, findings at the 5-year mark showed a strong connection between good psychological adjustment in the children and the overall quality of life within the postdivorce or remarried family.

Preliminary Findings Regarding Late Latency and Adolescent Children at 10 Years.   Preliminary findings of 40 young people from 26 of the families, who ranged in age from 19 to 29 at the 10-year mark, showed strongly that they continued to regard their parents' divorce as a major influence in their lives. A significant number were burdened by vivid memories of the unhappy events at the time of the marital rupture. Their predominant feelings as they looked backward were restrained sadness, some remaining resentment at their parents, and a wistful sense of having missed out on the experience of growing up in an intact family. Although many were proud of their enhanced maturity, they regretted the ways in which the divorce had cut into the play and school time of their growing-up years.

One half of these young people were still full time at school, one third were fully self-supporting, and the greater majority were law abiding. Only two thirds of these young people, however, were attending or had graduated from college, or were seeking advanced degrees, in a county where 85% of the high school graduates go on directly to junior college or 4-year college programs. It may well be that the lower incidence of college enrollment among this group is related, at least in part, to the fact that in the majority of the families, child support stopped abruptly when the youngster reached the age of 18. Those who were at the university at the time of the follow-up were often also carrying jobs—

sometimes even alternating school semester with full-time work—in order to earn tuition and living expenses. The burdening of the opportunity for post-secondary education for children in divorced families, if found to exist in a wide popula- tion, represents a grave issue, not only for these youngsters but for society as a whole.

A significant number of young men and women, and especially young wom- en, appeared troubled and drifting. A minority consisting of one third of the women appeared especially wary of commitment and fearful of betrayal. They seemed caught up in a web of short-lived sexual relationships. The greater number, however, were strongly committed to the ideals of a lasting marriage and to values that include romantic love and fidelity. They were apprehensive about repeating their parents' unhappy marriage during their own adulthood and especially eager to avoid divorce for the sake of their own future children. This identification with being a child of divorce may be one of the lasting sequelae of the experience of parental divorce during childhood.

Finally, in a subgroup of families, the sibship emerged as a powerful suppor- tive network with the capacity not only to buffer the family ordeal, but also to provide the significant nutrients of family relationships and to actualize for these young people their otherwise battered conceptions of fidelity, enduring love, and intimacy.

Parents at the 10-Year Mark

Preliminary findings for 47 women and 36 men in 52 families showed unexpect- edly wide discrepancies in the adjustment of the former spouses at the 10-year mark. Employing an overall assessment of quality of life aggregating four dimensions—nature and quality of interpersonal relationships, general content- ment with life, freedom from severe loneliness and neurotic suffering, and so- cioeconomic status and stability—we found that, in about two-thirds of the families, only one of the former spouses was able to make use of the divorce to signifi- cantly improve the quality of his or her life; in only 10% of the couples did both do so. And, in fact, in 20% of the couples, both were experiencing a diminished quality of life as compared with their lives during the marriage. Men or women who sought the divorce initially were significantly more likely to have enhanced the quality of their lives than did those who had opposed the divorce decision.

Viewed more narrowly than from concern with the overall quality of life, and considered just from the standpoint of change in psychological capacity and in- tegrity, the discrepancy between the former marital partners at the 10-year mark is even more striking. Psychological growth among women subsequent to divorce was conspicuous; it was much less evident among the men, many of whom showed surprisingly little change over the postdivorce decade in their attitudes or in the patterning of their relationships.

The capacity of women to rebuild intimate adult relationships and to reestablish social and economic stability within the postdivorce or remarried family was clearly age-related. Women who were 40 or over at the time of the marital rupture appeared to be socially and perhaps psychologically disadvantaged in this rebuilding task. At the 10-year mark, many women felt lonely and rejected, and were living in economic, social, and psychological conditions well below those that they had experienced during their marriage. By contrast, women in their 20s and 30s at the marital rupture showed in many instances a resiliency that enabled them to establish new lives and new careers successfully. As a result of their own psychological growth and the greater economic opportunities available at that time in California, a significant subgroup of women in their 20s and 30s had made splendid economic progress and established stable, gratifying relationships. Their self-esteem was high, and they appeared to have benefited considerably from the divorce and from the years following the divorce in achieving a more finely honed sense of reality, a clearer self-concept, and better judgment. Insight among the parents into the cause of the marital breakdown was rare in men and women alike. Few recognized their own contribution to the failure of the marriage. Very few men, and no women, accepted responsibility for the divorce.

CONCLUSIONS

Findings from a 10-year study of the experience of marital rupture during childhood and adolescence are currently being analyzed with respect to the impact of this experience and the many life changes associated with it, on children and their parents, on their relations with each other, and on their present attitudes and future expectations. Sample, method, and preliminary findings from the analysis of two subgroups of children—namely, 30 preschoolers who were between 2½ and 6 years of age at the time of the decisive separation, and 40 late latency and adolescent youngsters who were aged 9–18 at the time of the separation— have been reviewed. A first paper describing the parents, 47 mothers and 36 fathers, has also been presented. In this preliminary material, some long-lasting consequences of divorce and its differential impact on diverse groups within the divorce population of adults, adolescents, and children emerge with clarity. These sequelae are linked significantly in these preliminary reports to sex differences in children and adults as well as to the age of the child and the age of the parent at the time of the marital rupture. Contrary to earlier findings from the same study, the greater impact appears to be on the older children, especially among the girls at the time of their entry into adulthood. Significant linkages are also apparent between child outcome and the quality of the parent–child and stepparent–child relationships within the postdivorce or remarried family. An unexpected finding is that there is a wide discrepancy of outcome between formerly married partners.

These preliminary findings show that the consequences of the marital rupture for children and adults are potentially grave and enduring. The initial responses of children and parents at the height of the crisis during the separation are serious. They need to be addressed at that time through a range of intervention programs that can relieve suffering and ameliorate or prevent the consolidation of psychological dysfunction. Over the long haul, however, the central hazards to the psychological health of children are not necessarily the results of the divorce, per se, although the persistence in older children of memories, affects and images associated with the intact family and the marital rupture is striking. The lasting danger lies in the disrupted parenting that so often follows in the wake of marital breakdown, in the parental conflicts that can remain and become chronic within the postdivorce family, in the flawed or tragic role models provided by parents who fail over many years to reconstitute or stabilize their lives, in the overall diminished quality of life, the economic deprivation, and the curtailed educational and social opportunities for the children that represent the legacy of divorce in so many postdivorce homes.

ACKNOWLEDGMENTS

This research has been supported by the San Francisco Foundation, The Zellerbach Family Fund, and the Kenworthy-Swift Foundation.

REFERENCES

Hetherington, E. (1979). Divorce: A child's perspective. *American Psychologist, 34*, 851–858.

Hetherington, E., Cox, M., & Cox, R. (1978). The aftermath of divorce. In H. Stevens & M. Mathews (Eds.), *Mother-child relations* (pp. 149–176). Washington, DC: National Association for Education of Young Children.

Hetherington, E., Cox, M., & Cox, R. (1982). Effects of divorce on parents and children. In M. E. Lamb (Ed.), *Nontraditional families: Parenting and child development* (pp. 233–285). Hillsdale, NJ: Lawrence Erlbaum Associates.

Hollingshead, A. B. (1957). *Two factor index of social position*. Unpublished manuscript, Yale University, New Haven, CT.

Horowitz, M. (1976). *Stress response syndromes*. New York: Aronson.

Kelly, J. B. (1981). The visiting relationship after divorce: Research and clinical implications. In I. Stuart & L. Abt (Eds.), *Children of separation and divorce* (pp. 338–361). New York: Van Nostrand Reinhold.

Kelly, J. B. (1982a). Divorce: The adult perspective. In B. Wolman & G. Stricker (Eds.), *Handbook of developmental psychology* (pp. 734–750). Englewood Cliffs, NJ: Prentice-Hall.

Kelly, J. B. (1982b). Observations on adolescent relationships five years after divorce. In S. Feinstein (Ed.), *Adolescent psychiatry* (Vol. 9, pp. 133–141). Chicago: University of Chicago Press.

Kelly, J. B., & Wallerstein, J. S. (1976). The effects of parental divorce: Experiences of the child in early latency. *American Journal of Orthopsychiatry, 46*, 20–32.

Kelly, J. B., & Wallerstein, J. S. (1977a). Brief interventions with children in divorcing families. *American Journal of Orthopsychiatry, 47*, 23–39.

Kelly, J. B., & Wallerstein, J. S. (1977b). Part-time parent, part-time child: Visiting after divorce. *Journal of Clinical Child Psychology, 6,* 51–54.

Kelly, J. B., & Wallerstein, J. S. (1979). The divorced child in the school. *National Elementary Principal, 59,* 51–58.

Lewis, J. M., & Wallerstein, J. S. (1987). Family profile variables and long-term outcome in divorce research: Issues at a ten-year follow-up. In J. P. Vincent (Ed.), *Advances in family intervention, assessment and theory* (Vol. 4, pp. 121–142). Greenwich, CT: JAI Press.

Terr, L. (1983). Chowchilla revisited: The effects of psychic trauma four years after a school bus kidnapping. *American Journal of Psychiatry, 140,* 1543–1550.

Wallerstein, J. S. (1974). Effect of divorce on children, research findings, and implications for intervening. *Conciliation Courts Review, 12,* 8–9.

Wallerstein, J. S. (1977a). Responses of the pre-school child to divorce: Those who cope. In M. McMillan & S. Hanao (Eds.), *Child psychiatry: Treatment and research* (pp. 269–292). New York: Brunner/Mazel.

Wallerstein, J. S. (1977b). Some observations regarding the effects of divorce on the psychological development of the pre-school girl. In J. Oremland & E. Oremland (Eds.), *Sexual and gender development of young children* (pp. 117–129). Cambridge, MA: Balinger Press.

Wallerstein, J. S. (1980a). The child in the divorcing family. *The Judge's Journal, 19,* 16–19; 40–43.

Wallerstein, J. S. (1980b). Children and divorce. *Pediatrics in Review, 1,* 211–217.

Wallerstein, J. S. (1980c). Contributions of studies of divorce: The impact of divorce on children. In B. Blinder (Ed.), *Psychiatric clinics of North America* (Vol. 3, No. 3, pp. 455–468). Philadelphia: W. B. Saunders.

Wallerstein, J. S. (1981). Children of divorce: A growing awareness of the long term impact. *Medical Aspects of Human Sexuality, 15*(8), 36–47.

Wallerstein, J. S. (1983a). Children of divorce: The psychological tasks of the child. *American Journal of Orthopsychiatry, 53,* 230–243.

Wallerstein, J. S. (1983b). Children of divorce: Stress and developmental tasks. In N. Garmezy & M. Rutter (Eds.), *Stress, coping, and development in children* (pp. 265–302). New York: McGraw-Hill.

Wallerstein, J. S. (1983c). Separation, divorce, and remarriage. In M. Levine, W. Carey, A. Crocker, & R. Gross (Eds.), *Developmental behavioral pediatrics* (pp. 241–255). Philadelphia: W. B. Saunders.

Wallerstein, J. S. (1984a). Children of divorce: The dilemma of a decade. In L. Grinspoon (Ed.), *The American Psychiatric Association Annual Review* (Vol. 3, 144–158). Washington, DC: American Psychiatric Press.

Wallerstein, J. S. (1984b). Children of divorce: Preliminary report of a ten-year follow-up of young children. *American Journal of Orthopsychiatry, 54,* 444–458.

Wallerstein, J. S. (1985a). Changes in parent-child relationships during and after divorce. In. E. Anthony, & G. Pollock (Eds.), *Parental influences in health and disease* (pp. 317–347). Boston: Little Brown.

Wallerstein, J. S. (1985b). Children of divorce: Emerging trends. In J. Beitchman (Ed.), *Psychiatric clinics of North America, 8*(4), (pp. 837–855). Philadelphia: W. B. Saunders.

Wallerstein, J. S. (1985c). Children of divorce: Preliminary report of a ten-year follow-up of older children and adolescents. *Journal of the American Academy of Child Psychiatry, 24,* 545–553.

Wallerstein, J. S. (1985d). The overburdened child: Some long-term consequences of divorce. *Social Work, 30*(2), 116–123.

Wallerstein, J. S. (1986a). Child of divorce: An overview. *Behavioral Sciences and the Law, 4*(2), 105–118.

Wallerstein, J. S. (1986b). Women after divorce: Preliminary report from a 10-year follow-up. *American Journal of Orthospychiatry, 56*(1), 65–77.

Wallerstein, J. S., & Corbin, S. B. (1986). Father-child relationships after divorce: Child support and educational opportunities. *Family Law Quarterly, 20*(2), 109–128.

Wallerstein, J. S., & Huntington, D. S. (1983). Bread and roses: Nonfinancial issues related to fathers' economic support of their children following divorce. In J. Cassetty (Ed.), *The parental child support obligation: Research, practice, and social policy* (pp. 135-155). Lexington, MA: D. C. Heath.

Wallerstein, J. S., & Kelly, J. B. (1974). The effects of parental divorce: The adolescent experience. In J. Anthony & C. Koupernik (Eds.), *The child in his family: Children at psychiatric risk* (Vol. 3, pp. 479-505). New York: Wiley.

Wallerstein, J. S., & Kelly, J. B. (1975). The effects of parental divorce: The experiences of the preschool child. *Journal of the American Academy of Child Psychiatry, 14,* 600-616.

Wallerstein, J. S., & Kelly, J. B. (1976). The effects of parental divorce: Experiences of the child in later latency. *American Journal of Orthopsychiatry, 46,* 256-269.

Wallerstein, J. S., & Kelly, J. B. (1977). Divorce counseling: A community service for families in the midst of divorce. *American Journal of Orthopsychiatry, 47,* 4-22.

Wallerstein, J. S., & Kelly, J. B. (1979a). Children and divorce: A review. *Social Work, 24,* 468-475.

Wallerstein, J. S., & Kelly, J. B. (1979b). Divorce and children. In J. Noshpitz, I. Berlin, & L. Stone (Eds.), *Basic handbook of child psychiatry, Vol. IV, Prevention and current issues* (pp. 339-347). New York: Basic Books.

Wallerstein, J. S., & Kelly, J. B. (1980a). California's children of divorce. *Psychology Today, 13*(8), 66-76.

Wallerstein, J. S., & Kelly, J. B. (1980b). Effects of divorce on the father-child relationship. *American Journal of Psychiatry, 137,* 1534-1539.

Wallerstein, J. S., & Kelly, J. B. (1980c). *Surviving the breakup: How children and parents cope with divorce.* New York: Basic Books.

Wallerstein, J. S., & Kelly, J. B. (1982). The father-child relationship: Changes afer divorce. In S. Cath, A. Gurwitt, & J. Ross (Eds.), *Father and child: Developmental and clinical perspectives* (pp. 451-466). Boston: Little Brown.

Weitzman, L. J. (1985). *The divorce revolution: The unexpected social and economic consequences for women and children in America.* New York: The Free Press.

11

Single Parenting in the Context of Three-Generational Black Families

Melvin N. Wilson
Timothy F. J. Tolson
University of Virginia

The number of single-parent families has dramatically increased over the past 2 decades. This has been the result not only of increasing rates of marital dissolution but also of increasing rates of extramarital births as well. The increase in single-parent families has led to a change in the characteristics of the American family. Although research has shown that many Americans believe that family refers to a mother-father-children unit, such compositions have become inconsistent with the actual experiences of many (Chilman, 1982; Gilby & Pederson, 1982). Defining family as a nuclear family model, while treating other family forms either as incomplete (e.g., childless couples) or as deviant (e.g., single parents) variations of the nuclear family model misrepresents the current norms regarding family life (Chilman, 1982; Feiring & Lewis, 1984; Glick & Norton, 1979). Some believe (Chilman, 1982; Hodkin, 1983) these diverse family forms portend the breakup of the family as a socializing unit. However, the "family" is surviving, but in structures new to middle-class America. Interestingly, the normative structure of the Black family has always reflected diverse forms of familial organization and embeddedness in extended-family networks and may become the prototype of family survival (Hill, 1972; Hill & Schackleford, 1972; Uzoka, 1979).

This chapter presents data from a research project that examined the relative influence of two- and three-generational, and one- and two-parent, Black families on perceived childrearing behaviors and the extent of agreement among mothers', grandmothers', target children's and, where appropriate, fathers' perception of adult childrearing behaviors. Before examining this research, a brief review of relevant literature on single-parent Black families and the impact of the Black extended family on childrearing is presented.

Prevalence of Single Parent and Extended Families in the Black Community

Single-parent family units have been a persistent phenomena in the Black community. Past demographic reports have indicated that Black families have had the highest incidences of single-parent family units in the United States (Reid, 1982; Sweet, 1977; U.S. Bureau of the Census, 1986). In 1985, about 60% of Black families with children were maintained by only one parent, whereas 21% of White families with children were one-parent family units (U.S. Bureau of the Census, 1986). These high rates are cause for concern about the impact one-parent familial structures could have on the development of children.

A phenomena that is juxtaposed to the high incidence of one-parent families involves the prevalence of extended-family households in the Black community and the reliance of Black parents on their extended families for child-care assistance. Demographic evidence has shown that household compositions involving nonimmediate family members, that is, other adult and child relatives of the immediate family, are three times as likely to occur in Black families than White families (Reid, 1982; Sweet, 1977). Tienda and Angel (1982) have estimated that about 20%–25% of Black households consist of an extended family.

In addition, research has shown that for the Black one-parent family, grandparents, uncles and aunts, siblings, cousins, and even fictive kin often serve as surrogate parents in the rearing of young children (Martin & Martin, 1978; H. McAdoo, 1978; Wilson, 1984). Several studies indicated that one-parent families were more involved in extended-family networks than were two-parent families (Colletta, 1981; McLanahan, Wedemeyer, & Adelbery, 1981). Colletta (1981) indicated that single parents relied on extended-family networks for social support and child-care assistance more frequently than did two parents. Moreover, the quality of child-care in one-parent families was increased and the level of stress experienced by single mothers was reduced when the extended family was involved (Kellam, Adams, Brown, & Ensminger, 1982). Single mothers reported family networks were contacted more frequently than friendship or conjugal networks (McLanahan et al., 1981).

Not all single Black mothers have the ability to maintain and use familial and friendship support in accomplishing parental tasks. As with most abilities and attitudes, variations do exist. In a longitudinal study, Kellam et al. (1982) found that mothers who gave birth during adolescence were more likely to be rearing their children alone than mothers who were older at the birth of their first child. Kellam and his associates suggested that the mothers' inability to use familial networks involving other adults was related to an arrested social development that coincided with the birth of their first child.

In summary, the presence of additional adults in one-parent families affects childrearing activity by (a) providing alternative sources of intimacy and emotional support to the mother and children, (b) providing assistance in childrearing to the mother, and (c) assisting the mother in setting and enforcing limits on children (Colletta, 1979, 1981; Field, Widmayer, Stringer, & Ignatoff, 1980; Kellam et al., 1982; Wilson, 1984). Whereas accumulated evidence suggests that one-parent families are more involved in extended-family networks than are two-parent families, other questions are raised regarding the perceived involvement of adult relatives other than the mother in childrearing activities.

Father's and Grandmother's Involvement in Childrearing

After the mother, the adult family members most likely to be involved in child care are the father and the grandmother respectively (Slaughter & Dillworth-Anderson, 1985). It has been observed that father's behaviors are affected by the child's gender (Cazenave, 1979; J. McAdoo, 1981a), perceived mood state (Power, 1985; Ventura & Stevenson, 1986), and by the quality of the parent's marital interaction (Lamb & Elster, 1985). Fathers more often than mothers are observed to interact in a different way with their sons than their daughters. Generally, they are more responsive and communicative with their sons than with their daughters. Moreover, they interact less with infant children than do mothers (Lamb & Elster, 1985; Power, 1985). Lamb and Elster found that the degree of paternal involvement and engagement with children was significantly related to the degree of mother–father engagement as well as to social support; whereas maternal involvement and engagement were unrelated to marital engagement. Others have observed that the father's interaction may be influenced by his perception of the child. Ventura and Stevenson (1986) noted that fathers perceived their infant as less approachable and soothable during distress than did mothers. Therefore, it seems that fathers are more affected by the age, gender, and mood of their children than mothers.

In general, most empirical research (Field et al., 1980; Stevens, 1984) on the extended family examined the effect of a grandmother's presence on childrearing. Egeland and Sroufe (1981) observed that 12-month-old infants who were first classified as avoidant and anxious and 6 months later as securely attached were more likely to be living in three-generational households composed of their mothers, their grandmothers, and their mothers' siblings. Crockenberg (1981) found that the presence of a responsive sensitive grandmother seemed to buffer the infant against the deleterious influence of an insensitive mother. Other researchers have suggested that there are indirect as well as direct effects of grandmother's presence for children of single mothers (Field et al., 1980; Martin & Martin, 1978; H. McAdoo, 1978). Dornbush et al. (1985) found that when grandmothers were present in one-parent families, mothers exercised more parental control and adolescents had less autonomy in family decision making and participated in fewer deviant activities than in family situations involving one-adult households.

Tolson and Wilson (1987) have reported that the perception of family climate is significantly affected by the number of adults present in the home. In homes where there were two or more adults present, the respondents, including adults and children, perceived more familial moral–religious emphasis and less organization than did the respondents when there was only one adult present.

Moreover, using a multiple-case analysis procedure, Wilson and Tolson (1986) observed that the profiles of adult–child interactions could be categorized according to the number of adults and children present. Eight families were coded for the frequency with which each family member spoke. Three profiles of family interactions emerged from these analyses: (a) the single adult–multiple children family had an asymmetric interaction pattern in which children directed their conversation to mother and not each other; (b) the multiple adult–only child and single adult-only child families displayed a more egalitarian conversation pattern in which the child had equal opportunity to converse with adults; (c) the multiple adult–multiple children had conversation patterns that were egalitarian, although children had less opportunity to talk with adults and spent less time talking to each other. These profiles suggest an understanding about the amount of interactant vigilance required of a single mother rearing several children alone (Wilson & Tolson, 1986).

In summary, it appears that childrearing is best accomplished as a cooperative venture involving adequate adult resources. And, as the research evidence suggests, adequate adult resources imply the availability of at least two adults.

Childrearing Behaviors

Family researchers have suggested that some of the most frequent childrearing activities in which parents engage are: (a) nurturance, parental support, affection, and/or encouragement; (b) demand, parental action involving supporting achievement-oriented behavior or skill acquisition; (c) control, parental action involving reinforcing setting and enforcing limits on socially appropriate behavior; and (d) punishment, parental punitive actions such as the withdrawal of affection and/or privileges (Baumrind, 1967, 1971, 1972; Becker, 1964; Belsky, Robins, & Gamble, 1984; Emmerich, 1977; Maccoby, 1980).

This study is an addition to the increasing body of research addressing the involvement of grandmothers' (Hale, 1982; Tinsley & Parke, 1984) and fathers' (Cazenave, 1979; Lamb, 1981; J. McAdoo, 1981a) roles in childrearing. The questions addressed in this study concerned (a) the effects of family structure, that is, one-parent family unit or two-parent family unit, and grandmother's residence, either living with the family unit or at least 10 miles away, on the perception of mothers', grandmothers', and fathers' performance of childrearing behaviors; and (b) the extent of agreement among mothers', grandmothers', target children's, and fathers' perceptions of adult childrearing activity.

It was expected that family members' perceptions of the grandmothers' performance of childrearing behaviors would be influenced by her residence with her single adult daughter. In addition, family members' perception of the mother's performance of childrearing behavior would be influenced by her marital status and the residential status of her mother. It was expected that grandmothers' residence would influence the perception of paternal childrearing behaviors. That is, fathers would be perceived as less involved when grandmothers shared residence with the family than in other conditions. These expectations were derived from family literature that suggests that increasing numbers of significant adults in the home reduces the relative influence of any one adult on the child. Finally, it was expected that the sex of the child would effect the behavior of grandmothers and fathers but not mothers. Grandmothers of granddaughters will be perceived as more involved than grandmothers of grandsons. On the other hand, fathers of sons were expected to be more actively involved than the fathers of daughters.

METHOD

The goal of the study was to examine the perceived involvement of extended-family members in childrearing activity. The extended family was operationalized as a three-generational family unit in which a maternal grandmother, one or two parents, and at least one child between the ages of 8–14 years were present, whereas one or two parents and at least one child between the ages of 8–14 represented a two-generational family unit. The research design involved families participating according to the requirements of a 2 × 2 × 2 factorial design, involving family structure (one-parent or two-parent households), grandmother's residence (grandmother sharing a residence with the family or living at least 10 or more miles away), and sex of the target child.

The Family Interview

All families were identified through an informal network involving referrals from church groups or friends. If they agreed to participate, an appointment was arranged. At the family interview, the families were told that the study investigated functional aspects of Black family life and that in order to document their family life, an interview would occur. Participants were paid $25 when they complete the interview, which lasted approximately 1½ hours.

Sample Demographic Information

Table 11.1 presents the demographic information of the participants according to family structure and grandmother's residence. These data include age of parents, education of parents, family income, and an income/needs ratio, which is the family income divided by the number of family members dependent on the income. The families were not significantly different on age and education, however they did differ on income, $[F(3,56) = 28.2, p < .01]$ and number of

TABLE 11.1
Demographic Information Including Parents' Average Age, Education, Family Income, and Number of Children[a]

Demographic Averages	Structure of Nuclear Family	
	Single	Dual
Mean age of mother	32.6 years	35.5 years
Range of ages	24–46 years	27–51 years
Mean age of father	—	39.1 years
Range of ages	—	25–63 years
Mean education level of mother	12.5th grade	11th grade
Range of education	9th–16th grade	6th–14th grade
Mean education level of father	—	9.5th grade
Range of education	—	0–16th grade
Mean family income	$9,291	$14,750
Range of income	$7,500–27,000	$8,000–30,000
Mean income/needs ratio[b]	$2,511 per family member	$2,379 per family member
Mean number of children	1.7 children	3.2 children
Range of number of children	1–4 children	1–13 children

Living with the nuclear family

Grandmaternal Domicile

	Living in the local community	
Mean age of mother	32.1 years	34 years
Range of ages	25–46 years	25–50 years
Mean age of father	—	47.6 years
Range of ages	—	25–61 years
Mean education level of mother	11.6th grade	11th grade
Range of education	6th–16th grade	8th–16th grade
Mean education level of father	—	8th grade
Range of education	—	0–16th grade
Mean family income	$7,940	$11,211
Range of income	$6,800–19,500	$8,000–30,000
Mean income/needs ratio[b]	$2,406 per family member	$2,288 per family member
Number of children	2.3 children	2.9 children
Range of number of children	1–4 children	1–8 children

[a] N = 15 families per cell
[b] Family income divided by number of family members

children, $[F(3,56) = 6.9, p \leq .01]$. Although, these differences disappeared when adjusted using the family income/needs ratio, they were treated as significant covariates in later analyses. For each group, the mean family income/needs ratio ranged from $2,288–$2,511 per family member.

Measures

The perception of mothers', grandmothers', and fathers' performance on four basic parental behaviors was examined as a function of family structure, grandmother's residence, and sex of the target child. Mothers, grandmothers, target children, and if present, fathers completed the Bronfenbrenner Parental Behavioral Scale (PBS; Devereux, Bronfenbrenner, & Rodgers, 1969; Seigelman, 1963), a 30-item structured self-report interview. Seigelman (1963) reported the mean consistency for all subscale of the PBS as .63, whereas the mean factor-score reliability was .76, which represents reasonable estimate of reliability. Although developed as a children's scale, the PBS has been used successfully with adolescents and adults (Bartz & Levine, 1978; Buriel, 1981) and with cross-national and cross-ethnic groups (Devereux et al., 1969; Ellis, Thomas, & Rollins, 1976; Weigert, 1968).

The PBS focuses on four parental behaviors (a) support, the expression of affection and approval; (b) demand, the encouragement of responsible and achievement-oriented behaviors of the child; (c) control, the exertion of parental authority and protectiveness; and (d) punishment, the withdrawal of approval or the delivery of punitive action. In this study, this measure was used to assess the childrearing activity of parents and the maternal grandmother.

RESULTS

Multivariate analyses of variance examining the effects of family structure, grandmother's residence, and sex of the child on perceptions of the four childrearing behaviors were done separately for grandmothers, mothers, and fathers and for the reports of the children, mother, grandmother, and where appropriate, the father. Significant multivariate interaction effects were followed by univariate and simple effect analyses. All differences reported were significant at least at the $p < .05$ level. The means of the groups by family structure, grandmother's residence, and sex of the child are presented in Table 11.2 through 11.5.

Perception of Grandmothers. The most significant multivariate effect involved the perceptions of grandmothers. There was a significant multivariate interaction in children's perceptions of grandmothers for the Grandmother's Residence × Sex of the Child interaction. The simple effects analyses revealed that residential grandmothers of granddaughters and nonresidential grandmothers of grandsons were significant. Only one of the four univariate Fs tested within the analysis of the granddaughters' perceptions was significant. That is, granddaughters with residential grandmothers perceived them as using less control than did granddaughters with nonresidential grandmothers (see Table11.2). In contrast, grandsons reported that residential grandmothers were more demanding and controlling than were nonresidential grandmothers.

Mothers' perception of grandmothers revealed a Family Structure × Grandmother's Residence interaction effect. However, the simple effect analyses indicated that grandmother's residence had a significant effect on mother's perceptions only within one-parent families. Table 11.2 indicates that single mothers perceived more supporting, demanding, controlling, and punishing behaviors being used by their mothers when the mothers' mother lived in their home than in the community.

Finally, grandmothers' self-perceptions were significantly affected by grandmother's residence. Grandmothers who lived with the family perceived themselves as using the targeted behaviors (i.e., demanding, controlling, and punishing) more than did nonresidential grandmothers (see Table 11.3).

Perception of Mothers.   Grandmothers' perception of mother revealed a Family Structure × Grandmother's Residence interaction effect. The simple effect analyses indicated that grandmother's residence had a significant effect on grandmothers' perception only within one-parent families. Table 11.4 indicates that nonresidential grandmothers perceived less supporting and punishing behaviors being used by the mothers than did residential grandmothers (see Table 11.5).

Children's perception of mothers was affected significantly by the multivariate Grandmother's Residence × Sex of the Child interaction (see Table 11.6). The simple effect analyses indicated that the granddaughters of residential grandmothers and the grandsons of nonresidential grandmothers perceived their mothers as using less supporting, demanding, and controlling than mothers in the other conditions.

Perception of Fathers.   Grandmothers' and children's perceptions of fathers were affected significantly by the sex of the child (see Table 11.7). Significant univariate Fs showed that grandmothers reported fathers of boys to be more supportive and demanding but less controlling than fathers of girls. Sons but not daughters reported their fathers to differ only on being more controlling. Mothers reported no differential treatment of sons and daughters by fathers.

MANCOVAs were done with number of children and income covariates effects entered separately into the analyses. Although there were slight changes in the pattern of results, all patterns of significant results were essentially the same as for those analyses without covariates. The covariate effects of number of children and family income did not change the significance of the effects tested and thus do not influence the interpretation of the results.

TABLE 11.2
Mean Responses for Children's Perception of Grandmother's Behavior

		Support				Demand				Control				Punishment			
		Single		Dual		Single		Dual		Single		Dual		Single		Dual	
Structure of Nuclear Family		Female	Male	Female	Male	Female	Male	Female	Male	Female	Male	Female	Male	Female	Male	Female	Male
Living with the nuclear family	M	3.1	3.6	3.8	3.5	3.2	3.8	3.6	4.2	2.5	3.9	3.3	3.4	3.1	2.8	2.6	2.9
	SD	.6	.6	.6	.7	.9	.8	.6	.8	.9	1.1	.6	1.0	1.0	.9	.7	1.0
	n	8	7	7	8	8	7	7	8	8	7	7	8	8	8	7	8
Grandmaternal Domicile																	
Living in the local community	M	3.9	3.4	3.4	3.2	3.8	3.2	3.7	3.2	3.8	2.6	3.0	1.9	2.6	2.2	2.0	1.9
	SD	.7	1.0	.7	.5	.7	.9	1.0	.7	.9	1.0	1.0	.4	.5	.7	.5	.8
	n	7	8	7	8	8	8	7	8	7	8	7	8	7	8	7	8

TABLE 11.3
Mean Responses for Mother's Perception of Grandmother's Behaviors[a]

Structure of Nuclear Family		Support		Demand		Control		Punishment	
		Single	Dual	Single	Dual	Single	Dual	Single	Dual
Grandmaternal Domicile									
Living with the nuclear family	M	4.2	3.6	4.4	3.6	4.2	3.0	2.9	2.1
	SD	0.4	0.6	0.6	0.9	0.3	0.8	0.6	0.6
Living in the local community	M	3.3	3.8	3.6	3.8	3.2	3.4	1.9	1.8
	SD	0.8	0.5	0.9	0.7	0.8	0.7	0.8	0.7

Note: The mean perception of responses range from 1.0 to 5.0.
[a] n = 15 per cell

TABLE 11.4
Mean Responses for Grandmother's Perception of Self[a]

Structure of Nuclear Family		Support		Demand		Control		Punishment	
		Single	Dual	Single	Dual	Single	Dual	Single	Dual
Grandmaternal Domicile									
Living with the nuclear family	M	3.9	3.7	4.4	4.2	3.8	3.9	2.8	2.3
	SD	0.4	0.4	0.5	0.7	0.6	0.5	0.8	0.8
Living in the local community	M	4.0	3.8	3.8	3.2	3.1	3.4	1.9	2.0
	SD	0.5	0.7	0.6	0.8	0.3	0.8	0.6	0.8

Note: The mean perception of responses range from 1.0 to 5.0.
[a] n = 15 per cell

TABLE 11.5

Mean Responses for Grandmother's Perception of Mother's Behaviors[a]

Structure of Nuclear Family		Support		Demand		Control		Punishment	
		Single	Dual	Single	Dual	Single	Dual	Single	Dual
Grandmaternal Domicile									
Living with the nuclear family	M	4.2	4.1	4.2	4.3	3.4	3.8	3.2	2.6
	SD	0.4	0.3	0.4	0.6	0.5	0.6	0.6	0.6
Living in the local community	M	3.9	4.2	4.0	4.1	3.4	3.7	2.1	2.6
	SD	0.4	0.4	0.8	0.4	0.6	0.8	0.8	0.9

Note: The mean perception of responses range from 1.0 to 5.0.
[a]n = 15 per cell

TABLE 11.6
Mean Responses for Children's Perception
of Mother's Behavior

Structure of Nuclear Family		Support				Demand				Control				Punishment			
		Single		Dual		Single		Dual		Single		Dual		Single		Dual	
		Female	Male	Female	Male	Female	Male	Female	Male	Female	Male	Female	Male	Female	Male	Female	Male
Living with the nuclear family	M	3.1	3.7	3.6	4.0	3.9	4.3	4.0	4.4	3.0	3.7	3.1	3.7	2.7	2.4	2.1	2.7
	SD	.6	.5	.4	.4	.8	.6	18	.7	.6	.9	.7	16	.4	.8	.6	.7
	n	8	7	7	8	8	7	7	8	8	7	7	8	8	7	7	8
Grandmaternal Domicile Living in the local community	M	4.0	3.2	4.0	3.2	4.4	4.4	4.4	4.2	3.8	2.6	3.6	2.6	2.5	2.4	2.1	2.3
	SD	.6	.7	.4	.4	.6	.6	.5	.6	.6	1.0	.7	.9	.5	.9	.4	.6
	n	7	8	7	8	7	8	7	8	7	8	7	8	7	8	7	8

TABLE 11.7

Mean Response for Grandmother's, and Children's Perception of Father's Behavior

Sex of the Child			Grandmother's perception of:				Children's perception of:			
			Support	Demand	Contorl	Punishment	Support	Demand	Control	Punishment
Female[a]	M		3.8	3.7	3.5	2.17	3.4	3.7	3.0	1.9
	SD		.7	.8	.9	.8	.9	1.0	1.0	.6
Male[b]	M		4.1	4.2	2.9	2.23	3.7	4.5	2.9	2.1
	SD		.3	.6	.6	.7	.8	.6	.8	.8

[a]N = 14 per cell
[b]N = 16 per cell

229

Correlational Analyses. Pearson product moment correlations examining the agreements of family members' perceptions were done for the reports of the mothers, grandmothers, children, and where appropriate, fathers. The correlational matrice presented in Table 11.8 through 11.10 list the mothers', grandmothers', children's and father's perceptions of adult childrearing activities. Although the range of correlation coefficients varied from —.10 to .72, the minimum value at which significant $p < .05$ was reached was .22. However, the strength of association (r^2) among the correlated perceptions of childrearing activity suggest that only those r values greater than .50 were sufficiently different from 0 to warrant consideration. Across the perceptions of mothers', grandmothers', and fathers' childrearing activities, only support and punishment behaviors obtained sufficient strength of associations. Also, there were higher concordances between family members' perceptions of the targeted adult's childrearing activities than between that targeted adults' self-perceptions and others' perceptions of them. For example, when mother was the target, the correlation between her perception of her childrearing activities and children's perception of mother's activities was lower than the correlation children's and grandmother's perceptions of mother. The target persons attributed more of the childrearing activity to themselves than others attributed to them.

CONCLUSION

At first glance, the patterns of variations across the family types and the patterns of agreements within the families do not appear to form a consistent model of adult family members' involvement in childrearing. However, closer scrutiny reveals the fabric of conceptual understanding of nontraditional families. In several ways, these results support other research that indicate the important contribution made by adult family members other than the mother to childrearing activities in nontraditional households.

First, although mothers' and children's perceptions of grandmothers were qualified by specific interactions, their reports, and grandmothers' self-reports, indicated that residential grandmothers performed more of the targeted behaviors than nonresidential grandmothers. Mothers' perceived residential grandmothers to be more involved when the family structure was a one-parent household rather than a two-parent household. Grandsons perceived greater involvement by their residential grandmothers than was perceived by granddaughters. Residential proximity of grandmothers has been shown to effect the frequency and the nature of interaction between grandmothers and their grandchildren (Hale, 1982; Jackson, 1980; Martin & Martin, 1978). That is, grandmothers are more likely to participate in structured and unstructured interactions and to provide child-care assistance when she lives in close proximity to the family than when she does not (Hale, 1982; Martin & Martin, 1978; Slaughter & Dillworth-Anderson, 1985).

TABLE 11.8A
Correlation Matrix of Perception of Single Mother's Childrearing Activity (N = 30)

Source	Support				Control			
	Mother	Grandmother	Children	Father	Mother	Grandmother	Children	Father
Mother								
Grandmother	.50				.10			
Children	.55	.70			.20	.35		
Father								
		Demand				Punishment		
Mother								
Grandmother	.24				.34			
Children	.30	.40			.34	.72		
Father								

231

TABLE 11.8B
Correlation Matrix of Perception of Mother's Childrearing Activity with Father Present (N = 30)

Source	Support				Control			
	Mother	Grandmother	Children	Father	Mother	Grandmother	Children	Father
Mother								
Grandmother	.35				.30			
Children	.33	.50			.25	.26		
Father	.32	.47	.48		.20	.09	.15	

Source	Demand				Punishment			
	Mother	Grandmother	Children	Father	Mother	Grandmother	Children	Father
Mother								
Grandmother	.20				.23			
Children	.22	.30			.35	.43		
Father	−.10	.27	.29		.0	.57	.40	

TABLE 11.9A

Correlation Matrix of Perception of Grandmother's Childrearing
Activity in Single Parent Homes (N = 30)

	Support				Control			
Source	Mother	Grandmother	Children	Father	Mother	Grandmother	Children	Father
Mother								
Grandmother	.53				.40			
Children	.46	.44			.21	.47		
Father								

	Demand				Punishment			
Mother								
Grandmother	.25				.70			
Children	.21	.30			.62	.62		
Father								

233

TABLE 11.9B
Correlation Matrix of Perception of Grandmother's Childrearing Activity

Support

Source	Mother	Grandmother	Children	Father
Mother				
Grandmother	.60			
Children	.40	.60		
Father	.13	.0	.15	

Demand

Source	Mother	Grandmother	Children	Father
Mother				
Grandmother	.06			
Children	.56	.0		
Father	.56	.17	.51	

Control

Source	Mother	Grandmother	Children	Father
Mother				
Grandmother	.22			
Children	.10	-.05		
Father	.05	.0	.05	

Punishment

Source	Mother	Grandmother	Children	Father
Mother				
Grandmother	.60			
Children	.65	.40		
Father	.70	.46	.60	

TABLE 11.10
Correlation Matrix of Perception of Father's Childrearing
Activity (N = 30)

Source	Support				Control			
	Mother	Grandmother	Children	Father	Mother	Grandmother	Children	Father
Mother								
Grandmother	.19				.0			
Children	.07	.55			.45	.53		
Father	.30	.10	.0		.40	.16	.35	
		Demand				*Punishment*		
Mother								
Grandmother	.19				.70			
Children	.35	.08			.65	.58		
Father	.30	.09	.25		.50	.60	.69	

Second, the directional differences in the grandsons' and granddaughters' perceptions of grandmothers and of mothers suggest that the additional adult had a gender-specific effect on the children's perceptions of grandmothers and mothers. Grandsons reported receiving preferential attention when grandmother lived with the family; and conversely, granddaughters reported preferential attention when grandmothers resided in the community. It seems that families of nonresidential grandmothers may act to encourage the independence of their sons and the protection of their daughters, whereas the additional adult figure in the family household allows for greater nurturance of the sons. Also, it is possible that the granddaughter perceived less attention as a result of the greater number of adult females in the household. Furthermore, the consistency between the children's perceptions of mother and of grandmother suggest that the number of adult family members do affect children's perception.

Third, although mother's report of her childrearing activities were not significant, there were significant interactions obtained for children's and for grandmothers' perceptions of mothers. Namely, nonresidential grandmothers and grandsons of nonresidential grandmothers perceived the single parent as not performing enough of the targeted behaviors. As others have suggested, such a perception may be related to the limited adult resources in the home. For example, it has been demonstrated that one-parent households' limited adult resources effect (a) the kind of adult–child interaction (Patterson, 1982; Wilson & Tolson, 1986), (b) the nature of family organization and behavioral control of children (Dornbush et al., 1985; Hetherington, 1987; Tolson & Wilson, 1987), (c) the parents' ability to maintain control over adolescent acting out behavior (Dornbush et al., 1985), and (d) the level of the child's social and academic adjustment (Hetherington, 1987; Hetherington, Cox, & Cox, 1978; Kellam et al., 1982).

Whereas fathers did not perceive themselves as treating their sons and daughters differently, children and grandmothers did. In accord with the outcomes of other studies (e.g., Cazenave, 1979, 1981; J. McAdoo, 1981a, 1981b), fathers are reported as attending more to their sons than their daughters. For example, fathers are reported to show more concern about the sex-type development of boys than girls (Intons-Peterson, 1985) and are more rewarding to girls and more controlling and punishing to boys during play (Langlois & Downs, 1980). Moreover, Langlois and Downs reported that fathers differentially rewarded play with same sex toys and punished play with cross-sex toys for both sons and daughters.

There are other studies that have not supported father's differential treatment of girls and boys. Roopnarine (1986) found that although fathers and mothers responded differently to children toy play, parents were not affected by the sex difference in children. Intons-Peterson (1985) found that fathers reported having no gender-specific expectations and aspirations of boys and girls. The disparity in whether fathers respond to children in gender-specific patterns need further empirical investigation.

The evidence from the correlational analyses suggested a general consensus among family members' perceptions of mothers', grandmothers', and fathers' supporting and punishing behaviors. This is not surprising because support, expressing affection, approval and warmth, and punishment, withdrawing affection and approval, and reprimanding inappropriate behaviors, are consistently observed to be critical activities in the socialization of children (Becker, 1964; Belsky et al., 1984; Maccoby, 1980). For example, other researchers have indicated that adult support (Baumrind, 1972; Belsky, Goode, & Most, 1980) and punishment (Baumrind, 1972) are associated with the development of social competence and maturity in children. Baumrind suggested that exertion of parental authority leads to positive child outcome more often for Black families than White families. In this study, a common belief shared anecdotally by one grandmother was that children needed "to see both the carrot and stick to get them to do right."

On the other hand, mothers', grandmothers', and fathers' reports of their own behaviors did not correspond to what others reported them doing. These targeted adults were seen as supporting and punishing their children, but not to the extent that they saw themselves doing these behaviors. A common attributional inconsistency in the correlational patterns between the targets' self-perceptions and other family members' perceptions of the target was demonstrated (Forsyth, 1987). Namely, the target adults' self-perceptions often possess bias that is motivated by either a desire to protect ones self-esteem, "I am a good parent; therefore, I do these behaviors" or an expectancy of the parental role, "I am a parent; therefore, I do these behaviors." The more accurate perceptions probably occurred when other family members reported on the target adults' behaviors. Adult family members' involvement in child care could evoke considerable anxiety if the adults believed that a failure on the part of child occurred because the adults did not perform their child-care duties.

Nevertheless, the correlational and factorial analyses together suggest that personal and situational variables influence the perceived involvements of adults other than the mother in childrearing activities. Moreover, these outcomes do substantiate the role of grandmother in the family and suggest the importance of assessing the availability of alternative adult resources for childrearing activities in single-parent families.

It is noteworthy that most studies have analyzed either father's or grandmother's role but not both. An exception is the Slaughter and Dillworth-Anderson (1985) study. They indicated that among nonmaternal adults, father's support was more important than the grandmother's to mothers, independent of the father's presence or absence in the household (Slaughter & Dillworth-Anderson, 1985). Maternal grandmothers and sisters were reported as the next most important family members to the mothers. Interestingly, Slaughter and Dillworth-Anderson reported that fathers provided more emotional and instrumental support to the mothers than did the other family members, whereas maternal grandmothers provided more instrumental than emotional support.

Although this research suffers from the common problem of lack of a representative sample found in many psychological studies of the family it is hoped that the study will serve a heuristic function in raising issues and aspirations about family functioning in diverse nontraditional family forms. The expected impact of this study lies in its potential for understanding the childrearing practices in single- and dual-parent family structures and the role of the grandmother in the Black family. Given the high rate of marital dissolution and adolescent extramarital births, it is important to understand the factors that contribute to successful childrearing and positive child adjustment in nontraditional family structures.

The next step in this research project is to observe the actual performance of adults' childrearing behaviors and the impact of those behaviors on children's responses. Such a study is currently underway. Although other reciprocal interaction effects are present, our work is currently focused on the impact of adults on children. The eventual goal of the research project is the analyses of all dyadic and familial interactions patterns that are possible in two- and three-generational families.

The data of this study are focused on functional nonpathological Black families. Obviously, research that addresses dysfunctional aspects of two- and three-generational, and one- and two-parent Black families is needed. However, a major issue with past Black family research has been its focus on pathological aspects of Black family life before it understood the functional aspects of Black families. A significant example of this limited perspective was that although high frequency of extended-family structures among Black families was well documented, it was largely ignored in psychological studies on minority families. Devising interventions to enhance the well-being of Black families can only reliably be done once the functional roles and norms of Black family life are understood. This study represents an attempt to document the perception of childrearing behavior in two- and three-generational Black families.

ACKNOWLEDGMENTS

This study was supported by grants from the National Science Foundaton PRM-8210411, the Spencer Foundation, and the Rockefeller Foundation.

REFERENCES

Bartz, K. W., & Levine, E. S. (1978). Childrearing by Black parents: A description and comparison to Anglo and Chicano parents. *Journal of Marriage and the Family,40*, 709–719.

Baumrind, D. (1967). Childcare practices anteceding three patterns of pre-school behaviors. *Genetic Psychology Monographs, 75*, 43–88.

Baumrind, D. (1971). Current patterns of parental authority. *Developmental Psychology Monographs, 4*, (1, Part 2).

Baumrind, D. (1972). An exploratory study of socialization effects on Black children: Some Black-White comparisons. *Child Development, 43*, 261–267.

Becker, W. (1964). Consequences of different kinds of parental discipline. In M. L. Hoffman & L. W. Hoffman (Eds.), *Review of child development research* (Vol. 1, pp. 169–209). New York: Sage.

Belsky, J., Goode, M. K., & Most, R. K. (1980). Maternal stimulation and infant exploratory competence: Cross-sectional, correlational and experimental analyses. *Child Development, 51,* 1168–1178.

Belsky, J., Robins, E., & Gamble, W. (1984). The determinants of parental competence. In M. Lewis (Ed.), *Beyond the dyad* (pp. 257–280). New York: Plenum.

Buriel, R. (1981). The relation of Anglo- and Mexican-American children's locus of control beliefs to parents' and teachers' socialization practices. *Child Development, 52,* 104–113.

Cazenave, N. A. (1979). Middle-income Black families: An analysis of the provider role. *The Family Coordination, 28,* 583–593.

Cazenave, N. A. (1981). Black men in America: The quest of "manhood". In H.P. McAdoo (Ed.), *Black families* (pp. 176-185). Beverly Hills, CA: Sage.

Chilman, C. S. (1982). Major trends of families and their mental health in the United States: 1957–1978. *International Journal of Sociology of the Family, 12,* 1–10.

Colletta, N. D. (1979). Support systems after divorce: Incidence and impact. *Journal of Marriage and the Family, 41,* 837–846.

Colletta, N. D. (1981). Social support and risk of maternal rejection by adolescent mothers. *Journal of Psychology, 109,* 191–197.

Crockenberg, S. B. (1981). Infant irritability, mother responsiveness and social support influences in the security of infant-mother attachment. *Child Development, 52,* 857–865.

Devereux, E. C., Bronfenbrenner, U., & Rodgers, R. R. (1969). Childrearing in England and the United States: A cross-national comparison. *Journal of Marriage and the Family, 31,* 257–270.

Dornbush, S. M., Carlsmith, J. M., Bushwall, S. J., Ritter, P. L, Leiderman, H., Hastorf, A. H., & Gross, R. T. (1985). Single parents, extended households, and the control of adolescence. *Child Development, 56,* 326–341.

Egeland, B., & Sroufe, L. A. (1981). Attachment and early maltreatment. *Child Development, 52,* 44–52.

Ellis, G. J., Thomas, D. L., & Rollins, B. C. (1976). Measuring parental support: The interrelationship of three measures. *Journal of Marriage and the Family, 38,* 713–722.

Emmerich, W. (1977). Structure and development of personal-social behaviors in economically disadvantaged preschool children. *Genetic Psychology Monographs, 95,* 191–245.

Feiring, C., & Lewis, M. (1984). Changing characteristics of the U.S. family. In M. Lewis (Ed.), *Beyond the dyad* (pp. 59–89). New York: Plenum Press.

Field, T. M., Widmayer, S. M., Stringer, S., & Ignatoff, E. (1980). Teenage, lower class, black mothers and their preterm infants: An intervention and developmental follow-up. *Child Development, 51,* 426–436.

Forsyth, D. R. (1987). *Social psychology.* New York: Brooks/Cole.

Gilby, R. L., & Pederson, D. R. (1982). The development of the child's concept of the family. *Canadian Journal of Behavioral Science, 14,* 110–121.

Glick, P., & Norton, A. J. (1979). Marrying, divorcing and living together in U.S. today. *Population Bulletin, 32*(5), 1–40.

Hale, J. (1982). *Black children: Their roots, culture, and learning styles.* Provo, UT: Brigham Young University Press.

Hetherington, E. M. (1987). Family relations six years after divorce. In K. Palsey & M. Ihinger-Tollman (Eds.), *Remarriage and stepparenting today: Research and theory.* New York: Guilford Press.

Hetherington, E. M., Cox, M., & Cox, R. (1978). The aftermath of divorce. In J. H. Stevens, Jr. & M. Matthew (Eds.), *Mother-child, father-child relations* (pp. 87–123). Washington, DC: National Association for the Education of Young Children.

Hill, R. (1972). *The strength of Black families.* New York: Emerson-Hall.

Hill, R., & Schackleford, L. (1972). *Informal adoption among Black families*. Washington, DC: The National Urban League.

Hodkin, B. (1983, June). *The concept of family: Building an empirical base*. Paper presented at the annual meeting of the Canadian Psychological Association, Winnipeg, Canada.

Intons-Peterson, M. J. (1985). Father's expectation and aspiration for their children. *Sex Roles, 12,* 877–895.

Jackson, J. J. (1980). *Minorities and aging*. Belmont, CA: Wadsworth.

Kellam, S. G., Adams, R. G., Brown, C. H., & Ensminger, M. E. (1982). The long-term evolution of the family structure of teenage and older mothers. *Journal of Marriage and the Family, 46,* 539–554.

Lamb, M. E. (1981). The development of father-infant relationship. In M. E. Lamb (Ed.), *The role of father in child development* (2nd ed., pp. 359–389). New York: Wiley.

Lamb, M. E., & Elster, A. B. (1985). Adolescent mother-infant-father relationship. *Developmental Psychology, 21,* 768–773.

Langlois, J. H., & Downs, A. C. (1980). Mothers, fathers and peers as socialization agents of sex typed play behaviors in young children. *Child Development, 51,* 1217–1247.

Maccoby, E. E. (1980). *Social development: Psychological growth and the parent-child relationship*. San Diego: Harcourt, Brace, & Jovanovich.

Martin, E. P., & Martin, J. M. (1978). *The Black extended family*. Chicago: University of Chicago Press.

McAdoo, H. P. (1978). Factors related to stability in upwardly mobile Black families. *Journal of Marriage and the Family, 40,* 761–776.

McAdoo, J. (1981a). Involvement of fathers in socialization of Black children. In M. P. McAdoo (Ed.), *Black families* (pp. 225–237). Beverly Hills CA: Sage.

McAdoo, J. (1981b). Black fathers and child interaction. In L. E. Gary (Ed.), *Black men* (pp. 115–130). Beverly Hills, CA: Sage.

McLanahan, S. S., Wedemeyer, N. V., & Adelbery, J. (1981). Network structure, social support and psychological well-being in the single-parent family. *Journal of Marriage and the Family, 43,* 601–611.

Patterson, G. R. (1982). *Coercive family process*. Eugene, OR: Castalia.

Power, T. G. (1985). Mother- and father-infant play: A developmental analysis. *Child Development, 56,* 1514–1524.

Reid, J. (1982). Black America in the 1980s. *Population Bulletin, 37*(4), 1–37.

Roopnarine, J. L (1986). Mother's and father's behaviors toward the toy play of their infant sons and daughters. *Sex Roles, 14,* 59–68.

Seigelman, M. (1963). Evaluation of Bronfenbrenner's questionnaire for children concerning parental behavior. *Child Development, 36,* 163–174.

Slaughter, D. T., & Dillworth-Anderson, P. (1985, April). *Childcare of black sickle cell anemic children: Impact of father's presence and absence from households*. Paper presented at the Biennial Meeting of the Society for Research in Child Development, Toronto, Canada.

Stevens, J. H. (1984). Black grandmothers' and Black adolescent mothers' knowledge about parenting. *Developmental Psychology, 20,* 91–97.

Sweet, J. A. (1977, August). *Further indicators of family structure process for racial and ethnic minorities*. Paper presented at the Conference on Demography of Racial and Ethnic Groups, Austin, TX.

Tienda, M., Angel, R. (1982). Determinants of extended household structure: Cultural patterns in economic need? *American Journal of Sociology, 87,* 1360–1383.

Tinsley, B. R., & Parke, R. D. (1984). Grandparents as support and socialization agents. In M. Lewis (Ed.), *Beyond the dyad* (pp. 161–195). New York: Plenum.

Tolson, T. F. J., & Wilson, M. N. (1987, May). *Perceived social climate in two- and three-generational black families*. Paper presented at the First Biennial Conference on Community Research and Action, Columbia, SC.

U.S. Bureau of the Census. (1986). *Household and family characteristics: March, 1985.* (Current Population Report Series P-20, No. 411). Washington, DC: U.S. Government Printing Office.

Uzoka, A. (1979). The myth of the nuclear family. *American Psychologist, 34,* 1075–1106.

Ventura, J. N., & Stevenson, M. B. (1986). Relations of mothers' and fathers' reports on infant temperament, parents' psychological functioning and family characteristics. *Merrill-Palmer Quarterly, 32,* 275–289.

Weigert, A. J. (1968). Parent-child interaction patterns and adolescent religiosity: A cross-national study. *Dissertation Abstracts, 29,* 3691.

Wilson, M. N. (1984). Mothers' and grandmothers' perception of parental behavior in three-generational Black families. *Child Development, 55,* 1333–1339.

Wilson, M. N., & Tolson, T. F. J. (1986). A social interaction analysis of two- and three-generational Black families. In P. Dail & R. Jewson (Eds.), *In praise of fifty years: Groves conference on the conservation of marriage and the family* (pp. 43–53). Lake Mills, IA: Graphic Publishing.

PART IV

REMARRIAGE AND STEPPARENTING

12

Child Care After Divorce and Remarriage

Frank F. Furstenberg, Jr.
University of Pennsylvania

INTRODUCTION

After a long period of relative obscurity, remarriage and stepfamily life have begun to attract the attention of family practitioners, policymakers, and the public. The demand for information has caught social scientists short for remarkably little is known about stepfamilies. In the 1970s, when I first examined how divorce and remarriage were altering kinship conceptions and practices, I discovered that virtually nothing of significance had been written by sociologists on remarriage since the classical studies of Jessie Bernard (1956) and William J. Goode (1956). Textbooks on the family, replete with discussions of exotic family forms, all but ignored families reconstituted after divorce and remarriage. When the subject of remarriage was treated at all, it usually appeared at the conclusion of a chapter on divorce (Furstenberg, 1979). Often we learned that the return to matrimony resolved problems of divorce. It was as if remarriage operated to put Humpty Dumpty back together again, in the form of a nuclear family, cleverly concealing the cracks.

For a variety of reasons that I only allude to in this chapter, Americans have become less wedded to the ideal of the nuclear family (Pasley & Ihinger-Tallman, 1987). There is a growing recognition that alternative structures can provide congenial environments for children (Bohannon, 1985, 1986; Settles, 1986). Few researchers question the desirability of the two-parent family, especially when this form is constant and continuous, because it promises economic and emotional security for children. Social scientists are, however, beginning to question the doctrine that only the nuclear family can provide a truly appropriate setting for socialization.

245

One reason why Americans cling so tenaciously to the ideal of the nuclear family is that they mistakenly believe this family form—what has come to be known as the "traditional family"—was more common in the past (Hareven, 1986). This belief represents a serious misreading of history. Until quite recently, American children were unlikely to spend all of their early years with both of their biological parents (Skolnick & Skolnick, 1986). True, divorce was extremely rare until this century, but high rates of mortality often robbed children of one or both parents. Moreover, desertion, lengthy separations occasioned by economic necessity, and serious morbidity were common events that are rarely recalled in our nostalgic recollections of family life in earlier times. (Hareven, 1978; Shorter, 1975).

Families were also expanded when catastrophic events forced them to take in relatives, boarders, and lodgers. Many children at a tender age were forced to take refuge in the household of a relative, acquaintance, or employer when their parents were unable or, sometimes, unwilling to provide care. In certain respects, the family of the past resembles the situation of minority families today: Then, as now, family members were forced to improvise in the face of adverse economic conditions or personal misfortune.

It was not until the middle of the 20th century that the nuclear family came into full bloom (Uhlenberg, 1974). Very likely, more children spent a greater proportion of their childhoods in nuclear families during the period just before and after World War II than in any previous era in American history. But no sooner did the nuclear family enter its heyday than it began to succumb to a new set of pressures. By now we all know something about the meteoric rise of divorce since the 1960s. In fact, divorce rates had generally been rising over the past century, although sometimes in fits and starts (Cherlin, 1981). But beginning in the 1960s, a fundamental change occurred that crystallized what had previously been only an incipient trend. What I have referred to elsewhere as "the pattern of conjugal succession" emerged as a socially acceptable, although still not preferred, practice of family formation (Furstenberg, 1982). Marriage was no longer seen as an unconditional commitment. Rather, individuals felt a right, even an obligation, to seek marital gratification even at the expense of permanency. Economic, legal, and social support for divorce have all increased, reducing the obstacles to dissolving an unsatisfactory union.

Nothing in these changes indicates a waning commitment to the institution of marriage. Divorced individuals are almost as likely to reenter marriage as they ever were, although increasing numbers are cohabiting for a time between marriages, giving the appearance that interest in marriage is declining. The great majority of divorced individuals remarry, and even more would do so if they could find a suitable mate. Some years ago, Paul Jacobsen (1959) discovered that divorced persons have a greater likelihood of marrying again than never-married individuals of the same age have of marrying a first time. There is no reason to believe that this fact has changed.

If the pattern of conjugal succession represents a permanent change in our kinship system, we must then ask what are the implications for the development and well-being of children? In attempting to answer this question, I draw on the results of two separate studies. The first, conducted in 1979 is a longitudinal study of nearly 200 recently divorced individuals in transition from divorce to remarriage in Central Pennsylvania (Furstenberg & Spanier, 1984). It focused on problems adults encountered in raising their children after divorce and remarriage. The second study, The National Survey of Children (NSC) primarily examined the well-being of children. The NSC began collecting data in 1976 from a nationally representative sample of nearly 2,200 children between the ages of 7 and 11 and one of each child's parents. In 1981, reinterviews were completed on: (a) the children who had experienced marital disruption in their families by the time of the first interview; (b) all children whose parents reported a high level of marital conflict; and (c) a subsample of children from families in which the level of conflict was low or moderate. A tremendous amount of information was collected from nearly 1,300 children, 1,050 parents or parent surrogates who were the principal caretakers (almost always the mothers), and from mailed questionnaires sent to one or more of the children's teachers. Over the past several years, a series of papers has been published on the results of this study. (For a detailed discussion of the methods and findings see Furstenberg, 1987; Furstenberg, Morgan, & Allison, 1987; Furstenberg & Nord, 1985; Furstenberg, Nord, Peterson and Zill, 1983, Furstenberg & Seltzer, 1986).

In 1983, Andrew Cherlin and I completed a survey of the grandparents of the children in the NSC to examine the effect of marital disruption on intergenerational relations. These data were designed to test several hypotheses derived from the Central Pennsylvania study concerning how and why divorce and remarriage alters kinship bonds. Some of these findings are discussed later in this chapter. A complete account of the grandparent study is presented in *The New American Grandparent* (Cherlin & Furstenberg, 1986).

The Incidence of Disruption

From the NSC data, we are able to calculate the precise risk of disruption for children at any given age and to identify the specific contribution of separation and divorce as distinct from other disturbances such as death or out-of-wedlock childbearing. We are also able to examine the probability that children will enter a stepfamily and of their risk of encountering a disruption in their new family situation (see also, Bumpass, 1984; Hofferth, 1985).

Table 12.1 displays the probability of children experiencing family disruption at given ages. In order to show the increase in rates of disruption due to the growing likelihood of divorce in recent years, our sample has been divided into two birth cohorts. We have also divided the sample by race to show the differing experiences of Whites and minority children.

TABLE 12.1
Cumulative Proportion of Children with Disrupted Families by Age
and Race in the National Survey of Children, 1981
(Children aged 12–16)

Child's Year of Birth	1	2	3	4	5	6	7	8	9	10	11	12	13	14	15	16	Number of Children
Total[a]																	
1965–1967[b]	5	7	10	12	14	16	17	19	20	22	24	25	26	28	30	31	680
1965–1967[c]	14	16	19	21	22	24	25	27	28	30	31	33	34	35	38	38	772
1968–1969[b]	6	10	13	15	17	19	21	25	26	27	29	30	31				437
1968–1969[c]	15	19	21	23	25	27	29	32	33	34	36	37	38				492
White																	
1965–1967[b]	4	5	8	10	12	14	15	16	17	19	20	21	22	23	25	26	571
1965–1967[c]	9	10	13	15	16	18	19	20	22	23	25	26	27	28	31	31	613
1968–1969[b]	5	10	12	14	17	18	20	23	24	26	28	29	29				375
1968–1969[c]	10	15	17	19	21	23	25	27	28	30	32	33	33				396
Black																	
1965–1967[b]	16	24	27	28	30	30	31	35	35	37	41	51	52	53	58		81
1965–1967[c]	38	43	45	46	47	47	49	51	51	53	56	62	65	68	71		117
1968–1969[b]	20	20	22	27	29	33	33	47	47	49	49	51	51				45
1968–1969[c]	45	45	47	49	51	54	54	62	62	63	66	69	70				71

[a]Total figures for NSC data includes 57 cases of Hispanic and Oriental children.
[b]Includes only those children who were born after their mother's first marriage and who are currently living with at least one biological parent.
[c]Includes all children regardless of where they are currently living or whether their mother ever married.

Three important findings are immediately evident from Table 12.1. First, the risk of disruption during childhood is substantial. When we include children whose parents have never married in our calculations, close to two out of every five children in the sample are not living with both biological parents by age 16. Even without them, about one third of the sample whose parents ever married, are not living with both parents by age 16. Second, huge differences exist between Whites and Blacks: Blacks are almost twice as likely as Whites not to be living with both parents in their early teens. When we count children born out of wedlock as having experienced disruption, fewer than one third of the Blacks are living with both of their biological parents. Third, the risk of dissolution has increased substantially among children born after 1968, the time when divorce rates were shooting up. The younger cohort has experienced as much disruption by age 13 as the older cohort encountered by age 16.

Were our sample to extend to children born in the 1970s when divorce rates attained much higher levels and were we able to trace the probability of divorce through the middle teens, we have no doubt that our results would show that close to half of all children would not be living with both of their biological parents through their entire childhood. Even if we were to remove the Black children from the sample, who contribute disproportionately to the high rate of disruption, we would find that close to a majority of the White children would not reach adulthood without experiencing family disruption.

Very little of the disruption that occurs can be attributed to the death of a parent. Removing the children who lost a parent by death would drop the overall rate of disruption from .3044 to .2610, indicating that deaths only explain about 13% of the total amount of disruption. Even for teenage children, when deaths of parents are increasing and divorces decreasing, mortality continues to be a much less important source of disruption than marital breakup.

Over time, most children whose parents do not remain married enter stepfamilies. Among the Whites, 58% of the children whose parents separated eventually entered a stepfamily; the comparable figure for Blacks was far lower, 37%, reflecting the fact that Black couples who separate are less likely to divorce and, hence, less likely to remarry. The marriage pool for Black women is much less attractive, providing a lower incentive to divorce and remarry.

Remarriage does not necessarily stabilize the child's family situation. About one third of the children whose custodial parent had remarried had been subjected to another disruption. Had we been able to calculate the risk of redivorce among the noncustodial parent, we would have discovered still more disruption. Although Whites have a lower risk of experiencing disruption initially, their chances of undergoing multiple transitions due to a remarriage and redivorce are actually greater than Blacks. Of course, we have not reported cohabitational experience of the parents. But the data we have from the NSC does not indicate that counting cohabitation would make very much difference in the racial differences reported above. Even excluding cohabitation, the total number of children who will experience three or more transitions during their childhood years is considerable and growing rapidly. For our sample, we estimate that approximately 1 child in every 10 will see their parents divorce, their custodial parent remarry, and then divorce again before they reach the age of 16.

Patterns of Contact and Co-Parenting
After Marital Disruption

Divorce severs the marital bonds but does not necessarily cut the ties between parents and children. The U.S. has no clearcut guidelines on how to assign parental rights and obligations when marriage and parenthood are not coterminous (Weitzman, 1985). Custody practices have wavered during the past century, first favoring paternal then maternal custody (Halem, 1980). Currently, great ferment exists for a more even-handed custody policy, permitting both parents to assume rights to and responsibilities for the children. Shared or joint custody does not, of course, mean that children would maintain residence with both parents or that each would spend equal time with the child.

Relatively little is known about how parenting is carried out after marriages break up and even less about how parental patterns are altered when parents reenter marriage and assume new family obligations (Pasley & Ihinger-Tallman, 1987). In both the pilot study in Central Pennsylvania and the national survey, extensive information was collected on childrearing practices after divorce and remarriage. We can summarize only a few of the most important findings here. For more detailed discussion, the readers should consult previous papers describing the results of the two studies (Furstenberg, 1987; Furstenberg & Nord, 1985; Furstenberg & Spanier, 1984).

Although all parents were interviewed in the Central Pennsylvania study within 4 years of the dissolution of their marriages, a substantial number reported that little or no contact occurred between the nonresidential parent and child. Accounts varied somewhat according to the gender of the parent and whether he or she had custody of the child, but less than one-fifth of the respondents indicated that contact occurred as often as a few times a week, most said they saw them once or twice a month or occasionally during the year and, about one-fifth replied that contact was even less frequent. Custodial parents reported lower levels of contact than noncustodial parents, but differences were not very great. A distinct decline in interaction took place within the 2-year interval of study, indicating that parents tend to drift apart from their children not long after separation occurs. Finally, noncustodial parents assumed very little responsibility for childrearing beyond seeing their children occasionally. Virtually all important decisions were made by custodial parents, although noncustodial parents perceived themselves as more involved in their decisions than did the custodial parents.

Some evidence from the Central Pennsylvania study suggests that remarriage, especially by the noncustodial parent, seems to complicate the process of co-parenting. Withdrawal was most evident when noncustodial fathers remarried and their spouses did not. We could not tell from the limited data available whether this was because, in taking on new family obligations, fathers outside the home tended to lose interest in the children from their first marriage, whether they were overwhelmed by competing demands, or whether situational factors such as increased geographical distance associated with remarriage increased the barriers to assuming parental responsibilities. We speculated that custodial mothers may have become more vigilant gatekeepers after their former spouses established a new family.

Remarriage occasionally produced quite the opposite effect, increasing interaction between parents and children. Tensions were sometimes reduced when intermediaries entered the scene to cool down hostilities. Also fathers who had been ill-prepared to assume a caretaking role could play a more active part when they were aided by a spouse or partner. Thus, the effect of remarriage on patterns of parenting was not simple or uniform.

Data from the National Survey of Children revealed a much broader picture of the consequences of marital disruption for childcare arrangements, but many of the trends just mentioned reappeared in even starker form. The pilot study, for example, tended to overstate the amount of childcare provided by the parent living outside the home. As Table 12.2 reveals, close to half (43.7%) of all children living with a biological parent, have not seen their other parent during the preceding 12 months; of those who have had contact with the parent living outside the home, only a minority (34.7%) see him or her regularly, that is, an average of once a week or more throughout the year. Not only is contact relatively infrequent for most children who are living apart from one of their parents, but only a small portion of the sample talk to their parents on the phone as often as once a week (27.1%), ever spend a week or more at a time in the home of

TABLE 12.2
Extent of Children's Contact With Their Outside Parent[a]
(weighted percent, U.S. children aged 12–16, 1981)

	Percent of all children	Percent of children with contact in last year
Last contact, 1–5 years ago	28.6	
No contact in last year	15.1	
1–2 days of contact last year	5.2	9.3
3–13 days of contact last year	12.8	22.7
14–51 days of contact last year	18.7	33.2
52–103 days of contact last year	11.1	19.7
104+ days of contact last year	8.4	15.0
Weighted N	(360)	(203)

[a]Restricted to children living with one biological parent whose other biological parent is known or believed to be alive.

their outside parent (26.6%), sleep over at his or her house on at least a monthly basis (27.3%), have a place in the outside parent's home to store their things (27.3%), and consider that household to be like a home of their own (28.6%). In very general terms, close to half of the sample rarely or never have contact with their parents, another third have contact irregularly or infrequently, and about one-fifth have what might be called regular relations.

In Table 12.3, data on parenting activities, expectations, and rules are contrasted for children living with both biological parents, living in stepfamilies, and living with a single parent. Children who are not living with both biological parents were asked a parallel set of questions about both their residential and nonresidential parents if they have contact with their outside parents at least once a month. Thus, it is necessary to keep in mind that the comparisons in Table

TABLE 12.3
Selected Data on Parenting Activities, Expectations, and Rules by Family
Type in the National Survey of Children, 1981[a]
(children aged 12–16)

	Unbroken	Reconstituted		Single Parent	
	Biological Parents	Inside Parent	Outside Parent	Inside Parent	Outside Parent
Within the last month, have you:					
gone to the movies	22.5	16.6	7.1	23.4	19.7
gone out to dinner	65.8	53.2	51.4	54.9	41.9
gone shopping for you	69.7	60.0	37.7	68.3	44.1
taken trip to museum					
or sports event	41.0	29.3	21.5	30.2	17.7
Within the last week, have you:					
done a project together	49.0	53.4	17.0	42.2	22.9
worked on schoolwork together	30.2	18.8	8.0	16.6	11.3
played game or sport	41.7	39.4	36.5	30.1	24.4
Expectations: Are you expected to:					
clean your room	96.2	97.9	73.0	95.9	57.9
clean rest of house	81.7	77.8	55.4	92.4	46.9
do dishes	60.6	66.3	46.9	77.1	42.6
cook	32.0	42.9	24.2	43.9	20.9
Rules: Are there rules about:					
watching TV	32.6	37.4	20.8	20.1	3.6
telling your whereabouts	94.5	95.5	77.5	94.4	75.8
doing homework	76.5	77.4	36.1	76.0	36.9
dating	69.3	66.2	56.4	57.6	49.3
Rule Making: Do your parents:					
discuss decisions with you	39.2	27.1	48.5	40.9	28.6
listen to your arguments	41.9	40.4	57.8	54.4	41.0

[a]Restricted to children whose outside parent is a biological parent and who are living with a biological parent. Family type refers to living stituation of inside parent, not of outside parent.

12.3 do not include children who have no outside parent or who saw him or her only infrequently.

Even if we limit ourselves only to those outside parents who actively participate in child care, the nature of the care provided is more recreational than instrumental. Outside parents frequently take their children out for dinner, play a game or sport with them, or take them on a shopping trip, but only rarely do they assist them with schoolwork or work on some project with them. When compared to residential parents, outside parents are far less likely to expect their children to participate in household chores and are much less likely to have strict rules. Thus, outside parents seem to adopt a more lenient or permissive standard toward childrearing, particularly after the custodial parent has remarried. This finding might suggest either that children resent the intrusion of a stepparent or, possibly, that outside parents become more indulgent when their place in the household is filled by a surrogate.

Turning now to the behavior of residential parents, only small differences in parent–child relations are evident among the different family forms. Generally speaking, children get more attention when they are living with both of their biological parents, although the differences in activities are not large or completely consistent. Children are equally likely to say that their residential parents make demands on them to help out regardless of their family structure. If anything, demands seem to be slightly greater on children living in single-parent families.

Cooperation Between the Custodial and Noncustodial Parent

The evidence presented thus far from the NSC indicates that marital disruption drastically curtails children's relations with their noncustodial or nonresidential parents, but has a far less pronounced impact on relations with the custodial parent. In large measure, this is because most nonresidential parents withdraw from parental participation. This fact has obvious implications for the management of child care when parents are living apart.

Table 12.4 presents selected items tapping the extent of collaboration between the parents as reported by the residential parent. The picture strongly supports the impression provided by the Central Pennsylvania study that parents have little to do with one another once their marriage breaks up. Questions pertaining to the participation of the outside parent were only asked when contact had occurred in the past year. Only a minority of the parents indicate that the outside parent assumes a fair share of responsibility and a small fraction report that he or she has some or a great deal of influence in important decision that concern the child. And, most residential parents say that they discuss childrearing matters rarely or never with the parent living outside the home. Thus, even when we restrict our attention to the segment of the sample where the outside parent

TABLE 12.4
Interaction of Parents Living Apart by Identity of Outside Parent,[a]
National Survey of Children, 1981

	Mother	Father	Total
Do you and (OUTSIDE PARENT) discuss matters concerning (CHILD):			
frequently	4.0	10.0	9.1
sometimes	37.8	22.9	25.1
rarely, or	26.0	28.6	28.2
never?	32.2	38.5	37.5
Weighted N	(30)	(169)	(199)
In raising (CHILD), does (OUTSIDE PARENT) take:			
too much,	8.9	1.5	2.5
about the right amount, or	21.6	23.2	23.0
too little responsibility?	69.6	74.9	74.2
Weighted N	(27)	(185)	(212)
When you and (OUTSIDE PARENT) make decisions about (CHILD), does (OUTSIDE PARENT) have:			
a great deal of influence	6.7	3.2	3.7
some or,	16.7	23.5	22.6
very little influence?	30.0	29.4	29.5
(DO NOT READ) Make no decisions together?	46.7	43.9	44.2
Weighted N	(30)	(187)	(217)

[a]Restricted to children living with one biological parent, the other is the outside parent.

remained involved to some degree, parents seem to operate as independently as possible.

Moreover, collaboration between parents does not increase noticeably when contact is higher between the parent and child (Furstenberg & Nord, 1985). Of course, when children have little or no contact with their outside parent, the level of collaboration is very low. But at the other extreme, collaboration does not greatly increase when there is regular and frequent contact between the outside parent and child. Noncustodial parents who play an active role in childrearing typically do not coordinate their activities with parents living in the home. If we mean by the term *co-parenting* that parents continue to discuss matters concerning the children and share childrearing decisions, our research indicates that co-parenting rarely occurs after divorce. A more apt term for describing the process of childrearing after divorce is *parallel parenting*: the formerly married parents operate in tandem, segregating their activities as much as possible from one another.

Although there are obvious disadvantages to this strategy, it does have the effect of dampening conflict between the parents. Very few of the residential parents report disagreements with their former spouses, even though they freely acknowledge that conflict was extremely high before the marriage broke up. Fewer than 10% complain that the outside parent breaks plans to see the child, meddles in the way that they bring up the child, or undermines their parental rules. Very few of those who have remarried indicate that the outside parent increases strain in their relations with their new spouse or interferes in the relationship of their spouse and the child. There is no statistically significant association between the amount of contact the outside parent has with the child and the various measures of conflict, suggesting that even when contact with the child is relatively high, relations between the former spouses are unaffected (Furstenberg & Nord, 1985). No doubt, the high level of disengagement dampens the possibilities of conflict.

Remarriage does not greatly change the picture. As we found in the Central Pennsylvania study, contact with the child dropped slightly when the outside parent married. However, when we controlled for factors such as geographical distance and the length of time since separation, reentering marriage had only a trivial effect on the level of participation by the outside parent. Similarly, remarriage did not significantly decrease the degree of collaboration between the parents. Remarriage was as likely to reduce as to elevate tensions between the formerly married couple. Generally, however, remarriage does not affect the former couple's relations one way or the other because most former couples have so little to do with one another that the marriage of one or both has little bearing on how they get along or how successfully they share childrearing duties.

If remarriage does not affect the childrearing arrangement, what circumstances do influence the level of involvement by the outside parent and the quality of relations between the parents? An additional analysis attempted to identify conditions that influence the pattern of parenting after separation and divorce. The critical factors seem to be the level of child support provided by the outside parent and his or her geographical distance from the child (Furstenberg & Nord, 1985). Both conditions are in turn related to the age of the child at the time of the separation, the length of time since separation occurred, the separation process itself, and the socioeconomic status of the family. Although we can only speculate about the causal chain of these various factors, it is reasonable to surmise that parents who have a strong relationship with their child before the marriage breaks up, who have the resources to offer the child, and who are able to avoid a bitter divorce process maintain a relatively high level of involvement. High participation (i.e., regular contact and support), however, does not necessarily imply that the nonresidential parent will work closely with the custodial parent. None of the factors just mentioned is related to the ability of the parents to collaborate with one another. Apparently, more idiosyncratic factors influence whether the formerly married couple is able to coparent successfully or resorts instead to a pattern of parallel parenting.

THE IMPACT OF MARITAL DISRUPTION
ON CHILDREN

Further analysis of the NSC data examines how the process of parenting following marital disruption affects the children in the study (Furstenberg & Allison, 1985; Furstenberg, Morgan, & Allison, 1987; Furstenberg & Seltzer, 1986). The data reveal that children who have experienced disruption are more discontent with the quality of relations within their families, although the differences are not very great. A series of controls for background factors reduces the differences by family type, but the findings generally are robust. Reports from parents, teachers, and children themselves show that divorce has modest, long-lasting effects on children's academic and social adjustment.

It is not clear whether the adverse effects on different developmental outcomes (academic achievement, problem behavior, and psychological distress) result from who experiences marital disruption, the process of disruption itself, or negative experiences resulting from the disruption. The data from the NSC indicate that children who are under age 6 at the time of the marital separation are more likely to experience long-term ill effects. Conversely, youth who were adolescents when their parents' marriage dissolved showed few negative consequences. Also, the NSC data reveal no differences between boys and girls in the magnitude of ill effects, although gender differences were evident in the way boys and girls respond to marital dissolution.

A separate analysis examined the effect of participation by the outside parent on the child's relationship with his or her residential parent and stepparent. The results conclusively showed that involvement by the noncustodial parent had little impact on the child's relationship with the residential parent. This finding seems to bear out the reports of residential parents that outside parents only rarely interfered in their dealings with the child. Interestingly, contact with outside parents had no general effect—positive or negative—on children's well-being. The absence of any general association between contact with the noncustodial parent and child outcomes may be due to the fact that relatively few outside parents see their children frequently enough to exert much influence. These findings also indicate that researchers need to probe for the specific conditions under which contact occurs if they hope to establish a causal link between parental contact and children's well-being.

Stepparent relations were not adversely affected by the child's contact with the outside parent when the biological mother was the custodial parent and a stepfather was living with the child (Furstenberg, 1987). All our data pointed to the conclusion that the child functioned rather well with more than two fathers. Indeed, there was a slight hint that children had slightly closer relations with their stepfather when regular contact continued with the biological father, although the differences that occurred were not statistically significant.

There are very few cases of stepfamilies consisting of the biological father and a stepmother, making it difficult to draw any firm conclusions about this family form. Nonetheless, the evidence strongly suggested that this arrangement proved to be far more problematic from the child's viewpoint. Children generally had more negative evaluations of their stepmothers, especially when they continued to have regular contact with their biological mothers. Thus, children seem far less able to cope with the replacement of a mother than a father, an observation that should not be surprising in light of what we know about the relative importance of mothers and fathers in early childrearing. However, before drawing any lessons from the data for public policy or guidelines for clinicians, we should keep in mind that the number of cases on which these observations are based are very few, the subgroup of fathers who retain custody is highly selective, and the data cannot be applied to recent custody arrangements as it is largely based on divorces that occurred in the early and middle part of the last decade. Whether these findings can be generalized to more recent cohorts of children who are experiencing divorce and remarriage in the 1980s is a matter for conjecture.

Marital Disruption and Intergenerational Relations

Up to this point I have only considered how divorce and remarriage reshapes relations in the child's immediate family. But the data from the Central Pennsylvania study revealed that marital disruption restructures the boundaries of the extended family as well. Divorce, particularly when it attenuates the link between the outside parent and child, reduces the child's access to one line of the family. Or from the perspective of grandparents, it can weaken intergenerational bonds between the family of the noncustodial parent and the child.

This finding must be qualified in certain respects. In a substantial minority of cases, the grandparents continue to see the child on a fairly regular basis. If the noncustodial parent maintains regular contact with the child, then the link to the grandparents is often preserved. Even when contact slackens between the outside parent and child, the grandparents typically continue to see the child if they live close by and maintain reasonably amicable relations with the custodial parent. Most custodial parents are committed to preserving these intergenerational ties; some even continue to regard their former in-laws as their relatives because they are the child's kin. Despite these commitments, relations between the noncustodial grandparents and their grandchildren are rarely as active as they might have been had the divorce not occurred.

By contrast, divorce frequently intensifies the child's bonds with the custodial parent's family. Often, the parent turns to relatives for help at the time of divorce.

An unemployed mother may, for example, temporarily reside with her parents or, if she does not, she may seek financial or child-care assistance from them. A study of the grandparents of the children in the NSC confirmed the findings from Central Pennsylvania that contact between the parent and her family is much greater when the parent is separated or divorced. Grandparents were often drawn into a more functional relationship with the child following marital dissolution (Cherlin & Furstenberg, 1986). Thirteen percent of the children in disrupted families were living with their grandparents, compared to only 1% of the children in nondisrupted families. (For further details, see Table A-7 in Cherlin & Furstenberg, 1986.)

Remarriage seems to restore some of the balance achieved by the initial marriage. The Central Pennsylvania study revealed that stepgrandparents quickly assume the familiar grandparent role, even for children in their middle years. Children, for their part, seem to make little distinction between real and stepgrandparents, and parents usually encourage them to become assimilated into their new family as quickly as possible, so long as the children were young when the remarriage occurred. Indeed, young children seem to experience far fewer problems acquiring stepkin than stepparents (Furstenberg & Spanier, 1984).

Divorce and remarriage then can have the consequence of expanding the child's kinship network. Relatives are added on rather than replaced when children move from one family to the next. Whether emotional relations are diluted in the process is not clear from available data. It is also not known whether divorce disrupts children's claims to material resources or assistance from relatives of the noncustodial parent. Moreover, it is not possible to tell whether children receive fewer benefits from their stepkin than would be provided by biological kin. In regard to kinship support, children may actually derive some benefit from divorce and remarriage because they have a larger pool of available kin than do children whose parents remain in first marriages. But the hypothesis can be challenged on a number of grounds, and we must await the data now being collected to assess its validity.

CONCLUSION

I have touched upon a number of topics in this brief chapter concerning the impact of divorce and remarriage on child care. None of the issues explored have been fully researched, leaving a number of critical questions unsettled. Nonetheless, the evidence to date provides some intriguing findings on child-care arrangements, the consequences of marital disruption for parenting practices, and the well-being of children.

The most striking result to emerge from the National Survey of Children is the low level of contact between the noncustodial parent and child. The prevailing pattern seems to resemble a system of "child swapping." Fathers move out of the home and are usually replaced by stepfathers. The outside parents in turn establish a new household in which they may share responsibility for their partner's children. This system is far from efficient. There are delays in the transition from one marriage to the next, leaving the custodial parent with the full burden of child support (Ellwood, 1987). And, in a sizable fraction of families, particularly among older women and low-income Blacks, the father is never replaced.

It is not clear how well this system of surrogate parenthood works out for the child. We know that a substantial number of remarriages do not succeed, and children are exposed to disruption again. The NSC data reveal that approximately 1 child in 10 will undergo two or more family disruptions before reaching the age of 16. We need to pay close attention to the special effects, if there are any, of complex family sequences on the development and well-being of children.

It would be wrong, however, to count only the causalities of marital disruption. The preliminary data from NSC on the welfare of the children indicate that many children develop reasonably close attachments to their stepparents, and most stepfamilies function rather well. Thus, rather than engage in a form of sociological stereotyping, we need to explore the varieties of stepfamily experience. What are the conditions that promote successful relations between stepparents and their children? Are there distinctive styles of stepparenting that seem to be associated with favorable outcomes for children?

Evidence from the NSC suggests that the continued involvement of the outside parent in child care generally does not conflict with the establishment of a stepfamily. Reports from both parents and children revealed only minor traces of conflict between biological and stepparents. The picture was quite different for children living with stepfathers and stepmothers. Relations were less satisfactory for the latter group, perhaps because of the special circumstances that led the father to receive custody. Whatever the reason, children in our study seem to be better able to operate with two active fathers than two active mothers. If generally true, this finding requires explanation.

In general, more information is needed about how parents coordinate their child care after divorce and remarriage. The NSC data suggest that there is little conscious effort to collaborate. Each parent seems to operate fairly independently, consulting and communicating as little as possible. Parallel parenting keeps down the level of conflict, but it may not serve the child's interests very well. What are the consequences of different parenting arrangements for the adjustment of children after divorce? Does cooperation between parents lessen the trauma of divorce for children and reduce the adverse effects?

An important area for both research and policy analysis is what factors might promote a greater level of cooperation between parents after divorce. The NSC shows, as have other investigators, that child support is strongly correlated to involvement by the outside parent and cooperation between the parents (Furstenberg & Nord, 1985). Provision of child care was in turn related to the age of child at separation, the socioeconomic status of the family, and the ability of the parents to arrive at a reasonable, amicable settlement. To reduce the growing costs of marital disruption for families and society at large, more information is required about how to manipulate the conditions that influence child support and whether such intervention will ultimately benefit the child.

Finally, some preliminary information was provided in this chapter on how marital disruption and reconstruction alters the network of kinship ties. The role of extended kin can be dramatically changed by a divorce. In some cases, greater demands are placed on family, grandparents in particular, for support. In others, the grandparent may be forced to relinquish ties to the child. Similarly, remarriage may introduce an element of ambiguity in intergenerational relations. What rights and responsibilities are stepgrandparents expected to assume? Are distinctions drawn between step and biological relations that affect the claims that can be made on extended kin?

One of the most frustrating features of research in areas where rapid change is taking place is that data become dated almost as soon as they are collected. It is entirely possible that the lessons we have learned from the National Survey of Children will not apply to younger cohorts of children who grow up in an era when divorce and remarriage are even more common. Changing custody practices and changing opinions about the rights and responsibilities of parents following divorce and remarriage may produce new responses to marital disruption, resulting in different outcomes in the next generation of children. Research results must therefore be placed within a specific historical and cultural context, with full knowledge that this context may be in transition. If the consequences of family change are to be mapped accurately, we must be prepared to take repeated readings of the social world in which children are growing up. In doing so, we would be in a better position to learn about both the shifting dimensions of family worlds and the ever changing process of socialization.

ACKNOWLEDGMENTS

This research was funded by grants from the Foundation for Child Development and the National Institute of Mental Health (5 R07 MH 34707-02). The National Survey of Children-Wave 2 was jointly carried out by Frank F. Furstenberg, Jr. at the University of Pennsylvania and James L. Peterson and Nicholas Zill of Child Trends, Inc. The author appreciates assistance from Christine Winquist Nord in preparing this chapter.

REFERENCES

Bernard, J. (1956). *Remarriage*. New York: Dryden.
Bohannan, P. (1985). *All the happy families: Exploring the varieties of family life*. New York: McGraw-Hill.

Bumpass, L. (1984). Children and marital disruption: A replication and update. *Demography, 21,* 71–82.

Cherlin, A. J. (1981). *Marriage, divorce, remarriage.* Cambridge, MA: Harvard University Press.

Cherlin, A. J., & Furstenberg, F. F., Jr. (1986). *The new American grandparent: A place in the family, a life apart.* New York: Basic Books.

Ellwood, D. T. (1987). *Divide and conquer: Responsible security for America's poor.* New York: Ford Foundation.

Furstenberg, F. F., Jr. (1979). Recycling the family: Perspectives for researching a neglected family form. *Marriage and Family Review, 2*(3), 12–22.

Furstenberg, F. F., Jr. (1982). Conjugal succession: Reentering marriage after divorce. In P. B. Baltes & O. G. Brim, Jr. (Eds.), *Life span development and behavior* (Vol. 4, pp. 107– 146). New York: Academic Press.

Furstenberg, F. F., Jr. (1987). The new extended family: Experiences in step families. In K. Pasley & M. Ihinger-Tallman (Eds.), *Remarriage and step-parenting; Current research theory* (pp. 42–61). New York: Guilford.

Furstenberg, F. F., Jr., & Allison, P. (1985, April). *How marital dissolution affects children: Variations by age and sex.* Paper presented at the annual meeting of the Society For Research in Child Development, Toronto.

Furstenberg, F. F., Jr., & Morgan, S. P. (1987). Exploring race differences in the timing of early sexual behavior. *American Sociological Review, 52*(4), 511–518.

Furstenberg, F. F., Jr., Morgan S. P., & Allison, P. D. (1987). Paternal participation and children's well-being after marital disruption. *American Sociological Review, 52,* 695–701.

Furstenberg, F. F., Jr., & Nord, C. W. (1985). Parenting apart: Patterns of childrearing after divorce. *Journal of Marriage and the Family, 47*(4), 893–904.

Furstenberg, F. F., Jr., Nord, C. W., Peterson, J. L., & Zill, N. (1983). The life course of children and divorce: Marital disruption and parental conflict. *American Sociological Review, 48*(5), 656–668.

Furstenberg, F. F., Jr., & Seltzer, J. A. (1986). Divorce and child development. In P. Adler & P. A. Adler (Eds.), *Sociological studies of child development* (pp. 137–160). New Brunswick, NJ: JAI Press.

Furstenberg, F. F., Jr., & Spanier, G. B. (1984). *Recycling the family.* Beverly Hills, CA: Sage.

Goode, W. J. (1956). *Women in divorce.* New York: The Free Press.

Halem, L. C. (1980). *Divorce reform.* New York: The Free Press.

Hareven, T. K. (1978). *Transitions: The family and the life course in historical perspective.* New York: Academic Press.

Hareven, T. K. (1986). Historical analysis of the family. In M. B. Sussman & S. K. Steinmetz (Eds.) *Handbook of marriage and the family* (pp. 37–57). New York: Plenum Press.

Hofferth, S. L. (1985). Updating children's life course. *Journal of Marriage and the Family, 47*(1), 93–115.

Jacobsen, P. H. (1959). *American marriage and divorce.* New York: Rinehart.

Pasley, K., & Ihinger-Tallman, M. (Eds.). (1987). *Remarriage & stepparenting: Current research theory.* New York: Guilford.

Settles, B. H. (1986). A perspective on tomorrow's families. In M. B. Sussman & S. K. Steinmetz (Eds.), *Handbook of marriage and the family* (pp. 157–180). New York: Plenum Press.

Shorter, E. (1975). *The making of the modern family.* New York: Basic Books.

Uhlenberg, P. (1974). Cohort variations in family life cycle: Experiences of U.S. females. *Journal of Marriage and the Family, 36*(2), 284–292.

Weitzman, L. J. (1985). *The divorce revolution.* New York: The Free Press.

13

Adolescent Self-Esteem: *A Focus on Children in Stepfamilies*

Kay Pasley
Colorado State University

Cathy L. Healow
Montana State University

The study presented in this chapter examines the relationship between family structure, family functioning, and the development of self-esteem in adolescents. Marital transitions and reorganizations in the family have been found to have marked effects on family functioning and various aspects of child development including that of self-esteem (Ahrons, 1980; Ganong & Coleman, 1984, 1986, 1987; Hetherington, Cox, & Cox, 1978, 1982; Wallerstein & Kelley, 1980; Weiss, 1979). Moreover, if as has been proposed by many theorists, adolescence is a salient period in identity formation, the effects of variations in family structure and family processes on self-concept and self-esteem may be particularly apparent at that time.

Both theories of self-concept development (Gecas, 1982) and research evidence indicate that the formation of the self-system is strongly influenced by relationships with primary groups especially with the family. The review of the relevant empirical literature reveals an adolescent develops high self-esteem in a family with two parents, where (a) parents love and support the adolescent; (b) a type of discipline is used that reflects to the adolescent a belief in his or her ability to chart his or her own life course; and (c) the family is cohesive and adaptive, with effective communication patterns (Openshaw & Thomas, 1986, p. 123).

Adolescence is a time in the child's life when the development of identity predominates (Erikson, 1965, 1968). The establishment of a sense of identity involves three components: "a sense of *unity* among one's self conceptions, a sense of *continuity* of these self-attributes over time, and a sense of *mutality* between

263

the individual's concepts of self and those that significant others hold of the self''
(Harter, 1983, p. 309). Although identity is best seen as part of the person's self-
conception (Gecas, 1982; Rosenberg, 1979), it is not considered the totality of
one's self-conception.

Adolescence is also viewed as a time of heightened self-awareness (Elkind,
1967; Rosenberg, 1979)—a time of intense preoccupation with the imagined evaluation of others and the comparison the adolescent makes of him or herself with
others in their environment. This self-evaluation component is generally referred
to as self-esteem and is seen as a subset of the various self-conceptions that make
up the social dimensions of the self (Gecas, 1982; Openshaw & Thomas, 1986).

It has been suggested by several scholars that children who hold confident pic-
tures of themselves develop a sense of identity more readily than do children who
have confused or ambiguous self-concepts. Moreover, having a positive sense
of self serves an important function in the development of more desirable social–
psychological traits (see Gecas, 1982; Harter, 1983; Maccoby, 1980, for reviews
of the relevant literature). More specifically, studies of adolescents have reported that their level of self-esteem is associated with problem behavior, chemical
dependency and drinking problems, depression, suicidal behavior, poor peer relationships, and low achievement in school (Battle, 1980; Harter, 1983; Mitic, 1980;
Openshaw & Thomas, 1986; Samuel & Samuel, 1974; Scanlan, 1982).

It is because of the development of identity and the need of the adolescent
to develop positive self-esteem that adolescence is seen as a time when the child
is particularly vulnerable to the effects of family reorganization and changes in
family functioning due to divorce and remarriage. Although considerable attention has been paid to the influence of divorce and single parenting on child outcomes and adjustment much less attention has been given to the influence of
remarriage on children. Yet, the literature suggests that remarriage involves a
series of unique problems not common in first marriages—problems that can complicate the adjustment process for all family members. Moreover, scholars warn
that stepfamily adjustment is more difficult when adolescent children are involved.
There is some data to support these warnings. Stepfamilies with younger children or adult children report greater acceptance of the stepparent into the existing single-parent household and fewer problems overall (Duberman, 1975;
McKain, 1972; Ihinger-Tallman & Pasley, 1985; Vinick, 1978).

When adolescent children are present, adjustment to the new stepfamily can
be more stressful for all members. Several explanations are offered regarding
the additional stress. Typically, adolescence is a time when autonomy and separation from the family are expected as part of normal development. The need
for autonomy comes at a time when the adult members of the new stepfamily
may ask for or imply that demonstrations of commitment to the new unit are essential. Often, the parent and new stepparent expect all family members to spend
a good deal of time together so that a strong sense of closeness or cohesion develops. In fact, findings from an investigation by Pasley and Ihinger-Tallman

(1984) indicated that 100% of their sample of 784 remarried individuals reported "a close family and many shared times" was highly valued. For adolescents, however, the decision to invest energy into the new family may be inhibited, in part, by the desire for independence and separateness from the family in general and particularly from the stepfamily to which they feel little or no allegiance.

An alternative explanation is derived from family development literature. This literature suggests that the needs of the newly married pair in their establishment or "honeymoon" phase include adequate time for personal privacy and intimate interaction. Adolescent children, who are themselves "coming of age" sexually and who may need greater autonomy from the family, may be embarrassed or confused by the demonstrations of affection and sexuality between their parent and stepparent. When the adolescent is unable or unwilling to discuss his or her feelings openly, inappropriate behavior can result. Also, the adolescent likely prefers the company of his or her peers to that of their parent and stepparent, and for those who feel uncomfortable in the company of the remarried couple more time may be spent away from the family.

A family systems perspective offers yet another way of explaining the reported complications of stepfamily adjustment when adolescent children are present. This perspective suggests that the principle of homeostasis (desire to maintain status quo) would operate early in the remarriage. That is, the biological parent and child share the longest personal history. Also, they likely established a strong emotional bond and consistent routine during the single-parent phase following divorce. Resentment on the part of the adolescent can arise when his or her relationship with the residential parent and the daily routine are disrupted by remarriage. Often, the parent–child relationship operates in such a way that the stepparent feels excluded. In reality, he or she likely is excluded, at least unconsciously.

Although some investigators have examined the influence of family structure or family functioning on adolescent self-concept and self-esteem, few have examined the interaction between a variety of other family or individual factors and self-esteem. The study presented here attempts to do just that—we examine a wider variety of family and individual factors and their relation to measures of adolescent self-evaluation in a large sample of high school students.

A CLOSER LOOK AT THE RESEARCH: FAMILY STRUCTURE AND SELF-CONCEPT

Several studies have investigated the influence of family structure on self-concept and self-esteem, focusing on the effects of divorce and separation. Commonly, studies have compared the self-concept of adolescents residing in two-parent families to those residing in single-parent households. The evidence suggests that there is a negative relationship between the single-parent structure and adolescent self-esteem (Openshaw & Thomas, 1986). Few of these studies discriminated between two-parent families that were first marriages and those that were remarriages. One exception is an early study by Rosenberg (1965). Level of self-esteem was compared in a sample of 5,024 high school juniors and seniors from 10 randomly selected public high schools in New York state. Several different family structures were represented beyond first-marriage families. Sixteen percent of the adolescents were from families terminated by divorce, separation, or parental death where the residential parent had not remarried. Another 5.2% were from families where the mother had remarried, and 6.2% were from single-parent households where the mother had never married. He found that although adolescent self-esteem was substantially affected by family structure (i.e., adolescents of divorce and remarriage had lower self-esteem than those in first-marriage families), other factors appeared to mediate this influence. Religious background, age of mother at divorce or separation, child's age, and number and sex of siblings influenced level of self-esteem. He concluded that self-esteem alone was not appreciably different in the three family types (first marriage, divorced but not remarried, and remarried). If the child was young at the time of marital disruption, he or she was found to have a lower self-esteem whether the mother remarried or not. If the child was older at the time of marital disruption, his or her self-esteem was "normal." If the child was older at the time of dissolution, his or her self-esteem was below "normal," however, if the mother remarried.

Several other studies have examined the influence of family structure on self-esteem in children. Ganong and Coleman (1984) summarize the findings from these studies:

> A majority of studies found no difference in self-image between stepchildren and children in nuclear or single parent families (Parish, 1981; Parish & Nunn, 1981; Parish & Parish, 1983; Parish & Taylor, 1979; Raschke & Raschke, 1979; Santrock, Warshak, Lindberg, & Meadows, 1982; Wilson, Zucher, McAdams, & Curtis, 1975). However, two studies reported lower self-images in stepchildren (Kaplan & Pokorny, 1971; Rosenberg, 1965) and a third study reported "no change" in stepchildren's self-image after teachers' efforts to enhance it (Parish & Philip, 1982). (p. 399)

It is important to note, however, that only two studies used probability samples (Kaplan & Pokorny, 1971; Rosenberg, 1965). All other studies used nonprobability samples with small numbers of stepfamilies represented. Further, very few studies examined other factors that might mediate the effects of family structure on self-concept. In the studies reported here, the other factors investigated include religious affiliation, marital disruption due to parental death versus divorce, sex of child, grade level, race, and socioeconomic status.

Recent research suggests that the structural characteristics of the remarried family may be an important mediator of child outcomes. For example, evidence suggests that children adjust differently in residential stepfather and stepmother families (Clingempeel & Segal, 1986; Furstenberg, Nord, Peterson, & Zill, 1983; Peterson & Zill, 1986). Conflicting results emerge from studies examining the influence of structural complexity on the adjustment of members to the new stepfamily. Some studies have reported fewer adjustment problems in children from remarriages with only biological children from the current union than in remarriages that involve children from a prior marriage or marriages (Pasley & Ihinger-Tallman, 1983, 1984). Similarly, remarriages that include only one set of children from a prior marriage experience fewer complication in adjustment than those that included both sets of children from a prior marriages (Clingempeel, 1981; Clingempeel, Ievoli, & Brand, 1984; Pasley & Ihinger-Tallman, 1982, 1983). Yet, another study reported no differences in outcome measures for stepfamilies of varying structural complexity (Clingempeel, Brand, & Ievoli, 1984). The majority of studies on remarried families, however, fail to discriminate structural variations (stepfather from stepmother families) or structural complexity (simple from more complex stepfamilies; Ganong & Coleman, 1984, 1986, 1987).

Studies have also suggested that family functioning (cohesion and adaptability) influences the development of positive self-conception in adolescence. Specifically, the findings from several studies examining self-esteem suggest a positive relationship between family cohesion, adaptability, and adolescent self-esteem. Few studies (Koren, Lahti, Sadler, & Kimboko, 1983; Lopez, 1983; Pink & Wampler, 1985) have examined the perceptions of adolescents residing in stepfamilies regarding their family functioning. None have focused on the influence of their perceptions on self-esteem.

THE STUDY

The Sample

The sample consisted of the entire student body of the only high school in a rural community in eastern Washington in 1981, less two students whose parents refused consent ($n=416$). Participating in the study were 233 male students (56%) and 183 female students (44%). These students completed questionnaires that were administered in class by a guidance counselor. The students ranged in age from 14 to 19 years with a mean age of 16.1 years. Fifty-nine percent ($n=246$) lived in first-marriage families, and 14.4% ($n=60$) lived in single-parent households. Another 15.1% or 63 lived with a stepfather and mother, and 4.8% or 20 lived with a father and stepmother. Almost 7% or 27 lived in other family forms such as with a grandparent, other relative or "friend." Further, all adolescents residing in a stepfamily were in one of two types of structurally unique stepfamilies. "Simple" stepfamilies included those where only one set of children from the prior marriage existed and resided in the home. (Almost 84% of the stepfamilies fit this description.) ''Complex'' stepfamilies included two sets of children from the parents' prior marriages regardless of where they resided (16%).

These figures are somewhat comparable to those derived from the 1980 Census (Bumpass, 1984) and from the Panel Study of Income Dynamics (Hofferth, 1985). These sources report that between 70–72% of all children resided in a first-marriage family, 7–9% resided in a stepfamily, and 19% in a single-parent household. No estimates distinguish between stepfather and stepmother families. While these estimates include all children under 18 years, our sample included only children who were now attending high school—a time when more children would be expected to experience marital disruption and reconstitution. Thus, fewer of these adolescents resided in first-marriage families and more resided in stepfamilies.

In addition, the majority of children living with a lone parent or in a stepfamily had experienced parental divorce. Of the total sample 90.9% reported that their parents' first marriage ended in divorce, while 9.1% experienced death of a parent.

Additional information obtained from this sample indicate that the majority of parents (69%) spent 1 to 3 years in transition between marriage. The mean time in transition was 3.62 years—comparable to national estimates (Glick, 1984). Data on length of marriage indicated that about half of the parents' marriages for those maintaining first marriages had endured between 19–24 years. The marriages that had ended (single-parent households) were of shorter duration with the majority existing 6 or fewer years. The average length of the remarriage was 5.95 years for stepfather families and 7.3 years for stepmother families. For adolescents in stepfather families, the majority spent 0–6 years in that family structure.

Data from the 1980 Census (Bureau of the Census, 1983, Tables 188–189) indicated that this rural community had a population of 2,341. Thus, many of the children attending this high school are bused in from the surrounding area. The median income of the community was $19,872 per family ($16,309 per household). Of the population, 10% held poverty status in 1979. The vast majority of the population was White (97.7%) with the remaining 2.3% being Native American or Asian.

Instruments

Several instruments were used in this study. Two measures were used to assess the dependent variable (self-esteem). The Rosenberg Self-Esteem Scale (Rosenberg, 1965) is a measure of global self-esteem. It consists of 10 items measured on 4-point Likert scales, ranging from ''strongly agree'' to ''strongly disagree.'' In tests of reliability and validity, the scale is reported to have good reproducibility and scalability (Demo, 1985; Rosenberg, 1965, 1979).

The Gecas Self-Evaluation Scale (Gecas, 1971) examines two aspects of self-evaluation: sense of power (efficacy) and sense of worth. The scale consists of 12 adjective pairs measured with a 5-point semantic differential rating. Subjects are asked to rate themselves "as you ordinarily think of yourself" on each of the 12 adjective pairs. (Fourteen items were on the original scale; two were dropped, "tolerant" and "wise," because their factor loadings were too low.) Test–retest reliability was calculated at .86 for the entire scale and .91 and .86 for the two subscales (Gecas, personal communication, April, 1985). (The correlation between the two subscales using this sample was $r = .42$. This correlation suggests that, although the subscales assess somewhat distinct aspects of self-evaluation, they are moderately associated.)

A modified, shortened version of Olson's FACES (Olson, Bell, & Portner, 1978) questionnaire was also used. This measure assesses adolescent perception of family functioning. The original scale measures two dimensions of family interaction. One dimension is called *adaptability* and refers to the family's ability to change its roles, rules, and power structure in response to situational stress. The other dimension is called *cohesion* and refers to the emotional bonding between family members. The modified instrument consisted of 38 items (Koren et al., 1983). In a study of 68 stepfamilies, Koren et al. reported reliability correlations ranging from .67 to .74, depending on which family member completed the questionnaire. Validity was not established on this modified version. Subjects were asked to report to what degree a particular item described their family situation with responses ranging from "always" to "never." In their recent research with a sample of 1,000 first-married families, Olson et al. (1983), found that families with adolescent children functioned best when there was a balance between cohesion and adaptability. Thus, for this study the respondents' scores were dichotomized as either functional or dysfunctional. If their score was in the upper or lower extreme (mean plus or minus one standard deviation), they were classified as dysfunctional. Mid-range scores were classified as functional.

Demographic information was obtained from both the adolescent and the adult male living in the household, or if in a single-parent or "other" family structure, the child's legal guardian. No information was obtained on parent or stepparent occupation, income level, religious affiliation, or race due to limitations imposed by the school. Thus, more detailed demographic data are not available beyond what was offered. Other information was obtained on who was currently residing in the home, their age, sex, and relationship to the adolescent. Similar information was obtained for those family members residing elsewhere. Current marital status, length of parental marriage, and stepparent status was asked also. From these questions, additional information was determined (i.e., length of time in transition between marriages or in a single-parent household).

Analysis of Data

Multiple regression analysis and mean differences (t) tests were used to determine the best predictors of level of self-esteem as measured by the dependent variables (sense of power, sense of worth, and global self-esteem). These statistical procedures were used to examine the influence of sex, family structure, and adolescent perception of family functioning on level of self-esteem for the entire sample. (Age of adolescent was not included as an independent variable because evidence suggests that self-esteem is fairly stable from age 14 to 18; Blechman, O'Malley, & Johnson, 1978; Dusek & Flaherty, 1981. Further, our own preliminary analysis included age as a covariate in a series of ANOVAs only to have age prove to be insignificant.) These procedures were also used to examine the influence of additional variables (i.e., size of family, duration of current family, duration of single-parent household status, and total time since termination of the original biological family) on level of self-esteem for adolescents residing in stepfather and stepmother families.

Because of the limitations of sample size for adolescents residing in stepmother families ($n=20$), multiple regression could not be used. Instead a series of t tests and Pearson correlation coefficients were performed to examine differences in groups and relationships between variables.

FINDINGS

First, the influence of sex, family structure, and perception of family functioning on level self-esteem was examined. The findings showed that only sex was a significant predictor of sense of power or self-efficacy (beta = .27, p = .0000): Males reported a significantly higher sense of power than did females. Neither family structure nor perception of family functioning significantly predicted sense of power. These variables accounted for only 8% of the explained variance in this measure of esteem (F = 12.23, df = 3, p = .0000).

Neither sex of respondent nor family structure significantly predicted self-worth. Perception of family functioning, however, was found to be a significant determinant of worth (beta = $-.13$, p < .01). Here adolescents' sense of worth was greater when they perceived their family as functional (moderate levels of

TABLE 13.1
Standardized Beta Coefficients, Means, and Standard Deviations for Three
Measures of Self-Esteem, Regressed on Five Factors for Adolescents
Residing in Stepfather Families.

Variables	Power	Worth	Global Self-esteem
	Beta	Beta	Beta
Size of stepfamily	.02	$-.25$	.23
Time spent in single-parent household	.28*	.23	.31*
Duration of stepfamily	$-.29*$	$-.24$	.05
Perception of family functioning	.28*	.30*	.16
Sex	.30**	$-.06$	.06
R^2	.41	.24	.26
Dependent variable mean	18.83	17.00	22.32
Standard deviation	3.72	3.14	.31

*p < 0.5
**p < .01

cohesion and adaptability). Yet, these variables accounted for only 2% of the explained variance in the measure of self-worth ($F = 2.43$, $df = 3$, $p = .06$).

None of the three independent variables significantly predicted global self-esteem in this sample of adolescents.

Factors Influencing Self-esteem for Adolescents in Stepfamilies

The additional variables believed to influence level of self-esteem in adolescents residing in stepfamilies were examined. These additional variables included size of stepfamily, time spent in single-parent household, and duration of the stepfamily.

Stepfather Families. The data examining the influence of these additional factors on self-esteem are presented in Table 13.1.

The findings suggest that for adolescents in stepfather families, time spent in a single-parent household, duration of the stepfamily, perception of family functioning and sex were all significant predictors of one's sense of power or efficacy. These variables accounted for 41% of the variance in this measure of esteem ($F = 5.96$, $df = 5$, $p = .0003$). More specifically, the longer the adolescent resided in a single-parent household, the less time spent residing with a stepfather, and the more functional the adolescent perceived the stepfamily to be, the more powerful, confident, and competent the adolescent felt. Moreover, male adolescents in stepfather families felt more powerful than did females.

Regarding sense of worth, only perception of family functioning was a significant determinant of self-worth (beta = .30, $p = .03$). Adolescents who perceived their stepfamily as dysfunctional reported higher levels of self-worth. Neither family size, time spent in a single-parent household, nor duration of stepfamily were significant predictors of worth, although all approached significance (betas = .25, .23, −.24, $p = .08$, respectively). These variables accounted for 24% of the variance ($F = 2.66$, $p = .03$).

Only duration of single-parent status was a significant predictor global self-esteem (beta = .31, $p = .03$), although the prediction was not significant ($F = 2.120$, $p = .08$). These variables explained 20% of the variance in this measure of self-esteem.

TABLE 13.2
Correlational Analyses Between Family Size, Time Spent in Single-Parent Household, and Duration of Stepfamily and Power, Worth, and Global Self-Esteem for Adolescents in Stepmother Families ($n = 20$).

Variables	Power	Worth	Global Self-esteem
Family size	−.13	.34	−.46*
Time spent in single-parent household	−.48*	−.30	.08
Duration of stepfamily	.09	−.05	.33

*$p < .05$

Stepmother Families.   No significant differences were found between male and female adolescents regarding sense of power, worth, or global self-esteem for those residing in stepmother families ($t = -1.15$, $.51$, $-.09$ respectively).

Similarly, no significant differences were found between adolescents who perceived their family as functional from those perceiving their family as dysfunctional on measures of either power or worth. However, adolescents who perceived their family as functional had significantly higher scores on the measure of global self-esteem than did those who perceived their family as dysfunctional ($t = 2.19$, $p = .04$).

Lastly, a series of correlation coefficients were performed to assess the relationship between family size, time spent in a single-parent household, and duration of the stepmother family and the three measure of self-esteem. These findings are presented in Table 13.2. These data indicate that no significant association was found between family size and measures of power or worth. A significant association was found, however, between family size and the measure of global self-esteem. This finding suggests that as family size increased, the adolescent's overall level of esteem decreased.

These analyses also indicate there was as significant correlation between length of time spent in a single-parent household and the one's sense of power. No significant association was found between length of time spent in a single-parent household and one's sense of worth or global self-esteem. Thus, teens currently residing in a stepmother family who spent more time in a single-parent household reported feeling less powerful.

DISCUSSION

When considering the influence of sex, family structure, and perception of family functioning on self-esteem, the findings from this study varied somewhat depending on the specific outcome measure used. For example, sex was a significant predictor of one's sense of power, yet not a significant determinant of either sense of worth or global self-esteem. Similarly, a teen's perception of their family's functioning significantly predicted their sense of self-worth. Yet, their perception was not a significant predictor of either sense of power or global self-esteem. Moreover, family structure did not significantly predict any of the dependent measures (power, worth, or global self-esteem). Too, little of the variance in the dependent measures was explained by this combination of independent variables.

Clearly, these findings suggest that factors other than sex, perception of family functioning and family structure better explain variations in an adolescent's assessment of their power, worth, and global self-esteem. Factors external to the family (e.g., peers) or other factors within the family (e.g., perception of the quality of the step relationship, stepsibling interaction, socioeconomic status) may prove to be more predictive of an adolescent's sense of worth. This may be particularly relevant to self-worth because of the social comparisons involved in this aspect of self-esteem (Gecas, 1982; Rosenberg, 1979). Self-efficacy might better be explained by gender when examined in conjunction with birth order and the sex of siblings (Gecas & Pasley, 1983; Gecas & Swalabe, 1986). Furthermore, sense of efficacy might be better explained by the nature of the control and support dimensions of parent–child interaction (Openshaw & Thomas, 1986; Peterson, Southworth, & Peters, 1983).

When the influence of additional variables was examined for adolescents in two different types of residential stepfamilies (stepfather families and stepmother families), the findings varied by type of stepfamily and outcome measure. Findings from other studies suggest that adolescents with more time since parental divorce have more positive feelings about themselves than those with recent divorce experience (Rosenberg, 1965). Evidence also suggests that the potential negative effects of divorce on the majority of children dissipate over time (Hetherington, Cox, & Cox, 1978, 1982; Rosenberg, 1965; Wallerstein & Kelly, 1980), and that both time since divorce and parental remarriage may mediate any negative effects (Hetherington, 1987). The findings of this study, however, only partially support those of earlier studies. That is, for adolescents residing in stepfather families the longer the time spent in a single-parent household, the higher the sense of power and global self-esteem. No such association was found for one's sense of worth.

The findings regarding sense of power and global self-esteem are not surprising. The literature suggests that sense of power would increase as adjustment to parental divorce occurs. With more time, stabilization occurs and consistent habits and routines result. Such stability likely fosters the sense of control that is part of one's sense of power. Self-worth may be influenced more by other aspects of interpersonal interaction and family process than those measured here.

Although this may be the case for the teens residing in stepfather families, the reverse was true for the adolescents residing in stepmother families. More time spent in a single-parent household was associated with the teen feeling less powerful. Length of time spent in a single-parent household was not associated, however, with either worth or global self-esteem. For teens residing in stepmother families, it may be that over time single-parents gain greater confidence in their ability to manage alone. This may be particularly true for single-parent fathers who may not have assumed an active role in household and parenting tasks prior to divorce. As the parent's self-confidence increases, they also may assume more control over their children. Thus, the teen may lose some of the autonomy and independence that was relinquished earlier by the father.

It is also easy to see how adolescents would see themselves as having a greater sense of self-efficacy earlier in the remarriage. These findings for teens in stepfather families indicate that the more time the teen spends residing in a stepfather family the less powerful they feel. Pasley and Ihinger-Tallman (1982), as well as others, have discussed the subsystem of the stepfamily involving the biological parent and child as having the longest history. This relationship may also be characterized by strong emotional bonds that were strengthened during the single-parent household phase. It is not uncommon that the parent comes to treat the child, and particularly an older child, as an equal. Such treatment blurs the generational boundaries between parent and child. Upon remarriage, the generational boundaries may become more clearly defined, as the stepparent, particularly a stepfather, begins to assume more responsibility for the "running" of the family. Overtime, the adolescent who is unable to derive his or her sense of power via other aspects of their life (e.g., school achievement), may feel less powerful. A recent study (Dornbusch et al., 1985) found that the presence of a stepfather in a mother-only household was, in fact, correlated with increased parental control.

In addition, the literature suggests that family cohesion and adaptability is positively correlated to adolescent self-esteem. Research suggests that self-concept development would be stifled in highly cohesive families via restricting personal autonomy or in extremely low-cohesive families where there is not sense of commitment to the unit. Moderately adaptive families are those "wherein the system provides stability and yet is able to facilitate change when appropriate" (Openshaw & Thomas, 1986, p. 121). In a study by Koren et al. (1983) moderate levels of cohesion and adaptability were found to be highly associated with stepfamily adjustment over a 3-year period. The findings from this study again offer partial support for those of earlier studies, with some variation by type of stepfamily and outcome measure. That is, adolescents in stepfather families who perceive their stepfamily as functional report feeling more powerful and worthwhile. For adolescents residing in stepmother families, however, a significant positive correlation was found only between perception of family functioning and global self-esteem.

Only for teens residing in stepmother families was size of stepfamily correlated negatively with global self-esteem. It may be that a teen who has received a good deal of attention from his or her single-parent father may perceive him or herself as less positive when such attention is then shared with the other members of the stepfamily. Such sharing may be particularly difficult when it involves a stepmother and stepsiblings.

CONCLUSIONS

These findings suggest that family structure when considered alone is not an effective predictor of level of self-esteem. Sex and perception of family functioning may be more salient indicators, at least for the adolescents in this sample. When examining the effects of stepfamily living on adolescent self-esteem, however, it appears that sex may be a less salient indicator of esteem for these teens. Recent evidence suggests that stepchild or the marital relationship may be more influential on child outcomes (Crosbie-Burnett, 1984; Furstenberg & Seltzer, 1983; Hetherington, 1987; Santrock & Sitterle, 1987).

Overall, the findings from this study suggest that for adolescents in stepfather families, additional family characteristics and family process variables may be important determinants of self-esteem. These variables should be systematically examined in future studies. This holds true for teen residing in stepmother families as well.

Moreover, the results presented here indicate the importance of differentiating type of stepfamily. Typically, researchers have treated stepmother and stepfather families as if they are the same. Future investigators must distinguish such structural variations. Only in this way will researchers begin to tease out the characteristics of family life that influence the outcomes of stepfamily living for adolescents.

Not only must researchers be more attentive to such obvious distinctions between types of stepfamilies, but attention must also be directed to the use of multiple measures for dependent variables. The first concern here requires the use of larger samples so differentiation between types of stepfamilies is possible. The latter concern requires investigators to attend to measurement issues and concerns widely expressed by family researchers (cf. Clingempeel, Brand, & Segal, 1987; Esses & Campbell, 1984; Pasley, 1985).

In summary, these findings suggest the need to examine the relative contribution of a variety of family structure, family process, and individual factors to the development of self-esteem. Clearly, for adolescents in stepfamilies, certain structural and family process characteristics may be more influential than others. It is these that deserve further study.

REFERENCES

Ahrons, C. R. (1980). Joint custody arrangements in the postdivorce family. *Journal of Divorce*, *3*(3), 189–205.

Blechman, J. G., O'Malley, P. M., & Johnson, J. (1978). *Adolescence to adulthood: Change and stability in the lives of young men*. Ann Arbor, MI: Institute for Social Research.

Battle, J. (1980). Relationship between self-esteem and depression among high school students. *Perceptual and Motor Skills, 51*, 157–158.

Clingempeel, W. G. (1981). Quasi-kin relationships and marital quality. *Journal of Personality and Social Psychology, 41*, 890–901.

Clingempeel, G. W., Brand, E., & Ievoli, R. (1984). Stepparent-stepchild relationships in stepmother and stepfather families: A multimethod study. *Family Relations, 33*, 465–473.

Clingempeel, W. G., Brand, E., & Segal, S. (1987). A multilevel–multivariable-developmental perspective for future research on stepfamilies. In K. Pasley & M. Ihinger-Tallman (Eds.), *Remarriage and stepparenting: Current theory and research* (pp. 57–93). New York: Guildford.

Clingempeel, W. G., Ievoli, R., & Brand, E. (1984). Structural complexity and the quality of stepfather-stepchild relationships. *Family Process, 23*, 547–560.

Clingempeel, W. G., & Segal, S. (1986). Stepparent-stepchild relationships in stepmother and stepfather families. *Child Development, 57*, 474–484.

Crosbie-Burnett, M. (1984). The centrality of the step relationship: A challenge to family theory and practice. *Family Relations, 33*, 459–463.

Demo, D. H. (1985). The measurement of self-esteem: Refining our methods. *Journal of Personality and Social Psychology, 48*, 1490–1502.

Dornbusch, S. M., Carlsmith, J. M., Bushwall, S. J., Ritter, P. L., Leiderman, H., Hastorf, A. H., & Gross, R. T. (1985). Single parents, extended households and the control of adolescents. *Child Development, 56*, 326–341.

Duberman, L. (1975). *The reconstituted family: A study of remarried couples and their children*. Chicago: Nelson-Hall Publishers.

Dusek, J. B., & Flaherty, J. F. (1981). The development of the self-concept during the adolescent years. *Monographs of the Society for Research in Child Development, 46*(4, Serial No. 191).

Elkind, D. (1967). Egocentrism in adolescence. *Child Development, 38*, 1025–1034.

Erikson, E. (1965). *The challenge of youth.* Garden City, NY: Doubleday/Anchor Books.

Erikson, E. (1968). *Identity, youth and crisis.* New York: Norton.

Esses, L., & Campbell, R. (1984). Challenges in researching the remarried. *Family Relations, 33,* 415–424.

Furstenberg, F. F., Jr., Nord, C. W., Peterson, J. L., & Zill, N. (1983). The life course of children of divorce: Marital disruption and parental conflict. *American Sociological Review, 48,* 656–668.

Furstenberg, F. F., Jr., & Seltzer, J. (1983, April). *Divorce and child development.* Paper presented at the annual meeting of American Orthopsychiatric Association, Boston, MA.

Ganong, L., & Coleman, M. (1984). The effects of remarriage on children: A review of the empirical literature. *Family Relations, 33,* 389–406.

Ganong, L., & Coleman, M. (1986). A comparison of the clinical and empirical literature on children in stepfamilies. *Journal of Marriage and the Family, 48,* 309–318.

Ganong, L., & Coleman, M. (1987). Effects of parental remarriage on children: An updated comparison of theories, methods and findings from the clinical and empirical research. In K. Pasley & M. Ihinger-Tallman (Eds.), *Remarriage and stepparenting: Current theory and research* (pp. 94–140). New York: Guilford.

Gecas, V. (1971). Parental behavior and dimensions of adolescent self-evaluation. *Sociometry, 34,* 466–482.

Gecas, V. (1982). The self-concept. In R. H. Turner & I. F. Short (Eds.), *Annual review of sociology* (Vol. 8, pp. 1–33). Palo Alto, CA: Annual Reviews.

Gecas, V., & Pasley, K. (1983). Birth order and self-concept in adolescence. *Journal of Youth and Adolescence, 12*(6), 521–535.

Gecas, V., & Swalabe, (1986). Parental behavior and adolescent self-esteem. *Journal of Marriage and the Family, 48,* 37–46.

Glick, P. C. (1984). Marriage, divorce and living arrangements: Prospective changes. *Journal of Family Issues, 5,* 7–26.

Harter, S. (1983). Developmental perspective on the self-system. In R. D. Parke (Ed.), *Review of Child Development Research* (Vol. 7, pp. 275–385). Chicago: University of Chicago Press.

Hetherington, E. M. (1987). Family relations six years after divorce. In K. Pasley & M. Ihinger-Tallman (Eds.), *Remarriage and stepparenting: Current theory and research* (pp. 185–205). New York: Guilford.

Hetherington, E. M., Cox, M., & Cox, R. (1978). The aftermath of divorce. In J. H. Stevens, Jr., & M. Mattews (Eds.), *Mother/child, father/child relations* (pp. 110–155). Washington, DC: National Association for the Education of Young Children.

Hetherington, E. M., Cox, M., & Cox, R. (1982). Effects of divorce on parents and children. In M. E. Lamb (Ed.), *Nontraditional families: Parenting and child development* (pp. 233–288). Hillsdale, NJ: Lawrence Erlbaum Associates.

Ihinger-Tallman, M., & Pasley, K. (1985). *Remarried conflict: Structural and interpersonal effects.* Unpublished manuscript.

Kaplan, H. B., & Porkorny, A. D. (1971). Self-derogation and childhood broken home. *Journal of Marriage and the Family, 33,* 328–337.

Koren, P., Lahti, J. I., Sadler, C. A., & Kimboko, P. J. (1983). *The adjustment of knew stepfamilies: Characteristics and trends.* Portland, OR: Regional Research Institute for Human Services.

Lopez, R. L. (1983). An investigation of the relationship of self-esteem in adolescents to family cohesiveness and family violence. *Dissertation Abstracts International, 43*(7B), 2345.

Maccoby, E. (1980). *Social development.* New York: Harcourt Brace & Jovanovich.

McKain, W. C. (1972). A new look at older remarriages. *The Family Coordinator, 21,* 61–69.

Mitic, W. R. (1980). Alcohol use and self-esteem in adolescents. *Journal of Drug Education, 10*(3), 197–206.

Olson, D. H., Bell, R. Q., & Portner, J. (1978). *FACES: Family adaptability and cohesion evaluation scale.* St. Paul, MN: Family Social Sciences, University of Minnesota.

Olson, D. H., McCubbin, H., Barnes, H., Muxen, M., Larson, A. & Wilson, M. (1983). *Families: What makes them work*. Beverly Hills, CA: Sage.

Openshaw, D. K., & Thomas, D. L. (1986). The adolescent self and the family. In G. K. Leigh & G. W. Peterson (Eds.)., *The adolescent in families* (pp. 104–129). Cincinnati, OH: Southwestern.

Parish, T. S. (1981). Young adults evaluations of themselves and their parents as a function of family structure and disposition. *Journal of Youth and Adolescence, 10*, 173–178.

Parish, T. S., & Nunn, G. D. (1981). Children's self-concepts and evaluations of parents as a function of structure and process. *Journal of Psychology, 107*, 105–108.

Parish, T. S., & Parish, J. G. (1983). Relationship between evaluations of oneself and one's family by children from intact, reconstituted, and single-parent families. *Journal of Genetic Psychology, 143*, 293.

Parish, T. S., & Philip, M. (1982). The self-concepts of children from intact and divorced families: Can they be affected in school settings? *Education, 103*, 60–63.

Parish, T. S., & Taylor, J. C. (1979). The impact of divorce and subsequent father absence on children's and adolescents' self-concept. *Journal of Youth and Adolescence, 8*, 427–432.

Pasley, K. (1985, November). *Remarriage and stepparenting: The state of the art*. Invited address at the Wingspread Conference on Families in Trouble, Racine, WI.

Pasley, K., & Ihinger-Tallman, M. (1982). Stress in second families. *Family Perspective, 16*, 181–196.

Pasley, K., & Ihinger-Tallman, M. (1983). Remarried family: Supports and constraints. In N. Stinnett, J. DeFrain, K. King, H. Lingren, G. Rowe, S. Van Zandt, & R. Williams (Eds.), *Family strengths 4: Positive support systems* (pp. 367–383). Lincoln, NE: University of Nebraska Press.

Pasley, K., & Ihinger-Tallman, M. (1984, October). *Consensus on family values in happy and unhappy remarried couples*. Paper presented at the annual meeting of the National Council on Family Relations, San Francisco, CA.

Peterson, G. W., Southworth, L. E., & Peters, D. F. (1983). Children's self-esteem and maternal behavior in three low-income samples. *Psychological Reports, 52*, 79–86.

Peterson, J. L., & Zill, N. (1986). Marital disruption and behavior problems in children. *Journal of Marriage and the Family, 48*, 295–308.

Pink, J., & Wampler, K. (1985). Problem areas in stepfamilies: Cohesion, adaptability, and the stepfather-adolescent relationship. *Family Relations, 34*, 327–335.

Raschke, H. J., & Raschke, V. J. (1979). Family conflict and children self-concepts: A comparison of intact and single-parent families. *Journal of Marriage and the Family, 41*, 367–374.

Rosenberg, M. (1965). *Society and the adolescent self-image*. Princeton, NJ: Princeton University Press.

Rosenberg, M. (1979). *Conceiving of self*. New York: Basic Books.

Samuel, D. J., & Samuel, M. (1974). Low self-concept as a cause of drug abuse. *Journal of Drug Education, 4*(4), 421–438.

Santrock, J. W., & Sitterle, K. A. (1987). Parent-child relationships in stepmother families. In K. Pasley & M. Ihinger-Tallman (Eds.), *Remarriage and stepparenting: Current theory and research* (pp. 273–299). New York: Guilford.

Santrock, J. W., Warshak, R., Lindberg, C., & Meadows, L. (1982). Children and parents' observed social behavior in stepfather families. *Child Development, 53*, 472–480.

Scanlan, P. A. (1982). The relationship of three aspects of the family environment to levels of I.Q., achievement, self-esteem, and alientation to adolescents. *Dissertation Abstracts International, 42*(12B), 4941.

U.S. Bureau of the Census. (1983). *1980 Census of Population, Vol. 1: Characteristics of the population (Part 49, Washington, Tables 188–189)*. Washington, DC: U.S. Government Printing Office.

Vinick, B. H. (1978). Remarriage in old age. *The Family Coordinator, 27*, 359–363.

Wallerstein, J. S., & Kelly, J. B. (1980). *Surviving the break-up*. New York: Basic Books.

Weiss, R. S. (1979). *Going it alone*. New York: Basic Books

Wilson, K. L., Zucher, L. A., McAdams, D. C., & Curtis, R. L. (1975). Stepfather and stepchildren: An exploratory analysis from two national surveys. *Journal of Marriage and the Family, 37*, 526–536.

14

Children's Development During Early Remarriage

James H. Bray
Texas Woman's University-Houston Center

This chapter presents initial results from the Developmental Issues in Stepfamilies (DIS) research project. The DIS project is investigating the relationship of family process, family structure, and adult–child psychosocial factors in stepfather families and nondivorced intact families. Stepfather families who have been together 6 months, 2½ years, and 5 years after remarriage were studied to determine developmental differences in family organization and process during these time periods. The research focuses on the impact of family orgnization and process on the social, emotional, and cognitive development of children ages 6 to 14 in these families. The time periods following remarriage and ages of the children were chosen to control for the length of time in a stepfamily. This is an important variable that has not been fully evaluated in previous research on stepfamilies (Ganong & Coleman, 1984; Hetherington & Camara, 1984). Both boys and girls were studied to determine sex differences in response to specific family relationships, such as mother–son or stepfather–stepson. Only stepfather families were studied because they are the most common type of stepfamily (Glick, 1980) and because of noted differences between various types of stepfamilies (Hetherington, Arnett, & Hollier, 1986; Santrock, Warshak, & Elliott, 1982).

The DIS project uses a family systems life-cycle model as a theoretical basis for understanding family process and change in divorce and remarriage (Carter & McGoldrick, 1980; Williamson & Bray, 1988). The model is based on a systems approach to families in which each family member is viewed as part of an interdependent interactional system that affects and is affected by all other aspects of the family system. Change within one aspect of the system is believed to produce change in other parts of the family through a process of reciprocal feedback of information and behavior by family members. The model proposes that there are

279

predictable developmental stages that families grow through that encompass common stresses and require certain changes in family structure and functioning. The transition from one stage to the next may be quite stressful and, if not handled properly, can result in family and/or individual dysfunction. The transitional events and issues from a single-parent family to the formation of a stepfamily is an area that is still relatively unknown and is the focus of this research.

Hetherington (1979) and Walker and Messinger (1979) pointed out that the time since remarriage, as well as family process, is important in evaluating stepfamily functioning. Thus, faulty communication patterns, interpersonal distance and ambivalence, and less cohesion reported among stepfamily members (Bowerman & Irish, 1962; Bray, Berger, Silverblatt, & Hollier, 1987; Duberman, 1975; Perkins & Kahan, 1979; Wilson, Zucker, McAdams, & Curtis, 1975) may not reflect static and intrinsic system characteristics, but rather the dynamics of stepfamily formation. Although it is assumed that reorganization of the stepfamily produces broad changes throughout the complex family system, these changes, as well as the short- or long-term effects on adults and children, are not clearly understood or documented by research (Ganong & Coleman, 1984; Hetherington & Camara, 1984; Heiherington et al., 1986; Sager, Steer, Crohn, Rodstein, & Walker, 1980).

RESEARCH ON STEPFATHER FAMILIES

Research on stepfamilies is limited in volume and because of methodological shortcomings of the research (Ganong & Coleman, 1984; Hetherington & Camara, 1984; Hetherington et al., 1986; Sager et al., 1980; Walker, Roger, & Messinger, 1977). The research in this area has not generally considered the developmental nature of families and individuals and has not investigated interactional processes within families and their relation to outcome variables. There are no studies reported in the literature that have systematically investigated stepfamily development across time and focused on early school-aged children.

Psychological Effects of Stepfamilies on Children.   Most studies dealing with psychological outcomes for children in nonclinical populations find inconsistent differences between children from intact families and remarried families (Burchinal, 1964; Chapman, 1977; Oshman & Manosevitz, 1976; Perry & Pfuhl, 1963; Santrock, 1972; Santrock, Warshak, & Elliott, 1982; Santrock, Warshak, Lindberg, & Meadows, 1982). Other studies have found that children in stepfamilies were less well adjusted; and manifested more anxiety, more symptoms of withdrawal, and more conduct and behavior problems (Bowerman & Irish, 1962; Dahl, McCubbin, & Lester, 1977; Hetherington, Cox, & Cox, 1985; Langer & Michael, 1963; Kellam, Ensminger, & Turner, 1977; Zill, 1985). Hetherington et al. (1985) reported that children in stepfather families during early remarriage had greater negative stress and conduct disturbances than children in nondivorced families Brady, Bray, and Zeeb (1986) found that stepchildren from a clinical population were rated as having more severe behavior problems than children from divorced, separated, or intact families. Ganong and Coleman (1984) pointed out in their review of the stepfamily literature that studies that found negative outcomes for stepchildren in nonclinical populations usually sampled the stepfamilies when they had been together less than 1 year.

Studies of differences in self-image in children from stepfamilies reveal a similar pattern of conflicting results. Santrock, Warshak, Lindberg, and Meadows (1982) and Wilson et al. (1975) found no differences in self-esteem between children in stepfather families and children in nondivorced families. Kaplan and Pokorny (1971) reported that adults raised in stepfamilies had lower self-esteem than adults from other family types only if the remarriage occurred after they were 8 years old. Hetherington et al. (1985) reported that children in stepfather families had lower self-esteem than those in intact families. However, these differences appeared to decrease as the duration of the remarriage increased. Although not controlling for time since remarriage or age of the child at remarriage, Rosenberg (1965) found significant differences in adolescent's self-esteem related to stepfamily structure. The relationship between time since remarriage, age of the child at remarriage, and the possible short- and long-term effects of these family transitions on self-esteem remains unclear.

The role of the stepfather in attenuating possible cognitive and social–psychological deficits is supported, at least for males, by three studies (Chapman, 1977; Oshman & Manosevitz, 1976; Santrock, 1972). Santrock (1972) found that the entrance of a stepfather into a home had a positive effect on cognitive development for boys, age 6–11, but not for girls of like ages. A similar study by Chapman (1977) investigated the cognitive development of college-age males from intact, father-absent, and stepfather families. Although the age of father-absence was controlled, the reason for father-absence and length of time in the stepfather family was not. His study indicated that the presence of a stepfather attenuated the negative effects of father-absence on cognitive development. Oshman and Manosevitz (1976) also reported that adolescent males from stepfather families rated themselves higher on a scale of psychosocial adjustment than males from father-absent families. These two issues are particularly pertinent for future research: (a) how the presence of a stepparent mediates psychosocial and cognitive outcomes for children over time, and (b) what the relevant outcome variables are for female children.

Sex and Age Differences. Current research is pointing to consistent sex differences in behavioral outcomes and interactions between family members (e.g., stepdaughter–stepfather versus stepson–stepfather) as important differences in family processes of stepfamilies and intact families (Brand & Clingempeel, 1985; Clingempeel, Brand, & Ievoli, 1984; Clingempeel, Ievoli, & Brand, 1984;

Hetherington et al., 1986; Hetherington et al., 1982, 1985; Santrock, Warshak, Lindberg, & Meadows, 1982; Zill & Peterson, 1983). Hetherington and colleagues (Hetherington, Arnett, & Hollier, 1986; Hetherington et al., 1982, 1985) and Clingempeel and colleagues (Clingempeel, Brand, & Ievoli, 1984; Clingempeel, Ievoli, & Brand, 1984;) found that girls (ages 9 to 12) have more problematic family and social relationships and exhibit more behavior problems than boys in stepfather families. Ten-year-old girls during early (less than 2 years) stepfather family formation perceived greater negative life stress than boys, or girls in later stepfamilies, or children in divorced or intact families (Hetherington et al., 1985). Clingempeel, Brand, and Ievoli (1984) and Clingempeel, Ievoli, and Brand (1984) also found that girls had more problematic relationships than boys, as girls evidenced a lower proportion of positive verbal and a greater proportion of negative problem-solving behaviors toward their stepfathers. Stepfathers did not differ in their responses to stepsons or stepdaughters. Hetherington (1987) reported similar relationship patterns between girls in stepfather families, but noted that these problematic patterns seem to improve over time. Santrock, Warshak, Lindberg, and Meadows (1982) observed children's (ages 6 to 11) social behavior in stepfather, divorced, and intact families. Overall, boys in stepfather families showed more competent social behavior than boys in intact families. In contrast, girls in stepfather families expressed less warmth in this relationship than did boys. Girls in stepfamilies were more anxious than girls in intact families and demonstrated more anger toward their remarried mothers than boys. A consistent finding from most of these studies is that girls in stepfamilies have more problematic relationships with stepfathers than do boys. A key question concerns whether these findings are consistent for younger children in a different developmental status.

Family Relationships.   Interactional processes within stepfamilies have been found to be important determinants of adjustment in children. Hetherington et al. (1982) indicated that the most successful stepfathers, during the first 2 years of remarriage, developed warm, involved and communicative relationships with their stepchildren. Succesful stepfathers did not attempt to take over the family system. Instead of trying to establish new and possibly conflicting expectations, rules, and disciplinary practices, stepfathers were supportive of the custodial mother's parenting. After 2 years, more active, authoritative parenting seemed to lead to better outcomes, especially for boys (Hetherington, 1987). Likewise, Santrock, Warshak, Lindberg, and Meadows (1982) found that boys' social competence in stepfather families was related to the more competent parenting practices observed in mothers and stepfathers, which were described as more authoritative, less permissive, and as involving more parental control. Stepfathers did not appear to behave differently with stepdaughters than with stepsons. Several studies reported that stepfather families were less well adjusted, with less cohesion and adaptability, and were less satisfied with their family functioning than intact families (Garbarino, Sebes, & Schellenbach, 1984; Perkins & Kahan, 1979; Pink

& Wampler, 1985). In addition, children in stepfamilies rated their stepfathers as less good, less powerful, and having poorer relationships than with biological fathers (Perkins & Kahan, 1979; Pink & Wampler, 1985). A recent study by Anderson and White (1986) examined how family process is related to dysfunctional family relationships. They found that functional stepfamilies differed from functional intact families by having less intense stepfather–child relationships and more biological parent–child coalitions. Functional stepfamilies were similar to functional intact families by having positive bonds between biological parent and child and were able to make appropriate family decisions. Dysfunctional stepfamilies differed from functional stepfamilies by having poorer stepparent–child relationships and coalitions that excluded the stepparent. Unfortunately, these authors did not report anlyses that examined differences in family relationships for male and female children. These studies indicate that family process in stepfamilies is different than in nondivorced families, but these differences do not necessarily lead to more negative outcomes for the children involved.

The literature suggests that there are a variety of interrelated factors that affect the stepfamily in formation. In addition, there is a clear need for researchers to identify stressors and individuals and system reponses that contribute to early and successful adaptation to family reconstitution. This chapter reports initial analyses on a research project that examined these issues during early remarriage.

INITIAL RESULTS
OF THE 6-MONTH STEPFAMILY GROUPS

The DIS project is currently investigating the 6-month stepfamily groups and nondivorced control groups to study the early transitional issues, changes, and outcomes that occur in remarriage and the impact on the children in these families. The preliminary evaluations presented here focus on children's psychosocial development, life stresses, and perceptions of family process by adults. Based on the literature and a family life cycle model it is expected that children in stepfamilies will exhibit more behavior problems, experience more life stress, and report poorer self-esteem than children in intact families. Stepfamilies are expected to report more life stress, less effective and more dysfunctional family processes, and less emotional bonding than nondivorced families. It is also predicted that the more dysfunctional family processes and stress in stepfamilies will be related to poorer outcomes for the children.

METHODS

Sample

The results presented herein are based on a sample of 60 families. The families were recruited from many sources. These included letters sent home to all children in four suburban school districts, letters to local parent groups, athletic teams, posters in local stores and neighborhood centers, referrals from local clergy and advertisements from local media. At this writing, over 1,000 people volunteered to participate in the DIS study and were screened for criteria variables. Those selected were the ones that met our criteria. Whenever possible, nondivorced families were selected to match the characteristics of the stepfather families.

The sample includes 30 stepfather families, 16 with a girl and 14 with a boy. There are 30 nondivorced intact families, 16 families with a girl and 14 families with a boy. All children were between the ages of 6 and 9 years old. The stepfather families were remarried between 4 and 7 months at the time of participation. Mothers in stepfamilies had an average age of 30.8 years and 14 years of education, stepfathers had an average age of 30.9 years and 15 years of education. For intact families, mothers had an average age of 32.9 years and 14 years of education; fathers had an average age of 35 years and 16 years of education. All families were White, middle-class with a modal annual income between $30,000 – $40,000. The stepfamily mother's first marriage lasted an average of 7.9 years. The average time between separation and divorce for the first marriage was 9.3 months and between divorce and remarriage was 2.7 years.

Procedures and Measures

All families completed a structured interview designed by Hetherington and Clingempeel (1984) for their study on adaptation to remarriage. This interview was modified to meet the time requirements of our study and for our age group. In addition, psychometric instruments, standardized tests, and videotapes of structured family interactions were used to evaluate individual and family functioning. All of the data were collected in the family's home during two 3 to 3½-hour home visits or between home visits on their own time. The home visits were usually 7 to 14 days apart. The adults were interviewed by one research assistant while the target child was interviewed separately by a second research assistant. The results from the following instruments are presented in this chapter.

Wechsler Intelligence Scale for Children–Revised (WISC–R; Wechsler, 1974). Intellectual functioning was assessed by five subtests of the WISC–R: Vocabulary, Arithmetic, Block Design, Object Assembly, and Coding. The vocabulary and arithmetic subscales were used to estimate verbal IQ and the remaining subscales were used to estimate performance IQ (Satler, 1982). Scale scores adjusted for age norms were used. Higher scale scores reflect higher intelligence.

Piers–Harris Children's Self-Concept Scale (PHCSCS; Piers & Harris, 1978). This measure was used to assess the child's self-concept and self-esteem. This is an 80-item self-report that was administered by an interviewer. Larger scores indicate better self-concept and self-esteem.

Children's Life Experiences Survey (CLES; Johnson, 1982).   This is a modified version of the Life Experiences Survey (Sarason, Johnson, & Siegel, 1978) to measure life stress of children. This is a self-report measure that was administered by an interviewer. Larger scores indicate more life stress. The CLES yields six scores, number of positive, negative, and total life events experienced and subjectively weighted positive, negative, and total life events. The weighting was provided by the child.

Child Behavior Checklist (CBCL; Achenbach, 1978).   This is a commonly used self-report instrument that allows parents to rate the presence and severity of their child's behavior problems. The CBCL yields two broad band factors called Internalizing and Externalizing, and a Total child behavior score (Achenbach & Edelbrock, 1983). Larger scores indicate more behavior problems.

Family Assessment Device (FAD; Epstein, Baldwin, & Bishop, 1983).   The FAD is a 53-item self-report measure of family health and functioning based on the McMaster Model of Family Functioning (MMFF; Epstein, Bishop, & Levin, 1978). The FAD has seven scales: General Family Functioning (GF), Problem Solving (PS), Communication (CO), Roles (RO), Affective Responsiveness (AR), Affective Involvement (AI), and Behavior Control (BC). Each adult rated their families on a 4-point likert scale, with 1 = strongly agree to 4 = strongly disagree. Larger scores indicate more dysfunctional or unhealthy family functioning.

Family Adaptability and Cohesion Evaluation Scales II (FACES II: Olson, Portner, & Bell, 1982).   This scale measures the style and degree of adaptability and cohesion perceived by adult members in the family. The questionnaire yields two subscales: family adaptability and family cohesion. The cohesion subscale, which ranges from disengaged to enmeshed, measures the degree of emotional bonding that family members have toward one another. The adaptability subscale, which ranges from chaotic to rigid, measures the ability of a family to change its power structure, role relationships, and relationship rules in response to situational and developmental stress. The parents in each family completed the FACES II twice, first rating their current family functioning and then rating their ideal family functioning. The FACES II yields summary scores for current family cohesion and adaptability, ideal family cohesion and adaptability, and difference scores between current and ideal on the two dimensions. The difference scores are viewed by Olson as measures of family satisfaction on these dimensions. Higher scores reflect more cohesion and more adaptability.

Stepfamily Role Questionnaire (Hetherington & Clingempeel, 1984).   This questionnaire measures perceived role relationships within stepfamilies. The questions were grouped into four subscales that measure the following aspects of stepfamily roles: (a) *openness* is the degree to which family members believe it is appropriate to discuss stepfamily issues among themselves, with former spouses, and with children; (b) *parental role* is the degree to which family members believe it is appropriate for stepparents to quickly assume the role of the parent; (c) *takeover* is the degree to which family members believe that it is *not* appropriate for stepparents to parent their stepchildren; and (d) *discipline* is the degree to which family members believe it is appropriate for stepparents to discipline stepchildren.

Life Experiences Survey (Sarason et al., 1978)   The LES is a 57-item self-report measure that allows adults to rate the presence and positive or negative impact of events during the past 6 months. The LES yields subjectively weighted and unweighted positive, negative, and total scores of life stress. Larger scores indicate more life stress.

Data Analysis

Multivariate analyses of variance (MANOVA) and analyses of variance (ANOVA) were conducted in a 2 × 2, Family Type by Child's Sex design for all of the outcome variables (Bray & Maxwell, 1985). Planned comparisons were also conducted to look at specific differences between boys and girls within and between family types. Multiple regression and correlational analyses were used to examine the relationships between child outcome variables and family process variables.

RESULTS AND DISCUSSION

Children's Social, Emotional, and Intellectual Functioning

The children in stepfamilies and nondivorced families scored significantly different on measures of intellectual functioning (see Table 14.1). Boys in nondivorced families scored higher on the overall verbal measure than both boys and girls in stepfamilies. There were no differences between boys and girls in stepfamilies or girls in stepfamilies and nondivorced families on verbal intelligence. Boys in stepfamilies scored higher on the overall performance measure than girls in stepfamilies and girls in nondivorced families. However, all of the means were in the average to above average range. Analyses of the self-esteem and self-concept data indicate no overall differences between children in the two family groups. Children in stepfamilies reported that their self-esteem was generally equivalent to children in nondivorced families. There were also no differences between the self-esteem of boys and girls in stepfamilies.

On children's self-reports of life stress, girls in stepfamilies reported more negative stress than girls in nondivorced families and boys in stepfamilies, whereas

TABLE 14.1
Means and Standard Deviations for Child Outcome Variables

	Family Type			
	Nondivorced Family		Stepfamily	
	Sex of Child		Sex of Child	
Variable	Males	Females	Males	Females
WISC-R				
Verbal Intelligence	27.6 (5.4)	25.9 (4.3)	24.9 (5.4)	24.0 (4.8)
Performance Intelligence	37.4 (7.7)	34.2 (4.9)	39.4 (5.3)	35.7 (4.6)
P–H Self-Concept	63.9 (9.0)	65.3 (9.2)	59.6 (10.1)	63.7 (7.5)
Weighted Negative Stress	7.2 (5.5)	4.4 (3.6)	4.4 (3.3)	7.1 (4.6)
Mothers CBC				
Internalizing T-score	50.4 (6.8)	50.9 (10.0)	57.6 (7.5)	54.2 (9.2)
Externalizing T-score	49.8 (7.4)	51.6 (8.1)	57.7 (6.7)	58.4 (8.4)
Total Raw Score	17.4 (8.9)	19.6 (13.0)	30.8 (12.0)	29.0 (16.5)
Fathers CBC				
Internalizing T-score	54.1 (10.3)	49.8 (10.1)	54.3 (8.0)	50.6 (5.8)
Externalizing T-score	53.9 (7.6)	51.8 (6.9)	58.4 (8.7)	58.8 (5.5)
Total Raw Score	25.4 (12.3)	18.4 (11.0)	29.7 (15.2)	25.5 (10.0)

WISC–R = Wechsler Intelligence Scale for Children-Revised
P–H Self-Concept = Piers-Harris Children's Self-Concept Scale
CBC = Child Behavior Checklist

boys in nondivorced families reported more negative stress than girls in nondivorced families and boys in stepfamilies. The strongest effect was that girls in stepfamilies reported more negative stress than girls in nondivorced families. There were similar trends on the total life stress scores.

Mothers in stepfamilies rated their children with significantly more externalizing, internalizing, and overall behavior problems than did mothers in nondivorced families. Stepfathers also rated their stepchildren as having significantly more externalizing behavior problems and a trend toward more overall behavior problems than fathers did their biological children. The ratings by fathers and stepfathers were not significantly different for internalizing problems. Boys had more internalizing and overall behavior problems than girls on fathers and stepfathers ratings. However, there were no differences in specific comparisons between boys and girls in stepfamilies on either mother's or stepfather's ratings, although the means are consistently higher for boys in stepfamilies (see Table 14.1).

Thus, biological parents *and* stepparents reported consistent and large differences between children in stepfamilies and children in nondivorced families in their ratings of externalizing behaviors. Only mothers reported that their children in stepfamilies had more internalizing behaviors than did mothers of children in nondivorced families. One hypothesis about the differences between parents' ratings is that internalizing problems tend to be less obvious and require more inference on the rater's part than externalizing problems. Because stepfathers at 6 months post-remarriage know their stepchildren less well and have been around them less than their biological mothers, they may not have the knowledge and experience to observe these types of problems. The differences between mothers' and stepfathers' ratings could also reflect a "honeymoon" effect in which the stepfathers were reluctant to rate as many problems because of the formation of the new family.

Overall, the results indicate some interesting trends for boys and girls in stepfamilies at this early transition. Girls in stepfamilies reported more negative stresses in their lives than girls in nondivorced families and boys in stepfamilies and they exhibited more behavioral problems than children in nondivorced families. In addition, stepfamily girls had poorer intellectual performance relative to the male children. The decrease in intellectual performance is consistent with the fact that they are experiencing more stress than boys in stepfamilies. However, their self-concept was not negatively affected relative to other children. It seems that girls in stepfamilies respond to the added stresses by acting out and misbehaving and with decreased cognitive performance, rather than internalizing their problems and feeling bad about themselves. Boys in stepfamilies also had more behavioral problems than children in nondivorced families and poorer verbal intelligence than boys in nondivorced families. Boys in stepfamilies reported fewer life stresses than girls in stepfamilies and boys in nondivorced families, which may explain their better performance in some cognitive abilities. The measures of performance intelligence tend to be influenced more by anxiety and stress than the verbal measures (Matarazzo, 1972; Satler, 1982). It is not clear from this data if these effects on children in stepfamilies are due to the formation of the new stepfamily, or from the experience of the divorce, or a combination of both.

Family Process and Adult Stress

Mothers in stepfamilies reported that their families had poorer communication patterns and were less effective in resolving problems than did mothers in nondivorced families (see Table 14.2). Stepfamily mothers also reported less effective discipline practices, behavior control, and more poorly defined roles than nondivorced mothers. The emotional responsiveness, affective involvement, and empathetic interest in family members' lives was reported as more healthy by nondivorced mothers than remarried mothers.

Stepfathers also reported that their families were functioning less well than fathers in nondivorced families. In particular, stepfathers indicated that discipline

TABLE 14.2
Means and Standard Deviations for Adult FACES, FAD, and Life Stress

	Family Type			
	Nondivorced Family		Stepfamily	
	Sex of Child		Sex of Child	
Variable	Males	Females	Males	Females
Mothers FACES				
Current cohesion	69.6 (4.3)	68.9 (4.7)	63.2 (9.3)	64.7 (7.0)
Current adaptability	49.9 (2.8)	50.8 (5.3)	48.3 (5.5)	48.8 (4.9)
Ideal cohesion	73.0 (4.1)	71.9 (4.7)	71.8 (4.1)	71.3 (7.5)
Ideal adaptability	59.6 (3.7)	57.4 (5.5)	57.5 (4.1)	58.8 (4.2)
Mothers FAD				
Affective response	9.1 (2.4)	8.0 (1.8)	10.4 (2.7)	9.8 (2.4)
Affective involvement	12.2 (1.7)	11.8 (2.6)	14.4 (2.7)	12.7 (1.7)
Roles	16.4 (1.8)	15.8 (2.7)	18.4 (2.8)	17.2 (3.0)
Behavior control	14.7 (2.4)	14.1 (2.6)	15.8 (2.3)	16.8 (3.4)
Problem solving	8.4 (2.0)	7.8 (1.9)	9.4 (2.2)	8.8 (1.9)
Communication	9.8 (1.7)	10.6 (1.7)	12.1 (2.1)	11.9 (2.4)
Global functioning	17.3 (3.8)	17.7 (4.9)	21.5 (5.6)	18.4 (3.3)
Mothers Life Stress				
Weighted good	7.9 (9.9)	7.5 (5.2)	13.5 (7.5)	17.9 (9.0)
Weighted bad	4.6 (5.3)	4.6 (3.1)	13.3 (6.8)	12.9 (10.7)
Fathers FACES				
Current cohesion	66.8 (8.0)	67.6 (4.8)	59.3 (11.3)	64.4 (6.7)
Curent adaptabiltiy	48.7 (4.8)	49.6 (5.3)	45.5 (6.1)	48.6 (6.8)
Ideal cohesion	70.8 (9.2)	70.5 (5.8)	69.1 (6.8)	70.6 (4.8)
Ideal adaptability	55.9 (5.8)	55.2 (5.5)	53.8 (5.6)	55.3 (4.6)
Fathers FAD				
Affective response	10.9 (3.4)	9.3 (2.7)	12.4 (2.5)	10.3 (2.7)
Affective involvement	12.9 (2.8)	14.0 (2.9)	13.9 (2.4)	13.3 (3.5)
Roles	17.3 (2.9)	16.9 (2.9)	18.4 (2.7)	15.8 (2.9)
Behavior control	15.2 (2.9)	15.5 (3.0)	17.9 (3.2)	16.3 (2.4)
Problem solving	9.6 (1.7)	9.2 (2.2)	10.1 (1.6)	8.6 (2.5)
Communication	11.3 (1.4)	11.1 (2.8)	13.4 (2.7)	11.8 (2.5)
Global functioning	19.4 (4.1)	18.6 (4.1)	24.1 (4.9)	18.4 (4.8)
Fathers Life Stress				
Weighted good	6.1 (4.0)	5.4 (3.5)	16.7 (7.0)	13.3 (4.2)
Weighted bad	3.7 (5.4)	3.2 (1.9)	7.4 (5.9)	8.3 (5.6)

FACES = Family Adapatability and Cohesion Evaluation Scales II.
FAD = Family Assessment Device.
Life Stress = Life Events Survey.

and behavior control practices were not as clearly defined as in nondivorced families and that communication patterns were also less effective. In general, fathers with boys rated their families as more problematic than did fathers in families with girls. It is important to note that all the means on these scales were within a nonclinical range for family functioning (Epstein et al., 1983). Thus, the reports by adults in stepfamilies that family functioning is less effective does not mean they are experiencing a decrease in family functioning that is necessarily pathological or in need of clinical intervention.

Both mothers and stepfathers rated their families as less cohesive than parents in nondivorced families. In addition, the parents in stepfamilies reported less satisfaction with their level of cohesion. There were no differences on mothers' or fathers' ratings of current adaptability, ideal adaptability, or ideal cohesion. In addition, no differences were found between groups on satisfaction with levels of adaptability. These results are consistent with previous findings on a subsample of these families (Bray et al., 1987).

The cohesion reports for the mothers and fathers in the nondivorced family groups were in the Circumplex Connected category (Olson et al., 1982), whereas, the reports for stepfamilies were in the Separated category. For adaptability reports, all group means were in the Structured category. All of the family groups fit within the balanced range of the Circumplex model, which is hypothesized as the most healthy for family functioning (Olson, Sprenkle, & Russel, 1979; Olson et al., 1982).

Adults reported different perceptions of the roles of stepparents depending on whether they were in a stepfamily or in a nondivorced family. Stepfamily members (mothers and stepfathers) believed that there should be a higher degree of openness about relationships among family members than nondivorced family adults. Both biological and stepfathers were more in favor of stepparents forming a close relationship with stepchildren than mothers. All adults felt that it was unacceptable for stepparents to takeover the parental role of the biological parent. Additionally, adults in stepfamilies stated that stepparents should discipline children significantly more than adults in nondivorced families. Overall, these findings support the view of Cherlin (1978) and others that the roles for stepparents are not clearly defined and widely supported in society.

Parents' Life Stress.   There were large significant differences in the amount of life stress reported by adults in stepfamilies and intact families. Overall, adults in stepfamilies reported almost twice as many positive and negative life stressors than adults in intact families. The differences in life-stress ratings included areas directly related to the remarriage, such as the marriage itself or income changes, and also indirect changes, such as moving to a new home, changing jobs status, or parenting difficulties. Anecdotal reports from stepfamilies during the interviews suggest that the positive stresses make the negative experiences tolerable and keep the new families from feeling overwhelmed.

The decreased cohesion and emotional bonding, less effective discipline practices and communication patterns, and more problematic family processes reported by stepfamilies confirms previous hypotheses about stepfamily functioning reported in the clinical and research literature (Anderson & White, 1986; Garbarino et al., 1984; Pink & Wampler, 1985; Sager et al., 1980; Visher & Visher, 1979; Walker & Messinger, 1979). These families are struggling to form a cohesive unit and family identity, which is a process filled with stress for family members. At this point in our research it is not clear if the differences reflect the process of family formation, in which members of the stepfamily are just beginning to emotionally bond with one another and stabilize family relationships, or if the differences indicate structural processes unique to stepfamilies. The previously reviewed research on differences in family relationships between stepfamilies and intact families (Anderson & White, 1986; Garbarino et al., 1984; Perkins & Kahan, 1979; Pink & Wampler, 1985; Rossen, Bray & Ambler, 1985) supports the structural and process differences hypotheses. Comparisons that will be conducted with the later stepfamily groups (2½ and 5 years post-remarriage) in the DIS project will address this question more directly. The self-ratings of family process indicate that these stepfamilies are having some problems in forming their reconstituted family that are not consistent with healthy family functioning.

Family Process and Children's Behavior

Given the differences between children's psychological functioning and family process in stepfamilies and nondivorced families, a salient question is how do these impact one another? Second, are there differences in family process in nondivorced families and stepfamilies that relate to different outcomes for children? In answering these questions differences between mother's and father's ratings were observed and are presented separately.

Multiple regression analyses were conducted using family type, parental ratings on the FACES and FAD, and parent's negative life stress to predict children's behavior problems. The group classification variable was always entered first to evaluate structural differences in family processes. Children had more externalizing behavior problems when they were in a stepfamily; when mothers reported more chaotic adaptability to change, less cohesion, emotional bonding, and affective responsiveness; and fathers reported *more* cohesion, affective responsiveness, overinvolvement and intrusion in family matters. A similar pattern of family relationships and father's negative life stress was predictive of more internalizing and overall behavior problems. However, the group structure variable was not significant for internalizing and overall behavior problems that indicates that similar family patterns in stepfamilies and in nondivorced families lead to these types of behavior problems in children. When the mothers and fathers ratings of children's behavior problems were analyzed separately, the family pattern just described was again found to predict behavior problems. The group structure variable was significant for all of the mother ratings, but none for the father ratings. Again, the major difference was that for father ratings of negative life stress, in combination with specific family patterns, accounted for the differences between behavior problems for children in stepfamilies and intact families. This was not the case for mother ratings of behavior problems.

It is interesting to note the differences and similarities between father's and mother's family process ratings as they relate to children's behavior problems. For both mothers and fathers behavior problems were associated with affective components of family functioning; however, *in different ways*. For mothers *less* affective involvement and expressiveness was associated with more behavior problems, whereas for fathers, *more* involvement and expression of emotional issues was associated with more behavior problems. The family pattern associated with more externalizing behavior problems involves a complementary relationship in which mothers are less involved with their children and respond to change in more chaotic ways, whereas stepfathers become overinvolved in family matters and report enmeshed family relationships. Also of note is that controlling for the life stress of parents did not eliminate the differences in externalizing behavior problems between children in nondivorced families and stepfamilies.

A closer examination also indicates that there were differences in outcomes between boys and girls in stepfamilies for different family processes. Boys in stepfamilies demonstrated better intellectual performance when they reported more positive life experiences, but there was less life stress for their parents. More consistent behavior control by mothers, effective communication in the family, and appropriate affective reponsiveness in the family were also related to better intellectual performance for male children in stepfamilies. Boys' self-esteem was also better if there was more emotional bonding and more flexible adaptability in the family. More behavior problems for boys were related to more life stress for all family members, *less* affective responsiveness, and less emotional bonding, by mothers, but *more* affective responsiveness by stepfathers.

Girls in stepfamilies demonstrated better intellectual performance when their mothers' experienced fewer life stresses, when there was *less* cohesion in the family, and more consistent behavior control and discipline. Better self-esteem for girls was also related to *less* cohesion and affective responsiveness according to mothers and to better overall family functioning. When their parents experienced more life stress these girls also exhibited more internalizing and externalizing behaviors. However, when the girls experienced more life stress, they tended to have more internalizing problems and less externalizing problems. More consistent and effective discipline practices and rules by mothers, appropriate amounts of involvement by mothers and stepfathers, but *less* affective responsiveness by stepfathers was associated with fewer behavior problems for girls.

Girls and boys in stepfamilies appear to function better intellectually, have better self-esteem, and fewer behavior problems under different family circumstances. Boys do better when there is more emotional bonding and cohesion in the family, but girls do better when there is less cohesion and overinvolvement in the family. Following divorce, girls often develop a close emotional bond with their mothers (Hetherington et al., 1978, 1982) and this may be disrupted by the mother's remarriage. Thus, if there is less cohesion between mother and daughter and less involvement by the stepfather, the remarriage may be less disruptive for the girl. In contrast, boys usually develop more conflicted and distant relationships with their mothers following a divorce (Hetherington et al., 1978, 1982). Therefore, more cohesion and emotional bonding following the remarriage may be more beneficial to boys' self-esteem, intellectual performance, and behavioral adjustment. Family process factors reported by both mothers and stepfathers correlated with boys' adjustment, whereas mothers' reports correlated more than stepfathers reports with girls' adjustment. It is also apparent that the increased life stress for both parents and children has negative effects on their behavior and adjustment, although it does not completely explain the differences between children's adjustment in stepfamilies and intact families. It is also important to consider an alternative explanation because these are simple correlations. That is, children with more behavior problems may negatively influence family functioning and increase life stress for parents rather than the reverse. A longitudinal follow-up of these children will clarify the causal links between family process and children's behavior problems in future research.

CONCLUSIONS AND FUTURE DIRECTIONS

This chapter provides some initial findings on the social, behavioral, cognitive, and family functioning of children and adults in new stepfather families. Although final conclusions on stepfamily development and functioning and the impact on family members are premature at this point in our study, some interesting trends are beginning to emerge. Our findings indicate that there are some important differences between stepfamilies and nondivorced families that highlight unique aspects of life in a stepfamily. However, it is important to keep in mind that these results are based on a nonrandom, White, middle-class sample and may not generalize to stepfamilies of different ethnic and socioeconomic status.

Children in stepfamilies did not suffer from self-esteem problems relative to children from nondivorced families. This is contrary to our predictions, although these results are consistent with previous findings reviewed by Ganong and Coleman (1984) for children's self-esteem in stepfamilies. Consistent with our predictions, both boys and girls in stepfamilies had more behavior problems than children in nondivorced families. This finding is similar to previous research in both nonclinical (Hetherington et al., 1982, 1985; Zill, 1985) and clinical settings (Brady et al., 1986), which found that children in stepfamilies had more severe behavior problems than children in nondivorced families. It will be important to determine if these increases in behavior problems for children in stepfamilies are due to the immediate stress of stepfamily formation or are more long-term adjustment difficulties for children experiencing a divorce and remarriage.

There appears to be differential adjustment for boys and girls in stepfamilies. Boys seem to benefit from having a stepfather in the family through increased intellectual performance and less life stress, although they had the most behavior problems. Girls reported more life stress and had poorer intellectual performance than boys in stepfamilies, but they also had more behavior problems than children in nondivorced families. The differences in adjustment are also related to different family process patterns. Boys seem to adjust better when there is more cohesion and emotional bonding with their mothers and stepfathers, whereas girls seem to adjust better when there is less emotional bonding and affective involvement with their mothers. This family relationship pattern appears to be similar to patterns described by Hetherington et al. (1982, 1985; Hetherington, Arnett, & Hollier, 1986) in which children's adjustment is better when the mother plays the primary parental role and the stepfather plays a less active role with the children.

However, the findings concerning children's adjustment are different than those of Hetherington and colleagues (Hetherington, 1987; Hetherington et al., 1982, 1985) and Clingempeel and colleagues (Brand & Clingempeel, 1985; Clingempeel, Brand, & Ievoli, 1984; Clingempeel, Ievoli, & Brand, 1984) that found that girls have more problematic relationships and exhibit more behavior problems than boys in stepfather families. An explanation for this discrepancy lies in two differences between this study and those of Hetherington and Clingempeel. This study specifically focused on early remarriage, less than 7 months, and the children were generally younger, 6 to 9 years old, than the children in the other studies. These discrepancies may point to important developmental issues for children experiencing a remarriage of their mother and the effects of the length of family formation. Analysis of our other groups and comparisons with current studies by Hetherington and Clingempeel will further clarify these issues.

The differences in family process between remarried families and nondivorced families are consistent with previous research that found stepfamilies had less cohesive, more problematic, and more stressful family relationships than nondivorced families (Anderson & White, 1986; Garbarino et al., 1984; Perkins & Kahan, 1979; Pink & Wampler, 1985; Rossen et al., 1985). According to the family life-cycle model, these differences are expected because of the transitions in family formation and because of the more complex family relationships involved in stepfamilies. It is important to note that although these patterns and relationships are different than nondivorced families, they are still within a range considered "normal" by family researchers (Epstein et al., 1983; Olson et al., 1982). The present findings provide one step toward a goal of defining the unique aspects of family functioning for nonclinic stepfamilies.

This chapter did not report on a number of areas of family life that have been identified as important for stepfamily adjustment. The impact of the noncustodial parent and extended family relationships on the new stepfamily is one area that is being investigated and will be reported in later papers. It is expected that the noncustodial parent and extended kin will have a significant impact on the adjustment of the children, as well as the developing stepfamily. In addition, the adjustment of the child in school and other environments will be important indicators to assess.

There are many implications of this and other research on remarriage for social policy, prevention research, and treatment of problems in stepfamilies. Stepparents have many legal responsibilities for children in stepfamilies, but few, if any rights. For example, a child might live in a stepfamily for many years and be raised and supported by a stepparent, yet if the custodial, biological parent dies or becomes disabled the child may be given to the noncustodial parent or biological grandparents rather than being allowed to live with the stepparent. There are obviously arguments on both sides of this issue. However, the differences in roles and expectations about parenting for biological parents and stepparents and the lack of institutional or societal support of stepparenting is likely to increase the stress and possibly lead to other negative outcomes for remarried families (Cherlin, 1978).

Second marriages are at greater risk for dissolution than are first marriages and the risk is greater when children are involved. In fact, many children experience the dissolution and reconstitution of their family two or more times because of the high divorce rate of second marriages. Given the degree of stress reported in this study by adults and girls in stepfamilies, primary prevention programs need to be developed for stepfamilies, particularly when there are children involved. Coping with the stresses of parenthood was reported as one of the primary difficulties for stepfamilies in both this study and the Rossen et al. (1985) study. Many of the techniques and programs developed for nondivorced families and new parents are probably applicable, with appropriate modifications, for remarried families. Support groups for stepfamilies have also been found to help them cope with the stresses of remarriage (Brady & Ambler, 1982; Rossen et al., 1985).

Finally, more research that identifies successful coping patterns for stepfamilies is needed to help clinicians work with stepfamilies who develop problems. In clinical contexts, remarried families are often felt to be much more of a challenge to treat than nondivorced or single-parent families because of the complicated nature of family relationships. Thus, research that identifies the unique stresses and means of successfully coping with these stresses is imperative.

ACKNOWLEDGMENTS

This research is supported by NIH grant R01 HD18025 from the National Institute of Child Health and Human Development and a grant from the Kempner

Foundation of Galveston. I would like to acknowledge the contributions and support of Sandra Berger, Tom Mann, Alan Silverblatt, Sarah Milford, Brad Michael, Sarah Pollack, Joyce Ambler, Patti Arenz, and the other students who worked on this project. Special appreciation is expressed to Dr. E. Mavis Hetherington and her research team at the University of Virginia for providing consultation and invaluable help throughout this project.

REFERENCES

Achenbach, T. M. (1978). The child behavior profile: I. Boys aged 6–11. *Journal of Consulting and Clinical Psychology, 46*, 478–488.

Achenbach, T. M., & Edelbrock, C. (1983). *Child Behavior Checklist and Manual*. Burlington, VT: Department of Psychiatry, University of Vermont.

Anderson, J. Z., & White, G. D. (1986). An empirical investigation of interaction and relationship patterns in functional and dysfunctional nuclear families and stepfamilies. *Family Process, 25*, 407–422.

Bowerman, C. E., & Irish, D. P. (1962). Some relationships of stepchildren to their parents. *Marriage and Family Living, 24*, 113–212.

Brady, C. A., & Ambler, J. (1982). Use of group educational techniques with remarried couples. In L. Messinger (Ed.), *Therapy with remarried families* (pp. 145–157). Rockville, MD: Aspen System Corp.

Brady, C. P., Bray, J. H., & Zeeb, L. (1986). Behavior problems in children seen clinically and their relation to parental marital status, age and sex of child. *American Journal of Orthopsychiatry, 56*, 399–412.

Brand, E., & Clingempeel, W. G. (1985, May). *A multimethod study of family relationships and child outcomes in stepmother and stepfather families: Conclusions and future directions*. Paper presented at the National Institute of Child Health and Human Development Conference on "The impact of divorce, single-parenting and step-parenting on children," Washington, DC.

Bray, J. H., Berger, S. H., Silverblatt, A. H., & Hollier, A. (1987). Family process and organization during early remarriage: A preliminary analysis. In J. P. Vincent (Ed.), *Advances in family intervention, assessment, and theory* (Vol. 4, pp. 253–279). Greenwich, CT: JAI Press.

Bray, J. H., & Maxwell, S. E. (1985). *Multivariate analysis of variance* (Sage University Paper series on Quantitative Applications in the Social Sciences, series no. 07–054). Beverly Hills, CA: Sage.

Burchinal, L. G. (1964). Characteristics of adolescents from unbroken, broken and reconstituted families. *Journal of Marriage and the Family, 24*, 44–51.

Carter, E. A., & McGoldrick, M. (Eds.). (1980). *The family life cycle: A framework for family therapy*. New York: Gardner.

Chapman, M. (1977). Father absence, stepfathers, and the cognitive performance of college students. *Child Development, 48*, 1155–1158.

Cherlin, A. (1978). Remarriage as an incomplete institution. *American Journal of Sociology, 84*, 634–650.

Clingempeel, W. G., Brand, E., & Ievoli, R. (1984). Stepparent-stepchild relationships in stepmother and stepfather families: A multimethod study. *Family Relations, 33*, 465–473.

Clingempeel, W. G., Ievoli, R., & Brand, E. (1984). Structural complexity and the quality of stepfather-stepchild relationships. *Family Process, 23*, 547–560.

Dahl, B. B., McCubbin, H. L., & Lester, G. R. (1976). War induced father absence: Comparing the adjustment of children in reunited, non-reunited, and reconstituted families. *International Journal of Sociology of the Family, 6*, 99–108.

Duberman, L. (1975). *The reconstituted family: A study of remarried couple and their children*. Chicago: Nelson-Hall.

Epstein, N. B., Baldwin, L. M., & Bishop, D. S. (1983). The McMaster family assessment device. *Journal of Marital and Family Therapy, 9*, 171–180.

Epstein, N. B., Bishop, D. S., & Levin, S. (1978). The McMaster model of family functioning. *Journal of Marriage and Family Counseling, 4*, 19–31.

Garbarino, J., Sebes, J., & Schellenbach, C. (1984). Families at risk for destructive parent–child relations in adolescence. *Child Development, 55*, 174–183.

Ganong, L .H., & Coleman, M. (1984). The effects of remarriage on children: A review of the empirical literature. *Family Relations, 33*, 389–406.

Glick, P. C. (1980). Remarriage: Some recent changes and variations. *Journal of Family Issues, 1*, 455–478.

Goetting, A. (1979). Nornative integration of former-spouse relationships. *Journal of Divorce, 2*, 395–414.

Hetherington, E. M. (1979). Divorce: A child's perspective. *American Psychologist, 34*, 851–858.

Hetherington, E. M. (1987). Family relations six years after divorce. In K. Pasley & M. Ihinger-Tollman (Eds.), *Remarriage and Stepparenting today: Research and theory*. New York: Guilford.

Hetherington, E. M., Arnett, J. A., & Hollier, E. A. (1986). Adjustment of parents and children to remarriage. In S. Wolchik & P. Karoly (Eds.), *Children of divorce: Perspectives on adjustment*. New York: Gardner.

Hetherington, E. M., & Camara, K. (1984). Families in transition: The processes of dissolution and reconstitution. In R. D. Parke (Ed.), *Review of child development research, Vol. 7: The family*. Chicago: University of Chicago Press.

Hetherington, E. M., & Clingempeel, W. G. (1984). *Adaptation to remarriage* Study in progress, University of Virginia and Temple University.

Hetherington, E. M., Cox, M., & Cox, R. (1978). The aftermath of divorce. In J. H. Stevens & M. Mathews (Eds.), *Mother–child, father–child relations* (pp. 149–176). Washington, DC: National Association for The Education of Young Children.

Hetherington, E. M., Cox, M., & Cox, R. (1982). Effects of divorce on parents and children. In M. E. Lamb (Ed.), *Nontraditional families: Parenting and child development* (pp. 233–288). Hillsdale, NJ: Lawrence Erlbaum Associates.

Hetherington, E. M., Cox, M., & Cox, R. (1985). Long-term effects of divorce and remarriage on the adjustment of children. *Journal of the American Academy of Child Psychiatry, 24*, 518–530.

Johnson, J. H. (1982). *Development of the children's life experiences survey*. Unpublished manuscript. Department of Clinical Psychology, University of Florida, Gainesville, Florida.

Kaplan, H. B., & Pokorny, A. D. (1971). Self-derogation and childhood broken home. *Journal of Marriage and the Family, 33*, 328–337.

Kellam, S. G., Ensminger, M. A., & Turner, J. I. Family structure and the mental health of children. *Archives of General Psychiatry, 34*, 1012–1022.

Langer, G. S., & Michael, S. T. (1963). *Life stresses and mental health*. New York: The Free Press.

Matarazzo, J. D. (1972). *Weschsler's measurement and appraisal of adult intelligence*. Baltimore, MD: Williams & Wilkins.

Olson, D. H., Portner, J., & Bell, R. (1982). FACES II: Family adaptability and cohesion evaluation scales. In D. H. Olson (Ed.), *Family inventories* (pp. 5–24). Family Social Science, 290 McNeal Ave., University of Minnesota, St. Paul, MN. 55108.

Olson, D. H., Sprenkle, D. H., & Russel, C. S. (1979). Circumplex model of marital and family systems I: Cohesion and adaptability dimensions, family types, and clinical applications. *Family Process, 18*, 3–28.

Oshman, H., & Manosevitz, M. (1976). Father-absence: Effects of stepfathers upon psycho-social development in males. *Developmental Psychology, 12*, 479–480.

Perkins, T. F., & Kahan, J. P. (1979). An empirical comparison of natural-father and step-father family systems. *Family Process, 18*, 175–183.

Perry, J. B., & Pfuhl, E. H. (1963). Adjustment of children in "solo" and "remarriage" homes. *Marriage and Family Living*, 221-223.

Piers, E. V., & Harris, D. B. (1978). *Piers–Harris children's self-concept scale*. Los Angeles, CA: Western Psychological Services.

Pink, J. E. T., & Wampler, K. S. (1985). Problem areas in stepfamilies: Cohesion, adaptability, and the stepfather–adolescent relationship. *Family Relations, 34*, 327-335.

Rosenberg, M. (1965). *Society and the adolescent self-image*. Princeton, NJ: Princeton University Press.

Rossen, K., Bray, J. H., & Ambler, J. (1985). *A follow-up study of marriage in reconstituted families*. Unpublished manuscript, Texas Woman's University, Houston Center, Houston, TX.

Sager, C. J., Steer, H., Crohn, H., Rodstein, E., & Walker, E. (1980). Remarriage revisited. *Family and Child Mental Health Journal, 6*, 19-33.

Santrock, J. W. (1972). The relations of type and onset of father absence to cognitive development. *Child Development, 43*, 455-469.

Santrock, J. W., Warshak, R. A., & Elliott, G. L. (1982). Social development and parent–child interaction in father–custody and stepmother families. In M. E. Lamb (Ed.), *Nontraditional families: Parenting and child development*. Hillsdale, NJ: Lawrence Erlbaum Associates.

Santrock, J. W., Warshak, R. A., Lindberg, C., & Meadows, L. (1982). Children's and parent's observed social behavior in stepfather families. *Child Development, 53*, 472-480.

Sarason, I. G., Johnson, J. H., & Siegel, J. M. (1978). Assessing the impact of life changes: Development of the Life Experiences Survey. *Journal of Consulting and Clinical Psychology, 46*, 932-946.

Satler, E. M. (1982). *Assessment of children's intelligence* (2nd ed.). Boston, MA: Allyn & Bacon.

Visher, E. B., & Visher, J. S. (1979). *Stepfamilies: A guide to working with stepparents and stepchildren*. New York: Brunner/Mazel.

Walker, K. N., & Messinger, L. (1979). Remarriage after divorce: Dissolution and reconstruction of family boundaries. *Family Process, 18*, 185-192.

Walker, K. N., Roger, J., & Messinger, L. (1977). Remarriage after divorce: A review. *Social Casework, 58*, 276-285.

Wechsler, D. (1974). *Wechsler intelligence scale for children-revised*. New York: The Psychological Corp.

Williamson, D. S., & Bray, J. H. (1988). Family development and change across the generations: An intergenerational perspective. In C. J. Falicov (Ed.), *Family transitions: Continuity and change over the life cycle*. New York: Guilford.

Wilson, K. L., Zucker, L., McAdams, D. C., & Curtis, R. L. (1975). Stepfathers and stepchildren: An exploratory analysis from two national surveys. *Journal of Marriage and The Family, 37*, 526-536.

Zill, N. (1985, May). *Children in stepfamilies: Their behavior problems, school performance, and use of mental health services*. Paper presented at the National Institute of Child Health and Human Development Conference on "The impact of divorce, single-parenting and step-parenting on children," Washington, DC.

15

Family Relationships and Children's Psychological Adjustment in Stepmother and Stepfather Families

Eulalee Brand
W. Glenn Clingempeel
The Pennsylvania State University at Harrisburg

Kathryn Bowen-Woodward
Clinical Psychologist, Philadelphia, PA

It has been estimated that 35% of all children born in the United States in the early 1980s will spend part of their childhood living in a stepfamily (Glick, 1984). Despite this statistic, few empirical studies have examined the interdependencies of multiple dyadic relationships within stepfamilies and the extent to which qualitative dimensions of these relationships mediate children's psychological adjustment. Yet, the quality of husband–wife, stepparent–stepchild, and nonresidential parent–child relationships may be critical to stepfamily functioning and positive child outcomes.

The quality of the stepparent–stepchild relationship may have an impact on child outcomes and the quality of relationships within the stepfamily household. The addition of a stepparent into a single–parent home may threaten the child's relationship with both the residential and nonresidential biological parent. Moreover, the absence of societal guidelines regarding the appropriate role of the stepparent in childrearing may strain the family system and the coping mechanisms of children (Cherlin, 1978). In a 6-year follow-up of a longitudinal study of divorce, Hetherington, Cox, and Cox (1986) found that stepfathers who initially supported the remarried mother in parenting and later on developed an authoritative parenting style (high on warmth and moderate on control dimensions) seemed to have a positive effect on the psychological adjustment of stepsons. Crosbie-Burnett (1984) found that a mutually supportive stepfather–stepchild relationship was a better predictor of overall happiness within the family than the quality of the marital relationship. In analyses of a National Survey of Children (Furstenberg, Nord, Peterson, & Zill, 1983), Furstenberg and Seltzer (1983) found that the quality of the stepparent–stepchild relationship was a better predictor of child adjustment than the quality of the child's relationship with the nonresidential biological parent.

The quantity and quality of children's contacts with the nonresidential biological parent may also mediate the quality of relationships within the stepfamily household and child outcomes. Studies of the impact of divorce on children have found that, regular contact with the nonresidential father generally is related to better postdivorce adjustment (Hess & Camara, 1979; Hetherington, Cox, & Cox, 1978; Wallerstein & Kelly, 1980). However, the extant research provides little information regarding whether this positive effect continues after the residential parent remarries.

Remarriage of the residential parent may disrupt the nonresidential parent-child relationship and children's hopes for reconciliation of biological parents (Fast & Cain, 1966; Visher & Visher, 1978, 1979). Nonresidential parents may visit children less frequently after the residential parent remarries due, in part, to the awkwardness of relating to the new stepparent (Furstenberg & Spanier, 1984). This reduction in visitation may be upsetting to children who, after remarriage, may fear replacement of the "outside" parent. Clinicians (e.g., Mills, 1984; Papernow, 1984) report that children's fantasies of parental reconciliation may persist for years after the divorce, and these fantasies may be disrupted when the residential parent remarries.

The quality of the stepparent–stepchild relationship and the frequency of visits from the nonresidential parent may be interdependent and the nature of this interdependency may mediate child outcomes. Frequent visits from the nonresidential parent could reduce children's fears that the stepparent is a parent replacement resulting in more positive stepparent–stepchild relationships and better outcomes for children. Alternatively, frequent contact with the nonresidential parent could increase role ambiguities for the residential parent and stepparent (due to a greater probability of increased interaction between ex-spouses and between stepparent and nonresidential biological parent), prevent the development of a cohesive stepparent–stepchild relationship, and ultimately translate into negative consequences for children. Using data from a National Survey of Children (Furstenberg et al., 1983), Furstenberg and Seltzer (1983) reported that, in stepfather families, regular contact with nonresidential biological fathers did not adversely affect the quality of stepfather–stepchild relationships. However, in stepmother families, regular contact with nonresidential biological mothers was related to lower quality relationships between stepmothers and stepchildren.

Rare in the stepfamily literature are studies of the "effects" of qualitative dimensions of the remarried couples' relationship on stepparent–stepchild relationships and children's adjustment. Studies of nuclear families have found that more positive marital relationships are related to more competent parenting practices (e.g., Belsky, 1979; Dielman, Barton, & Cattell, 1977; Johnson & Lobitz, 1974; Kempler & Reichler, 1976; Olweus, 1980) that, in turn, are related to better adjustment of children (e.g., Baumrind, 1971, 1982; Hetherington, Cox, & Cox, 1982). A happy marriage may serve as a support system for the parent role and, in a reciprocal manner, competent parenting practices may lead to more positive interactions between spouses (Belsky, 1979, 1984).

During the early stages of stepfamily formation, more positive marital relationships may have different consequences for stepparent–stepchild relationships and children's adjustment than those suggested by the extant research on nuclear families. Stepparent couple relationships characterized by a higher proportion of positive exchanges between spouses (and higher overall marital quality) may be associated, at least initially, with greater disruptions of positive roles and relationships negotiated during the single-parent stage.

From a family systems perspective (e.g., P. Minuchin, 1985; S. Minuchin, 1974; Watzlawick, Beavin, & Jackson, 1967), remarriage of the residential parent requires a reallocation of the personal resources of family members, a reassignment of roles, and redistribution of parent–child boundaries. Time and affection previously given by the resident parent to the child may be reallocated to the new spouse (Visher & Visher, 1978). Children's power and status within the household that may have increased during the single-parent stage (e.g., Hetherington et al., 1982) also may diminish. Adult-like roles and responsibilities often acquired by children after parental divorce, including that of disciplinarian of younger siblings and confidant to resident parent (Weiss, 1979), may be assumed by the stepparent (Pasley & Ihinger-Tallman, 1986). A more positive marital relationship may encroach even more on the special roles acquired by children during the single-parent stage and may translate into an even greater reallocation of the resident parent's time and affection from child to new spouse. A more positive remarriage may also be perceived by children as a greater blow to their hopes for reconciliation of biological parents and as a greater threat to their relationship with the nonresident parent.

It is also possible that positive remarriages may support rather than detract from positive roles and dimensions of intrafamilial relationships. A relationship with the stepparent may compensate for any reduction of time and affection from the resident parent to the child. The stepparent's assuming roles and responsibilities placed upon the child during the single-parent stage actually may be a "welcome relief" to children who now have more time to engage in pleasurable activities (e.g., interactions with peers). Moreover, the stepparent may be perceived as an additional support system rather than replacement for the nonresident parent.

The relations between intra-stepfamily dyads and children's psychological adjustment may depend on the sex of stepchild and sex of resident stepparent. Several studies of stepfamilies have found that stepfather–stepdaughter relationships are more problematic than stepfather–stepson relationships (Hetherington et al., 1986; Santrock, Warshak, Lindbergh & Meadows, 1982). Studies of nuclear and divorced families have suggested that the sex of the child or sex of child–sex of parent interactions may mediate the quality of parent-child relationships (e.g., Hetherington et al., 1986; Margolin & Patterson, 1975; Santrock & Warshak, 1979), the quality of husband–wife relationships (e.g., Lerner & Spanier, 1978), the effects of marital relationship dimensions (e.g., conflict) on children's psychological adjustment (e.g., Emery & O'Leary, 1979; Oltmanns, Broderick, &

O'Leary, 1977), and the relations between qualitative dimensions of mother–child and sibling dyads (Dunn & Kendrick, 1981). Moreover, Hetherington et al.'s (1986) 6-year follow-up of custodial mothers revealed that both styles of stepparenting (authoritarian, authoritative, permissive, or disengaged) and marital satisfaction were associated with different consequences for male and female children. Whereas, in the long run, boys appeared to benefit from an authoritative stepparent and from greater marital satisfaction of mother and stepfather, girls more than 2 years into the remarriage continued to show adverse effects associated with positive dimensions of stepparental and marital dyads.

This chapter integrates the findings of a series of studies of family relationships and child outcomes based on a Philadelphia, Pennsylvania sample of Caucasian, middle-income, divorce-engendered stepfamilies. The early studies from this database used a between-groups comparison strategy and assessed the "effects" of various structural and demographic factors on the quality of husband–wife and stepparent–stepchild relationships and children's psychological adjustment (Clingempeel & Brand, 1985; Clingempeel, Brand, & Ievoli, 1984; Clingempeel, Ievoli, & Brand, 1984). Three major questions were addressed: (a) Are there sex of stepchild or type of stepfamily differences on the quality of stepparent–stepchild relationships and children's adjustment? (b) Are there sex of spouse or type of stepfamily differences on the quality of marital relationships? (c) Do resident stepfathers who are also nonresident biological parents have different kinds of relationships with stepchildren than resident stepfathers who have no children from a prior marriage? Overall, these studies yielded few statistically significant findings. The only robust finding was that girls had more difficult relationships with both stepfathers and stepmothers than did boys.

The final two studies from the Philadelphia Stepfamily Research Project (Brand & Clingempeel, 1986; Clingempeel & Segal, 1986) employed an intragroup dynamics strategy. Rather than compare structural types of stepfamilies, Brand and Clingempeel (1986) and Clingempeel and Segal (1986) examined the interdependencies of dyadic relationships and childrens' psychological adjustment *within* four stepfamily groups (stepfather family—male target child; stepfather family—female target child; stepmother family—male target child; stepmother family—female target child). Brand and Clingempeel (1986) examined the effects of marital quality on stepparent–stepchild relationships and children's psychological adjustment and Clingempeel and Segal (1986) assessed the relations among frequency of visits of nonresident parents, the quality of stepparent-stepchild relationships, and child outcomes. Both studies found that the interdependencies of family relationships and children's adjustment depended on the sex of stepchild and type of stepfamily.

The intragroup dynamics strategy yielded the most striking findings, and, consequently, integrating the results of the Brand and Clingempeel (1986) and Clingempeel and Segal (1986) studies are the major focus of this chapter. In combination, the two studies examined five major questions separately for each of the four sex of resident stepparent–sex of stepchild groups: (a) What are the relations between qualitative dimensions of husband–wife relationships and qualitative dimensions of stepparent–stepchild relationships? (b) What are the relations between frequency of visits from nonresident parents and stepparent–stepchild relationships? (c) What are the relations between husband–wife relationships and child psychological outcomes? (d) What are the relations between stepparent–stepchild relationships and child psychological outcomes? (e) What are the relations between frequency of visits from nonresidential parents and child psychological outcomes?

METHODOLOGY AND RESEARCH DESIGN

Stepfamily Recruitment and Description

Forty, Caucasian, middle-income stepfather families (where a divorced woman with custody of children from a prior marriage remarried a divorced or single man without custody of children) and 22 White, middle-income stepmother families (where a divorced man with custody of children from a prior marriage remarried a divorced or single woman without children) were recruited from the Marriage License Records of Philadelphia and Norristown, Pennsylvania. All stepparent couples had been married less than 3 years, and in all families either the husband or wife had custody of a 9- to 12-year-old "target" child from the prior marriage. No couples had children from the current marriage. Comprehensive information regarding recruitment procedures, selection criteria, and sampling results (e.g., percentage of families who fit criteria but refused to participate) and a breakdown of the stepfamily groups on demographic variables, marital history variables (e.g., total time living in a stepfamily household, age of target child at time of divorce) and family composition variables (e.g., number of custodial children) are provided in Clingempeel and Segal, 1986. Statistical analyses revealed few significant differences between groups on these variables. However, the groups did differ significantly on age of biological parent and length of biological parent's previous marriage. Biological parents were older in stepmother families and their previous marriages were longer than their counterparts in stepfather families. The differences in age of biological parents is probably consistent with natural differences between stepmother and stepfather families. Men are older than women in both first and second marriages with the magnitude of the differences significantly greater in remarriages (Furstenberg & Spanier, 1984).

The 9–12 age range of target children is large and age differences may be related to children's adjustment. However, correlations between stepchildren's ages and the adjustment measures for the four stepfamily groups were, with one exception (in stepfather families with boys, age was correlated with parent ratings of aggression), nonsignificant.

Measurement of Stepparent–Stepchild Relationship Dimensions

Qualitative dimensions of the stepparent–stepchild relationship were assessed by a multimethod–multisource strategy. The stepparent and stepchild each rated love dimensions of their relationship on standardized questionnaires. Proportions of positive communication behaviors emitted by stepparents and stepchildren were derived from a 10-minute structured interaction task videotaped in the homes of the families.

Child Report of Stepparent Behavior Toward the Child Inventory.   The Acceptance and Positive Involvement scales of Schaefer's (1965) *Child Report of Parent Behavior Inventory* were reworded to focus on the child's relationship with the stepparent. The questionnaire requested that the child indicate for 32 specific stepparent behaviors (e.g., she/he makes me feel better after talking over my worries with her/him), whether each item was "like," "somewhat like," or "not like" his or her stepparent. The two scales assess the love dimension of the stepparent–stepchild relationship, have high internal consistency reliabilities (Schaefer, 1965, personal communication, 1982), and were considered most relevant to qualitative aspects of the stepparent–stepchild relationship. A single "child love" score was derived from the questionnaire.

Stepparent Report of Child Behavior Toward the Stepparent Inventory.   The Love factor (which includes the confiding, demonstrates competence, initiates shared activities, and active concern subscales) of Schaefer, Edgarton, and Finkelstein's (1979) *Parent Report of Child Behavior Inventory* was reworded to focus on the stepparent's relationship with the target child. Stepparents were asked to indicate on a 5-point Likert scale whether specific child behaviors (e.g., he or she tells his or her stepparent about things that bother him or her) were "not at all like" to "very much like" the target child. An internal consistency reliability of .88 has been reported for this scale (Schaefer, personal communication, 1982).

Behavioral Observations: Family Problem Solving System (FPSS).   A modified FPSS (Forgatch & Wieder, 1981) consisting of 30 verbal and 8 nonverbal codes was used in the behavioral coding of videotaped stepparent-stepchild interactions. The 38 codes are subsumed under six summary categories:

1. *Positive Problem Solving*: accept responsibility, contingent, closure, countersolution, hypothetical, promise, and positive solution
2. *Negative Problem Solving*: deny, demand, don't, morality lesson and noncooperate
3. *Positive Verbal*: agree, approve, comply, defend other, empathize, humor, and restate

4. *Negative Verbal*: blame, command, complain, criticize, disagree disqualify, guilt trip, leading question, mind read, threat, and why
5. *Positive Nonverbal*: laugh, lean forward, positive gesture, and touch positive
6. *Negative Nonverbal*: destructive, hostile gesture, touch negative, and wander

The videotapes were coded at the Oregon Social Learning Center by trained coders blind to the research questions. Intercoder reliabilities (agreements/agreements + disagreements) × 100 on nine videotapes were calculated on a moment-by-moment basis for all individual codes. Reliabilities ranged from 71% to 97% for nonverbal codes ($M = 83\%$) and 69% to 85% for verbal codes ($M = 75\%$).

Proportions of positive communication behaviors emitted by stepparents and stepchildren were derived by dividing the sum of rates for the three positive summary categories by the sum of rates for the three positive and three negative categories. The conversion of rates to proportions was designed to control for potential differences in basal activity-level differences that could result in higher rates of both positive and negative communication behaviors but not reflect differences in the quality of communications (Hadley & Jacob, 1973; Jacob, 1974). Arcsine transformations were performed on all proportional data (Winer, 1971).

Measurement of Husband–Wife Relationship Dimensions

Positive dimensions of the husband–wife relationship were assessed by a multimethod–multisource strategy. The husband and wife independently completed a self-report questionnaire assessing marital quality. Proportions of positive communication behaviors emitted by each spouse were derived from a 10-minute structured interaction task videotaped in the homes of families.

Dyadic Adjustment Scale (DAS). The DAS (Spanier, 1976) is a 32-item multidimensional measure of the marital quality. Individuals rate topics relevant to relationship quality (e.g., sex, companionship, displays of affection, disagreements) on 5- and 6-point Likert scales (e.g. , "always agree" to "always disagree," "all the time" to "never"). The total score of the DAS was used as the self-reported index of marital quality. Internal consistency reliabilities for the DAS total score are in the mid .90s (Sharpley & Cross, 1982; Spanier, 1976; Spanier & Thompson, 1982). A study of criterion-related validity (Spanier, 1976) found mean total scale scores significantly discriminated married respondents form divorced respondents. Pearson correlations between DAS total scores and the Locke–Wallace Marital Adjustment Scale ranged from .86 to .88 (Spanier, 1976).

Behavioral Observations: Marital Interaction Coding System (MICS). A modified form of the MICS (Hops, Wills, Patterson, & Weiss, 1972) consisting of 7 nonverbal and 14 verbal codes was used in the behavioral coding of videotaped husband–wife interactions. The 21 behavioral codes are subsumed under five summary categories:

1. *Positive Problem Solving*: accept responsibility, compromise, paraphrase, positive solution
2. *Positive Verbal*: agree, approve, humor
3. *Positive Nonverbal:* assent, attend, smile/laugh, positive physical contact
4. *Negative Verbal*: complain, disagree, criticize, deny responsibility, excuse, mindread, put down
5. *Negative Nonverbal*: no response, not tracking, turn off

Studies using MICS have consistently found interjudge reliabilities above .70 (e.g. Belsky, Spanier, & Rovine, 1983; Jones, Reid, & Patterson, 1975). Validity studies have shown that MICS successfully discriminates distressed from nondistressed couples (Birchler, Weiss, & Vincent, 1975; Vincent, Friedman, Nugent, & Messerly, 1979; Vincent, Weiss, & Birchler, 1975). Moreover, treatment outcome studies have reported increased positive and decreased negative behaviors from pre- to postintervention assessments (Jacobson, 1977, 1978; Margolin & Weiss, 1978a, 1978b).

Videotapes of the couple's discussion of the "Discuss Changes" task were coded at the University of Oregon Marital Studies Program by trained coders blind to the research questions. Interjudge reliabilities (agreements/agreements + disagreements) × 100 on eight videotapes were calculated on a moment-by-moment basis for all individual codes. Reliabilities ranged from .80 to .97 (M = 91%).

Frequencies of spousal behaviors in the five summary categories were adjusted for variations in total discussion time by calculating rates of behaviors per minute for each category. As was done with the stepparent–stepchild behavioral data, the basal verbal activity of the spouses was controlled by deriving proportions of total positive communication behaviors (the sum of rates for the three positive summary categories was divided by the sum of rates for the three positive and two negative categories) and the proportions were subjected to arcsine transformations.

Measurement of Child Outcome Dimensions

Children's responses to a standardized self-esteem questionnaire and parent ratings of aggression and inhibition were used as indices of psychological adjustment.

Piers–Harris Self-Concept Scale.   (P–H; Piers & Harris, 1969). The P–H is an 80-item self-report questionnaire designed to assess self-esteem in 9- to 17-year-old children. Children indicate whether statements (e.g., My classmates make fun of me) are true or false of themselves. The P–H yields a global self-concept score. Internal consistency reliabilities for the P–H have ranged from the upper .80s to low .90s (Piers, 1977; Yonker, Blixt, & Dinero, 1974). Convergent validity studies have found that the P–H correlates .85 with the Coopersmith Self-Esteem Inventory (Schauer, 1965).

Louisville Behavior Checklist (LBC; Miller, 1967, 1977). The LBC (Form E2) is a 164-item behavioral rating scale designed to assess a wide variety of deviant and prosocial behaviors in 7- to 13-year-old children. Parents indicate whether specific behaviors (e.g., cries easily, constantly fighting or beating up others) are "true" (describe their child) or are "false" (do not describe their child). Items from two broad-band factors—Aggression and Inhibition—were used in the current study. The Aggression and Inhibition factors are equivalent to the "overcontrol" and "undercontrol" broad-band dimensions consistently obtained in factor-analytic studies of children's behavioral rating scales (Achenbach & Edelbrook, 1978). Spearman–Brown reliability coefficients have ranged from .84 to .90 for the Aggression scale and .68 to .88 for the Inhibition scale (Miller, 1967). Criterion-related validity studies indicate that the LBC scales successfully discriminate among pathological groups of children and between deviant and nondeviant populations (e.g., Miller, 1967, 1977).

Measurement of Social Demographic and Marital History Variables

Social Demographic and Marital History Questionnaire. This questionnaire was constructed specifically for this research and included 40 questions with fixed alternative response categories. Section I focused on demographic (e.g., annual income, age, and educational level of parents/stepparents), and family size/structure characteristics (e.g., number, age, and sex of custodial children). Section II focused on marital history and courtship characteristics including length of current and previous marriages, duration of intermarriage interval, and length of time the stepparent couple "lived together" premaritally ("living together" was defined as spending at least 4 nights a week in the same household). The total time living in a stepfamily household (TTSH) was computed as the sum of the length of the current marriage and the length of time the couple lived together premaritally.

Frequency of Visitation from Nonresidential Parent

A modified *Quasi-Kin Relationships Questionnaire* (QRQ; Clingempeel, 1981) was used to assess the frequency of visits from nonresidential parents. The revised QRQ required the parent and stepparent to collaborate in recording the total number of days in which the target child received a visit from the nonresidential parent for each of the last 6 months. In recording monthly frequencies, subjects started with the most recent month and moved backward to the most distant month. Participants were asked to consider both the regular visitation schedule and any special events (e.g., birthdays, holidays). Test–retest reliabilities on the total frequency of visits in 6 months were obtained between 1 and 2 months after the home visit on 15 randomly selected families. The Pearson correlation of time 1 and time 2 frequencies was .71.

PROCEDURE

The data were collected during a 3½ hour home visit by two Caucasian doctoral students in clinical psychology. Parent and stepparent met with one interviewer and the target child met with a second interviewer (who was the same sex as the target child) in a separate room. The spouses collaborated on the Social Demographic and Marital History and Quasi-Kin Relationships Questionnaires; then they independently completed the Dyadic Adjustment Scale and parent and stepparent forms of the Parent Report of Child Behavior Inventory. In addition, the target child's biological parent completed the Louisville Behavior Checklist. The interviewer of the child administered the Piers–Harris Self-Concept Scale and the Child Report of Stepparent Behavior Inventory.

Stepparent–stepchild and husband–wife pairs were each asked to engage in two discussion tasks that were videotaped. The order of administering the questionnaire measures and the videotaped interaction tasks was counterbalanced across groups to control for sequence effects. In addition, the order of husband–wife and stepparent–stepchild discussion tasks was also counterbalanced across groups. Discussions always took place in an isolated room of the house in an effort to minimize reactivity and to control for differences due to the presence of other family members. The interviewer gave instructions for one task at a time, left the room during the discussions, and did not return until the time limit had expired (or until participants signalled completion).

The stepparent and stepchild were instructed first to spend 5 minutes planning an activity together. The task served as a "warm-up" and was designed to facilitate habituation to the video equipment. The second task had a 10-minute time limit and required the participants to discuss and try to reach agreement on changes they would like to see in their family. The "discuss changes" task generated the discussion that was coded by trained observers using the Family Problem Solving System (FPSS). The "plan activity" task was chosen as a warm-up and was presented first because it has been found to elicit less anxiety (Lewis, Beavers, Gossett, & Phillips, 1976).

The husband and wife "warm-up" task also had a 5-minute time limit and required couples to discuss and reach agreement on three rewarding areas of their marriage. The second task had a 10-minute time limit and required the participants to discuss and reach agreement on two problems they have faced as a stepparent couple and how they have dealt with, or plan to deal with, these problems. This task generated the discussion that was coded by trained observers using the Marital Interaction Coding System. This task was selected because previous studies have suggested its relevance to stepfamilies and that the issues involved are problematic and potentially conflict-inducing (Messinger, 1976).

RESULTS

The Between-Groups Comparison Studies

The data analytic plan of the between-groups comparison studies (Clingempeel & Brand, 1985; Clingempeel, Brand, & Ievoli, 1984; Clingempeel, Ievoli, & Brand, 1984) involved conducting a series of MANOVAs with structural and demographic factors as independent variables and the measures of family relationship dimensions and childrens' adjustment as dependent variables.

Type of Stepfamily, Sex of Stepchild, and the Quality of Stepparent–Stepchild Relationships. A series of 2 (type of stepfamily) × 2 (sex of stepchild) MANOVAs performed separately on questionnaire and behavioral measures of both positive and negative dimensions of stepparent–stepchild relationships revealed significant multivariate Fs for sex of target child. Moreover, univariate Fs revealed several significant differences between male and female stepchildren. When the target child was a boy, parents, stepparents, and stepchildren reported significantly higher scores on love and lower scores on detachment. Boys also engaged in a significantly higher proportion of positive verbal behaviors and a significantly lower proportion of negative problem-solving behaviors during structured interactions with their stepparents. Thus, girls exhibited lower quality relationships with stepparents in both stepmother and stepfather families.

Multivariate t tests were used to test for differences between *simple* stepfather families (where the resident stepfather had no children from a prior marriage) and *complex* stepfather families (where the resident stepfather was also a nonresident biological parent) on the quality of stepparent–stepchild relationships. No consistent significant differences were obtained on any of the questionnaire or behavioral measures.

Type of Stepfamily, Sex of Stepchild, and Stepchildren's Psychological Adjustment. Two by 2 (type of stepfamily × sex of target child) ANOVAs with proportional cell sizes were performed on each of the three child outcome measures (biological parents' inhibition and aggression ratings and stepchildrens' self-concept scores). No significant main effects or interactions were obtained. Boys and girls in stepmother and stepfather families did not differ on the psychological adjustment measures.

Type of Stepfamily and Marital Quality.   An Hotelling *t* test with type of stepfamily (stepmother vs. stepfather) as the independent variable and three measures of marital quality (including the DAS total score, the rate of positive verbal exchanges, and the rate of negative verbal exchanges) as dependent variables revealed no differences between the two types of stepfamilies. A separate Hotelling *t* performed on the two nonverbal behavioral measures (rates of positive and negative nonverbal behaviors) also revealed no differences between stepmother and stepfather families.

The Intragroup Dynamics Studies

The data-analytic strategy for the Brand and Clingempeel (1986) and Clingempeel and Segal (1986) studies involved conducting a series of Pearson correlations between measures of qualitative dimensions of family relationships (e.g., husband–wife, stepparent–stepchild) and children's psychological adjustment. Correlations were performed separately for each of the four sex of resident stepparent–sex of stepchild groups.

Relations Between the Quality of Husband–Wife and Stepparent–Stepchild Relationships.   For stepfather families, correlations between the marital quality measures (husband and wife DAS scores and proportions of positive behaviors emitted toward spouses) and measures of stepfather–stepchild relationships (stepfather and stepchild love ratings and proportions of positive behaviors emitted toward each other) are presented separately for male and female stepchildren in Table 15.1.

For stepfather–stepsons dyads, three of eight correlations involving the stepfather's behaviors toward and perceptions of stepchildren were statistically significant. Stepfathers' and biological mothers' DAS scores were both positively correlated with stepfathers' love ratings of stepsons. The proportion of positive behaviors mothers emitted toward stepfathers was positively correlated with the proportion of positive behaviors stepfathers emitted toward stepsons. Only one of eight correlations involving stepsons' behaviors toward and perceptions of stepfathers was significant. The proportion of positive behaviors mothers emitted toward stepfathers was negatively associated with stepsons' love ratings of stepfathers.

For stepfather–stepson dyads, three of eight correlations involving the stepfathers' behaviors toward and perceptions of stepdaughters were statistically significant. Stepfathers' and mothers' DAS scores were both positively correlated with stepfathers' love ratings of stepdaughters. Stepfathers' DAS scores were also positively correlated with the proportion of positive behaviors they emitted toward stepdaughters. The proportion of positive behaviors mothers emitted toward stepfathers was positively correlated with the proportion of positive behaviors stepfathers emitted toward stepdaughters. Only one of eight correlations involving stepdaughters behaviors toward and perceptions of stepfathers was significant. Biological mothers' DAS scores were negatively correlated with the proportion of positive behaviors girls emitted toward their stepfathers.

Thus, the marital quality measures were positively correlated, overall, with stepfathers' positive behaviors toward and perceptions of stepchildren of both sexes, but either uncorrelated or negatively associated with stepchildrens' positive behaviors toward and perceptions of stepfathers.

For stepmother families, correlations between the marital quality measures and measures of stepmother–stepchild relationships are presented separately for male and female stepchildren in Table 15.2.

For stepmother–stepson dyads, two of eight correlations involving the stepmothers' behaviors toward and perceptions of stepsons were significant and both were positive. Biological fathers DAS scores were positively correlated with stepmothers' love ratings of stepsons. The proportion of positive behaviors biological fathers emitted toward stepmothers was positively correlated with the proportion of positive behaviors stepmothers emitted toward stepsons. Two of eight correlations involving stepsons' behaviors toward and perceptions of stepmothers were significant and both were positive. Fathers' DAS scores were positively correlated with stepsons' love ratings of stepmothers; and the proportion of positive behaviors fathers emitted toward stepmothers was positively correlated with the proportion of positive behaviors stepsons emitted toward stepmothers.

For stepmother–stepdaughter dyads, two of eight correlations involving stepmothers' behaviors toward and perceptions of stepdaughters were significant and both were negative. Stepmothers' DAS scores were negatively correlated with their love ratings of stepdaughters. The proportion of positive behaviors stepmothers emitted toward biological fathers was negatively correlated with the proportion of positive behaviors stepmothers emitted toward stepdaughters. Of the eight correlations involving stepdaughters' behaviors toward and perceptions of stepmothers, two were significant and both were negative. Stepmothers' DAS scores and the proportion of positive behaviors stepmothers emitted toward fathers were both negatively correlated with stepdaughters' love ratings of stepmothers.

Relations Between Frequency of Visits from Nonresident Parents and the Quality of Stepparent–Stepchild Relationships. The frequency of visits from nonresident parents was correlated with the three measures of the stepparent–stepchild relationship (stepchild's love ratings, stepchild's proportion of positive behaviors emitted toward stepparent, and stepparents' proportion of positive behaviors emitted toward stepchild) separately for each of the four sex of resident stepparent–sex of stepchild groups. No correlations were significant for boys in stepfather or stepmother families. For girls in stepfather families, one correlation was significant. Visitation frequency was positively correlated with the proportion of positive behaviors stepfathers emitted toward stepdaughters. For girls in stepmother families, the frequency of visits from nonresident mothers was negative-

TABLE 15.1

Pearson Correlations Between Measures of Marital Quality and Measures of Stepfather–Stepson and Stepfather–Stepdaughter Relationships

Marital Quality Measures	Stepfather Behaviors and Love Ratings of Stepchildren				Stepchild Behaviors and Love Ratings of Stepfathers			
	Positive Behaviors to Stepchildren		Love Ratings of Stepchildren		Positive Behaviors to Stepfathers		Love Ratings of Stepfathers	
	Boys (N = 20)	Girls (N = 20)	Boys (N = 20)	Girls (N = 20)	Boys (N = 20)	Girls (N = 20)	Boys (N = 20)	Girls (N = 20)
Stepfather's DAS score	.15	.54*	.54**	.50*	.03	−.11	−.14	.25
Stepfather's positive behaviors to mother	.23	.15	.06	.20	.39	.02	−.34	.11
Mother's DAS score	.24	.02	.59**	.62**	.24	−.51*	−.14	.32
Mother's positive behaviors to stepfather	.50*	.54	.07	−.17	.38	.23	−.48*	−.08

*$p < .05$.
**$p < .01$.

312

TABLE 15.2

Pearson Correlations Between Measures of Marital Quality and Measures of Stepmother–Stepson and Stepmother–Stepdaughter Relationships

| Marital Quality Measures | Stepmother Behaviors and Love Ratings of Stepchildren | | | | Stepchild Behaviors and Love Ratings of Stepmothers | | | |
| | Positive Behaviors to Stepchildren | | Love Ratings of Stepchildren | | Positive Behaviors to Stepmothers | | Love Ratings of Stepmothers | |
	Boys (N = 11)	Girls (N = 11)	Boys (N = 11)	Girls (N = 11)	Boys (N = 11)	Girls (N = 11)	Boys (N = 11)	Girls (N = 11)
Stepmother's DAS score	.12	−.30	.02	−.58*	.24	−.35	.01	−.67*
Stepmother's positive behaviors to father	.17	−.76**	−.23	−.37	.13	−.50	.23	−.63*
Father's DAS score	.46	−.32	.58*	−.42	.12	−.21	.58*	−.29
Father's positive behaviors to stepmother	.73**	−.33	.45	−.07	.61*	.12	.22	−.25

*p < .05.
**p < .01.

313

ly associated with child love ratings and the proportion of positive behaviors stepmothers emitted toward stepdaughters (although this latter correlation was only marginally significant, $r = -.46$, $p = .09$).

Relations Between Marital Quality and Children's Psychological Adjustment. The measures of marital quality (husband and wife DAS scores and proportions of positive behaviors emitted toward spouses) were correlated with the three measures of children's psychological adjustment (biological parent ratings of aggression and inhibition, and children's self-concept scores) separately for each of the four sex of resident stepparent–sex of stepchild groups. For stepfather–stepson dyads, 3 of 12 correlations were significant. Mothers' DAS scores were negatively correlated with aggression ratings and positively correlated with boys' self-concept scores. The proportion of positive behaviors mothers emitted to stepfathers was also positively correlated with boys' self-concept scores. For stepfather–stepdaughter dyads, only 1 of 12 correlations was significant. Stepfathers' DAS scores correlated positively with girls' self-concept scores.

For stepmother–stepson dyads, 3 of 12 correlations were significant. Biological fathers' DAS scores were positively correlated with boys' self-concept scores. The proportion of positive behaviors biological fathers emitted to stepmothers was negatively correlated with both aggression ratings and inhibition ratings. Two additional correlations were marginally significant. Biological fathers' and stepmothers' DAS scores both correlated negatively with inhibition ratings.

For stepmother–stepdaughter dyads, one correlation was significant. Stepmothers' DAS scores correlated negatively with girls' self-concept scores. However, five additional correlations were marginally significant. Fathers' DAS scores were positively correlated with girls' inhibition ratings. Stepmothers' DAS scores also correlated positively with both inhibition ratings and aggression ratings. The proportion of positive behaviors stepmothers emitted to fathers and the proportion fathers emitted to stepmothers were both positively correlated with aggression ratings. Thus, in stepmother families, marital quality was differentially related to child outcomes for stepsons and stepdaughters. For boys, a more positive father–stepmother relationship was related to better psychological adjustment; whereas, for girls, a more positive marital relationship was associated with poorer psychological adjustment.

Relations Between the Quality of Stepparent–Stepchild Relationships and Children's Psychological Adjustment. The measures of the stepparent-stepchild relationship (stepchild's love ratings, stepchild's proportion of positive behaviors emitted toward stepparent, and stepparent's proportion of positive behaviors emitted toward stepchild) derived from data reduction procedures (see Clingempeel & Segal, 1986, for details) were correlated with the three measures of children's adjustment separately for each of the four stepfamily groups. For stepfather families with male and female stepchildren, no correlations were significant. The results for stepmother families are presented in Table 15.3.

TABLE 15.3

Pearson Correlations Between Measures of Stepparent–Stepchild Relationship and Children's Psychological Adjustment in Stepmother Families with Male and Female Stepchildren

Stepparent–Stepchild Relationship Measures	Male Stepchildren (n = 10)			Female Stepchildren (n = 10)		
	Inhibition Ratings	Aggression Ratings	Self-Concept Scores	Inhibition Ratings	Aggression Ratings	Self-Concept Scores
(1) Stepchild's love rating of stepmother	–.21	–.27	.27	–.68*	–.75**	.59*
(2) Stepchild's positive behaviors to stepmother	–.81**	–.61*	.18	–.32	.07	.61*
(3) Stepmother's positive behaviors to stepchild	–.63*	–.19	.25	–.10	–.18	.41 (p = .11)

*p < .05
**p < .01

For stepmother families with boys, the proportion of positive behaviors stepsons emitted toward stepmothers was negatively correlated with both Inhibition and Aggression ratings. The proportion of positive behaviors stepmothers emitted toward stepsons was also negatively correlated with Inhibition ratings. For stepmother families with girls, stepdaughter's love ratings of stepmothers were negatively correlated with Inhibition and Aggression ratings and positively correlated with self-concept scores. The proportion of positive behaviors girls emitted toward stepmothers was also positively correlated with their self-concept scores. The correlation between stepmothers' positive behaviors to stepdaughter and girls' self-concept scores was also positive (although only marginally significant, $p = .11$). Thus, in stepmother families, more positive stepmother–stepchild relationships were associated with better psychological adjustment of both stepsons and stepdaughters.

Relations Between Frequency of Visits from Nonresident Parents and Children's Psychological Adjustment.   Pearson correlations between the frequency of visits from nonresident parents and the measures of children's psychological adjustment revealed no significant correlations for any of the sex of resident stepparent – sex of stepchild groups. However, for girls in stepmother families, a trend was obtained ($p = .09$) with frequency of visits negatively associated with self-concept scores.

DISCUSSION

This research demonstrated that the interdependencies of family process dimensions and child outcomes vary as a function of type of family and sex of child. The greatest interdependencies among qualitative dimensions of dyadic relationships and children's psychological adjustment were obtained for stepmother families, and particularly for stepmother families with female "target" children.

Stepmother Families

Stepmother–stepdaughter relationships were found to be more problematic than stepmother–stepson relationships. For stepdaughters, more positive marital relationships were associated with less positive stepmother-stepdaughter relationships and poorer psychological adjustment (i.e., poorer self-concepts and higher inhibition and aggression ratings). More frequent visits by nonresidential biological mothers were associated with less positive relationships with stepmothers (as perceived by stepdaughters); and more positive stepmother–stepdaughter relationships were associated with better psychological adjustment of stepdaughters.

The greater interdependencies among family relationships and child outcomes in stepmother families (and especially for girls in stepmother families) may be due to unique characteristics of this group. Custody policy rarely awards children, and especially girls, to fathers after divorce (Sanders & Spanier, 1979). Father-custody awards may occur primarily in cases where the father–daughter relationship is very close and/or the mother–daughter relationship is distant. Consequently, the father–daughter relationship may be more likely to be enmeshed and the nonresidential mother–daughter relationship may be more problematic than other sex of child-sex of custodial parent groups due to group formation factors.

In addition, there is evidence that custodial fathers have different expectations for daughters than for sons (Gilbert, Hanson, & Davis, 1982; Greif, 1985b). Custodial fathers support and encourage independence in their sons (e.g., reinforce involvement in activities outside of the home) but not in their daughters (Gilbert et al., 1982). In fact, daughters may be reinforced for nonindependence or for maintaining an enmeshed relationship with their fathers (Greif, 1985b). Despite the fact that custodial fathers are themselves filling nontraditional roles (i.e., a single man rearing children), they appear to expect their daughters to conform to traditional roles (e.g., household manager). Greif (1985a) suggested that this traditional view of the sexes may result in fathers viewing daughters as parent substitutes (i.e., they should assume the roles previously performed by their ex-wives). Moreover, other family members and friends also may reinforce daughters for assuming maternal roles.

Custodial fathers also may be likely to rely on daughters for emotional support, given the absence of an intimate relationship in their lives (Weiss, 1979). The close father–daughter relationship is probably reciprocal. Fathers may rely a great deal on daughters who, in turn, may enjoy the special and privileged status concomitant with assuming adult–like roles.

A close father–stepmother conjugal union may be related to poorer stepmother–stepdaughter relationships and more problematic adjustment of stepdaughters to the extent stepdaughters perceive stepmothers as a threat to their relationship with biological parents. Daughters may view the stepmother as encroaching on their privileged role and special status within the household, and as competition for the biological father's time and affection. In fact, the high rate of positive exchanges between spouses may be the result of fathers' reallocating personal resources from daughters to new spouses.

Positive marital relationships also may constitute greater threats to girls' relationship with nonresidential parents than to children in other stepfamily groups. Because mother substitutes for girls are particularly alien to societal norms, girls in the custody of fathers may be more likely to harbor hopes for parental reconciliation and the re-establishment of close mother–daughter ties. The happier the remarried couple, the more these hopes may be threatened. In fact, the stepmother's very presence may serve as a painful reminder to stepdaughters of times when, the biological mother was present in the household and the mother–daughter relationship was closer.

Finally, due to differential socialization of females, stepmothers may try harder and earlier on, than stepfathers, to become parent figures to stepchildren. Stepmothers may try particularly hard with their same-sex stepchildren whom they perceive as having more difficult relationships with biological mothers. (Nonresidential mothers visited daughters less than half as often as they visited sons.) Premature parenting attempts may exacerbate loyalty conflicts for girls (who may fear that the stepmother is trying to supplant their biological mother and who may perceive responding positively to the stepmother as disloyal to their biological mother). Our data revealed (as did Furstenberg & Seltzer's, 1983, survey findings), that the more frequently the nonresidential biological mother visited, the less positive the stepmother–stepdaughter relationship. The two mother figures may vie for girls' affections; and the stepmother may be viewed less positively by girls to the extent such competition exists. Thus, the combination of stepmothers trying to assume a parental role (a role that daughters may have performed during the single-parent stage and may have enjoyed), and frequent visits from biological mothers (with whom they have problematic relationships) may maximize loyalty conflicts, and may lead to more problematic stepmother–stepdaughter relationships and adjustment problems for stepdaughters.

From a family systems perspective, patterns of interactions within families are circular rather than linear processes (e.g., Minuchin, 1985). Unrewarding stepmother–stepdaughter relationships and adjustment problems of stepdaughters may lead stepmothers to invest more energy in the marital relationship and less in the relationship with stepdaughters. The correlation between stepmothers' and stepdaughters' behavior to each other was virtually zero (and there were no mean differences across groups on proportions of stepparent behaviors to stepchildren). This suggests that, at least initially, positive overtures of stepmothers to stepdaughters may not be reciprocated. (We are referring to *reciprocity* in the rate matching—dyad members emit positive behaviors at similar or dissimilar rates— rather than in the probability change sense—positive behaviors of one person increase the probability of positive behaviors by the other). Stepmothers may compensate for this lack of reciprocity by behaving more positively toward spouses. Ironically, the stepmother's withdrawal from the stepdaughter and subsequent increased focus on the father probably causes stepdaughters to withdraw even further from their stepmothers.

For stepsons, more positive marital relationships were associated with more positive stepmother–stepson relationships and better psychological adjustment (i.e., better self-concepts and lower inhibition and aggression ratings). The frequency of visits from nonresidential mothers was largely unrelated to stepsons adjustment; and more positive stepmother–stepson relationships were associated with better psychological adjustment of stepsons.

Boys in stepmother families may perceive the stepmother as an additional support system rather than as a threat to their relationship with biological parents.

During the single-parent stage, boys may develop a male friend type of relationship with fathers centering on companionship and joint activities (Greif, 1985b). Consequently, when fathers remarry, the stepmother's relationship with the father may not encroach directly on these positive dimensions of father–son relationships (unlike the case with father–daughter relationships). In addition, sons seem to benefit from a good relationship with their stepmothers and the closeness does not appear to threaten their relationship with biological mothers. (Boys in this sample saw their nonresidential mothers more frequently than children in the other stepfamily groups saw their nonresidential parents.)

Although the entry of a stepmother into a father–daughter household may engender initial disruptions in the boundaries of father–child relationships and the roles of family members, over time a re-equilibrium with different boundaries and roles may be established. Correlations between the total length of time family members had lived in a stepfamily household (TTSH) and each of the measures of husband–wife and stepparent–stepchild relationships and children's psychological adjustment suggested some time-related changes in family dynamics (although longitudinal inferences from cross-sectional data should be viewed cautiously). The longer girls lived in a biological father–stepmother household, the fewer the visits from nonresidential biological mothers, the lower the proportion of positive behaviors fathers emitted toward stepmothers, the higher the proportion of positive behaviors stepdaughters emitted toward stepmothers, and the better the psychological adjustment of stepdaughters (the findings are similar for stepmother families with boys except the correlations between TTSH and the stepparent–stepchild relationship measures were not significant).

Competition between stepmother and biological mother may attenuate as child-rearing roles of the two mother figures are successfully negotiated. An optimal permeability of boundaries, including a balance between the daughters' needs to feel loyal to their biological mothers and the stepfamily's developmental need for cohesion, may be reached. Moreover, as the new conjugal union passes beyond the "honeymoon period," fathers may direct more energy outside the marital relationship (TTSH was negatively correlated with fathers' positive behavior toward stepmothers), and stepmothers may redirect some of their attention and affection from their spouse to their stepdaughters. Furthermore, as biological mothers visit less frequently, and initially intense loyalty conflicts (experienced by stepdaughters) dissipate, stepdaughters may begin to reciprocate their stepmother's friendly overtures (TTSH was positively correlated with stepdaughter's positive behavior toward stepmothers), and a legitimate relationship between stepmother and stepdaughter may develop. Thus, stepdaughters may come to perceive their stepmothers as additional support systems rather than as threats to their relationship with biological parents. Given the limitations of longitudinal inferences from cross-sectional data (cf. Achenbach, 1978), these interpretations should be viewed cautiously.

Stepfather Families

The finding that stepfather–stepdaughter relationships are more problematic than stepfather–stepson relationships is consistent with the results of other studies of stepfamilies (e.g., Hetherington et al., 1986; Santrock et al., 1982). Because the mother–son relationship after divorce is often more problematic than the mother–daughter (Hetherington et al., 1982, 1986), boys may welcome the same-sex parent figure, whereas girls who usually become closer to their mothers after divorce may fear a stepfather will disrupt the mother–daughter bond.

Very few additional findings were obtained with this sample of stepfather families. The only consistent pattern of significant correlations involved relations between marital quality and stepparenting behaviors. Stepfathers both perceived and behaved toward stepchildren of both sexes more positively to the extent they were involved in more positive marital relationships. Moreover, 3 of 12 correlations revealed that higher marital quality of stepparent couples was associated with better psychological adjustment of stepsons (only 1 of 12 correlations was significant for stepdaughters). As newcomers to a parent–child subsystem, stepfathers may recognize the importance to their marriage of a positive relationship with stepchildren. Consequently, as supported by these data, stepfathers who are more positive toward stepchildren may be treated more positively by their wives; and bidirectionally, more positiveness in the marital relationship may increase the proclivity of stepfathers to be more positive toward stepchildren.

Positiveness in the marital relationship was ostensibly less salient for stepchildren's positive behaviors toward and perceptions of stepfathers. Only 2 of 16 correlations were significant and both were negative. Stepchildren may have less invested than stepfathers in marital positiveness during the early years of the remarriage. Greater allocations of the custodial parents' time and affection from child to new spouse may be perceived as concomitants of greater marital felicitude. In addition, higher levels of marital positiveness may signal greater disloyalty to the noncustodial father, may further dash hopes for reconciliation of biological parents, and may thus engender resentment of the stepfather.

The paucity of significant correlations between measures of the stepparent–stepchild relationship, husband–wife relationship, and children's adjustment is not consistent with some of the more recent studies of stepfather families (e.g., Hetherington et al., 1986). There are at least three explanations for the lack of findings in this research. First, it is possible that our sample sizes were too small to detect "interdependencies" that would have emerged with larger samples. Second, we may have focused on dimensions of relationships (e.g., love and detachment dimensions of stepparenting) that have less of an impact on family dynamics and children's adjustment. For example, measures of stepparenting on autonomy (permissiveness) – control (restrictiveness) dimensions may have been more strongly related to children's adjustment than measures of warmth and affection. Third, stepfather families may exhibit a high degree of variability in coping strategies and family dynamics, and thus inconsistencies in results across studies may reflect the great heterogeneity of those reconstituted families.

CONCLUSIONS

This research has underscored the importance of examining structural variables including sex of stepchild and type of stepfamily as potential mediators of both the relations between family subsystems (e.g., husband–wife and stepparent–stepchild) and of the "effects" of marital quality, nonresidential parent–child and stepparent–stepchild relationships on child outcomes. The results of this study should be viewed cautiously given the following limitations: (a) the design was cross-sectional and correlational (and thus has third variable and directionality problems in interpreting results); (b) the sample sizes were small thus limiting generalizability of findings; (c) no data was obtained on the custodial parent–child relationship and how it changed from pre- to postremarriage.

Family researchers should attempt to replicate these findings using longitudinal designs and larger samples. Ideally, future studies should follow single parents from pre- to postcohabiting relationships and should include measures of the child's relationship with both biological parents as well as measures of marital and stepparent–stepchild dyads.

REFERENCES

Achenbach, T. M. (1978). Psychopathology of childhood: Research problems and issues. *Journal of Consulting and Clinical Psychology, 46,* 759-776.

Baumrind, D. (1971). Current patterns of paternal authority. *Developmental Psychology Monographs, 41,* (Pt. 2).

Baumrind, D. (1982). *To textbook writers seeking information about time 2 data from the Family Socialization Project.* Unpublished manuscript, University of California, Berkeley, Institute of California, Berkeley, Institute of Human Development, Berkeley, CA.

Belsky, J. (1979). The interrelation of parental and spousal behavior during infancy in traditional nuclear families: An exploratory analysis. *Journal of Marriage and the Family, 41,* 62-68.

Belsky, J. (1984). The determinants of parenting: A process model. *Child Development, 55,* 83-96.

Belsky, J., Spanier, G. B., & Rovine, M. (1983). Stability and change in marriage across the transition to parenthood. *Journal of Marriage and the Family, 45,* 567-577.

Birchler, G. R., Weiss, R. L., & Vincent, J. P. (1975). A multimethod analysis of social reinforcement exchange between martially distressed and non-distressed spouse and stranger dyads. *Journal of Personality and Social Psychology, 31,* 349-360.

Brand, E., & Clingempeel, W. G. (1987). Interdependencies of marital and stepparent–stepchild relationships and children's psychological adjustment: Research findings and clinical implications. *Family Relations, 36,* 140-145.

Cherlin, A. J. (1978). Remarriage as an incomplete institution. *American Journal of Sociology, 84,* 634-650.

Clingempeel, W. G. (1981). Quasi-kin relationships and marital quality in stepfather families. *Journal of Personality and Social Psychology, 41,* 890-901.

Clingempeel, W. G., & Brand, E. (1985). Structural complexity, quasi-kin relationships, and marital quality in stepfamilies: A replication, extension, and clinical implications. *Family Relations, 34*, 401–409.

Clingempeel, W. G., Brand, E., & Ievoli, R. (1984). Stepparent-Stepchild relationships in stepmother and stepfather families: A multimethod study. *Family Relations, 33*, 465-474.

Clingempeel, W. G., Ievoli, R., & Brand, E. (1984). Structural complexity and the quality of stepfather-stepchild relationships. *Family Process, 23*, 547-560.

Clingempeel, W. G., & Segal, S. (1986). Psychological adjustment of children in stepfamilies: Family structure and process influences. *Child Development, 57*, 474-484.

Crosbie–Burnett, M. (1984). The centrality of the step relationship: A challenge to family theory and practice. *Family Relations, 33*(3), 459-463.

Dielman, J., Barton, K., & Cattell, R. (1977). Relationships among family attitudes and childrearing practices. *Journal of Genetic Psychology, 130*, 105-112.

Emery, R. E., & O'Leary, K. D. (1979). Children's perceptions of marital discord and behavior problems of boys and girls. *Journal of Abnormal Child Psychology, 86*, 574-596.

Fast, I., & Cain, A. C. (1966). The stepparent role: Potential for disturbances in family functioning. *American Journal of Orthopsychiatry, 36*(3), 485-491.

Forgatch, M. S., & Wieder, G. (1981). *Family problem solving system.* Unpublished manuscript, University of Oregon, Social Learning Program, Eugene, OR.

Furstenberg, F. F., Jr., Nord, C. W., Peterson, J. J., & Zill, N. (1983). The life course of children of divorce: Marital disruption and parental contact. *American Sociological Review, 48*, 5.

Furstenberg, F. F., & Seltzer, J. A. (1983, April). *Divorce and child development.* Paper presented at a meeting of the Orthopsychiatric Association, Boston, MA.

Furstenberg, F. F., & Spanier, G. B. (1984). Remarriage and reconstituted families. In M. B. Sussman & S. K. Steinmetz (Eds.), *Handbook of marriage and the family* (pp. 249-276). New York: Plenum.

Gilbert, L. A., Hanson, G. R., & Davis, B. (1982). Perceptions of parental role responsibilities: Differences between mothers and fathers. *Family Relations, 31*, 261-269.

Glick, P. C. (1984). Marriage, divorce, and living arrangements: Prospective changes. *Journal of Family Issues, 5*, 7-26.

Greif, G. L. (1985a). Children and housework in the single-parent family. *Family Relations, 34*, 353-357.

Greif, G. L. (1985b). Single fathers rearing children. *Journal of Marriage and the Family, 46*, 185-191.

Hadley, T., & Jacob, T. (1973). Relationship among measures of family power. *Journal of Personality and Social Psychology, 27*, 6-12.

Hess, R. D., & Camara, K. A. (1979). Post-divorce relationships as mediating factors in the consequences of divorce for children. *Journal of Social Issues, 35*, 79-96.

Hetherington, E. M., Cox, M., & Cox, R. (1978). The aftermath of divorce. In J. H. Stevens, Jr. & M. Matthews (Eds.), *Mother-child, father-child relations* (pp. 149-176). Washington, DC: National Association for the Education of Young Children.

Hetherington, E. M., Cox, M., & Cox, R. (1982). Effects of divorce on parents and children. In M. Lamb (Ed.), *Non-traditional families: Parenting and child development* (pp. 233-288). Hillsdale, NJ: Lawrence Erlbaum Associates.

Hetherington, E. M., Cox, M., & Cox, R. (1986). Family relations: Six years after divorce. In K. Pasley & M. Ihinger–Tallman (Eds.), *Remarriage and stepparenting today: Research and theory* (pp. 27-87). New York: Guilford.

Hops, H., Wills, T. A., Patterson, G. R., & Weiss, R. L. (1972). *Marital interaction coding system.* Unpublished manuscript, University of Oregon and Oregon Research Institute, Eugene, OR.

Jacob, T. (1974). Patterns of family conflict and dominance as a function of child age and social class. *Developmental Psychology, 10*, 1-12.

Jacobson, N. S. (1977). Problem-solving and contingency contracting in the treatment of marital discord. *Journal of Consulting and Clinical Psychology, 45*, 92-100.

Jacobson, N. S. (1978). Specific and nonspecific factors in a behavioral approach to marital discord. *Journal of Consulting and Clinical Psychology*, *46*, 442–452.

Johnson, S. & Lobitz, G. (1974). The personal and marital adjustment of parents as related to observed child deviance and parenting behaviors. *Journal of Abnormal Child Psychology*, *2*, 193–207.

Jones, R. R., Reid, J. B., & Patterson, G. R. (1975). Naturalistic observation in clinical assessment. In P. McReynolds (Ed.), *Advances in psychological assessment* (Vol. 3, pp. 149–176). San Francisco: Jossey–Bass.

Kempler, J. & Reichler, M. (1976). Marital satisfaction and conjugal power as determinants of intensity and frequency of rewards and punishments administered by parents. *Journal of Genetic Psychology*, *129*, 221–234.

Lerner, R. M., & Spanier, G. B. (1978). *Child influences on marital and family interaction: A life-span perspective.* New York: Academic Press.

Lewis, J., Beavers, W., Gossett, J., & Phillips, V. (1976). *No single thread: psychological health in family systems.* New York: Brunner/Mazel.

Margolin, G., & Patterson, G. R. (1975). Differential consequences provided by mothers and fathers for their sons and daughters. *Developmental Psychology*, *11*, 537–538.

Margolin, G., & Weiss, R. L. (1978a). A comparative evaluation of therapeutic components associated with behavioral marital treatments. *Journal of Consulting and Clinical Psychology*, *46*, 1476–1486.

Margolin, G., & Weiss, R. L. (1978b). Communication training and assessment: A Case of behavioral marital enrichment. *Behavior Therapy*, *9*, 508–200.

Messinger, L. (1976). Remarriage between divorced people with children from previous marriages: A proposal for preparation of remarriage. *Journal of Marriage and Family Counseling*, *2*, 193–200.

Miller, L. C. (1967). Louisville behavior checklist for males, 6–12 years of age. *Psychological Reports*, *21*, 885–896.

Miller, L. C. (1977). *Louisville Behavior Checklist Manual.* Los Angeles, CA: Western Psychological Services.

Mills, D. M. (1984). A model for stepfamily development. *Family Relations*, *33*, 365–372.

Minuchin, P. (1985). Families and individual development: Provocations from the field of family therapy. *Child Development*, *56*, 289–302.

Minuchin, S. (1974). *Families and family therapy.* Cambridge, MA: Harvard University Press.

Oltmanns, T. F., Broderick, J. E., & O'Leary, K. D. (1977). Marital adjustment and the efficacy of behavior therapy with children. *Journal of Consulting and Clinical Psychology*, *45*, 724–729.

Olweus, D. (1980). Familial and temperamental determinants of aggressive behavior in adolescent boys: A casual analysis. *Developmental Psychology*, *16*, 644–660.

Papernow, P. L. (1984). The stepfamily cycle: An experiential model of stepfamily development. *Family Relations*, *33*, 355–363.

Pasley, K., & Ihinger-Tallman, M. (1986). Stepfamilies: New challenges for the schools. In T. Fairchild (Ed.), *Crisis intervention strategies for school-based helpers* (pp. 70–11). Springfield, IL: Charles Scribner.

Piers, E. V. (1977). *The Piers-Harris Children's Self-Concept Scale. Research Monograph No. 1*, Nashville, TN: Counselor Recordings and Tests.

Piers, E. V., & Harris, D. B. (1969). *The Piers-Harris Children's Self-Concept Scale.* Nashville, TN: Counselor Recordings and Tests.

Sanders, R., & Spanier, G. B. (1979). Divorce, child custody and child support. *Current Population Reports*, U.S. Bureau of the Census, Series P-23, No. 84.

Santrock, J. W., & Warshak, R. A. (1979). Father custody and social development in boys and girls. *Journal of Social Issues*, *35*, 112–125.

Santrock, J. W., Warshak, R. A., Lindberg, C., & Meadows, L. (1982). Children's and parents' observed social behavior in stepfather families. *Child Development*, *53*, 472–480.

Schaefer, E. (1965). *Child Report of Parent Behavior Inventory.* Washington, DC: National Institute of Health.

Schaefer, E., Edgarton, M., & Finkelstein, N. (1979). *Relationship inventory for families: Parent-child form*. Chapel Hill, NC: Carolina Institute for Research on Early Education of the Handicapped, University of North Carolina.

Schauer, G. H. (1965). *An analysis of the self-report of fifth and sixth grade regular class children and gifted class children*. Unpublished doctoral dissertation, Kent State University.

Sharpley, C. F., & Cross, D. G. (1982). A psychometric evaluation of the Spanier Dyadic Adjustment Scale. *Journal of Marriage and the Family, 44,* 739-743.

Spanier, G. B. (1976). Measuring dyadic adjustment: New scales for assessing the quality of marriage and similar dyads. *Journal of Marriage and the Family, 38,* 15-28.

Spanier, G. B., & Thompson, L. (1982). A confirmatory analysis of the Dyadic Adjustment Scale. *Journal of Marriage and the Family, 44,* 731-738.

Vincent, J. P., Friedman, L. C., Nugent, J., & Messerly, L. (1979). Demand characteristics in observations of marital interaction. *Journal of Consulting and Clinical Psychology, 47,* 557-566.

Vincent, J. P., Weiss, R. L., & Birchler, G. R. (1975). A behavioral analysis of problem solving in distressed and nondistressed stranger dyads. *Behavior Therapy, 6,* 475-487.

Visher, E. B., & Visher, J. S. (1978). Major areas of difficulty for stepparent couples. *International Journal of Family Counseling, 6,* 70-80.

Visher, E. B., & Visher, J. S. (1979). *Stepfamilies: A guide to working with stepparents and stepchildren*. New York: Bruner/Mazel.

Wallerstein, J. S., & Kelly, J. B. (1980). *Surviving the breakup: How children actually cope with divorce*. New York: Basic Books.

Watzlawick, P., Beavin, J., Jackson, D. D. (1967). *Pragmatics of human communications: A study of interactional patterns, pathologies, and paradoxes*. New York: Norton.

Weiss, R. (1979). Growing up a little faster: The experience of growing up in a single-parent household. *Journal of Social Issues, 35,* 97-111.

Winer, B. J. (1971). *Statistical principles in experimental design* (2nd ed.). New York: McGraw-Hill.

Yonker, R. J., Blixt, S., & Dinero, T. (1974, November). *A methodological investigation of the development of a semantic differential to assess self-concept*. Paper presented at the National Council on Measurement in Education, Chicago, IL.

16

Behavior, Achievement, and Health Problems Among Children in Stepfamilies:
Findings From a National Survey of Child Health

Nicholas Zill
Child Trends, Inc., Washington, DC

INTRODUCTION

What happens to a child in a single-parent family when the mother (or father) who lives with the child remarries? Is it beneficial to the child's development and well-being to have a second, substitute parent in the household to provide companionship, guidance, emotional support, additional income, and help with the host of day-to-day problems that beset families with children? Does the addition of a new, and possibly unsympathetic adult to the household create further adjustment problems for a child who has already been through parental conflict and divorce, or the death of a parent? Or is it unwise to try to make generalizations about the "usual" effects of remarriage? Do the effects of remarriage on a child largely depend on the specific circumstances and characteristics of the child and parents involved?

The answers to these questions are of interest for both practical and scientific reasons. The practical concerns stem from the large numbers of young people who will experience family disruption and/or reconstitution at some point during their childhoods, given the current high rates of divorce and out-of-wedlock childbearing. Estimates are that one third of today's children will experience their parents' divorce; close to half will spend some time in a single-parent family because of divorce or birth outside of marriage or the death of a parent; and about one quarter will live with a stepparent by the time they are 16 years of age (Bumpass, 1984; Furstenberg, Nord, Peterson, & Zill, 1983; Hofferth, 1985; Nord, 1987). Although the probability of remarriage following divorce has declined in the last decade, it is still the case that close to 60% of divorced women, and a larger majority of divorced men, will remarry within 5 years after a divorce (Cherlin, 1981, pp. 29–31; personal communication, 1987).

Thus, many single parents are faced with questions of whether and when to remarry and, having made the decision to do so, how to facilitate their children's adjustment to the new family situation. Many adults who enter into the stepparent role for the first time also have questions about what to expect from and how to behave toward their stepchildren. Reliable information about the relative risks for boys and girls of various ages and of the single-parent family situation versus the stepfamily situation could also have a bearing on custody decisions.

On the scientific side, data on the development and well-being of stepchildren are relevant to theoretical issues concerning the nature of the parent–child relationship and the extent to which biological parents can be replaced (or supplemented) by step- or adoptive parents. Comparisons between children living with their mothers and stepfathers and those living with their fathers and stepmothers may illuminate the respective roles that mothers and fathers play in children's development. Data on stepchildren can also help to clarify whether remarriage should really be considered a stressful event for children; how the stress varies by sex and across developmental stages; and which aspects of the stepfamily situation serve to exacerbate or ameliorate the stress.

Previous Studies of Children in Stepfamilies

The scientific literature on child development and well-being in stepfamilies has grown substantially in recent years, but much remains to be learned. (See literature review by Ganong & Coleman, 1984; and overviews by Macklin, 1980, pp. 909–910; Emery, Hetherington, & DiLalla, 1985, pp. 215–216; Furstenberg, 1987; and Hetherington, 1987.) A number of studies have found that although the health, learning, and behavior of most children in stepfamilies appear to be normal, there is a significant minority of stepchildren who exhibit serious and persistent emotional disturbances, academic difficulties, and/or conduct problems at home or in school. This finding has emerged from several large-scale, school-based studies (Perry & Pfuhl, 1963; Rosenberg, 1965; Touliatos & Lindholm, 1980); from a longitudinal study of Black children in an inner-city community (Kellam, Ensminger, & Turner, 1977); from a 5-year follow-up study to a national household survey of school-aged children (Furstenberg & Allison, 1985; Peterson & Zill, 1986; Zill, 1978); and from smaller scale observational studies (Brand, Clingempeel, & Woodward, this volume; Bray, this volume; Hetherington, Cox, & Cox, 1985).

The finding of increased developmental problems among stepchildren is not universal, however. Other studies report no significant differences between children in stepfamilies and those in intact biological families (Bohannon, 1975; Burchinal, 1964; Santrock, Warshak, Lindberg, & Meadows, 1982; Wilson, Zurcher, McAdams, & Curtis, 1975). Additional evidence is needed to help resolve the discrepancy.

Where group differences have been observed, children in stepfamilies and those in single-parent families have usually been found to have about the same frequency of developmental problems, with both groups having more problems than children in families where both biological parents are present. Thus, the problems of the stepchildren have sometimes been attributed to the parental conflict, marital disruption, or other stress or deprivation that preceded the remarriage, rather than to the stepfamily situation per se. For example, Furstenberg (1987) has written: "marital disruption . . . impose(s) some kind of developmental risk that is neither erased . . . nor aggravated by remarriage" (p. 56). If this is the case, then information about the stepchild's family history prior to the remarriage of the custodial parent (e.g., the nature and timing of the original family disruption) may help to explain why some stepchildren exhibit developmental problems, whereas most do not (Furstenberg & Allison, 1985; Zill, 1978; Zill & Peterson, 1983). This notion is tested in the present study.

Why is it that, on the average, stepparents do not seem to have much of an effect, either beneficial or harmful, on their stepchildren's development? Data from previous studies indicate that many stepparents try not to get involved in the rearing of their stepchildren, or, when they do try to play a more active role, have difficulty establishing intimacy and exercising control over the stepchildren (Bohannon, 1975; Furstenberg, 1987, pp. 52–55; Perkins & Kahan, 1979; Stern, 1978; Walker & Messinger, 1979). One would expect, however, that some groups of stepparents would be more efficacious than others. For example, parents with more education probably approach the stepfamily situation in a more "activist" manner, yet may also show greater sensitivity to the emotional complexities inherent in the situation, than parents with relatively little education. Better educated parents also have greater resources for coping with problems that arise. Hence, higher educational attainment for the parents in a stepfamily should be associated with fewer developmental problems in the stepchildren. Some data that suggest better family functioning in stepfamilies with higher education levels have been reported (Furstenberg & Seltzer, 1986), but further evidence on the relationship between parent education and child development in stepfamilies is needed. This chapter provides such evidence.

There is one area of family functioning in which the presence of a stepparent often makes a clear and striking difference. That is the area of financial well-being. Using data from the 1976 National Survey of Family Growth, Bachrach (1983, Table 2, p. 175) found that 8% of children living in mother–stepfather families were below the poverty line, compared to 49% of children living with their mothers only. Yet the better financial situation of stepfamilies does not seem to translate into better functioning on the part of children in these families. Here, too, additional evidence is needed.

One would also expect that the specifics of the current family situation would make some difference as far as stepchild development and well-being are concerned. It is generally held to be a good thing, for example, for the child in a single-parent or stepparent family to maintain contact with the outside biological parent. However, very frequent contact may lead to continued conflict between the divorced parents and, hence, a greater risk of developmental problems for the child. Previous studies (e.g., Furstenberg & Nord, 1985) have not found evidence of a negative effect on stepfamily functioning of frequent contact with the outside parent, at least not in mother–stepfather families. On the other hand, neither has contact with the outside father been found to have a notably beneficial effect for the child. Little information is available on the effects of contact when the outside parent is the biological mother.

Another aspect of the stepfamily situation that should have a bearing on the child's adjustment is the number and type of brothers and sisters with whom the child resides. Stepchildren living in family configurations that tend to place the child of a former marriage in an "outsider" role would be expected to be at greater developmental risk than those in other situations. In particular, the child who lives with a stepparent and a biological parent and has one or more half siblings (who are the biological issue of the new marriage) should tend to show more emotional and behavior problems than the stepchild with no siblings, or biological siblings only, or stepsiblings who are also the products of earlier unions. There is, however, little or no information available in the stepfamily literature on the effects of different sibling situations on stepchild development.

The adjustment of children to stepfamily living can also be expected to vary according to developmental and personality characteristics of the child him- or herself. A good deal of attention has been paid in the literature on the effects of divorce and remarriage on children to possible age and sex differences in children's vulnerability to family change. It has been suggested (Hetherington, 1987), for example, that younger children or older adolescents more readily accept and benefit from a stepparent than do early adolescents. The age period from 9 to 15 has been identified as a difficult one for the acceptance of a stepparent (Hetherington, Arnett, & Hollier, in press). Hetherington has also proposed that boys often benefit from the presence of a stepfather, whereas girls appear to have more long-term difficulty adjusting to either a stepmother or stepfather. On the other hand, Furstenberg and Allison (1985) failed to find major sex differences in boys' and girls' responses to divorce or remarriage, although they did find that younger children were more susceptible to long-term effects of family disruption, and boys in both intact and disrupted families showed more behavior and learning problems than girls.

Study Overview and List of Hypotheses

This report examines the life circumstances, development, and well-being of a national sample of 1,300 children, each living with one biological parent and one stepparent, and compares these children with those in single-parent families and those in two-parent families where both biological parents are present. The study also contrasts children who live with a mother and stepfather with those who live with a father and stepmother. In addition, the report examines variations in the frequency of child behavior problems *within* stepfamilies, as these variations relate to factors such as the education and income levels of the parents, the parents' marital history, the amount of contact that the child has with the outside biological parent, the type of siblings (full, half, step) with whom the child resides, and the age and sex of the child.

The following hypotheses were tested in the study. The hypotheses were derived from results of earlier research (summarized previously) and/or from theories about developmental vulnerabilities and the disruptive effects of conflict between parents on a child's socialization and emotional well-being (Gassner & Murray, 1969; Hirschi, 1969; Peterson & Zill, 1986; Schwarz, 1979).

Hypothesized Differences Across Family Types

1. Children living with a stepparent and a biological parent will show more developmental problems than those living with both biological parents.
2. Children living with a stepparent and a biological parent will show about the same level of developmental problems as those living with one biological parent only.
3. Children in father–stepmother families will show more developmental problems than those in mother–stepfather families.

Hypothesized Differences Within Stepfamily Groups

Parent Education and Income

4. Stepchildren in families with high parent education levels will show fewer developmental problems than those in families where parents education levels are moderate or low.
5. Stepchildren in families with low incomes will show more developmental problems than those in families with moderate or high incomes.

Parents' Marital History

The level of developmental problems shown by stepchildren will vary according to the nature and timing of the original family disruption experienced by the child. Specifically:

6. Stepchildren who experienced the disruption of their biological parents' marriage by divorce will show more developmental problems than those whose families were disrupted by the death of a parent. And;

7. Stepchildren who experienced family disruption during the preschool years (ages 1–5) will show more developmental problems than those who experienced disruption later in their childhoods.

Current Family Situation

8. Stepchildren who have regular contact with their outside biological parents will show fewer developmental problems than those who have little or no contact with those parents.
9. Stepchildren living with one or more half siblings (who are the biological issue of the new marriage) will show more developmental problems than stepchildren living with no siblings, or full siblings only, or stepsiblings (who, like themselves, are the products of an earlier union).

Age and Sex Differences

Because of contradictory findings in the literature, no specific hypotheses were put forth regarding age trends and sex differences among stepchildren.

METHOD

Source of the Data

The source of the data reported here is the Child Health Supplement to the National Health Interview Survey. This was a survey of 15,416 children aged 0–17 that was conducted by the National Center for Health Statistics (NCHS) in 1981 (NCHS, 1982; Poe, 1986; Zill, Peterson, Moore, & Hernandez, 1984, pp. 86–88). The National Health Interview Survey is an ongoing data collection program on the health status and medical care use of the U.S. population, based on probability samples drawn by the Bureau of the Census of persons living in households in the United States (NCHS, 1975; NCHS, Kovar & Poe, 1985). For the Child Health Supplement, there was a further random selection of one child per family in any household that contained children in the 0–17 age range at the time of the survey.

The data collection method consisted of in-person interviews by trained Census interviewers with an informed parent or guardian of the child, usually the mother. The overall completion rate of the child portion of the survey was 93%. Unlike most federal surveys, the Child Health Supplement obtained a detailed specification of the child's familial relationships to all adults and children in the household, including step-, foster, and adoptive relationships. The survey also obtained a broad range of measures of physical health, behavior and emotional adjustment, school performance, and receipt of medical and psychological care.

The measures were all based on reports by the parent respondent. The survey questionnaire has been published (NCHS, 1982, pp. 74–106) and a public use data tape is available through the Division of Health Interview Statistics of the National Center for Health Statistics.

Definition of Stepparent Groups

The children who were the focus of the present study were those living with one biological parent (i.e., "natural" parent) and one parent who was biologically unrelated to the child but legally married to the biological parent. There were 1,300 such children in the sample, 1,084 living with their mother and a stepfather, and 216 living with their father and a stepmother (unweighted *n*s). Both those who had been legally adopted by the stepparent and those not adopted were included. Children who lived with a single parent and had another biological parent and stepparent living elsewhere were not included in the stepparent groups. Children who lived with single parents who had live-in partners to whom they were not legally married were also excluded from the stepparent groups.

Marital History Information

Information about the marital history of the child's biological mother was obtained in the survey questionnaire, so that, at least for the mother–stepfather families, it was usually possible to ascertain the nature and timing of events (i.e., divorce, death of a parent, birth outside of marriage, etc.) that led to the child living apart from one biological parent and with a stepparent. However, for nearly 6% of the children in mother–stepfather families, and 16% of those in father–stepmother families, it was either not possible to determine the nature of the original marital disruption (if any) or the available marital history information seemed implausible or contradictory. Moreover, because separate questions on the biological father's marital history were not included in the questionnaire, information about the timing of the father's remarriage was not available for most of the father–stepmother families.

Child Development Indicators

Parent respondents to the Child Health Supplement were asked an extensive series of structured questions concerning the child's habits, problem behaviors, and use of mental health services; academic achievement; and physical health and use of medical services. The specific questions asked varied somewhat depending on the age of the child. The measures described here, all based on parent responses, were used to make comparisons between the children in the stepparent groups and those in other family arrangements, as well as comparisons among various subgroups within each of the stepparent groups.

Behavior and Mental Health Indicators

Behavior Problems Index (Ages 4–17). This was a summary score based on responses to a series of 28 questions (27 questions for 12- to 17-year-olds) dealing with specific problem behaviors that the child may or may not have exhibited in the previous three months. The items were derived from the Achenbach Behavior scales (Kellam, Branch, Agrawal, & Ensminger, 1975; Peterson & Zill, 1986; Rutter, Tizard, & Whitmore, 1970). The selection criteria were that the items discriminated well between chidlren whose behaivor problems did or did not require professional attention, and represented several of the most common behavior syndromes of childhood (i.e., antisocial "acting out;" anxious-distractible behavior; and depression-withdrawal).

Three response categories were used in the questionnaire, but in the present study responses to individual items were dichotomized and summed to produce an index score for each child. The specific behaviors covered differed somewhat for children aged 4–11 and adolescents aged 12–17 (see NCHS, 1982, pp. 101–102). The resulting index had an overall mean of 6.6 and a standard deviation of 5.4 for the children; and an overall mean of 6.0 and a standard deviation of 5.8 for the adolescents. The internal consistency reliability of the index scores was alpha = .89 for the children and alpha = .91 for the adolescents. Further information about the construction and psychometric properties of the scale are available elsewhere (Zill, 1985).

Proportion Who Needed or Got Psychological Help (Ages 3–17). A dichotomous indicator was developed from a series of questions about whether and when the child had ever seen "a psychiatrist, psychologist, or psychoanalyst about any emotional, mental, or behavior problem" and, if not, whether the parent felt or had been told that the child needed psychological help. Children who had either received psychological help in the last 12 months or were perceived as needing help during that period were given a score of "1," whereas others were scored "0." Six percent of all children aged 3–17 received or needed psychological help in the previous year.

Proportion with Indulgent Sleeping Arrangements (Ages 3–17). A dichotomous indicator of family disorganization and/or emotional neediness on the part of the child was developed from a series of questions concerning the child's bedtime and sleeping arrangements. Children who had no regular bedtime, or whose regular bedtime was after 11 p.m., or who slept in the same room as the parent(s) were given a score on "1," whereas others were scored "0." Seventeen percent of all children aged 3–17 had such indulgent sleeping arrangements.

Academic Performance Indicators

Standing in Class Rating (Ages 6–17).   Parents of school-aged children were asked to rate the child's academic standing on a 5-point scale that ranged from "one of the best students in the class" (scored "1") to "near the bottom of the class" (scored "5"). The question produced a skewed response distribution, inasmuch as few parents were willing to acknowledge that their child was "below the middle" or "near the bottom" of the class. Nevertheless, in the 1976 National Survey of Children it was found that parent responses to this question correlated moderately well ($r = .55$) with teacher responses to the same question. The mean rating in the 1981 Child Health Supplement for all children aged 6–17 was 2.3, with a standard deviation of 1.0.

Grade Repetition (Ages 6–17).   A dichotomous indicator of academic difficulties was developed from a question as to whether the child had ever had to repeat a grade in school for any reason. In the National Survey of Children, parent and teacher responses to this question correlated reasonably well and showed about the same overall frequency of grade repetition. Fourteen percent of all children aged 6-17 in the 1981 Child Health Supplement had repeated a grade at some point in their academic careers.

Physical Health Indicators

School Absences (Ages 6–17).   A numerical measure of illness-related disability was obtained from parent estimates of the number of days in the previous year on which the child had missed school for health reasons. The mean number of days reported on the Child Health Supplement for children aged 6–17 was 4.5, with a standard deviation of 7.0. The question produced a skewed distribution because most children missed only a few days of school each year, whereas some missed a great deal.

Proportion in Excellent Health with No Activity Limitation (Ages 3–17).   A dichotomous health indicator was constructed by combining two different health items that appear regularly on the core questionnaire for the National Health Interview Survey. One was a question asking the parent to rate the overall health of the child on a scale of "excellent, good, fair, or poor." The other was a series of questions that ascertain whether the child is chronically limited in school or play activities because of a health condition. Responses to these questions were combined such that the child received a "1" if he or she was rated in "excellent" health *and* had no limitation of activity. Otherwise, the child received a

"0". Sixty percent of children aged 3–17 were reported to be in excellent health with no activity limitation.

Analysis Methods

Mean scores on each of the developmental indicators were computed for children in mother–stepfather and father–stepmother families, as well as for children in three comparison groups: mother–father families, mother-only families, and father-only families. Multiple classification analysis, a form of multiple regression that uses dummy coding to represent categorical variables, was used to adjust the means of the family structure groups for the main effects of demographic control variables (see below). Both observed and adjusted differences between groups were tested for statistical significance. Prior to making mean contrasts on a given developmental indicator, it was ascertained that the family structure variable had a significant relationship to the developmental indicator and that it contributed a significant increment of explained variance to the overall regression (i.e., two separate regressions were run, one with the control variables only and one with the controls plus family structure).

Multiple classification analysis was also used to study variations in behavior problem scores within each of the two stepfamily groups. The procedure allowed for ascertainment of the effect of a predictor variable such as income both by itself, and after controlling for the main effects of other, related predictor variables, such as parent education and ethnic group.

The sample of children and families obtained in the National Health Interview Survey was a far superior sample from the point of view of random selection and representativeness than those used in the vast bulk of child and family research. Nonetheless, because the sample was a multistage stratified probability sample, rather than a simple random sample of the population, mathematical statisticians note that the standard statistical formulas tend to underestimate the sampling fluctuations actually obtained with such a sample. Standard random-sample formulas for variance and F-tests were used in this study, but criteria for significance were made more stringent in order to compensate for possible underestimation of sampling variability. Specifically, probability levels of $p = .025$ and $.005$ were used as cutoffs, rather than the customary criteria of $p = .05$ and $.01$.

RESULTS

Size and Demographic Characteristics of the Stepchild Population

The survey sample contained 1,084 young persons living in mother–stepfather families, and 216 living in father–stepmother families. The weighted population estimates for the two groups were 4.5 million, or 7.1% of all children under 18, in mother–stepfather families; and 979,000, or 1.6% of all children, in father–stepmother families. The mother–stepfather family was the third most common living arrangement for children, exceeded only by mother–father families (67.5% of all children) and mother-only families (18.3% of all children). The demographic characteristics of stepchildren in the 1981 Child Health Supplement (see Table 16.1) were generally consistent with those reported by Bachrach (1983) based on the 1976 National Survey of Family Growth, with some differences attributable either to differences in the sampling frames of the two surveys, or to secular trends such as the increase in parent education levels or the decrease in average family size.

Age Distribution. Stepchildren in the survey tended to be older than children in general, with nearly half of those in mother–stepfather families, and more than half of those in father–stepmother families, falling in the 12–17 age bracket. Only 14% of the children in mother–stepfather families, and just 4% of those in father–stepmother families, were under 6 years of age. By contrast, 33% of children in mother–father families were 12–17 years old, and 36% were under 6. One reason why children in stepfamilies tend to be older is that the process of becoming a stepchild, which usually involves both family disruption and family reconstitution may take years to complete. Another reason is that children of divorce, particularly males, may spend their younger years living with one parent (typically, the mother) and then be sent to live with the other parent (typically, the father, who has usually remarried) as they become older and their preferences or developmental needs change, or the first parent finds them difficult to handle.

Sex Distribution. Consistent with the latter scenario, nearly two thirds of the youngsters in father–stepmother families were boys, whereas children in mother–stepfather families were equally divided between girls and boys. Males also made up a majority of the children in father-only families, although the imbalance was not as pronounced. As would be expected, a slight majority of the larger group of children in mother-only families were female. There were clearly some selection (or self-selection) processes at work in the residential decisions that operated on the premise that male children belong with the father.

Ethnic Composition. The ethnic composition of the mother–stepfather group mirrored that of the child population in general, whereas the father–stepmother group showed an underrepresentation of Black and Hispanic children, and an overrepresentation of nonminority children. The ethnic breakdown of both stepparent groups stood in marked contrast to that of the mother-only group, where Black children were greatly overrepresented and nonminority children were underrepresented. These differences partly reflect the fact that Black women are less

TABLE 16.1
Demographic Profile of Children Living in Mother-Stepfather, Father-Stepmother, and Other Types of Families, United States, 1981

Child or Family Characteristic	All Types (Full Sample)	Family Type				
		Mother-Stepfather	Father-Stepmother	Mother-Father	Mother Only	Father Only
Estimated number of children in U.S. pop. (000's)	63,142	4,498	979	42,607	11,570	946
Number of cases in sample (unweighted)	15,416 100%	1,084 100%	216 100%	10,386 100%	2,759 100%	265 100%
Age of child						
0–5 years	32%	14%	4%	36%	31%	13%
6–11 years	32	37	44	31	34	33
12–17 years	36	49	53	33	37	55
Sex of child						
Male	51%	50%	63%	51%	49%	56%
Female	49	50	37	49	51	44
Ethnic group						
Nonminority	74%	76%	86%	80%	50%	71%
Black	15	15	7	8	37	19
Hispanic	9	6	5	9	11	8
Asian & other	3	3	2	3	2	2

Parent education (More educated parent)						
Less than high school	19%	13%	8%	16%	34%	29%
High school graduate	41	50	46	39	43	38
Some college	19	22	21	19	16	18
College graduate or more	21	15	25	26	7	15
Family income						
Less than $10,000	22%	17%	14%	12%	60%	23%
$10,000–14,999	15	15	9	14	19	18
$15,000–24,999	28	28	33	32	13	33
$25,000 or more	35	40	44	42	8	25
Number of children in household						
1–2	56%	53%	39%	55%	57%	63%
3–4	35	38	46	36	33	29
5 or more	9	9	15	9	10	7
Type of siblings child has						
None	19%	19%	16%	16%	24%	26%
Full only	66	29	16	78	54	67
Half only	5	21	11	2	12	3
Step, or half & step	3	7	17	1	1	1
Full & step &/or half	6	24	39	3	9	3

(Continued)

TABLE 16.1
(Continued)

Child or Family Characteristic	All Types (Full Sample)	Mother-Stepfather	Father-Stepmother	Mother-Father	Mother Only	Father Only
Contact with outside parent[a]						
Daily	—	1%	3%	—	7%	5%
Weekly	—	7	14	—	18	25
Monthly	—	15	23	—	20	27
Less than once/month	—	29	35	—	23	27
Never	—	47	25	—	32	15
($n =$)	—	(853)	(162)	—	(2,221)	(190)
Identity of survey respondent						
Biological mother	84%	94%	—	88%	95%	—
Biological father	10	—	61%	12	—	88%
Stepmother	1	—	39	—	—	—
Stepfather	<1	6	—	—	—	—
Grandparent	2	—	<1	<1	2	8
Older sibling	1	<1	—	<1	3	3
Adoptive parent	2	—	—	—	—	—

Note: The estimated 2.5 million children (706 cases in the sample) who lived with their biological parent are not shown separately, but are included in the full sample figures. These include children living with grandparents or other relatives, adoptive parents, and foster parents. Persons under 18 who were married or living with children of their own were excluded from the sample. Percent distribution may total slightly more or less than 100 percent because of rounding.

[a]Figures on contact with outside parent exclude cases where the outside parent had died and cases where it was not known whether or not the outside parent was living.

likely to marry after giving birth to a child outside of marriage, or to remarry after divorce (Cherlin, 1981).

Parent Education. The average educational attainment of parents in stepfamilies was superior to that of parents in single-parent families, and approximated that of parents in mother–father families. Based on the educational level of the more educated parent in the household, for example, 87% of children in mother-stepfather families, and 92% of children in father–stepmother households, had parents who were at least high school graduates. By comparison, 66% of children in mother-only families, and 84% of those in mother–father families, had parents who had completed high school or more. The proportions of children who had parents who had graduated from college were 15% in mother–stepfather families, 25% in father–stepmother families, only 7% in mother-only families, and 26% in mother–father families.

Although these differences were partly attributable to the presence of a male parent in the two-parent households, there were also differences in the educational levels of the mothers in the different groups. For example, the proportions of children whose biological mothers had at least finished high school were: 72% in mother–stepfather families; only 62% in mother-only families; and 77% in mother–father families. In father–stepmother families, 81% of the children had stepmothers who finished high school or more. The varying educational levels of the different family types probably relate to the differing ethnic composition of the groups and to the better remarriage prospects of women (and men) with more schooling.

Family Income. Because of the higher education level of the parents, and the presence of a male wage earner in the household, the average financial situation of children in stepfamilies was markedly better than that of children in mother-only families. To illustrate: The proportion of children whose families had incomes in 1980 that were less than $10,000 was 60% in mother-only families, but only 17% in mother–stepfather families, and 14% in father–stepmother families. Conversely, the proportions, with family incomes of $25,000 or more were just 8% in mother-only families, but 40% and 44% in mother–stepfather and father–stepmother families, respectively. In mother–father households, 12% of the children had families with incomes below $10,000 and 42%, incomes of $25,000 or more.

Nature of Family Disruption. Children in stepfamilies were more likely than children in single-parent families to have had their birth families disrupted by divorce, and less likely to have been born outside of marriage. Among children in mother–stepfather families, 75% had had their birth families disrupted by divorce, 6% had had their birth families disrupted by the death of the father, and 19% had been born out of wedlock. (These figures exclude children for whom marital history data was missing or contradictory.) Among children in mother-only families, 41% had their birth families disrupted by divorce, 20% had parents who were currently separated, 7% had had their families disrupted by the death of the father, and 33% were born out of wedlock. Comparable data were not available for children in father–stepmother or father-only families because of the limited marital history information that was collected in the survey when the biological mother of the child was not present in the household.

Number and Type of Siblings in Household.   The average number of children in mother–stepfather families was about the same as that in mother–father families, whereas the size of father–stepmother families tended to be somewhat larger (see Table 16.1, part B). Thus, 53% of children in mother–stepfather families had no siblings or only one sibling in the household, while the same was true of only 39% of children in father–stepmother families. Fifteen percent of children in father–stepmother families, versus 9% in mother–stepfather families, had four or more siblings in the household. In mother–father families, 55% of children had zero or one sibling, and 9% had four or more.

As would be expected, children in stepfamilies were more likely than children in mother-only or mother–father families to have half- or stepsiblings in the household. Fifty-two percent of children in mother–stepfather families, and 68% of those in father–stepmother families, had one or more half- or stepsiblings in the household. The comparable figures for mother-only and mother–father families were 22% and 6%, respectively. More than 1 child in 5 in mother–stepfather families, and more than 1 in 10 in father–stepmother families, was in the potentially problematic situation of having only half-siblings in the household.

Father–stepmother families were especially likely to be complex, "blended" families. Nearly 40% of children in father–stepmother families had a mixture of full and step- and/or half-siblings in the household. This probably reflects the fact that divorced fathers remarry and have new children more rapidly than divorced mothers. In addition, when a divorced father with children remarries a woman who has been married before, she is more likely to have custody of children from her previous marriage than is a man who has been married before.

Contact with Outside Parent.   Relatively few of the children living in stepfamilies had frequent contact with their outside biological parents. Only 8% of children in mother–stepfather families saw their outside fathers as often as once a week, and more than 75% saw their fathers less than once a month or never. Outside biological mothers did somewhat better in maintaining contact with children in father–stepmother families. Yet only 17% of these children saw their outside mothers once a week or more, and 60% saw the mother less than once a month or never. (These figures actually overstate the amount of contact slightly, because they exclude cases where it was not known whether the outside parent was living or dead, as well as those cases where the parent was known to be dead.)

Children in mother-only or father-only families were apt to see more of their outside parents than children in stepfamilies (see Table 16.1, part B). This is partly because, on the average, less time had elapsed since the divorce of the child's parents in the single-parent families than in the stepfamilies. Frequency of contact declines as time since divorce increases (Furstenberg, Nord, Peterson, & Zill, 1983). In addition, however, there seems to be a relationship between remarriage of the custodial parent and less frequent visitation by the outside parent. In the single-parent families, as in the stepfamilies, outside mothers tended to see their children more frequently than did outside fathers.

Identity of Survey Respondent. There were differences across family types in the identity of the parent who provided the survey information. In mother-stepfather families, the respondent was almost always (94% of the cases) the biological mother. The same was true in mother-only families (95% of the cases) and mother–father families (88% of the cases). The biological father was usually the respondent in father-only families (88% of the cases) and father–stepmother families (61% of the cases). However, the stepmother was the respondent in a substantial minority (39%) of the father–stepmother families. This proportion is considerably higher than the proportion of stepfathers who were respondents in mother–stepfather families (6%) or the proportion of biological fathers who were respondents in mother–father families (12%). The relatively large minority of stepmother respondents partly reflects differences in the availability of women and men for household survey interviews. But it also says something about the respective knowledge and participation levels of stepmothers versus stepfathers with respect to stepchildren's lives.

In preliminary analyses of the survey data, it was found that there were small but significant differences between the reports of male versus female parents on some child development questions. For example, male parents generally tended to report somewhat fewer behavior problems in the children than female parents did. Therefore, in making comparisons across family types, statistical controls were introduced for the type of parent respondent involved (biological mother, biological father, other mother figure, other father figure). It was not possible to control completely for respondent type, because this variable was confounded with family type (e.g., stepmother respondents occurred only in father–stepmother families). However, the introduction of a respondent variable into the multiple classification analyses did serve to reduce spurious differences between groups that were caused by variations in the identity of the typical respondent for children in each group.

The differences just described in the demographic characteristics of children and parents in the different family types show the importance of controlling for demographic differences when making comparisons between the development of children in different types of families. Thus, in the comparisons reported here, multiple classification analysis was used to adjust observed group differences for the main effects of age of child, sex of child, ethnic group, parent education level, family income level, family size, as well as the identity of the parent respondent.

Differences Across Family Types
on Child Development Measures

Mother–Stepfather Versus Mother–Father Families.   Children and adolescents living in mother-stepfather families were reported to have more developmental problems than those living in mother-father families. On the average, children in mother–stepfather families exhibited two more types of problem behavior than children in mother–father families; were three times as likely to have gotten or needed psychological help in the last year; ranked a little lower in their classes at school; were about 50% more likely to have repeated a grade; missed 1 day more of school because of illness during the past 12 months; and were slightly less likely to be described as in excellent health with no health-related activity limitations. (See Table, 16.2; and column 1 of Table 16.3.) These differences are not enormous: the largest amounts to about four-tenths of a standard deviation. However, the differences with respect to behavior problems and use of mental health services were large enough to be of practical as well as statistical significance.

When the observed differences were adjusted for age, sex, and ethnic group of the child, parent education level, family income, family size, and identity of the parent respondent, most of the developmental differences were reduced slightly in magnitude. However, the adjusted differences were in the same direction as the observed differences and all except the difference in health ratings were statistically reliable. The slight reductions in the sizes of the differences are probably attributable to the somewhat lower education and income levels of mother-stepfather families, vis-à-vis those of mother–father families.

Father–Stepmother Versus Mother–Father Families.   Children and adolescents in father–stepmother families also showed more behavior and learning problems than youngsters in mother–father families. The differences are as large or larger than those for mother–stepfather families. (See Table 16.2; and column 2 of Table 16.3.) On the average, children living with their father and a stepmother exhibited more than two additional problem behaviors; were five times as likely to have gotten or needed psychological help in the past year; ranked a little lower in class; and were almost twice as likely to have repeated a grade than their counterparts in mother–father families. On the other hand, children in father-stepmother families missed one *less* day of school because of illness (although this difference was not statistically reliable), and they were just as likely to be described as in excellent health with no health-related activity limitations, as children in mother–father families.

When the developmental differences were controlled for the effects of related

TABLE 16.2
Group Means on Various Developmental Measures for Children
in Mother-Stepfather, Father-Stepmother, and Other Family Types, U.S.
Children Aged 3–17, 1981

BEHAVIOR PROBLEMS AND PSYCHOLOGICAL HELP INDICATORS

	Behavior Problems Index		Proportion Who Needed or Got Psychological Help in Last Year		Proportion with Indulgent Sleeping Arrangements	
	(n)	$\overline{X}$, (s.d.)	(n)	$\overline{X}$, (s.d.)	(n)	$\overline{X}$, (s.d.)
Overall Totals	(11,588)	6.4 (5.7)	(12,373)	.06 (.23)	(12,452)	.17 (.38)
(Age range covered)	(4–17)		(3–17)		(3–17)	
			Observed Means			
Family Type	(n)	$\overline{X}$	(n)	$\overline{X}$	(n)	$\overline{X}$
Mother-Stepfather	(984)	7.9	(1,024)	.10	(1,030)	.13
Father-Stepmother	(205)	8.0	(207)	.15	(211)	.10
Mother-Father	(7,411)	5.7	(7,986)	.03	(8,402)	.14
Mother Only	(2,148)	8.1	(2,288)	.10	(2,302)	.30
Father Only	(235)	6.5	(243)	.09	(244)	.22
Other	(605)	7.2	(625)	.12	(634)	.16
eta =		.19*		.16*		.16*
			Adjusted Means			
Family Type						
Mother-Stepfather		7.8		.09		.14
Father-Stepmother		8.6		.15		.13
Mother-Father		5.8		.03		.15
Mother Only		7.7		.11		.27
Father Only		7.3		.10		.21
Other		7.4		.13		.14
beta =		.17*		.18*		.13*

ACADEMIC PERFORMANCE INDICATORS

	Standing in Class Rating		Proportion Who Repeated A Grade	
	(n)	$\overline{X}$, (s.d.)	(n)	$\overline{X}$, (s.d.)
Overall Totals	(9,502)	2.3 (1.0)	(9,897)	.14 (.35)
(Age range covered)	(6–17)		(6–17)	

(Continued)

TABLE 16.2
(Continued)

ACADEMIC PERFORMANCE INDICATORS

	Standing in Class Rating		Proportion Who Repeated A Grade	
	(n)	$\overline{X}$, (s.d.)	(n)	$\overline{X}$, (s.d.)

		Observed Means		
Family Type	(n)	$\overline{X}$	(n)	$\overline{X}$
Mother-Stepfather	(845)	2.4	(887)	.16
Father-Stepmother	(187)	2.5	(198)	.19
Mother-Father	(5,992)	2.2	(6,202)	.11
Mother Only	(1,749)	2.5	(1,845)	.21
Father Only	(206)	2.4	(215)	.19
Other	(523)	2.6	(550)	.17
eta =		*.14**		*.12**

		Adjusted Means		
Family Type				
Mother-Stepfather		2.4		.17
Father-Stepmother		2.6		.18
Mother-Father		2.2		.13
Mother Only		2.4		.17
Father Only		2.4		.18
Other		2.5		.12
beta =		*.10**		*.06**

HEALTH INDICATORS

	Number of School Absences in Last Year		Proportion in Excellent Health with No Limitation	
	(n)	$\overline{X}$, (s.d.)	(n)	$\overline{X}$, (s.d.)
Overall Totals	(9,746)	4.5 (7.0)	(12,483)	.60 (.49)
(Age range covered)	(6–17)		(3–17)	

		Observed Means		
Family Type	(n)	$\overline{X}$	(n)	$\overline{X}$
Mother-Stepfather	(876)	5.1	(1,032)	.59
Father-Stepmother	(195)	3.2	(215)	.68
Mother-Father	(6,122)	4.3	(8,046)	.64
Mother Only	(1,809)	5.5	(2,303)	.50
Father Only	(213)	3.2	(250)	.57
Other	(531)	3.7	(637)	.56
eta =		*.08**		*.11**

(Continued)

TABLE 16.2
(Continued)

	HEALTH INDICATORS			
	Number of School Absences in Last Year		Proportion in Excellent Health with No Limitation	
	(n)	$\overline{X}$, (s.d.)	(n)	$\overline{X}$, (s.d.)
		Adjusted Means		
Family Type				
Mother-Stepfather		5.1		.59
Father-Stepmother		3.7		.61
Mother-Father		4.3		.62
Mother Only		5.3		.59
Father Only		3.7		.58
Other		4.0		.51
beta =		*.07* *		*.05* *

Note: Means adjusted by multiple classfication analysis for variations across groups in age, sex, education, income, ethnic composition, family size, and identity of parent respondent. See text for definitions of measures.
   *$p <$ .001

background variables, some differences involving the father–stepmother group remained unchanged or were actually amplified, while others were diminished. The higher frequency of problem behavior among children in father–stepmother families became more pronounced. (This was probably due to corrections for the general tendency of male parent respondents to report fewer behavior problems than female parent respondents. Fathers were more likely to be the survey respondents in father–stepmother families than in mother–father families.) The more frequent psychological counselling and the lower standing-in-class ratings received by children in father–stepmother families remained essentially unchanged.

One of the differences that was reduced in size was the difference in grade repetition. Indeed, after the background controls were introduced, this difference was no longer statistically reliable. (The change here may have been due to corrections for the overrepresentation of males and adolescents in the father–stepmother group.) Statistical controls also brought the two groups closer on the physical health indicators. As was the case before statistical correction, the school absences and health status ratings for children in father–stepmother families were not significantly different from the corresponding measures for children in mother–father families.

Mother–Stepfather Versus Mother-Only Families.   When children in mother-stepfather families were compared with children in mother-only families, the two groups were found to be quite similar with respect to behavior problems, need for psychological help, and frequency of school absences (see Table 16.2, and

TABLE 16.3

Differences Between Group Means On Various Child Development Measures for Children in Mother-Stepfather or Father-Stepmother Families and Children in Other Family Types, U.S. Children Aged 3–17, 1981

Child Development Measures	Mother-Stepfather vs. Mother-Father	Father-Stepmother vs. Mother-Father	Mother-Stepfather vs. Mother Only	Father-Stepmother vs. Mother Only	Father-Stepmother vs. Father Only	Father-Stepmother vs. Mother-Stepfather
			Observed Differences (in standard deviation units)			
Behavioral Problems	.39***	.41***	−.03	−.01	.27**	.02
Psychological Help	.31***	.52***	−.00	.21**	.26**	.22**
Standing In Class	.19***	.33***	−.11**	.03	.10	.14
Repeated Grade	.14***	.23**	−.14**	−.06	.00	.09
School Absences	.12**	−.16	−.05	−.32***	.00	−.27***
Health Rating	.10**	−.08	−.18***	−.37***	−.22*	−.18*
Sleeping Arrngmnts	−.03	−.11	−.45***	−.53***	−.32***	−.08

Adjusted Differences

Behavioral Problems	.37***	.49***	.04	.16*	.22*	.12
Psychological Help	.28***	.54***	−.09*	.17*	.22*	.26***
Standing In Class	.14***	.32***	−.02	.16	.20	.18
Repeated Grade	.13**	.16	.02	.05	.00	.03
School Absences	.12**	−.08	−.03	−.23**	.00	−.20*
Health Rating	.06	.02	.01	−.03	−.06	−.04
Sleeping Arrngmnts	−.03	−.07	−.35***	−.39***	−.21*	−.04

Note: A positive difference between groups indicates that the first-listed group has come out worse on the developmental measure than the second-listed group. A negative sign means the reverse. Adjusted differences have been corrected by means of multiple classification analysis for variations across groups in age, sex, parent education, income, ethnic composition, family size, and identity of parent respondent.

   *p < .02
  **p < .01
 ***p < .001

column 3 in Table 16.3.) Youngsters in both groups had elevated behavior problem scores and were equally likely to have gotten or needed psychological help in the past year. Both groups also had above average numbers of school absences. The mother–stepfather children seemed to be slightly better off than the mother only children as far as physical health ratings, grade repetition, and standing-in-class ratings were concerned. The two groups were notably different with regard to the proportion of children who were allowed indulgent sleeping arrangements. Those in the mother–stepfather group were less than half as likely to be permitted to stay up late or sleep in the same room as the parent. In this respect, at least, the mother–stepfather families were more similar to the mother–father families than to the mother only families.

When group means were adjusted for variations in group composition, all but one of the aforementioned differences between the mother–stepfather and mother only groups were eliminated. Only the difference with respect to indulgent sleeping arrangements persisted. The changes that occurred are probably attributable to differences in ethnic composition, parent education, and family income across the two groups. As noted earlier, children in mother–stepfather families were less likely to be Black and less apt to have had parents with low education and income levels than children in mother only families. But Black children and children from low socioeconomic status (SES) families were more apt to have repeated a grade in school and to have gotten below-average health and school performance ratings. When these ethnic and SES effects were controlled for, no additional effect of the presence or absence of a stepfather was found (except with respect to the sleeping arrangements variable).

It can be argued, of course, that there were some beneficial effects of the stepfathers, but that these effects were mediated by the financial and educational resources that the stepfathers brought to the families. Whether or not this is the case, the differences between the mother–stepfather and mother only groups were much smaller than those between the mother–stepfather and mother–father groups (with the exception, again, of the sleeping arrangements variable). In the behavioral area especially, the socioeconomic advantages of the mother–stepfather families did not translate into a significantly lower frequency of developmental problems for the children in these families. On the other hand, neither was their evidence that children in mother–stepfather families had significantly *more* developmental disturbances, on the average, than children in mother only families.

Father–Stepmother Versus Mother-Only Families.   There *was* some evidence that children in father–stepmother families tended to have more problems than children in mother only families. Specifically, young people in father–stepmother families were 50% more likely than those in mother only families to have received or needed psychological help in the past year. Not all of the indicators showed more problems for the father–stepmother group, however. The unadjusted behavior problem scores of both groups were about equally elevated. The two groups were also similar in having below average standing-in-class ratings, and an elevated risk of having to repeat a grade in school. In the area of physical health, the father–stepmother group appeared to be *better* off than the mother only group. Children in the former group had fewer school absences and a larger proportion rated in excellent health with no activity limitations than those in the latter group. And the father–stepmother children were less apt to be allowed indulgent sleeping arrangements than were the children in the mother only group.

Adjusting the developmental measures for variations in group composition produced additional indications that children in father–stepmother families may have more behavioral problems than those in mother only families. Children in the father–stepmother group now appeared to be slightly worse off than those in the mother only group with respect to current behavior problems as well as with respect to the need for psychological help. However, these differences were modest in size, each amounting to less than two-tenths of a standard deviation. The adjustments for age, sex, education, income, race, and respondent identity eliminated the difference in average health ratings and reduced, but did not eliminate, the difference in school absences, which favored the father–stepmother group. As in the mother–stepfather versus mother only contrast, the largest continuing difference between the father–stepmother and mother only groups was the difference in the proportion of children with indulgent sleeping arrangements, with less than half as many of the father–stepmother children having such arrangements.

Father–Stepmother Versus Father-Only Families. Comparisons between young people in the father–stepmother and father only groups were less sensitive than the other comparisons reported here because of the relatively small number of cases in each of these two groups. Nonetheless, significant differences between the groups were found. Children in father–stepmother families showed more behavior problems and a greater need for psychological help than did children in father only families. This was true both before and after statistical controls were introduced, although the controls did reduce the size of the differences somewhat. On the other hand, the father only group had a significantly higher proportion of children with indulgent sleeping arrangements than did the father–stepmother group. This difference, which was reduced but still significant after controls were introduced, paralleled those found in the other stepparent-versus-single-parent contrasts.

The two groups were virtually identical in regard to grade repetition and school absences, with both showing a higher than average rate of grade repetition and a lower than average number of absences. More of the young people in the father–stepmother group received excellent health ratings, but the difference was cancelled out by the background controls.

Father–Stepmother Versus Mother–Stepfather Families. A developmental comparison between young people in the two stepparent groups—father–stepmother versus mother–stepfather—produced results much like those found when contrasting the father–stepmother group with the mother only group. As in that contrast, the father–stepmother group appeared to be worse off than the mother–stepfather group with respect to the psychological help measure, but better off with respect to the physical health indicators. The two groups did not differ significantly as far as the measure of indulgent sleeping arrangements was concerned.

Adjustments for group composition strengthened the difference in psychological help seeking, eliminated the difference in physical health ratings, and weakened, but did not eliminate, the difference in school absences. The adjustments also expanded the difference between the two groups' standing-in-class ratings and behavior problem scores, but not to the point of making these differences statistically reliable. Thus, although the children in father–stepmother families were more likely than those in mother–stepfather families to have received psychological help, it could not be said that those in the former group exhibited significantly more current behavior problems than those in the latter group.

Differences Within Stepfamily Groups

Parent Education

As anticipated, the frequency of behavior problems in stepchildren showed a significant association with the educational attainment of the children's parents (as measured by the educational level of the more educated parent in the household). This was true in both mother–stepfather and father–stepmother families, although it was only in the mother–stepfather households that the pattern of the relationship was as predicted (see Table 16.4).

In the mother–stepfather group, the more education the parents had, the fewer the behavior problems shown by the children (eta $= .18$, $df = 5, 969$, $F = 6.4$, $p < .001$). After adjustment for the effects of other variables, there was more than a 4-point difference (two-thirds of a standard deviation) between the mean behavior scores of stepchildren whose parents had some graduate school education and those whose parents had less than a high school education (beta $= .17$, $df = 5, 969$, $F = 5.94$, $p < .001$). The stepchildren with graduate school educated parents had essentially the same average behavior problem scores as children in intact mother–father families with graduate school educated parents.

In the father–stepmother group, parent education was also a leading predictor of within-group variations in child behavior problems (eta $= .28$, $df = 5, 199$, $F = 3.3$, $p < .01$), but the relationship between education and behavior scores was curvilinear. Adjusted behavior scores fell by 3 points between the less-than-high school and high school graduate education levels, but then went back up again by an equivalent amount between the high school graduate and college graduate levels (beta $= .26$, $df = 5, 199$, $F = 2.8$, $p < .025$). Thus, stepchildren in father–stepmother households with graduate school educated parents showed the same level of behavior problems as those whose parents had less than a high school education. They also showed substantially more problems than children in mother–stepfather or mother–father families who had graduate school educated parents.

By way of comparison, among children living with both biological parents, there was an inverse monotonic relationship between parent education and behavior problem scores, but the difference between the lowest and highest education levels amounted to only 1.3 points, or about one quarter of a standard deviation (beta $= .09$, $df = 5$, $7,405$, $F = 12.4$, $p < .001$).

Family Income

Stepchildren in mother–stepfather families with low incomes (below \$5,000 in 1981 dollars) showed more behavior problems than those in families with higher incomes, although the overall relationship between income and behavior scores was weak (eta $= .14$, $df = 5$, 969, $F = 4.05$, $p < .005$) and showed reversals (see Table 16.4). After adjustment for the effects of other variables, there was a difference of 2.2 points (one third of a standard deviation) between stepchildren at the lowest and highest income levels (beta $= .12$, $df = 5$, 969, $F = 2.9$, $p < .025$).

There appeared to be a similar inverse relationship between family income and behavior problem scores among children in father–stepmother families, although the relationship was not strong enough to attain statistical reliability (eta $= .21$, $df = 5$, 199, $F = 1.9$, $p < .10$), given the smaller size of the father–stepmother group. There were also too few cases of father–stepmother families at the lowest income level to produce a reliable estimate for that level. Among children living with both biological parents, the relationship between income and behavior scores was also weak (eta $= .07$, $df = 5$, $7,405$, $F = 7.2$, $p < .001$), amounting to a 1-point difference (less than two-tenths of a standard deviation) between the lowest and highest income levels, and less than that after adjusting for the effects of other variables (beta $= .04$, $df = 5$, $7,405$, $F = 2.6$, $p = .025$).

Parents' Marital History

As expected, information about the marital history of the stepchild's biological parents added significantly to the ability to predict which stepchildren would show behavior problems and which would not. However, the amount of additional variation accounted for by the marital history variables was much smaller than had been anticipated, and the observed pattern of differences did not conform to the expected pattern in at least one important respect.

Type of Family Disruption. One of the hypotheses put forth earlier regarding the effects of marital history was that stepchildren whose parents had been through

TABLE 16.4
Mean Behavior Problem Scores for Children Aged 4–17 by Parent Education Level, and Family Income Level, in Mother-Stepfather, Father-Stepmother, and Mother-Father Families, United States, 1981

	Family Type					
	Mother-Stepfather		Father-Stepmother		Mother-Father	
	(n)	$\overline{X}$, (s.d.)	(n)	$\overline{X}$, (s.d.)	(n)	$\overline{X}$, (s.d.)
Group Totals	(975)	7.8 (6.2)	(205)	8.0 (6.5)	(7,411)	5.7 (5.3)
			Observed Behavior Scores			
Parent Education Level	(n)	$\overline{X}$	(n)	$\overline{X}$	(n)	$\overline{X}$
Less than high school	(98)	9.3	(18)	11.9	(1,052)	6.1
High school graduate	(474)	7.9	(89)	6.9	(3,019)	5.8
Some college	(231)	8.2	(47)	7.4	(1,404)	6.0
College graduate	(105)	6.3	(31)	9.2	(944)	5.1
Some graduate school	(67)	5.2	(20)	9.9	(992)	4.9
eta =		.18***		.28**		.09***
			Adjusted Behavior Scores			
Parent Education Level						
Less than high school		9.4		9.8		6.2
High school graduate		7.9		6.7		5.8
Some college		8.2		7.7		6.0
College graduate		6.4		10.5		5.1
Some graduate school		5.2		10.0		4.9
beta =		.17***		.26*		.09***

Observed Behavior Scores

Family Income Level	(n)	X̄	(n)	X̄	(n)	X̄
Less than $5,000	(33)	10.2	(3)	—	(137)	6.4
$5,000–$9,999	(84)	7.4	(19)	11.5	(496)	5.9
$10,000–$14,999	(131)	9.2	(16)	8.0	(809)	6.2
$15,000–$24,999	(260)	8.0	(60)	7.6	(2,042)	6.0
$25,000 and over	(408)	7.3	(91)	7.7	(3,365)	5.4
unknown	(59)	6.3	(16)	7.1	(562)	5.0
$eta =$		.14**		.21		.07**

Adjusted Behavior Scores

Family Income Level	X̄	X̄	X̄
Less than $5,000	9.8	—	6.3
$5,000–$9,999	7.0	11.1	5.6
$10,000–$14,999	8.9	9.0	5.9
$15,000–$24,999	7.9	7.4	5.8
$25,000 and over	7.6	7.3	5.6
unknown	6.2	9.5	5.0
$beta =$	.12*	.21	.04

*$p < .025$
**$p < .005$
***$p < .001$

(n) = Unweighted number of cases in group. Means adjusted by Multiple Classification Analysis for effects of age, sex, parent education, family income, ethnic group, and family size.

a divorce would show more behavior problems than those whose birth families had been disrupted by the death of a parent. Instead, among children in mother-stepfather families, those who had experienced parental divorce and those who had experienced parental death both showed about the same level of behavior problems (see Table 16.5). There was a weak relationship between the type of disruption and behavior problem scores (eta = .10, df = 3, 967, F = 3.12, p < .025), but the relationship was due to the somewhat higher behavior scores exhibited by stepchildren who were originally born outside of marriage. (No specific hypothesis had been formulated with respect to this subgroup.) Moreover, when adjustments were made for the effects of other factors, even this weak relationship was diminished (beta = .08, df = 3, 967, F = 2.3, p < .10).

It was not possible to do a full test of the marital history hypotheses with the father–stepmother group because the necessary marital history information had not been collected for many of these families. It was possible, however, to contrast the behavior problem scores of stepchildren in father–stepmother families whose biological mothers were dead at the time of the survey with the scores of those stepchildren whose biological mothers were alive (see Table 16.5). The comparison showed a 3-point plus difference (half a standard deviation) in the expected direction; that is, stepchildren whose biological mothers were dead showed fewer problems than those whose mothers were living (eta = .23, df = 2, 202, F = 5.5, p < .005). After controls for related factors, however, the difference was diminished somewhat and, given the small size of the father–stepmother group, could no longer be said to be reliable (beta = .16, df = 2, 202, F = 2.6, p < .10). One bit of additional evidence in support of the hypothesis was that children in mother only and father only families whose outside parents were dead also showed somewhat lower behavior problem scores than children in those groups whose outside parents were living.

Age at Family Disruption.   The second hypothesis that was put forth regarding the effects of marital history was that stepchildren whose families had been disrupted during the preschool years would show more behavior problems than those whose families were disrupted later in childhood. This hypothesis received support—albeit rather modest support—among the children in the mother-stepfather group (see Table 16.5). There was a slight but significant decline in mean behavior scores (beta = .14, df = 6, 964, F = 3.1, p < .01) going from stepchildren whose families were disrupted at ages 0–2 or 3–5, to those whose families were disrupted during the early elementary years (ages 6–8), to those whose families were disrupted in the later elementary years (9–11). The overall decline amounted to just over 2 points, or about one third of a standard deviation. There was then an upturn in behavior scores for those whose family disruptions occurred in early adolescence (ages 12–14), making the overall relationship curvilinear. Although this curvilinearity was not explicitly predicted, neither was it wholly unexpected, given the frequent suggestions in the literature that early

TABLE 16.5
Mean Behavior Problem Scores for Children Aged 4–17 by Type
of Family Disruption and Child's Age at Disruption, in Mother-Stepfather
and Father-Stepmother Families, United States, 1981

	Family Type					
	Mother-Stepfather				Father-Stepmother	
	(n)	$\overline{X}$ (s.d.)			(n)	$\overline{X}$ (s.d.)
Group Totals	(971)	7.8 (6.2)			(205)	8.0 (6.5)
	Observed Behavior Scores					
How Child's Birth Family was Disrupted	(n)	$\overline{X}$	Child's Biological Mother Alive?		(n)	$\overline{X}$
Divorce	(723)	7.6	Yes		(166)	8.6
Death	(49)	7.5	No		(32)	5.2
Born out of wedlock	(158)	9.2				
Missing or contradictory data	(41)	7.0	Unknown		(7)	—
eta =		.10*				.23**
	Adjusted Behavior Scores					
How Child's Birth Family was Disrupted						
Divorce		7.5	Yes			8.6
Death		7.9	No			6.0
Born out of wedlock		8.8				
Missing or contradictory data		9.1	Unknown			—
beta =		.08				.16
	Observed Behavior Scores					
Child's Age at Disruption	(n)	$\overline{X}$				
0–2 years	(541)	8.3				
3–5 years	(203)	8.1			(Not available)	
6–8 years	(97)	6.9				
9–11 years	(60)	5.9				
12–14 years	(15)	6.9				
15–17 years	(4)	—				
Missing or contradictory data	(51)	6.5				
eta =		.12*				

(Continued)

TABLE 16.5
(Continued)

	Family Type				
	Mother-Stepfather			Father-Stepmother	
	(n)	X̄, (s.d.)		(n)	X̄, (s.d.)
Group Totals	(971)	7.8 (6.2)		(205)	8.0 (6.5)
		Adjusted Behavior Scores			
Child's Age at Disruption					
0–2 years		8.3			
3–5 years		8.2		(Not available)	
6–8 years		7.1			
9–11 years		6.0			
12–14 years		7.9			
15–17 years		—			
Missing or contradictory data		5.2			
beta =		.14*			

Note: Marital history information collected in the survey did not permit determination of how family was disrupted or child's age at disruption in father-stepmother families.
*$p < .025$
**$p < .005$
(n) = Unweighted number of cases in group. Means adjusted by Multiple Classification Analysis for effects of age, sex, parent education, family income, ethnic group, and family size.

adolescence may also be a difficult time for children to experience family disruption. There were too few cases in the sample of stepchildren whose families had been disrupted in later adolescence (ages 15–17) to produce an estimate for this subgroup. And data were not available to allow the age at disruption hypothesis to be tested in the father–stepmother group.

Current Family Situation

Two kinds of additional information about the stepchild's family situation, namely, the amount of contact that the child had with the biological parent who did not live in the household, and the type of siblings with whom the child lived, also proved to be useful in predicting which stepchildren would show behavior problems. Information about the other children in the household was helpful in both mother–stepfather and father–stepmother families, whereas information about contact with the outside parent was only predictive when the outside parent was the child's biological mother.

Contact with the Outside Parent.   It was hypothesized that stepchildren who had regular and fairly frequent contact with their outside biological parents would show better adjustment than those who saw their outside parents rarely or not at all. This hypothesis had not been confirmed in earlier studies of mother–stepfather families, and it was not supported in the mother–stepfather group in the present study (see Table 16.6). Stepchildren who saw their outside fathers on a monthly basis did show slightly lower behavior scores than those who never saw their fathers, but the observed difference was just over one point and the overall relationship was not reliable (eta = .08, df = 5, 969, F = 1.3, p > .20). The adjusted differences were even smaller (beta = .06, df = 5, 969, F = .76).

Among children in father–stepmother families, on the other hand, there was clear support for the hypothesis. The lower the frequency with which stepchildren in this group saw their outside biological mothers, the higher their behavior scores tended to be (eta = .34, df = 5, 199, F = 5.1, p < .001). There was more than a 5-point difference (eight-tenths of a standard deviation) between stepchildren who saw their mothers on a weekly basis and those who never saw their mothers. (The "never saw" subgroup did not include stepchildren whose mothers were not living. As noted earlier, those whose biological mothers were dead also tended to have relatively low behavior problem scores.) When behavior scores were adjusted for effects of other variables, the relationship with maternal contact was weakened somewhat, but remained substantial (beta = .29, df = 5, 199, F = 3.8, p < .005).

Type of Siblings.   It was hypothesized that stepchildren living with half-siblings (who, by definition, would be the biological children of the parent and stepparent) would show more behavior problems than stepchildren who had no siblings or had other types of siblings in their households. Although it is certainly conceivable that other aspects of the sibling situation would also be significant for the stepchild's adjustment, the half-sibling hypothesis was the only specific prediction that was put forth in this area. In the mother–stepfather group, there was a significant but weak relationship (eta = .14, df = 4, 970, F = 4.7, p < .001) between the type of siblings in the household and behavior problem scores (see Table 16.6). As anticipated, stepchildren with half-siblings only showed the highest average behavior scores. The same pattern obtained after adjustment for the effects of other variables (beta = .13, df = 4, 970, F = 4.4, p < .005).

In the father–stepmother group, there was also a significant relationship between the sibling configuration and behavior scores (eta = .26, df = 4,200, F = 3.5, p < .01), although the rank order of the different sibling types was different from that found with the mother–stepfather group. Once again, however, the half-siblings-only category showed the highest average behavior score. And this continued to be the case after adjustment for effects of other variables (beta = .25, df = 4, 200, F = 3.4, p < .01).

Age Trends and Sex Differences

Neither the age nor the sex of the child proved to be useful in predicting which stepchildren would exhibit behavior problems (see Table 16.7). The lack of age and sex trends in behavior problems among stepchildren stood in contrast to the

TABLE 16.6
Mean Behavior Problems Scores for Children Aged 4–17 by
Frequency of Contact with Outside Parent, and Type of Siblings
in Household, in Mother-Stepfather and Father-Stepmother Families,
United States, 1981

	Family Type			
	Mother-Stepfather		Father-Stepmother	
	(n)	$\overline{X}$, (s.d.)	(n)	$\overline{X}$, (s.d.)
Group Totals	(975)	7.8 (6.2)	(205)	8.0 (6.5)
	Observed Behavior Scores			
Frequency of Contact with Outside Parent	(n)	$\overline{X}$	(n)	$\overline{X}$
Weekly	(70)	7.5	(25)	5.1
Monthly	(121)	7.1	(36)	8.1
Less than once/month	(245)	7.6	(56)	8.9
Never	(446)	8.3	(48)	10.4
Outside parent dead	(74)	7.0	(32)	5.2
Missing data	(19)	7.4	(8)	—
eta =		.08		.34***
	Adjusted Behavior Scores			
Frequency of Contact with Outside Parent				
Weekly		7.9		5.2
Monthly		7.4		7.8
Less than once/month		7.5		8.5
Never		8.2		10.5
Outside parent dead		7.1		6.0
Missing data		8.4		—
beta =		.06		.29**
	Observed Behavior Scores			
Type of Siblings in Household	(n)	$\overline{X}$	(n)	$\overline{X}$
None	(334)	7.0	(69)	8.2
Full only	(275)	7.5	(31)	9.1
Half only	(174)	9.5	(22)	11.0
Step only; or Half & step	(50)	7.5	(33)	9.0

(Continued)

TABLE 16.6
(Continued)

		Family Type		
	Mother-Stepfather		Father-Stepmother	
	(n)	$\bar{X}$, (s.d.)	(n)	$\bar{X}$, (s.d.)
Group Totals	(975)	7.8 (6.2)	(205)	8.0 (6.5)
Other combinations	(142)	8.1	(50)	6.2
eta =		.14***		.26*

Adjusted Behavior Scores

Type of Siblings in Household			
None		6.9	9.5
Full only		7.5	7.6
Half only		9.2	10.7
Step only; or Half & step		7.5	9.3
Other combinations		8.4	6.3
beta =		.13**	.25*

*$p < .025$
**$p < .005$
***$p < .001$
(n) = Unweighted number of cases in group. Means adjusted by Multiple Classification Analysis for effects of age, sex, parent education, family income, ethnic group, and family size.

situation in other family types, where age and sex differences were found. Even among stepchildren, there were significant age and sex differences observed in other developmental variables, such as receipt of psychological help and class standing.

Age Trends.   Among children in mother–stepfather families, there was little variation in behavior problem scores as a function of the age group of the child (eta = .04, $df = 4$, 970, $F = 0.4$). The picture was not changed by adjustments for the effects of other variables (beta = .05, $df = 4$, 970, $F = 0.6$). By contrast, among children in intact mother–father families, there was a slight but significant downward trend in mean behavior scores from the 4- to 5-year-old age group to the 15- to 17-year-old age group (eta = .12, $df = 4$, 7,406, $F = 26.6, p < .001$). There was also an apparent downward trend with age among children in the father–stepmother group, but the trend was not pronounced enough to be statistically reliable, given the relatively small size of the father–stepmother group (eta = .17, $df = 4$, 200, $F = 1.5, p = .20$). Adjustments for the effects of other variables seemed to enhance the relationship with age and make it curvilinear, with the highest behavior score occurring among 9- to 11-year olds. The reliability of the trend was only marginal, however (beta = .22, $df = 4$, 200, $F = 2.6$, $p < .05$).

TABLE 16.7
Mean Behavior Problem Scores for Children Aged 4–17 by Age of Child,
and Sex of Child, in Mother-Stepfather, Father-Stepmother, and
Mother-Father Families, United States, 1981

	Family Type					
	Mother-Stepfather		Father-Stepmother		Mother-Father	
	(n)	$\overline{X}$, (s.d.)	(n)	$\overline{X}$, (s.d.)	(n)	$\overline{X}$, (s.d.)
Group Totals	(975)	7.8 (6.2)	(205)	8.0 (6.5)	(7,411)	5.7 (5.3)
	Observed Behavior Scores					
Age of Child	(n)	$\overline{X}$	(n)	$\overline{X}$	(n)	$\overline{X}$
4–5 years	(91)	7.8	(8)	—	(1,170)	6.4
6–8 years	(161)	7.8	(33)	9.7	(1,267)	6.4
9–11 years	(225)	8.2	(42)	8.7	(1,457)	5.7
12–14 years	(233)	7.9	(62)	7.5	(1,570)	5.4
15–17 years	(265)	7.5	(60)	6.6	(1,947)	4.8
eta =		.04		.17		.12***
	Adjusted Behavior Scores					
Age of Child						
4–5 years		7.8		—		6.4
6–8 years		7.8		8.8		6.4
9–11 years		8.2		10.0		5.7
12–14 years		8.0		7.1		5.4
15–17 years		7.4		6.4		4.8
beta =		.05		.22		.12***
	Observed Behavior Scores					
Sex of Child	(n)	$\overline{X}$	(n)	$\overline{X}$	(n)	$\overline{X}$
Male	(480)	8.1	(128)	8.4	(3,845)	6.2
Female	(495)	7.6	(77)	7.5	(3,566)	5.2
eta =		.04		.07		.09***
	Adjusted Behavior Scores					
Sex of Child						
Male		8.0		8.1		6.1
Female		7.7		7.9		5.2
beta =		.02		.01		.09***

*p < .025
**p < .005
***p < .001
(n) = Unweighted number of cases in group. Means adjusted by Multiple Calssification Analysis for effect of age, sex, parent education, family income, ethnic group, and family size.

The apparent difference in age relationships in mother–stepfather as opposed to mother–father families could be interpreted as meaning that the stepfather situation is more problematic for adolescents than for younger children. Given the relatively weak effect of age even in the intact families, however, the difference could be merely a matter of sampling fluctuations. The findings with regard to age trends in father–stepmother families suggest that the middle years of childhood are the most difficult time for adjusting to the presence of a stepmother. Here too, however, it would be unwise to read too much into what may be chance variations.

Sex Differences.   Among children in the mother–stepfather group, both boys and girls showed elevated behavior problem scores (see Table 16.7). A very slight observed difference that favored the girls proved to be non-significant (eta = .04, $df = 1, 973$, $F = 1.6$, $p \leq .20$). The difference became smaller still after adjustments for the effects of other variables (beta = .02, $df = 1, 973$, $F = 0.5$). A similar result was obtained in the father–stepmother group (eta = .07, $df = 1, 203$, $F = 0.9$; beta = .01, $df = 1, 203$, $F = 0.02$). Among children in mother–father families, on the other hand, there was a modest but significant sex difference in behavior scores both before (eta = .09, $df = 1, 7,409$, $F = 65.0$, $p < .001$) and after statistical adjustment (beta = .09, $df = 1, 7,409$, $F = 62.2$, $p < .001$). The mean for the males was about 1 point higher (two-tenths of a standard deviation) than that for the females. Children in mother-only families also showed a sex difference in behavior scores that favored the females.

Given that there were significant sex differences in behavior problem scores in mother–father and mother-only families, but not in mother–stepfather and father–stepmother families, it could be argued that the evidence provides some support for the notion that the stepparent situation is comparatively beneficial for boys and comparatively detrimental for girls. A more conservative reading of the data is that boys and girls have similar reactions to being in a stepfamily (and/or to the sequence of events that got them there). The latter interpretation is supported by other developmental indicators, such as the psychological help measure and the standing-in-class rating, which did show significant sex differences (favoring females) in the stepparent groups. These sex differences were roughly of the same order of magnitude as those found for all children in the survey.

SUMMARY AND CONCLUSIONS

Summary of Findings

Differences Across Family Types

The following were the major findings that emerged from the comparison of children's development and well-being in stepfamilies with child development and adjustment in other family types:

1. The hypothesis that children in stepfamilies would show more developmental difficulties than those in intact nuclear families was confirmed. Young people in both types of stepfamilies were found to have significantly more developmental problems than young people in families where both biological parents were present. The differences were most pronounced and consistent with respect to behavior and emotional adjustment problems and use of mental health services, although smaller but significant decrements were noted in some of the academic performance and physical health indicators as well.

2. The hypothesis that the adjustment of children in stepfamilies would be similar to that of children in one-parent families was also confirmed. The frequencies of developmental problems among children in stepfamilies were generally comparable to those found among children in single-parent families. Although children in stepfamilies appeared to have fewer learning problems and to show better physical health than children in single-parent families, it was found that these differences could probably be attributed to the higher education levels of the stepfamilies and to the smaller proportion of Black children in the stepparent groups.

Stepfamilies did differ from the single-parent families on one indicator, the measure of indulgent sleeping arrangements. Children in both the mother only and father only groups were two to three times more likely than children in the mother–stepfather or father–stepmother groups to be allowed to stay up late or sleep in the same room as the parent. The differences were reduced somewhat by controls for age, education, race, and the like, but remained substantial.

3. Evidence was found in support of the hypothesis that children living with stepmothers would have more difficulties than children living with stepfathers, but the picture was less clear than with the first two hypotheses. Children in father–stepmother families were more frequently described as in need of psychological help than children in mother–stepfather families or those in single-parent families. After background factors were controlled, the father–stepmother children also showed slightly higher behavior problem scores and slightly lower standing-in-class ratings than the other groups. These differences were not statistically reliable, however. In other respects, the father–stepmother group resembled either the mother–stepfather group or the father only group.

Differences Within Stepfamily Groups

The second part of the study was an examination of variations in the level of behavior problems across different subgroups within each of the two major stepfamily types. The following results emerged from this portion of the study:

4. As hypothesized, the education level of the parents was found to be a leading predictor of developmental problems among children in stepfamilies, with the children of more educated parents generally showing fewer behavior and learning problems than the children of less educated parents. Among children in father–stepmother families, however, there seemed to be a curvilinear relationship between parent education and child behavior problems, with the children of college educated parents showing more difficulties than the children of high school educated parents.

5. As predicted, stepchildren in families with low incomes showed more behavior problems than those in families with moderate or high income levels, although the differences involved were relatively slight.

6. The hypothesis that stepchildren whose birth families had been disrupted by divorce would show more behavior problems than those whose families had been disrupted by the death of a parent was supported in father–stepmother families, but not in the larger group of mother–stepfather families. In the latter group, there was no difference between the divorced and widowed subgroups. (Data from single-parent families also tended to support the hypothesis.)

7. Data from mother–stepfather families provided weak support for the hypothesis that stepchildren whose birth families were disrupted early in life would show more behavior problems than those whose families were disrupted later in childhood. Stepchildren whose families were disrupted in early adolescence also showed somewhat elevated behavior problem scores in comparison to those whose families were disrupted in middle childhood.

8. The hypothesis that stepchildren who had regular contact with their outside biological parents would show fewer problems than youngsters with little or no contact with those parents was confirmed only for children from father–stepmother families. In mother–stepfather families, there was little covariation between the frequency of contact with outside fathers and the level of behavior problems in the child. Contact with an outside mother seemed to be more critical for a stepchild's well-being than contact with an outside father.

9. As hypothesized, stepchildren who had half-siblings in the household showed more behavior problems than stepchildren with no siblings or other types of siblings. This was true in both types of stepfamilies.

10. Information about the age and sex of the child added little to the prediction of behavior problems in stepchildren. There was some age variation in behavior problems among children in father–stepmother families, with children in middle childhood (9–11 years) showing slightly higher scores than younger or older children. Where sex differences were found, as on the psychological help and class standing measures, they tended to favor females and to be of the same order of magnitude as sex differences found among children in other types of families. Thus, there was little evidence that children of a particular age or sex were particularly sensitive to the stepfamily situation.

Discussion

The results just reported are generally consistent with the view that children living with a biological parent and a stepparent are at greater developmental risk than children in intact biological families. Stepchildren appear to have the same frequency of developmental problems as children in single-parent families, despite the presence of an additional parent figure in the household and the fact that the financial situation of stepfamilies is usually strikingly superior to that of mother-only families.

The observation that adding a stepparent to the household does not usually reduce the child's risk of emotional difficulties should not be taken to mean that a stepparent cannot make a difference in any circumstances. Indeed, the finding of a significant reduction in stepchild behavior problems as parent education increases supports the contention that stepparents can be a beneficial influence. One possible interpretation of this finding is that stepparents are beneficial only if they become actively involved in the stepchild's rearing while also showing sensitivity to the persistence of affectional ties between the child and the outside biological parent. This presumes, of course, that better educated individuals are, on the average, more likely to exhibit activism and sensitivity in the stepparent role than less educated individuals. Another interpretation is that better educated stepparents tend to bring more financial and problem-solving resources to the family than less educated stepparents.

The notion that there is a direct relationship between a family's financial well-being and the emotional well-being of the children received only weak support as far as stepfamilies were concerned. Although there was some significant co-variation between the income level of the stepfamily and the frequency of behavior problems in the stepchildren, the relationship was neither strong nor consistent. One might argue, however, that the parent education index, which showed a stronger relationship with behavior problems, is really a better measure of the family's financial prospects than is the current earnings index. Moreover, inasmuch as there *was* a stronger relationship between income and behavior problems found in single-parent families, one could argue that the relationship is weaker among stepfamilies because income levels are generally higher in the latter group. However, the overall level of behavior problems in stepfamilies was not lower than the overall level in single-parent families, even though the income levels of the two groups were markedly different. Looking at the results from a different perspective, though, perhaps one should conclude that the addition of a stepfather to a mother-only family usually produces a net gain for the family because it improves the family's financial condition without making the children's psychological well-being notably worse.

Another conclusion that the present data and earlier, related studies seem to point towards is that mother–stepfather and father–stepmother families are not mirror images of one another. It seems to be more difficult to supplement or substitute for a child's mother with a stepmother than it is to supplement or substitute for a child's father with a stepfather. One of the differences observed in the present study was that parents in father–stepmother families felt a greater need to obtain psychological help for their children than parents did in mother–stepfather families. There were also differences across the groups in the relationships between child behavior problems and three different predictor variables, namely: the parents' education level; the frequency of contact with the outside parent; and the child's age.

A possible explanation for the curvilinear relationship between parent education level and stepchild behavior problems in father–stepmother families is that a better educated stepmother is more apt to try to play an active role in the family and, in effect, take over as the child's mother. Given the child's continuing bonds to the outside biological mother, however, the stepmother's attempts to usurp the mother's role creates conflicts and resentment in the child. It is also possible that the children of better educated parents are more apt to be precocious and, hence, more likely to take on some adult responsibilities themselves in a post-divorce family. Thus, these children may view the arrival of an activist stepmother as a threat to their own positions in the family. Presumably, these kinds of dynamics do not operate as strongly in mother–stepfather families because: a) the bond to an outside biological father is not as strong, or at least not as exclusive, as the bond to an outside mother; and b) stepfathers, even well-educated stepfathers, generally play a more passive role with regard to their stepchildren than stepmothers do, and, when they do get involved, their involvement is more likely to be appreciated than resented.

Children in father–stepmother families showed fewer behavior problems when they had frequent contact with their outside mothers than when contact was rare. This suggests that there is little question as to who the child's "real" mother is when the outside biological mother remains involved with the child, and, hence, relatively little conflict. In this situation, the stepmother perforce plays a different and more limited parental role. The situation is also relatively conflict free when the biological mother is dead. Here the stepmother can step into the maternal role without producing loyalty conflicts in the child. In this instance, too, there were relatively few behavior problems among children in father–stepmother families.

Although the overall level of developmental problems was similar among stepchildren and children in single-parent families, it is clear that the stepfamily situation can entail some special problems for the child. This is exemplified by the finding that stepchildren with half-siblings have a higher level of behavior problems than those in other sibling situations. When the child's biological parent and stepparent produce additional children of their own, the stepchild may be cast, or may see himself or herself, in a less favored position, as an unwelcome reminder of the earlier, broken union. This may intensify the rivalry that occurs in virtually all sibling relationships and create additional emotional difficulties for the stepchild.

Finally, although this chapter has focused on those children in stepfamilies who have developmental problems, it would be a serious mistake to assume that all young people in stepfamilies are "problem" children. Although they may encounter temporary difficulties in making the transition from one type of family situation to another, many, perhaps most, stepchildren seem to go on to function and develop normally. The relationships between family type and child development measures are statistically and practically significant, but they are not particularly strong. There is a great deal of unexplained variation in children's functioning within each family type.

We still have much to learn about which characteristics of the individual child and family produce successful or unsuccessful adjustment to family change. It has been suggested in the literature about stepfamilies that the age and sex of the child, and the age at which the child experiences family disruption or family reconstitution, may have a great deal to do with how well the child adjusts to the stepfamily situation. Although the present study found that the timing of family transitions made some difference, the timing variables did not prove to have major explanatory power. Nor did the age and sex of the stepchild. It is certainly possible that other outcome measures would have shown somewhat stronger sex, age, and timing effects. It would appear, however, that we must look elsewhere, such as to temperamental characteristics of the child and particulars of the parent–child relationship, to gain a more complete understanding of variations in stepchild development.

ACKNOWLEDGMENTS

The research reported here was supported by Grant Number R01-HD-19380 from the Demographic and Behavioral Sciences Branch of the Center for Population Research, National Institute of Child Health and Human Development. The development of behavioral questions for the 1981 Child Health Supplement to the National Health Interview Survey was supported by a grant from the William T. Grant Foundation. The research was planned and executed in collaboration with James L. Peterson and Kristin A. Moore of Child Trends. Assistance in data recoding and analysis was provided by Christine Winquist Nord, Marianne Winglee, Brian Ault, and Nancy Snyder. The cooperation and assistance of Gail Poe, Clinton Burnham, and Robert Fuchsberg, formerly of the Division of Health Interview Statistics, National Center for Health Statistics, are also gratefully acknowledged.

REFERENCES

Achenbach, T. M., & Edelbrock, C. S. (1981). Behavioral problems and competencies reported by parents of normal and disturbed children aged four through sixteen. *Monographs of the Society for Research in Child Development*, *46*(1, Serial No. 188). University of Chicago Press.

Bachrach, C. (1983). Children in families: Characteristics of biological, step-, and adopted children. *Journal of Marriage and the Family*, *45*, 171–179.

Bohannon, P. (1975). *Stepfathers and the mental health of their children. Final report.* LaJolla, CA: Western Behavioral Science Institute.

Bumpass, L. (1984). Children and marital disruption: A replication and update. *Demography*, *21*(1), 71–82.

Burchinal, L. G. (1964). Characteristics of adolescents from unbroken, broken, and reconstituted families. *Journal of Marriage and the Family*, *26*, 44–50.

Cherlin, A. (1981). *Marriage, divorce, remarriage.* Cambridge, MA: Harvard University Press.

Emery, R. E., Hetherington, E. M., & DiLalla, L. F. (1985). Divorce, children, and social policy. In H. Stevenson & A. Seigel (Eds.), *Child development research and social policy* (pp. 189–266). Chicago: University of Chicago Press.

Furstenberg, F. F., Jr. (1987). The new extended family: The experience of parents and children after remarriage. In K. Pasley & M. Ihinger-Tollman (Eds.), *Remarriage and stepparenting today* (pp. 42–61). New York: Guilford.

Furstenberg, F. F., Jr., & Allison, P. A. (1985, April). *How divorce affects children: Variations by age and sex.* Paper presented at the Society of Research in Child Development, Toronto.

Furstenberg, F. F., Jr., & Nord, C. W. (1985). Parenting apart: Patterns of childrearing after marital disruption. *Journal of Marriage and the Family*, *47*(4), 893–904.

Furstenberg, F. F., Jr., Nord, C. W., Peterson, J. L., & Zill, N. (1983). The life course of children of divorce: Marital dissolution and parental contact. *American Sociological Review*, *48*(5), 656–668.

Furstenberg, F. F., Jr., & Seltzer, J. A. (1986). Divorce and child development. In P. Adler & P. A. Adler (Eds.), *Sociological studies of child development* (pp. 137–160). Greenwich, CT: JAI Press.

Ganong, L. H., & Coleman, M. (1984). The effects of remarriage on children: A review of the empirical literature. *Family Relations*, *33*, 389–406.

Gassner, S., & Murray, E. (1969). Dominance and conflict in the interactions between parents of normal and neurotic children. *Journal of Abnormal and Social Psychology*, *74*, 33–41.

Hetherington, E. M. (1987). Family relations six years after divorce. In K. Pasley & M. Ihinger-Tollman (Eds.), *Remarriage and stepparenting today* (pp. 185–205). New York: Guilford.

Hetherington, E. M., Arnett, J., & Hollier, A. (in press). The effects of remarriage on children and families. In P. Karoly & S. Wolchik (Eds.), *Family transition*. New York: Garland.

Hetherington, E. M., Cox, M., & Cox, R. (1985). Long-term effects of divorce and remarriage on the adjustment of children. *Journal of the American Academy of Child Psychiatry*, *24*(5), 518–530.

Hirschi, T. (1969). *Causes of delinquency.* Berkeley and Los Angeles: University of California Press.

Hofferth, S. L. (1985). Updating children's life course. *Journal of Marriage and the Family*, *47*(1), 93–115.

Kellam, S. G., Ensminger, M. E., & Turner, J. (1977). Family structure and the mental health of children: Concurrent and longitudinal community-wide studies. *Archives of General Psychiatry*, *34*, 1012–1022.

Kellam, S. G., Branch, J. D., Agrawal, K. C., & Ensminger, M. E. (1975). *Mental health and going to school: The Woodlawn program of assessment, early intervention, and evaluation.* Chicago, IL: The University of Chicago Press.

Macklin, E. D. (1980). Nontraditional family forms: A decade of research. *Journal of Marriage and the Family*, *42*(4), 905–922.

National Center for Health Statistics (1975). Health Interview Survey procedure, 1957–1974. *Vital and Health Statistics*, 1(11). DHEW Pub. No. (HRA)75-1311. Rockville, MD: National Center for Health Statistics.

National Center for Health Statistics (1982). Current estimates from the National Health Inverview Survey: United States, 1981. *Vital and Health Statistics*, 10(141). DHHS Pub. No. (PHS) 83-1569. Public Health Service, Washington, DC: U.S. Government Printing Office.

National Center for Health Statistics, Kovar, M. G., & Poe, G. S. (1985). The National Health Interview Survey Design, 1973-84, and Procedures, 1975-83. *Vital and Health Statistics*, 1(18). DHHS Pub. No. (PHS)85-1320. Washington, DC: U.S. Government Printing Office.

Nord, C. W. (1987). *Children's experience with family disruption: A review, an update, and an extension.* Washington, DC: Child Trends, Inc.

Perkins, T. F., & Kahan, J. P. (1979). An empirical comparison of natural father and stepfather family systems. *Family Process, 18*, 175-183.

Perry, J. B., & Pfuhl, E. H. (1963). Adjustment of children in "solo" and "remarriage" homes. *Marriage and Family Living, 25*, 221-223.

Peterson, J. L., & Zill, N. (1986). Marital disruption, parent-child relationships, and behavior problems in children. *Journal of Marriage and the Family, 48*(5), 295-307.

Poe, G. S. (1986). *Design and procedures for the 1981 Child Health Supplement to the National Health Interview Survey,* "Working Paper" series. Hyattsville, MD: National Center for Health Statistics.

Rosenberg, M. (1965). *Society and the adolescent self-image.* Princeton, NJ: Princeton University Press.

Rutter, M., Tizard, J., & Whitmore, K. (Eds.). (1970). *Education, health and behavior.* London: Longman Group.

Santrock, J. W., Warshak, R., Lindberg, C., & Meadows, L. (1982). Children's and parents' observed social behavior in stepfather families. *Child Development, 53*, 472-480.

Schwarz, J. (1979). Childhood origins of psychopathology. *American Psychologist, 34*, 879-883.

Stern, P. N. (1978). Stepfather families: Integration around child discipline. *Issues in Mental Health Nursing, 1*(2), 49-56.

Touliatos, J., & Lindholm, B. W. (1980). Teachers' perceptions of behavior problems in children from intact, single-parent, and stepparent families. *Psychology in the Schools, 17*, 264-269.

Walker, K. N., & Messinger, L. (1979). Remarriage after divorce: Dissolution and reconstruction of family boundaries. *Family Process, 18*(2), 185-192.

Wilson, K. L., Zurcher, L. A., McAdams, D. C., & Curtis, R. L. (1975). Stepfathers and stepchildren: an exploratory analysis from two national surveys. *Journal of Marriage and the Family, 37*(3), 526-536.

Zill, N. (1978). *Divorce, marital happiness and the mental health of children: Findings from the FCD National Survey of Children.* Paper presented at the NIMH Workshop on Divorce and Children, Bethesda, MD. Washington, DC: Child Trends, Inc.

Zill, N. (1985). *Behavior problems scales developed from the 1981 Child Health Supplement to the National Health Interview Survey.* Washington, DC: Child Trends, Inc.

Zill, N., & Peterson, J. L. (1983). *Marital disruption and children's need for psychological help.* (NIMH Paper No. 6). Washington, DC: Child Trends, Inc.

Zill, N., Peterson, J. L., Moore, K. A., & Hernandez, D. J. (1984). *National statistics on children, youth, and their families: A guide to federal data programs.* Washington, DC: Child Trends, Inc.

Author Index

Subject Index

Expectations
  of children, family type and, 252–253
  of custodial fathers, sex of children and, 317
Explosive discipline, 137
Extended families
  Black, single parenting in, 215–238, *see also*
    Three-generational Black families
  relations within, marital disruption and,
    257–258
Externalizing behaviors, in children, stepfamilies
    and, 287–288

F

FACES questionnaire, 268–269, 285
FAD (Family Assessment Device), 285
Family(ies), *see also* Relatives
  blended, *see* Stepfamilies
  coercive styles in, 129
  competitive, 189–190
  conflict in, *see* Interparental conflict
  definition of, 24
  extended
    relations within, 257–258
    single parenting and, 215–238, *see also*
      Three-generational Black families
  history of, 246
  individualistic, 190
  nuclear, ideal of, 145–146
  one-parent, *see* Single parent(s)
  promotive, 188–189
  sibling, in, *see* Siblings
  structures, 189
  two-parent, trends in, 8–9
  types of, classification of, 12
Family adaptability, adolescent self-esteem and,
    267, 268, 274
Family Adaptability and Cohesion Evaluation
    Scales, 268–269, 285
Family Assessment Device (FAD), 285
Family cohesion
  adolescent self-esteem and, 267, 268, 273–274
  in stepfamilies, 290
Family development "honeymoon" phase in,
    adolescents in stepfamilies and, 265
Family income
  parental living arrangements and, 17–18
  stepchildren and, 329, 339, 351
Family Problem Solving System (FPSS), 304–305
Family process
  adult stress and, 288–291

children's behavior and, 179–187, 291–293
  in stepfather families, 294
  child's sex and, 281–282
Family Rating Scales, 173, 176
Family relationships, stepfamily adjustment and,
    see also Stepfamilies
  in stepfather families, 282–283
Family situation, current, children's adjustment
    in stepfamilies and, 330, 356–357
Family structure, self-concept and, 265–267
Family systems perspective
  in Developmental Issues in Stepfamilies project,
    279–280
  interparental conflict effects on children's ad-
    justment and, 170
  stepfamily adjustment and, 301
    with adolescents, 265
  in stepmother families, 318
Family types, differences across
  child development measure and, 342–350,
    361–362
  hypothesized, 329
Father(s), *see also* Parent(s)
  children's residence with, *see also* Custody
    reasons for, 104
  conflict resolution style of, child behavior and,
    186
  custodial, expectations of children by, 317
  in extended Black families
    childrearing involvement of, 217–218
    perception of, 223, 229
  mothers versus, mediation satisfaction and,
    63–65
  remarriage of, *see also* Stepmother families
    co-parenting effects of, 250–251
  single, *see also* Single parent(s)
    ethnicity and, 38–39
Father physical custody, 94
Father-son bond, custody arrangements and,
    106–107
Financial status, *see* Economic status
FPSS (Family Problem Solving System), 304–305
Friendly interparental relationship, 188–189

G

Gecas Self-Evaluation Scale, 268
Gender, *see* Sex
Geographic factors, interparental relations and,
    255